The Positive Psychology
of
Meaning and
Addiction Recovery

"This is perhaps one of the most important additions in years in the literature on the intersection between existential and positive psychology, and its application for substance abuse disorders. The book will be invaluable to experienced practitioners and researchers wishing to update their knowledge of this important area. In brief, yet another excellent work from the pen of Paul Wong and his collaborators."

—Prof. Dr. Alexander Batthyany, Viktor Frankl Chair, International Academy of Philosophy in the Principality of Liechtenstein, Cognitive Science Research Group, University of Vienna, Viktor Frankl Institute, Vienna, principal editor, *Collected Works of Viktor Frankl* (14 volumes).

"A thorough, succinct, and comprehensive review of diverse and currently used approaches in the treatment of addictions. The book presents an in-depth synthesis of hands-on practice and up-to-date evidence-based research culminating in the meaning-centered 12-step program for addiction recovery, developed by Dr. Paul Wong. This fascinating and innovative approach is entirely consistent with the writings of Viktor E. Frankl. It is written with insight, wisdom and compassion. We highly recommend this relevant book to clients, students, and practitioners in mental health and addiction."

—Edward Marshall, Ph.D., and Maria Marshall, Ph.D., founders, the Canadian Institute of Logotherapy, Ottawa, Canada, and authors of *Logotherapy Revisited: Review of the Tenet's of Viktor E. Frankl's Logotherapy* (2012), and *Healing Ministry: Experiences with Viktor E. Frankl's Logotherapy in Psychiatry, Psychology, Clinical Counselling, and Psychotherapy* (2013).

"*A Meaning-Centered Approach to Addiction and Recovery* bravely surveys the field of recovery approaches, offering its own complimentary approach to attain long-term efficacy. In this text, the authors do not settle for 'abstinence,' but challenge the reader to reach back and reclaim his or her true self that is inherently imbued with meaning, fullness, and aliveness. The meaning-centered approach provides the way to restore one to wholeness by focusing on the person, not the drug. This book is transformative, renewing a sense of aliveness and community from the deadness of addiction."

—Brent Potter, Ph.D., author of *Elements of Self-Destruction*

"Addiction keeps you from developing beyond your past and makes your present miserable. In this new book, we learn how meaning can pull us forward toward a life free of substances and compulsions. Find meaning and the answer to life's most challenging questions become clear."

—Shane J. Lopez, Ph.D., Research Director, Clifton Strengths Institute; Senior Scientist, Gallup Professor of the Practice, University of Kansas School of Business

"This bracing volume offers an open-minded and open-hearted exploration of many key issues touching addiction and its treatment, from grief and loss to meaning and spirituality. It ranges far beyond the narrow and limiting confines of the usual reductionist perspectives of medical practice, biological psychiatry, and behavior modification."

—Gabor Maté M.D., Author, *In The Realm of Hungry Ghosts: Close Encounters With Addiction*

"*The Positive Psychology of Meaning and Addiction Recovery* is an important addition to the literature on humanistic approaches to helping excessive substance users toward recovery. It includes both quasi-philosophic approaches and rigorous quantitative approaches, and it includes both reviews of important research and guides for recovery and treatment directly addressed to clients and therapists. Its chapter authors include some who are among the most distinguished contributors to this field. Readers are likely to find much of value here that is unavailable elsewhere."

—Eric Klinger, Professor Emeritus of Psychology, Division of Social Sciences, University of Minnesota, Morris

"*The Positive Psychology of Meaning and Addiction Recovery* is an interesting and well-written compilation of chapters from well-known authors of wide-ranging interests. All have a stake in this emerging field of interest and each brings his/her own brand of positive psychology to bear on understanding addiction and the path to recovery from addictive behavior. This book will be of interest to both researchers and clinicians interested in the intersection of positive psychology and addictive behavior."

—Peter M. Monti, Ph.D., Donald G. Millar Distinguished Professor of Alcohol and Addiction Studies, Director, Center for Alcohol and Addiction Studies, Brown University

The Positive Psychology of Meaning and Addiction Recovery

LILIAN C. J. WONG
GEOFFREY R. THOMPSON
PAUL T. P. WONG
EDITORS

Published by
Purpose Research in cooperation with the
International Network on Personal Meaning

Published by Purpose Research, LLC
Charlottesville, Virginia USA
PurposeResearch.com
in cooperation with the
International Network for Personal Meaning, Toronto, Ontario
http://meaning.ca

.

Chapter 8, "Transforming the Addicted Person's Counterfeit Quest for Wholeness Using Wilber's Transpersonal Spectrum of Development: A Clinical Perspective" by Gary Nixon originally appeared in the *International Journal of Mental Health and Addiction*. Grateful acknowledgement is made to Springer Publishing for allowing us to include it in this book.

Chapter 9, "Beyond the Spiritual Wading Pool: A New Approach to Religion and Spirituality in the Healing of Addictions" by Linda Mercadante originally appeared in the *International Journal of Existential Psychology and Psychotherapy*. Grateful acknowledgement is made to INPM for allowing us to include it in this book.

In Chapter 15, the excerpts from the *Big Book, Alcoholics Anonymous* and the *Twelve Steps and Twelve Traditions* are reprinted with permission of Alcoholics Anonymous World Services, Inc. [Please see complete AAWS statement on page 238.]

Chapter 14, "A Meaning-Centered Therapy for Addictions" by Geoffrey R. Thompson originally appeared in the *International Journal of Mental Health and Addiction*. Grateful acknowledgement is made to Springer Publishing for allowing us to include it in this book.

In Chapter 16, the Life Orientation Scale and the Brief Personal Meaning Profile are ©2012 Paul T. P. Wong and used by permission.

First edition
ISBN 978-0-9824278-2-8
Soft cover edition

9 8 7 6 5 4 3 2

Contents

Dedication   vii

Acknowledgements   ix

Preface   xi

About the Editors   xiii

About the Contributors   xv

1. **Addiction Prevention and Recovery:**
   From Harm Reduction to Relapse Prevention
   G. Alan Marlatt 1

2. **Mindfulness Meditation in the Treatment of Addictive Behaviors**
   G. Alan Marlatt 13

3. **Alcoholics Anonymous: Cult or Cure?**
   George Vaillant 21

4. **Higher Goals and Leaving Addiction: Finding Meaning in Life**
   Stanton Peele 31

5. **The Affective Basis of Drug and Social Addiction**
   Jaak Panksepp 37

6. **The Many Faces of Spirituality**
   J. Scott Tonigan 47

7. **Thinking Addiction**
   Francis F. Seeburger 59

8. Transforming the Addicted Person's Counterfeit Quest
   for Wholeness Using Wilber's Transpersonal Spectrum
   of Development: A Clinical Perspective
   Gary Nixon 77

9. Beyond the Spiritual Wading Pool: A New Approach to
   Religion and Spirituality in the Healing of Addictions
   Linda Mercadante 105

10. Grief and Addictions
    Nancy Reeves. 113

11. The Importance of Assessing Meaning in a Clinical Population
    Kimberly A. Miller, Darrell L. Butler. 127

12. Addiction: Theory & Practice
    Geoffrey R. Thompson 135

13. A Meaning-Centered Approach to Addiction and Recovery
    Paul T. P. Wong 181

14. A Meaning-Centered Therapy for Addictions
    Geoffrey R. Thompson 193

15. Interpreting the 12 Steps of AA from the Perspectives of
    Ecumenical Christianity and Transpersonal Psychology
    Kenneth E. Hart 211

16. A Meaning-Centered 12-Step Program for Addiction Recovery
    Paul T. P. Wong, Jessica J. Nee, Lilian C. J. Wong 241

Dedication

GORDON ALAN MARLATT
November 26, 1941 to March 14, 2011

The International Network on Personal Meaning's (INPM) association with Alan Marlatt began in 2006, the first of two meaning conferences he participated in. In 2010, INPM presented him its lifetime achievement award for contributions to addiction research. At first, this might seem odd. Much of Marlatt's work was a cognitive-behavioral approach to relapse prevention, though in later life he promoted mindfulness meditation in preventing and treating addiction. The latter came from his personal experience with mindfulness. Still, his work was not anchored within an existential framework.

What endeared him to INPM was his conviction that those suffering from addictions should be treated with compassion and dignity. Addicts were not different than other people; indeed, his work showed that the same ideas and strategies applied to others who suffered could be applied to those with addictions. One of his most important books, though among his least famous, was *Harm Reduction*. In a society that heralded abstinence as the defining feature of recovery, Marlatt described a European approach that did not consider drug use as either the defining feature of addiction or recovery. Marlatt believed that we should help even those who decline abstinence, meet them where they are at.

Relapse prevention strategies, mindfulness, and even harm reduction are common today. Few therapists in the addiction field appreciate how pioneering these ideas were a few decades ago. When Marlatt earned his Ph.D. in clinical psychology from Indiana University in 1968, the public and professionals generally dismissed addicts as defective in morals and character. Even the *Diagnostic and Statistical Manual* listed addiction as a personality disorder. He had the perseverance and the vision to see beyond the times.

As for his official accomplishments, Alan Marlatt was professor of psychology at the University of Washington, and Director of its Addictive Behaviors Research Center. He published nine books on addictions, including *Relapse Prevention* (1985,

2005), *Assessment of Addictive Behaviors* (1988, 2005), *Harm Reduction* (1998), and *Brief Alcohol Screening and Intervention for College Students (BASICS): A Harm Reduction Approach* (1999). He contributed more than 200 book chapters and journal articles. He served on the editorial boards of numerous professional journals, including the *Journal of Consulting and Clinical Psychology, Journal of Abnormal Psychology, Addictive Behaviors,* and *Journal of Studies on Alcohol.* He has been honored by many addiction and scholarly societies, including the Distinguished Scientist Award from the Society for a Science of Clinical Psychology (2000). In 1990, Dr. Marlatt was awarded The Jellinek Memorial Award for outstanding contributions to knowledge in the field of alcohol studies. In 2001 he was given the Innovators in Combating Substance Abuse Award by the Robert Wood Johnson Foundation, and in 2004 he received the Distinguished Researcher Award from the Research Society on Alcoholism.

William R. Miller and Thomas McLellan (2011), in their tribute to Marlatt, wrote: "His was a voice for humane treatment in an era when the norm was harsh authoritarian, often punitive measures that could be considered malpractice in the treatment of nearly any other disorder" (p. 331). Those who met Dr. Marlatt were inevitably impressed with his graciousness.

This book is dedicated to Dr. Marlatt. His benevolent spirit runs throughout its pages.

Geoffrey R. Thompson, MA, PhD candidate, CCC
Program Director
Sunshine Coast Health Center

Miller, W. R. & McLellan, A. T. (2011). G. Alan Marlatt: 1941-2011 (In Memoriam). *Journal of Substance Abuse Treatment.* 41, 331-334.

Acknowledgments

We want to express our gratitude to the Sir John Templeton Foundation, the Meaning-Centered Counselling Institute, and the Sunshine Coast Health Center for their generous support of the International Conferences on Personal Meaning, from which many of the papers in this volume are drawn.

We also want to dedicate this volume to the memory of Dr. G. Alan Marlatt, who was a strong supporter of our Meaning Conferences.

Numerous individuals have contributed to the success of this volume, notably Dr. Charles McLafferty, Jr. of Purpose Research, LLC and Brendan Ritchie, a Ph.D. candidate at Harvard University.

Preface

It is no surprise that addiction has been a regular theme at Meaning Conferences of the International Network on Personal Meaning (INPM). Frankl had highlighted it as one of the three modern societal problems, which are addiction, depression, and aggression. Indeed, Frankl was convinced that the pursuit of a meaningful life was a "prerequisite for therapeutic success" for those suffering from addiction. From an existential/spiritual perspective, meaning—or, rather, lack of it—plays a prominent role in the development and course of addiction. Empirical research has increasingly discovered a consistent association between meaning and spirituality and overcoming addiction.

The chapters in this book are based primarily on the invited addresses from INPM's Fourth Biennial International Conference on Personal Meaning, which took place in 2006; but it also includes recent contributions. The conference theme for 2006 was *Addiction, Meaning, & Spirituality: Exploring New Frontiers, Discovering New Hopes, and Learning New Skills.*

INPM is open to different ways of knowing, embracing knowledge from different epistemologies, theoretical schools, and methodologies. The contributors to this volume reflect different theoretical perspectives, but readers will recognize that meaning and spirituality are fundamental to the nature and solution of addiction.

This volume contributes to a broader understanding of addiction and proposes that meaningful living is fundamental to overcoming it. The high that those with addictions find in the experience of intoxication is ephemeral and doomed. Only the real high—the authentic happiness of overcoming life's challenges and achieving dreams—is potent enough to overcome the drug experience.

The Editorial Team

Lilian C. J. Wong
Geoffrey R. Thompson
Paul T. P. Wong

August, 2013

About the Editors

Lilian C. J. Wong, B.Sc., M.A., Ph.D. received her Ph.D. in Counselling Psychology from the University of British Columbia. She served as psychoeducational consultant and school psychologist for several school boards in Ontario and British Columbia. She was Associate Professor and Clinical Coordinator for School Counselling of the Graduate Program in Counselling Psychology at Trinity Western University, and Associate Professor of Psychology at Tyndale University College. She is coeditor of the *Handbook in Multicultural Perspectives on Stress and Coping* (2006) and *The Positive Psychology of Meaning and Spirituality* (2007). She is President of the Meaning-Centered Counselling Institute and cochair of the Supervision and Training Section of the Society of Counseling Psychology (Division 17) of the American Psychological Association.

Geoffrey R. Thompson, M.A., Ph.D. (Candidate) is currently completing his dissertation at Saybrook University. He is the program director of Sunshine Coast Health Center, a drug rehabilitation center in Powell River, BC. He has an extensive background in both residential and outpatient addiction treatment. Before working at Sunshine Coast, Geoff spent several years as a clinical addictions counsellor at Maple Ridge Treatment Centre, as well as managing two provincial government nonresidential treatment programs. He volunteered his time as Executive Director of the International Network on Personal Meaning (INPM) and was managing editor of the *International Journal of Existential Psychology and Psychotherapy* from 2004 to 2008.

In 2006, he was program director of one of the largest scholarly addictions conferences ever held in North America, organized by INPM, the theme of which was Addiction, Meaning, & Spirituality. He is the author of *A Long Night's Journey into Day*, an in-depth look at cutting-edge treatment, as well as dozens of articles on recovery.

Paul T. P. Wong, Ph.D., C. Psych., Professor Emeritus, Trent University, earned his Ph.D. from the University of Toronto. He has held professorial positions at various universities, including Trent University, the University of Toronto, and Trinity Western University. He is a registered clinical psychologist in Ontario. His Meaning-Centered Counselling and Therapy has gained increasing recognition.

Dr. Wong is the president of INPM and editor of the *International Journal of Existential Psychology and Psychotherapy*. He has published extensively on the subject of meaning of life and meaning of death. Recently, he was the guest editor of the special issue on death acceptance in *Death Studies* and the "Positive Psychology Section" in *Canadian Psychology*. He is a fellow of the American Psychological Association and the Canadian Psychological Association.

About the Contributors

Darrell Butler, PhD, received his BS from the University of California and his PhD from Indiana University. He joined the faculty at Ball State University in 1981 and was honored with the Outstanding Faculty Award in 1997. During his 30+ years as a faculty member, cognitive psychology and technology have been noteworthy in his teaching, research, and service. He served as president of the Society for Computers in Psychology; as a reviewer for a number of journals and grant agencies, a consultant to technology companies; as an associate editor of *Behavior Research Methods, Instruments, and Computers* as well as the *Journal of Psychology: Interdisciplinary and Applied*; and as a fellow at the Office of Teaching and Learning Advancement at Ball State University.

Kenneth E. Hart, Ph.D., Associate Professor at the University of Windsor, is an interdisciplinary scholar who works at the interface of clinical-health psychology and positive psychology and who specializes in understanding and promoting change in health-destructive "addictive" behaviors. Theoretically, he draws from the fields of social-cognitive psychology and positive psychology. His research on addictions seeks to apply theory and research on "posttraumatic growth" to understanding and facilitating "post-abstinence flourishing." His chapters "Application of Social Psychology to Clinical Psychology" and "Applications of Social Psychology to Positive Mental Health" in Schneider et al. (2012) *Applications of Social Psychology* are examples of his applied orientation and his interdisciplinary interests.

G. Alan Marlatt, Ph.D., the late Professor of Psychology and Director of Addictive Behaviors Research Center, Department of Psychology, University of Washington, earned his Ph.D. in clinical psychology from Indiana University in 1968. After serving on the faculties of the University of British Columbia (1968-1969) and the University of Wisconsin (1969-1972), he joined the University of Washington faculty in the fall of 1972 until his death in 2011.

His major focus in both research and clinical work was in the field of addictive behaviors. He was awarded numerous accolades and awards, including a Lifetime Achievement Award by the International Network on Personal Meaning.

Linda Mercadante, Ph.D., Professor of Theology, B. Robert Straker Chair, The Methodist Theological School in Ohio, has had a life quest of "faith seeking understanding," and she has a passion to explore the intersection of belief and culture. Since earning her Ph.D. from Princeton and becoming ordained (Presbyterian Church, USA) more than two decades ago, she has helped persons discern meaning and vocation. Key areas of specialization include addiction recovery, victimization, gender issues, immigration, and popular culture. The author of *Victims & Sinners: Spiritual Roots of Addiction and Recovery*, she explores how addiction has become an umbrella term to cover many aspects of human dysfunction. Her spiritual narrative, *Bloomfield Avenue: A Jewish-Catholic Jersey Girl's Spiritual Journey* was published in 2006 by Cowley. Dr. Mercadante has served as Visiting Scholar in Media and Theology at The University of Edinburgh (Scotland), a consultant for the federal government on addiction and spirituality, and is active in the American Academy of Religion. She is a member of the Center for Theological Inquiry at Princeton and of The Ecumenical Institute, St. John's University, Collegeville, MN.

Kimberly A. Miller, Ph.D., is Cherokee, a licensed psychologist and an organizational consultant based in Colorado. She specializes in strength-based leadership. She has received several national and international awards. In addition to her academic credentials, Dr. Miller has significant experience in consulting, leadership, and mentoring with over 20 years of supervision. Clinically, Dr. Miller has worked with diverse clients in both inpatient and outpatient settings. Her areas of expertise include: assessment, substance abuse, eating disorders, meaning in life, and depression. She has received four grants for her research (two from The National Institute on Drug Abuse), which focused on the development and cross-cultural validation of a strength-based measure of psychological well-being. Dr. Miller's research interests include strength-based psychology and resiliency, culturally sensitive measurement development, and the epidemiology and treatment of substance use and eating disorders in ethnic minorities.

Jessica J. Nee, holds a B.Sc. (Honors) from Queen's University in psychology and biology, and an M.A. in counselling psychology from Trinity Western University. She works as a counselor with university and seminary students at Tyndale Counselling Services in Toronto. She also works as an assistant for the International Network on Personal Meaning and the Meaning-Centered Counselling Institute. Her research interests include spiritual development and the intersection of faith and psychology in developing models of healing.

Gary Nixon, LLB (Law), Ph.D. (Counseling Psychology), Professor in Addictions Counseling, University of Lethbridge, experienced a profound existential crisis in his early twenties at the end of law school, after which he embraced his true passion in life and embarked on a quest for wholeness involving the emerging field of transpersonal psychology. Gary joined the addictions counseling faculty in 1998 at the University of Lethbridge. Since then, Gary has been teaching and researching in the area of addictions counseling, including the process of long-term recovery, the spectrum of development, transpersonal psychology paths to wholeness, and more recently, in the emerging field of nondual psychology. He currently serves as the editor of *Paradoxica: The Journal of Nondual Psychology*. As well, Gary maintains a small private practice in transpersonal psychology. His research interests include transpersonal psychology, nondual psychology, and long-term recovery from addictions.

Jaak Panksepp, Ph.D., Baily Endowed Chair of Animal Well-Being Science, the Department of Veterinary and Comparative Anatomy, Pharmacology, and Physiology, Washington State University, is an Estonian-born American psychologist, a psychobiologist, and a neuroscientist. He has authored over 200 scientific articles dealing with the physiological mechanisms that underlie motivated behavior. He authored two books, *Affective Neuroscience: The Foundations of Human and Animal Emotions* (1998), and *The Archaeology of Mind, Neuroevolutionary Origins of Human Emotion* (2010). He is editor of *A Textbook of Biological Psychiatry* (2004), and serves as editor of the series *Advances in Biological Psychiatry*. He also coedited many books, such as *Handbook of the Hypothalamus* and *Emotions and Psychopathology*. He earned the NIMH Research Scientist Development Award for his work in hypothalamic mechanisms of energy balance. Presently, at Bowling Green State University, Dr. Panksepp serves as Professor Emeritus in the Department of Psychology. Bowling Green honored him with the title of "Distinguished Research Professor."

Stanton Peele, J.D., Ph.D., Adjunct Professor, School of Social Work, New York University, is a psychologist and attorney in New Jersey. He has written and worked in the addiction field for 30 years, beginning with his publication of *Love and Addiction* in 1975. Dr. Peele has also written *The Meaning of Addiction*, *Diseasing of America*, *The Truth About Addiction and Recovery*, and *7 Tools to Beat Addiction*. His most recent publications include *Addiction-Proof Your Child* and *The Life Process Program*. He was considered to be one of 10 most influential addiction experts in America, 2011, by *The Fix* online recovery magazine. He received a Lifetime Achievement Award in 2006 from the International Network on Personal Meaning. Since 2002, he has served as Associate Editor of *Addiction Research*.

Nancy Reeves, Ph.D., is a registered psychologist, spiritual director, and best-selling author, who has specialized in the area of healing and transformation with adults and children since 1978. She also conducts workshops and retreats in the area of spirituality. She is internationally respected as a workshop facilitator, psychotherapist, author, and poet. In her clinical practice she works with individuals, families, groups, and in trauma recovery sessions after community disasters. She was the recipient of Greater Victoria YM/YWCA Woman of Distinction Award Health and Wellness in 2002, and the C-FAX 1070 Citation Rose Award for Community Disaster Response in 2001. She has published numerous books related to spirituality, grief, and loss, such as *Gifts of the Eucharist* (2009), *Spirituality for Extroverts* (2008), *Found Through Loss: Healing Stories from Scripture and Everyday Sacredness* (2003), and *A Path Through Loss: A Guide to Writing Your Healing and Growth* (2001).

Francis F. Seeburger, Ph.D., Philosophy Department Chair, University of Denver, is the author of numerous articles on contemporary continental European philosophy and the author of three books, including one on the philosophy of addiction, *Addiction and Responsibility: An Inquiry into the Addictive Mind* (Crossroads Press, 1995). He is currently chair of the Department of Philosophy at the University of Denver, and Director of the Joint University of Denver-Iliff School of Theology Ph.D. Program in Religious and Theological Studies.

J. Scott Tonigan, Ph.D., Research Professor, Psychology, University of New Mexico, is Research Professor of Psychology and Codirector of the Center on Alcoholism, Substance Abuse and Addictions at the University of New Mexico. He has served on the Review Panel of NIH, NIAAA, and NIHR. He is the principal investigator of several major research projects on addiction, including the 10-year follow-up of MATCH on spirituality and AA Practices. He is especially interested in behavioral change in mutual-help programs. His current research activities include: longitudinal relationships between AA attendance, commitment to AA-related practices, and outcome; the role of AA-specific and nonspecific behavior change mechanisms in explaining outcome; distinctions between abstinence and sobriety in AA; and the role of psychopathology in mediating AA-related practices and outcome.

George E. Vaillant, M.D., Professor of Psychiatry, Harvard Medical School, has spent his research career charting adult development and the recovery process of schizophrenia, heroin addiction, alcoholism, and personality disorders. He has spent the last 30 years as director of the Study of Adult Development at the Harvard University Health Service. His published works include *Adaptation to Life* (1977), *The Wisdom of the Ego* (1993), and *The Natural History of Alcoholism Revisited* (1995). His summaries of the lives of men and women from adolescence to age 80 are entitled *Aging Well* (2008) and *Triumphs of Experience* (2012). His research on spirituality neuroscience was published in *Spiritual Evolution: How We are Wired for Faith, Hope and Love* (2009). Dr. Vaillant has received the Prize for Research in Psychiatry from the American Psychiatric Association, the Strecker Award from the Institute of Pennsylvania Hospital, the Burlingame Award from The Institute for Living, and the Jellinek Memorial Award for research in alcoholism. More recently, he received the research prize of the International Psychogeriatric Society, a Templeton Foundation Fellowship in positive psychology research, and a Lifetime Achievement Award from the International Network on Personal Meaning.

1. Addiction Prevention and Recovery: From Harm Reduction to Relapse Prevention

G. ALAN MARLATT

It's good to be back in my hometown of Vancouver, where I learned about a lot of these issues growing up. Relapse prevention was a controversial topic, and harm reduction is extremely controversial. They had a big international harm reduction conference in Vancouver a couple of years ago, and an ad was published in the *Vancouver Sun* which went as follows:

> Harm reduction is a step backwards. . . . At the last world conference on drug-related issues, drug policy experts from 25 nations agreed that softening of drug policy, commonly termed "harm reduction," has been a major failure; they concluded that harm reduction policies increase drug use and crime wherever they are implemented. In Canada today, the harm reductionists have dominated national, provincial, and local drug policy decisions. But their false promises threaten the well-being of our children, plus they're costing Canadians millions of dollars that otherwise could be directed to real health care.

And, of course, this was paid for by American drug education policy.

In the United States, the harm reduction movement has been frowned upon, to say the least. Just mention the term "harm reduction," and a lot of people will walk out of the room; it goes against the classical disease model, which says that the only way to help people recover is to maintain total abstinence, and harm reduction gives people permission to keep using. Vancouver, though, is the leading city in North America in terms of harm reduction policies, having set up a safe injection site for intravenous drug users and developing a heroin prescription maintenance program as well as others. More recently, we've been working with people in Vancouver, at Simon Fraser University, to help them develop their Housing First program for chronic public inebriates; it gives them a place to live, and they're still allowed to drink in their housing. I'm going to talk about that kind of program as well as the work that we've been doing on harm reduction with young heavy drinkers. I think the only way to resolve this harm reduction

1

controversy is in fact to do good studies and to show what the results are; then people can decide whether or not it's something that could be helpful.

We started doing harm reduction with binge-drinking college students at the University of Washington, and this program has been evaluated, and now has been adopted by many colleges both in the United States and Canada. For most people, young adulthood is the heaviest drinking period in their life. Most people who drink heavily when they're in their late teens or early twenties mature out of it as they get older—some continue to drink much more heavily, and that's more of an alcohol dependence problem. For many young people, it's a transition they're going through that can be very dangerous in terms of health risks. They have a lot of problems in common, yet are seen as more isolated—there's the whole issue about development in adulthood. In the United States, as you know, the drinking age in all 50 states is now 21. When I grew up in Vancouver and went to UBC as an undergraduate, the drinking age was also 21, though they've since reduced it—it's now down to 19. One of the big issues that comes up in a lot of discussions about drinking age is whether lowering the drinking age is helpful. Does it reduce problems? One of the concerns about a higher drinking age is that young people that do have drinking problems don't want to go for help because they're afraid that they're going to be accused of criminal activity—underage drinking. They tend to take their drinking underground, where it's much more difficult to evaluate or to assess or to get people help.

There are lots of problems associated with peer influence, social drinking, impulsivity, and conduct history—young people with a conduct history problem are much more likely to have alcohol problems as well. And yet most young heavy drinkers don't see drinking as a problem. So the question is how to work with these people to get them some help, and to overcome some of the resistances that they might have to seeking treatment. Many of them are probably concerned that treatment would mean abstinence, and so they're not willing to show up.

The Spectrum of Intervention Responses, developed by the Institute of Medicine, puts people who don't have any problems at one extreme, where we would mainly be dealing with primary prevention to try and help young kids not initiate drinking, and then we have people with mild and then moderate problems, and at the other extreme are people with severe alcohol problems who are going to be recommended for treatment. But what about the middle—people with moderate problems? Brief interventions seem to be working, and have been done in a number of different settings, not just with young people but also with people in trauma centers who are brought in because of car crashes involving drinking or other things. These brief interventions—meeting with the person once or twice, talking to them and using a motivational, nonconfrontational interviewing style, talking about what kinds of things could be helpful for them, and giving them some choices—have been found in research studies to be very effective. Larry Gentilello was one of the first to do that in Seattle, at the Harborview Trauma Center. Now in the United States all trauma centers are requiring this for all people who come into their programs in order to be licensed. More recently, Thomas McLellan, a psychologist and expert in drug and alcohol work who was appointed to be the associate drug czar in the United States, said that primary health care physicians in hospitals would be trained to do brief interventions with patients where alcohol or drugs show up, whatever their co-occurring or medical problem is, rather than not doing anything or confronting them so that they don't choose to do anything.

So we're going to talk here about brief interventions and how effective they are. The National Institute on Alcohol Abuse and Alcoholism published a call to action a couple of years ago saying that college-student drinking is a big health problem. In the United States, 1,400–1,500 students die every year from alcohol-related problems. That includes car crashes, but in a lot of cases it's just overdrinking: They overdose. There's a practice called "21" in which, on your 21st birthday, you have 21 shots of vodka in a row, and a lot of people collapse. In fact, Thomas McLellan's son died from an alcohol overdose at his college graduation party. Harm reduction is really bringing up the question why we're not doing anything to keep these people alive.

A couple of approaches have been explored. One, developed by Wesley Perkins, tries to tell students at any particular university what the average drinking rates are. They found that most students think that other students drink much more than they do themselves, which tends to escalate drinking rates. If you give them accurate information—how many people do and don't drink, what the average number of drinks per occasion is for incoming freshman, for males and for females—it seems to bring the drinking rates down. In Bellingham, Washington, at Western Washington University, they have a social norms campaign. If you go into the cafeteria, you'll see posters describing the incoming freshman class: how many people drink, how many people don't drink, etc. It's accurate, and is based on surveys. Since they started the campaign, drinking rates have dropped by about a third.

And then there have been some interactive Internet programs such as "Alcohol 101," which takes you through a virtual party. You can plug in how much people drink and see what happens to them; you get taught about blood alcohol levels, and there's also a sexual assault segment, where people see what happens when too much alcohol is involved in sexual activity. It takes about an hour and a half to go through the program, and it's a helpful brief intervention—we've done it at the University of Washington as well.

But we decided to develop something more promising in terms of alcohol strategies for students: the Alcohol Skills Training Program. We selected students at the University of Washington who were picked up in college dorms or at football games for being publicly intoxicated, or for other problems with alcohol, and we also had volunteer students take part. In this program we have therapists meeting with eight to ten students at a time for 8 weeks, training them to self-monitor blood alcohol levels so that they can keep track of how much they've been drinking, teaching them drinking moderation techniques, and dealing particularly with situations involving increased risk of heavy drinking—we have a lot of drinking games now. Or what if you don't want to get involved in drinking—how do you tell your friends about that? And we talk about how to cope with negative emotional states. Many of the students that we see are freshmen—they're new at the university and they don't know many people. When they go out to a party to meet people, they often want to drink a lot beforehand so that they'll feel more relaxed. And then they drink more when they get to the party, and they're much more likely to become overly intoxicated. So dealing with negative emotional states, and finding other ways to relax, is part of the program.

There's also training in how to recognize and modify alcohol outcome expectancies. People who have very positive expectations for drinking—it will make them more relaxed, make them happier, make them feel as if they are more likable—tend to drink more. People who have more balanced expectations—if I drink too much, I might have a blackout, I might not be able to remember what happened, I'm not going to perform very well on the exam—tend to drink less. The way we modify alcohol expectancies is by bringing students into our bar lab and giving them placebo drinks that they think have alcohol in them but in fact don't. We get a very strong placebo effect: People start to feel much more relaxed, they start talking more, they get louder, some of them start swaying around. After about an hour we tell them that there's no alcohol in the drinks, and a lot of them are incredulous. So we tell them that when you go drinking, there are three things that are happening: You're drinking, yes, but there's also the setting—if you're in a bar then there's the music and so on—and there's also your expectations about what will happen. And we've found in follow-up studies that just taking people through one of these placebo drinking trials tends to reduce their drinking by about 30–40%.

There was also training in alternative stress coping skills. There's relaxation, and we've done a lot of meditation work with college student drinkers, and it tends to significantly reduce their drinking, especially when they're stressed. The same is true of aerobic exercise, and there's an even bigger effect if you combine the two. And finally there's training in relapse prevention. Once you have a new plan to drink more safely, how do you stay on it, or get back on track if you get off it?

We did a follow up study over the course of a year after people went through the program. We had two comparison groups, one that had received information about alcohol but not been given any training or coping skills, and one that just kept track of their drinking without any intervention. Before the program, the average drinking rates were putting the blood alcohol levels well above legal intoxication (.08 in Washington), at about .12. The only group that kept a blood alcohol level below legal intoxication at each of the follow-up points was the group that took the Alcohol Skills Training Program.

That program is still being used, and lots of people prefer a group-based program to just seeing someone individually. By contrast, our BASICS program— Brief Alcohol Screening and Intervention for College Students—is one-on-one. Now in the stages of change model, which has been very effective in terms of deciding when to do what in addiction treatment, there is a precontemplation stage, "I don't have a problem" and a contemplation stage, "Maybe I have a problem, but I'm not sure what to do about it." Then there are stages of preparation to make changes, action, and maintenance of a plan. And finally there's the possibility of relapse, so you also need to have relapse prevention and management. But most of the people we're dealing with in BASICS are in precontemplation or contemplation, so the question is how to enhance their motivation to start thinking about making a plan of action to change. We did an anonymous questionnaire in the Greek system at our university—fraternity and sorority members tend to drink the most—asking them what kinds of things happened in association with their drinking in the last 30 days. We could see that there were a lot of negative consequences. For example, 40% said that they got into fights and acted badly; 40% said they needed more alcohol to get the same effect; 36% were driving after more than two drinks; 36% had blackouts; 30% were passing out; 16% had gone to work or school high or drunk. But only 16% said they felt they had a problem with alcohol. So I think there's something about admitting that you're a problem drinker that creates a lot of stigma, shame, and guilt, and people are not willing to go to treatment because of that. But if you ask them about the consequences they're facing, they are willing to admit that these kinds of problems do occur. So when we tell them about a program that will reduce the problem consequences, help them quit if they want to, or just help them to drink in a safer way, many more people are willing to show up.

For the BASICS program, we did a 4-year outcome study with a randomized control sample with incoming freshman at the University of Washington. We have 4,000 freshman coming in every year, and we sent the new admittees a questionnaire asking about their drinking and whether they would like to be in this study when they arrived. We wanted to pick the top 20% in terms of their high school drinking rates. We had a positive response rate around 54%, and those people were randomly assigned either to join the BASICS program and receive treatment there or to merely keep track of their drinking as the control group. BASICS consists of two 1-hour sessions, so we just met with them twice. In the first hour, we gave them feedback about their drinking and the risks they faced—they had filled out a lot of questionnaires, so we knew about their family history, and their history of alcohol problems, medical problems, and psychological problems. In the second session, we challenged them to come up with an action plan to change their drinking. We don't tell them what to do—we collaborate with them, and we use motivational interviewing—so they have a lot of input into the program. There were also stepped-care options. In the stepped-care model, the first step is to do something brief, and if it works, great; if not, you move up a step, and you keep going until something works. With some students we found early on that they were not responding and running into worse problems with their drinking. So we would recommend outpatient counseling and even residential treatment when necessary. We also had a control group of normal drinkers—people who were not in the top 20%—with whom we did periodic assessments to see how their drinking changed over the 4-year period.

We had a number of drinking measures for alcohol consumption: how much they drank, of course, and how often they drank, as well as peak blood alcohol levels. We had a daily drinking questionnaire, and even people in the control group, who were also filling out the daily questionnaires, said it was very helpful. They had never kept track of their drinking, and this gave them some feedback, so it was a good intervention for many of them. We also looked at negative alcohol consequences: We used the Rutgers Alcohol Problem Index, looking at things like blackouts and getting into fights, as well as two measures of alcohol dependency. Finally, to get some collateral verification, each student in the study was asked to provide the names of two close friends who would give us independent reports—we found overall an 85% agreement between what the students in the program said and what their friends said.

In the first BASICS session we look at risks or cues for overdrinking, how your friends drink, where you drink, when you drink, whether you drink before eating, special situational factors such as spring break, and emotional facts; and this is individualized for each student. We use motivational interviewing, which has five general principles. It's a nonconfrontational approach: We express empathy; develop discrepancy (here's what your drinking is like now; what would happen if you drank more moderately?); avoid argument; roll with resistance; and support self-efficacy (support any suggestions of your own that might be helpful). For students in the precontemplation stage, who don't see themselves as having any kind of problem, we try to raise doubts about their current behavior, look at the consequences they're suffering, and increase their awareness of the risks. If the student is in the contemplation stage, we try to tip the balance between the pros and the cons: We look at reasons to change their behavior, highlight the risks of not changing, and again strengthen their self-efficacy. So we try to match our intervention to where the student is in the stages of change, which we've already assessed from the questionnaires.

In the second session, we negotiate a plan for change. We want to set goals and limits for drinking: How much are you going to drink? When are you going to drink? What kinds of situation will you drink in? What are some enjoyable alternatives to drinking? We try to come up with a plan by the end of the hour, write it down, and encourage the students to follow it. We do follow-ups, so we know whether they stick to the plan, and if they don't we can help them get back on track.

One of the things we teach the students about is the biphasic response to alcohol. Many students think that the more you drink, the more enjoyable it will be. But that's not how alcohol works. Alcohol does have a euphoric effect when you first start to drink, but if you keep drinking it begins to have a dysphoric effect—you start having problems with coordination, memory, sexual functioning, and other things. So we ask students what the point of diminishing returns is for them, so that we can get them thinking about tolerance and differential effects.

We also give students a blood alcohol concentration chart, which takes into account gender and weight—many people don't realize that females get intoxicated more quickly than males even if they weigh the same, because of body fluid weight differentiation between the genders. We ask them to count their drinks, and to check that number on the chart against the time that has elapsed in order to determine their blood alcohol content. We have an area of the chart printed in red, and we ask them to keep out of that area. For example, if you have four drinks in one hour as a 185-pound male, you'll be legally intoxicated, whereas if you spread four drinks over three hours, you'll be at .03, and so forth. Many students find this to be a very helpful assistance.

For the action plan, there are a number of strategies to reduce alcohol consumption. You can keep track of your drinking; slow down your drinking; space out your drinks (many young people have a couple drinks, don't feel anything right away, and decide they need to have a couple more, without realizing that it takes about 30 minutes for one drink to have any effect on your physiology); have different types of drinks with lower alcohol content; drink for quality rather than quantity; and learn to enjoy the mild effects. At each feedback period, we give the students graphical feedback. If their drinking has increased, that will show up in the charts, and we'll try to meet with them to see what was not working and how we can get them back on track.

So what kinds of results did we get? Drinking in the high-risk sample went up in their first year after arriving at college, but the random sample, composed of people who were not heavy drinkers, also more than doubled their drinking rate. So the first year of college is a very high-risk period for many young people in terms of drinking rates.

Looking at drinking problems—blackouts, getting in fights, etc.—in the 4-year outcome results, we found that both the group that received the BASICS program training and the high-risk control group reduced their drinking. That's the maturing-out effect. But we did get significant reductions overall for people who took the BASICS course. In the control group of people who were not heavy drinkers, drinking went up in Year 2 when they turned 21, and then went down again.

So drinking problems were significantly reduced. We also found changes in drinking rates, though not as pronounced as the changes in drinking problems. Many students told us that they still like to have their six-packs, but they don't go driving, and will stay at home and watch the game instead. So situational changes reduce the problems even though they are still drinking a fair amount.

So we've pursued harm reduction for young heavy drinkers—here we were working with college students, but we're now also working with high school students, and we've had a lot of input from the military, which wants to do something similar for their populations. The program has a low threshold: We don't ask people to abstain. If people want to quit, we certainly help them, and we do relapse prevention, but many college students simply won't give up drinking altogether. We don't use labels; we don't tell people that they are "problem drinkers," for example. We just ask them to look at their drinking behavior, and see what kinds of consequences it has—what do they like about those consequences, and what do they not like? We treat young people as adults, and yes, we do tolerate illegal activity: We'll work with drinkers even if they're underage. Finally, we tailor our efforts to personal histories and risk statuses. BASICS is now listed in the National Registry of Evidence-Based Programs and Practices in the United States. So even though it's harm reduction—we don't call it that in the title—it has been recognized and accepted as an effective approach.

I'll note that drinking or drug use is one of the three dangerous drives in adolescent motivation, the other two being dating or sexual activity and driving. In the United States people still say that we should have abstinence-based sexual education programs, because if we teach people about safe sex, they'll do it more. The harm reduction approach in this case acknowledges that we have to teach people these things anyway, because sooner or later they're going to end up in situations where there is potential for a lot of harmful consequences, and they won't know what to do. So in fact I think that a harm reduction approach can apply to all three of these dangerous areas.

I'm going to now more briefly discuss the Housing First project. This is another harm reduction approach, but instead of dealing with college students, here we're dealing with homeless alcoholics in Seattle. The first program of this kind, providing housing to homeless alcoholics, and allowing them to drink in their housing, was started in Ottawa, Canada, and other programs have since been started elsewhere—earlier I mentioned the one in Vancouver. There was, of course, a lot of controversy when this program started up in Seattle, because most people thought these alcoholics would just drink more, and that taxpayer money was being used to support their alcoholism.

King County, where Seattle is located, had an estimated 1,000 people living in the streets, though this increased as the economy fell. Those with chronic alcohol problems are dying at rates higher than those of other homeless groups—the average life expectancy is 46 years. They're also consuming taxpayer-funded crisis services—sobering or detoxification centers, emergency departments and hospitals, involuntary treatment, jails and criminal justice, 911 or EMS calls—at elevated rates. So the medical and emergency costs are extremely high.

The program was developed by the Downtown Emergency Services Center, a nonprofit group that works with more than 5,000 homeless adults a year. They tend to work with the people who are the most sick and the most vulnerable. They offer emergency shelter as well as licensed mental health and CD services. They want to develop supportive housing, and have a high level of integration across programs. Their view was that housing is a basic human right, and not a reward for clinical success, and their experience was that people wanted a place to live, and wanted to get better. So the idea was to give people a place to live, and not tell them that they'll be kicked out unless they're abstinent. There are programs like that in New York and elsewhere, and 80% of people start drinking and get kicked out, and then they don't want any more help and just go out onto the streets. Giving them a chance to have a place to live might motivate them to drink less, and maybe even seek abstinence help.

The principles of the program were to move people directly from the street and homelessness into an acceptance-based housing treatment, to take a harm reduction approach, and to offer leases and tenant protection under the law. The facility, which opened on December 23rd, 2005, is designated as "pre-recovery" housing for people unwilling or unable to abstain. It has a low-demand, flexible structure, and intensive 24/7 staffing including medical personnel and therapists. The goals are to reduce the use of alcohol and reduce the use of crisis services.

It was very controversial. There was a lot of media coverage—there were editorials; the *Seattle Post-Intelligencer* did a project on it. There was a huge amount of negative publicity in particular—we saw headlines like "Wrong time, place for alcoholic house" and "Liberal lunacy mandates 'drug dorms' as homeless cure." There was also some favorable coverage, though less of it. But there was steadfast support from funders, elected officials, and the business community; the chief of police, Gil Kerlikowske, was also supportive. (He's now the drug czar for the United States, so we're hoping that he'll institute more harm reduction programs.)

For the program, we chose the people whose treatment was costing King County medical services the most. There were 85 apartments available, and both men and women were chosen, and the people on the wait list were our control group. They eventually got housing as well, but we wanted to see the difference between getting it sooner and getting it later. It was a fairly mixed group ethnically. There were a fairly high number of Native American participants, as well as of African Americans and Hispanics. Most of the participants were men—about 90%. (We published an article about the women's reactions to being in the housing. They liked it on the whole, but being around a lot of intoxicated guys all the time, a lot of them thought that maybe they needed their own facility just for women.)

The research aims were to evaluate the impact of the housing on the utilization and cost of public services, and to look at alcohol use outcomes. As noted, the residents were recruited from a list of high utilizers of public services. We made 79 offers to fill the first 75 openings, and 95 participants enrolled at least one year prior to the current analyses. Sixty eight, or 71.5%, of these participants remained in the house for at least one year. We used a number of assessment procedures: Participants consented to the release of services utilization records for 3 years pre- and postenrollment, and we evaluated alcohol use and functioning at baseline and at 3-, 6-, 12- and 18-month follow-ups.

So what kinds of results did we get? Looking at sober center utilization, there was a much greater reduction among people who had housing than among those who were on the wait list, and there were huge savings in sobering center costs. There was also a significant drop in shelter visits as well as in shelter costs. There was a significant drop in medical center visits and medical center costs. There were reductions in emergency medical service calls and costs. Jail bookings also dropped significantly, as did the costs associated with jail bookings. Likewise, the number of days in jail and associated costs were reduced. We published our results in the *Journal of the American Medical Association*, and our basic result was that for the 85 participants that were in the housing, the overall savings was over four million dollars. So people realized that it was actually saving taxpayer money. And it didn't increase drinking rates, either. There wasn't that much change in detox admission rates, but residents dropped from around 23 intoxicated days a month preadmission to about 12 days a month, and the number of days abstinent per month went up a bit as well. So they were still drinking a fair amount, but much less than had been the case previously.

We did not do any harm reduction interventions like the Alcohol Skills Training Program with these people, because the goal was to look at the effect of housing itself. But now that we're showing these positive results in terms of reduced costs, our new research will involving training the residents to drink more moderately. Many of the residents have also expressed an interest in the mindfulness meditation work we did at the university. So we're developing a comprehensive program to help people reduce their drinking, and, if they want to stop drinking, we have a relapse prevention program for them. So we're trying to meet their needs, keep them healthier, and hopefully keep them alive longer. One thing about harm reduction, whether it's needle exchange programs or anything else, is that yes, maybe we're giving them permission to continue their habits, but we're also trying to keep them alive.

2. Mindfulness Meditation in the Treatment of Addictive Behaviors

G. ALAN MARLATT

I'm going to talk about Vipassana meditation, or mindfulness meditation, and how it can be used in the treatment of addictive behaviors. This program is done at a prison in Seattle called the North Rehabilitation Facility, and it was funded by a grant from the National Institute on Alcohol Abuse and Alcoholism and the Fetzer Institute. They had a special request for proposals a few years ago on spirituality as an approach to treating alcohol and drug-related issues. There were a lot of grants for studies looking at 12-step programs such as Alcoholics Anonymous. We were the only researchers who were looking at a Buddhist meditation approach to treatment. Our project was called *Project Choices*.

One of the issues we wanted to study was how to get people who have addiction problems, and are usually on automatic pilot in terms of the way they're conditioned to think about and use drugs, to stand back and look at what's happening rather than giving in to their addiction automatically. Mindfulness meditation is a method to help them do that. It involves focusing on your breath as the center of awareness and, when you realize you're getting distracted by things, which could include urges or cravings to use, returning your attention to the breath so that you're able to observe your urges and cravings without automatically giving in to them. That offers people a choice point: Whether or not to engage in the addictive behaviors becomes more of a choice than an automatic process. Other people have talked about this as a pause, as interrupting otherwise binge behavior. Jean Kristeller, who has worked on mindfulness and how its practice can affect binge eating, is also looking at whether taking a moment or two to do a micromeditation just before the binge begins gives you the choice of whether or not to go on. Sometimes people will go on anyway, but they're more aware of the option of whether or not to do it. I think these ideas have a lot of implications for a variety of different addictive behaviors.

This started when I received a phone call from the psychologist at a prison in Seattle saying, "You know, we've been doing these 10-day meditation retreats for a couple of years out here"—it started in 1997—"and we think that it's really been having a big effect. We were comparing the recidivism rates for inmates who took the voluntary Vipassana course to the rates of those who didn't, and found a 40% reduction over a 2-year period." So they began to realize that something was going on there that seemed like it was having a pretty big effect, but they weren't sure how people were changing in terms of their alcohol or drug use or other mental health problems. They were very encouraged because they believed that this was a potential mechanism for getting a grant to evaluate these programs, and to look not only at recidivism, but also at relapse rates, drug and alcohol use rates, and mental health variables. So we got the grant and met with people at the prison. Ideally, it would have been good to do a randomized control trial in which people could be randomly assigned to participate in the Vipassana course or to be in the control group, but because this was a voluntary program, we were able to do a case-matched control. We matched people who took the program with those who didn't take it, matching on gender, age, and criminal background problems. So we had a pretty good comparison even though we couldn't control for the initial choice of whether or not to take the program.

Some work had already been done in the literature around the use of other kinds of meditation to treat drug and alcohol problems in correctional and other settings. The first people on board were people doing Transcendental Meditation (TM). They had a long interest in doing research studies, examining how effective this meditation could be for alcohol or drug problems, and they were getting pretty good results. That's how I got interested in meditation for myself, back in the 1970s. My doctor told me that I had a borderline hypertension problem, and that I needed to do something to relax. I wasn't really doing things that were lowering my blood pressure, so he suggested TM. I responded, "Oh come on, I'm a behavioral psychologist, you know. We're not interested in this strange stuff." So he handed me a reprint showing the effects of TM on diastolic blood pressure. There was a clear drop off for people who practiced it on a regular basis, so I started to do it. I measured my blood pressure after each session, and found that my diastolic blood pressure dropped about 10 points. Also, it was the most relaxing thing I'd ever done. TM consists of two 20-minute periods a day during which a mantra is repeated. It's a Hindu-based meditation technique—the Maharishi Mahesh Yogi taught the Beatles how to do TM, as you will remember. It basically elicits a deep relaxation state. Herb Benson has written a book called *The Relaxation Response*, where he says that this is one of the things that happens in meditation, and that it is something we can measure physiologically, looking at different brain scans and so forth. So for people who are using alcohol or drugs as a way of self-medicating tension or anxiety, meditation can provide an alternative way of getting relaxed.

I would also say that TM could be called "brief meditation therapy" because it's the shortest version of meditation.

After the development of TM in this direction, work was done on mindfulness-based stress reduction, starting with Jon Kabat-Zinn. It was at the University of Massachusetts Medical School that he started using this approach, treating people with chronic pain problems who were not responding to traditional approaches. His first book is called *Full Catastrophe Living*. In it, he documents what this program actually does and includes all the instructions for the practice of mindfulness. His latest book, which I would also recommend, is called *Coming to Our Senses*. And his book *Wherever You Go, There You Are* is a good book for clients if you want to introduce them to the field. Kabat-Zinn's program, at least the way it's practiced now, consists of 8 weekly group sessions over a 2-month period, followed by a day-long mindfulness retreat, giving people an extra chance to practice. They're getting significant results with this program, not only for chronic pain, but also for psoriasis and other medical conditions. It's now being practiced in hundreds of different hospitals and clinics around North America. They also offer regular training programs so you can learn how to do mindfulness-based stress reduction and how to practice it in different settings. At the University of Toronto, Zindel Segal and his colleague John Teasdale, who is in England, decided to take Kabat-Zinn's mindfulness-based stress reduction and turn it into a relapse prevention program for depression called mindfulness-based cognitive therapy. This program is also showing itself to be effective in randomized controlled trials. They're getting results that are even better than the traditional cognitive therapy developed by Beck in terms of reducing relapse rates among people who have already been treated for depression. So it's a kind of aftercare program: People first go through regular treatment and then participate in the mindfulness-based cognitive therapy program to help prevent relapse. We just got a grant from the National Institute on Drug Abuse to develop a program in Seattle which we're calling mindfulness-based relapse prevention. We're patterning our program after Kabat-Zinn and Segal's program in that there will be eight weekly meetings for groups of individuals that are interested in an aftercare or maintenance program following intensive outpatient treatment for alcohol and drug problems. This study will be a randomized control trial, so participants will get the mindfulness-based relapse prevention, the standard cognitive behavioral relapse prevention, or the treatment as usual control group. What we're doing right now is developing the treatment manual for mindfulness-based relapse prevention.

So we've talked about transcendental meditation and mindfulness-based cognitive therapy and relapse prevention, but what about Vipassana, the program that we evaluated in the prison? The 10-day meditation retreat run in the prison is the most intense form of meditation because it is done every day starting at about four o'clock in the morning through to about nine o'clock in the evening, with participants alternating between sitting and walking meditations. During the first 3 days, the participants focus their awareness on their breath. For a lot of the inmates who participated in the course, all kinds of things would come up during this stage. Many of them had histories of being physically or sexually abused and, as a result, had posttraumatic stress disorder, so strong emotional states would come up. The instructions were to pay attention to the feelings and the physical sensations associated with their reactions. So instead of trying to suppress them, avoid them, or, more typically, go out and use drugs or alcohol to try to modulate the feelings, they were really trying to use more of a radical acceptance approach, paying attention to the sensations and allowing them to pass without giving in to them or trying to avoid or escape them.

This is very similar to what's being taught by Marsha Linehan, my colleague at the University of Washington, from her work on dialectical behavioral therapy. She uses mindfulness, as you're familiar with it, and calls it "wise mind." These approaches are for treating borderline personality disorder or folks who are at risk for suicide. She gets them to use minimeditations—three minutes—asking them to try to pay attention to how they're feeling on a moment-to-moment basis for a short period, particularly at times when they're feeling overwhelmed or completely depressed. The clients and patients she works with, many of whom are also in correctional settings, really show strong benefits from this work.

You may also be familiar with the acceptance and commitment therapy developed by Steve Hayes at the University of Nevada. Hayes' work focuses on acceptance and mindfulness. He coedited a book, *Mindfulness and Acceptance*, in which we have a chapter. People are applying mindfulness in many different areas. There seems to be a sudden giant swell of interest in this kind of meditation and how it could be helpful for lots of problems.

Back in the 1970s and 1980s, we studied TM and binge-drinking college students. We wanted to see how practicing TM on a regular basis would affect their alcohol consumption. In the first study, we randomly assigned binge-drinking college students to one of four groups. The first group practiced TM as described by Patricia Carrington in her book *Clinically Standardized Meditation*; the second group practiced progressive muscle relaxation for two 20-minute periods a day; the third group engaged in quiet reading; and the fourth group just kept track of their drinking. To elaborate a bit on Carrington's book, she basically took TM and made it accessible for therapists. In it there are lists of mantras that you can choose from rather than being assigned one by the teacher. So it's not the official version of TM, but a clinical version of it, with tapes and other aids to facilitate its practice. So we taught the students how to meditate according to this format. They practiced the meditation for 3 months, after which we did a 3-month follow-up. Within the first 3 months, we found that people in all three relaxation conditions—TM, muscle relaxation, and quiet reading—showed significant reductions in daily and weekly alcohol consumption—about 40%. In the follow-up period, however, when all groups were given the option of stopping or continuing their assigned practice, we found that only in the TM group did the majority choose to continue. The drinking of those in other conditions went back up as the participations ceased their various practices. From a stress-reduction perspective, therefore, the long-term effects of TM seem particularly promising.

Going back to the Vipassana study, the 10-day Vipassana course would allow us to see how a much more intensive program would affect alcohol and drug behavior. We did a baseline interview, and then after the 10-day course we did the measures again, and then we followed up 3 months after they got out of prison. These interviews included lots of measures of alcohol and drug use: The Brief Symptom Inventory for mental health variables; measures of drinking-related locus of control; and measures of positive psychology variables such as optimism scores and recidivism rates, etc.

Let me explain a little bit about this prison. It's a minimal security prison, called the North Rehabilitation Facility. Most of the people in there were only there for a few months. Many inmates were there for drunk driving, drug possession, and prostitution, but there were no violent offenders. The facility offered inmates a very rich treatment array of courses. There were 12-step groups, parenting groups, all kinds of stress management programs, and some physical exercise groups. In 1997, the facility included this 10-day meditation retreat as another option.

When they first started the meditation groups, not that many inmates were interested, as they would have to go away for 10 days. Well, it was not really away—there was a special facility in the prison to which the participants would move. It was like a dormitory, a place where they could sleep, eat, and participate in the course, but where there was no opportunity to watch TV, read the newspaper, smoke cigarettes, check e-mail, or anything like that. So we thought the volunteer rate would be pretty small, and at the beginning it was; only a few people decided to take it. This changed with time, however, as those who took the course shared their experience with other inmates, describing how good it was for them and how much it had helped them. So enrollment increased. Unfortunately, the state of Washington, because of budgetary problems, closed the prison about two years ago. By then, though, they had people on the waiting list to take the meditation course, so clearly it was having a big effect.

In running this program, they taught separate courses for men and women, separated by a few weeks. In the prison there were maybe three times as many men as women. The inmate population was 63% Caucasian, 10% Native American, and 9% Latino. The average age was 37 years old. Of the inmates, 58% were employed, at least part-time, prior to incarceration; 79% had the equivalent of a high school diploma; 58% reported they were Christian in terms of their religious belief, 17% identified no formal religion, and 25% described themselves as belonging to other religious groups.

One of the questions participants in the course brought up was, "If this meditation practice comes from a different religious background"—in this case, Buddhism—"is it going to make it more difficult for me to adhere to my Christian beliefs?" The basic response we gave is that it doesn't really matter what your religious background is; this is a technique or procedure that can really help you to deal with stress and to get more in center with yourself. It can also be very consistent with Christian beliefs. There's apparently a Christian technique called centering prayer. It seems to be very similar to meditation in that you sit there repeating a sacred word to yourself, but at the same time you're allowing whatever comes in to come in—presumably the voice of God or whatever it is according to your belief. It's a similar kind of strategy, and seems to be very helpful. So I think the main message is, "No, we're not trying to turn you into Buddhists here."

In fact, the whole issue about how to describe where these practices came from keeps coming up at different professional meetings. People like Steve Hayes say, "This is cognitive therapy. We don't need to say anything about Buddhism here. If we do, people are going to leave because it sounds too strange. So let's just talk about it as metacognition, and as something that we can empirically validate." Jon Kabat-Zinn, even though he basically learned all his meditation practices in Buddhist classes, feels that we should just talk about this as a stress-reduction course. I, on the other hand, am not so sure because, since I've started more deeply exploring Buddhist psychology and have participated in a number of retreats, it seems to me that what Buddhism has to say about things like addiction is parallel to what we talk about in cognitive behavioral therapy. The Buddhists talk about the behavior of the mind. They talk about things like "skillful means," which sounds just like our focus on coping skills. They talk about cravings as one of the major features of ego attachment, describing this attachment as what gets us into problems in the first place. These ideas are very similar to outcome expectancies and things that we're looking at in psychological dependency and cognitive behavioral treatment. So I think cognitive-behavior therapy and mindfulness have a lot to offer each other, and I think we're going to see more integration of these two approaches as we go along.

Let me give a brief overview of the results of the study. We found a number of significant effects for people who took the meditation course compared to those in the case-matched control group. There was an effect for crack cocaine use as a variable, from baseline to 3-month follow-up. Both groups showed some decline in crack use over that period, as there were lots of other treatment programs available in the prison, but there was a significant decrease in use for those who also took the meditation course compared to those in the control group. This was also true for tobacco use; many of the participants were pretty heavy smokers. There was also an effect for alcohol-related variables, specifically peak weekly alcohol use and alcohol-related negative consequences, such as blacking out, getting into fights, and passing out, which showed a significant reduction. There was also a drop in overall scores on the Brief Symptom Inventory. In particular, there was a significant decrease in depression for the people who took the Vipassana course. They showed a significant increase in optimism about their future lives, whereas the control group showed a drop off at 3 months, becoming less optimistic as the Vipassana people were getting more optimistic. There was also a significant shift in scores on the Drinking-Related Locus of Control. This is Dennis Donovan's measure, and is similar to the general measure of internal-external locus of control, but is specific to drinking. There was a significant shift for people who took the Vipassana, towards a more internal locus of control. So they had more of a sense of their own choices and responsibility around their drinking.

There's a short video you can watch about people's experiences of the Vipassana course in prison. It's called *Changing from Inside*. It gives you a chance to see what some of the participants had to say. What they share seems to be pretty consistent with what the theory seems to suggest, namely the increased acceptance of negative emotional states. There's one gal who says, "When I get into situations in the dorm, I pay attention to my heart rate, how it's feeling—I know that it's going to pass." One of my graduate students, Sarah Bowen, has done some work looking at meditational factors that may be associated with some of these good changes that we're seeing with Vipassana. What we're finding, from looking at measures such as the White Bear Suppression Inventory, is that there's a lot more acceptance of negative emotions and of urges or cravings, and less attempts to suppress them. This was true for both alcohol use and alcohol-related consequences. There's also less thought-avoidance and fewer rebound effects. We have this technique that we're building into the mindfulness-based relapse prevention called "urge surfing." When you're having a strong urge, you imagine that it's like an ocean wave that starts to build up. Of course people sometimes think that if they don't give in to the urge it's just going to get stronger and wipe them out, but with this procedure, you use your breath as a surfboard while the urge is passing through you. So you're paying attention to the urge, but you're trying to keep your balance rather than getting wiped out by it. And you continue this until it goes down the other side. These sorts of meditation imagery techniques seem to be pretty helpful. The Vipassana course shown in the video doesn't really have any information in it about how to deal specifically with alcohol or drug problems. It's more about dealing with cravings, emotional reactions, and physical sensations in general.

These courses are a very powerful way to learn mindfulness, but people are saying, "Well, how can we have therapists teach people meditation skills without sending them to a 10-day course?" It would be great if everyone could go, but many people just aren't going to be able to do that. Also, you have to be a specially trained Vipassana teacher in order to be an assistant teacher for Goenka's course, the course that they did in the prison. We've designed it so that, for our program, the therapist will be able to teach some basic meditation techniques, like they do in mindfulness-based cognitive therapy. We encourage therapists to practice meditation themselves for 30 to 40 minutes a day, because that's what we ask the clients to do as part of their homework. The way the groups work is that in the first 40 minutes there will be some meditation instruction and practice. The rest of the two (or two and a half) hours of the weekly meeting focuses on exploring how to use this practice to deal with relapse issues, recognizing early warning signals, examining your own expectancies and issues about what's happening cognitively, identifying strong physical urges, and learning new ways to cope with them. We're also trying to integrate some yoga techniques into the meditation. I've been working most recently with a Buddhist teacher, Reginald Ray, who has done this course called "Meditating with the Body." It has been a very powerful course that helps you deal with strong emotional states and other things, and it integrates both yoga and sitting meditation. We're probably going to include some of that in our mindfulness-based relapse prevention course. So that's what the course looks like. Hopefully we'll be able to evaluate it and get the manual out for people who would like to integrate mindfulness meditation into some of their work. Overall, we're encouraged. It seems that this is something that more and more people are gaining access to. Hopefully it will help people deal with problems of addiction in the future.

3. Alcoholics Anonymous: Cult or Cure?

GEORGE VAILLANT

My task is to link three hungers: addiction to alcohol, positive emotion, and spirituality. In one sentence, it can be summed up as "Honey sho' do catch mo' flies than vinegar." In Latin, that translates into Carl Jung's *Spiritus contra spiritum*: Spirituality and emotions are the same thing. And since they are both dopaminergic and limbic, only they, and not the science of enlightenment, can cure addiction.

First, let me link spirituality and positive emotions. Our spirituality is made up of positive emotions. Unlike religious cognitions, dogma, and belief systems, and unlike negative emotions, the positive emotions help us to broaden and build. They're very different from sorrow, guilt, anger, and fear, in that, first, they are not all about me, and second, they are not focused on time-present, but on time-future. That's why the positive emotions are so important in learning and personal growth. Every recovering alcoholic knows that resentments, the "poor me's," and fear are the enemies of recovery, while the so-called theological virtues, faith, hope, love, forgiveness, and compassion, are what spirituality and recovery from addiction are all about. The "11th step prayer" of Alcoholics Anonymous (AA) is an illustration of this fact [see p. 234, this volume]. And of course the last great positive emotion, comfort, otherwise known as compassion, is at the root of the 12th step.

Academics, especially psychologists and psychiatrists, are frightened of the positive emotions. For example, Kaplan and Sadock (Sadock and Sadock, 2003), authors of a leading American textbook of psychiatry, devote hundreds of lines to anger, shame, terrorism, hate, sin, guilt, and thousands of lines to anxiety and depression. Although half a million lines in length, the book devotes only five lines to hope, one line to joy, and not a single line to love, faith, forgiveness, gratitude, or compassion. The three leading psychology departments with which I've been associated, Stanford, Harvard, and Dartmouth, have all avoided having clinical programs. God forbid they muddy their science with attachment and compassion! But in leaning over backwards to avoid "hoke," academics avoid the perfectly scientific positive emotions. So what makes positive emotions so aversive to science? Irrational superstition may be a good place to start. You see, scientists, too, are susceptible to hoke.

21

In contrast, the world's great religions all give these emotions pride of place. How can we integrate spirituality and science to maximize our powers to heal? A major obstacle for the modern world to take spirituality seriously has been disillusionment over false spiritual cures. Paradoxically, healing others and being healed is "so very scientific," and "so very spiritual," and sometimes (if you'll excuse my French) so full of bullshit. We want so badly for compassion to effect healing that the resulting backlash when spirituality fails to cure makes many cynical. The power of positive emotions like faith, hope, and love, must always be separated from the false comforts of wish, denial, and hoke.

The multibillion-dollar pharmaceutical industry on television, the multibillion-dollar alternative medicine industry in your local pharmacy, the multimillion-dollar "get-thin-quick" industry in your local bookstore, and the thousands of alternative healers in the yellow pages, all spawn millions of believers in cures that depend upon despair, denial, gullibility, and marketing, rather than upon love, reason, and, most importantly for this lecture, upon long-term follow-up. In short, the critical issue of spiritual healing is: "How do we distinguish scientific truth from wishful illusion?" How can those who need help find comfort in places that are empathic and safe, not cultish, exploitative, or even delusional? The pleadings of some lovers reflect unselfish love, and the pleadings of other lovers reflect reptilian lust, and how are we to tell? Only by what my children used to call, "wait and see pie." "Only by their fruits shall ye know them."

Despite the great power of the so-called theological virtues against suffering, they exert very limited effect upon disease. Interpersonal relief of suffering is the domain of the positive emotions. Pharmacological and surgical relief of pain is the domain of science. Of course, for the patient suffering from low-back pain, the value of hugs, Lourdes, chiropractic, Valium, and spinal surgery are all intertwined and of roughly equal value. But the question that I'm addressing today is "Can spirituality ever cure?"

A friend of mine told me she hated the word "spirituality" because of the "hoke" that went with it. I asked her to define "hoke." She defined it as "the promise of a cure, never delivered." Spirituality often becomes hoke when we try to explain its effects too concretely, overcharge for our services, confuse comfort with healing, or believe without adequate follow up that acamprosate and naltrexone cure alcoholics. For some of us, using spirituality for subjective well-being can seem narcissistic: Images of "spiritual" yuppies engaging in aromatherapy and body wrapping and of "valley girls" using yoga to make a serious commitment to their abdomens come to mind. In addition, spirituality and spiritual healing are often associated with cults that are both exploitative and totalitarian.

What would be a model of spiritual healing without side effects? In short, when is faith healing safe, and when is it hoke? If I am to frame my question in empirical, scientific terms, how can we enhance the healing potential of the positive emotions, while minimizing the toxic effects of hoke? As the focus for this discussion, I believe the healing provided by AA allows us to excavate the nature of what is meant by spiritual cure. No, I'm not an alcoholic, and I'm not a member of AA. But for 35 years as a clinician and as a research scientist I've marveled at how alcoholics, by giving Samaritan comfort to each other, and by focusing daily on a "power greater than me," are able to heal each other.

In the United States, alcoholism kills 100,000 people a year. That's far more than die of breast cancer. However, professional medicine can do little to halt alcoholism over the long term. Modern medicine can detoxify alcoholics, and over the short term can save lives, and for a few months modern medicine can delay relapse. All too often, however, alcoholics treated by modern medical science relapse. In contrast, within the spiritual setting of alcoholics helping each other, AA provides an example of spirituality as a force that cures as well as comforts. I'm talking here about 20-year cures, not six months' drying out and the brief efficacy of naltrexone and Antabuse. Often, AA is referred to as a self-help group; nothing could be further from the truth. Self-help is very limited. We all know that doctors who try to care for themselves have fools for physicians. Bestselling books on self-help are well intentioned, but more often than not they're ineffectual. When did you last read a diet book that kept someone thin for 5 years? Elizabeth Taylor would like to know. Why so seldom? Because such books depend upon wish, not upon human communion. Self-help is all about "me." Wishes and self-help books are autistic and isolate us. If you can't even tickle yourself, how are you going to give yourself love? In sharp contrast, most of the incorrectly named "self-help groups," like AA, are as communal as barn raising.

If I am to justify my thesis that AA provides a tangible model for understanding spiritual healing, I must provide scientific facts and not rhetoric. If I am to suggest that a program based on dependence on a Higher Power is more like penicillin than it is like the Unification Church of Rev. Sun Myung Moon, I must respect the rules of empirical medicine. I must present a mechanism of action. I must present efficacy better than a placebo. And I must examine toxic side effects.

First, AA does cure. If AA cures alcoholism, what's its mechanism of action? Much of what has been done scientifically to cure alcoholism is, at best, placebo, and, at worst, hoke. For example, cure from addiction does not come through psychodynamic insight. In my own prospective study of Harvard graduates, 26 alcoholics received 5,000 hours of psychotherapy. Only one recovered while in psychotherapy, and I say this as a dedicated psychotherapist. Nor is lifesaving detoxification effective for very long. In one study, being on the waiting list was about as successful as four comparable treatment studies.

In addition, cognitive behavior therapy works less well than we would like. Linda and Mark Sobell's 1970s study of training alcoholics to return to social drinking won them worldwide fame until someone thought to do a 10-year follow-up study and found that the treated patients fared no better than the untreated. Even Bill Miller, who's a brilliant investigator, found at 8 years that his patients turned out to do better in AA, not intended to be a control study, than they had in cognitive-behavior therapy.

The reason for this failure is twofold: First, the hold that drug addiction has on human beings doesn't rest in our neocortex. The hold that addiction has on our minds rests in what's been called our "reptile brain." The hold comes from cellular changes in midbrain nuclei with esoteric names, like the "nucleus accumbens" and the "superior tegmentum." Eventually these changes move abstinence beyond the reach of willpower, which doesn't predict remission, by the way. They are beyond the reach of condition, beyond the reach of psychoanalytic insight, and beyond the reach of deep fidelity to God. Catholic priests need AA just as badly as the rest of us to recover from alcoholism.

The second reason that professional treatment fails to prevent relapse in alcoholism is that the skills needed to climb out of a hole are different from the skills needed to fall into it. When we look at the six major reasons people become alcoholic, none of them are associated with recovery. Change in clinical course in both alcoholism and diabetes can be obtained not from doctors but from relapse prevention. And to quote Lady Macbeth's physician, "Therein, the patient must minister to herself."

There are four factors commonly present in relapse prevention from smoking, gambling, heroin addiction, and alcoholism. The four factors all prevent relapse and briefly they are: external supervision, ritualized dependency on a competing behavior, new love relationships, and deepened spirituality. Usually, we observe that two or more of these have to be present for alcoholism to remit. Recovery from alcoholism, like recovery from two-pack-a-day smoking, is anything but spontaneous. The reason these four factors are effective is that, unlike most of our professional treatments, they don't work to create temporary abstinence. They work to prevent relapse.

First, external supervision is necessary because in the treatment of addictions conscious motivation on admission is not associated with recovery—alligators don't come when they're called. Some kind of leash is needed to control the reptile brain. In our neocortex, most of us know how we ought to exercise more often, but we still take elevators. The great Christian theologian Paul Tillich wrote brilliantly about unselfish love, but he couldn't control his own repeated infidelity to his wife. AA, religion, and most personal trainers provide external supervision. They simply don't trust free will. They suggest that their clients return again and again. In AA, members are encouraged to find a sponsor to telephone and visit often. They're encouraged to keep coming back, and they're encouraged to engage in service to other alcoholics. Each of these activities provide external supervision, or in the language of AA "keep the memory green." But AA understands that compulsory supervision works best if it's from choice. We willingly suffer under the strict rules of our coach, even though we may avoid the rules of the tax collector or traffic policeman.

Second, it's important to find a *substitute dependency*, or a *competing reinforcer* for addiction. You can't easily give up a habit without getting "addicted" to something else. Alcoholics Anonymous understands what all behaviorists know, and what parents and psychiatrists and priests often forget. Bad habits need substitutes, not threats. Punishments and negative emotion alone don't change deeply ingrained habits. Thus AA and most religions provide a gratifying schedule of social and service activities in the presence of supportive and now-healed former sinners, especially at times of high risk, such as holidays. Think of all the times on a weekend, or a holiday, when you can get nothing but your doctor's answering service, but spiritual organizations are open for business. AA "home groups," more than most religions, focus on fostering positive emotions. "An attitude of gratitude." "To keep it you have to give it away." Ritual criticism is replaced by "loving suggestions" and "unconditional positive regard." AA meetings are filled with laughter, celebrations, anniversaries for sobriety, unlimited coffee and hugs, and humor—another positive emotion. And, of course, AA meetings compete with prime drinking time.

The bad news is that critics sometimes complain that AA is as addicting as alcohol. But so are puppies. Like heroin, positive emotion has a sneaky way of making us want to come back for more. The unhealthy pleasure of chemical addiction is replaced by the healthy physiological dopaminergic neurobiology of the positive emotions.

Another substitute for alcohol supplied by AA is the positive emotion of forgiveness. Alcoholics have often inflicted enormous pain and injury on others. Thus when sober, alcoholics may experience overwhelming guilt. Although a poor tranquilizer and a worthless antidepressant, alcohol is perhaps the most powerful solvent for a guilty conscience that modern pharmacology has yet devised. Thus, the forgiveness inherent in membership in the fellowship of AA provides absolution from a "power greater than ourselves," which becomes an important part of the healing process.

Third, there are new love relationships, which are important to recovery. It seems important for ex-addicts to bond with people who they have not hurt severely in the past and to whom they are not deeply emotionally in debt. Indeed it helps for alcoholics to bond with people for whom they can provide compassion and help. Perhaps it's no accident that the maternal-infant bonding is mediated by endorphins, our brain's natural morphine. Love trumps drugs. Or as Cole Porter, that great student of the limbic system, explained to us, "I get no kick from cocaine, I get a kick out of you." And "I'd even give up coffee for Sanka, even Sanka, Bianca, for you." As in evolution, love can tame the reptile brain. In short, compassion and love are even more consoling than shopping and chocolate, but just as addicting. Alcoholics Anonymous calls such a forgiving fellowship "the language of the heart."

The fourth common feature in recovery from addiction is the discovery or rediscovery of spirituality. Inspirational, altruistic group membership and belief in a power "greater than me" seems important in recovery from addiction. This was first identified by William James, and later by Jung with his Spiritus contra spiritum. The 12th step of AA carries the same message as Lourdes; to keep it you have to give it away. That makes no sense to a human neocortex. But it makes excellent sense to the mammalian limbic system, which has evolved in order to provide unselfish love. In short, human attachment and spirituality are mediated by the dopaminergic tracts in the limbic system that provide worthy substitutes for drugs. Since it's doubtful that our preliterate ancestors shot dope, the limbic brain circuitry underlying addiction may have evolved to facilitate unselfish love, attachment, social cohesion, and spiritual community.

One mechanism that helps spirituality to combat addiction may be that both spirituality and religion provide an alternative to the subjective ersatz high produced by drugs. In the 19th century, when opium smoking was a luxury of the rich, Karl Marx quipped that religion was the opiate of the masses. But let's turn old Marx on his head. Maybe the sense of spiritual peace and oceanic high the masses received from meditation, prayer, and daily reading was the real thing and the joy experienced by Quincy and Coleridge and their pals was merely ersatz.

Put in more scientific terms, spirituality may be an indirect way we have of stimulating both our dopaminergic and our endorphin systems. Consider the phenomenon at the height of battle. These are two related phenomena. Not only are there no atheists in foxholes, but often in battle the severely wounded feel no pain. Spiritual experiences, William James tells us, nearly all have "the great common denominators of pain, suffering, and calamity." God comes in through the wound.

Let me carry this hypothesis a little bit further. Dopaminergic brain tracts can be shown to underlie addictive behavior in mammals and reptiles. A scientist can produce pleasure in the brain by inserting dopamine into the primitive circuitry that links the nucleus accumbens and the superior tegmentum. But in mammals, the same dopaminergic tract runs from the midbrain, through the limbic system (that part of mammalian brain that serves attachment), onto the anterior cingulate gyrus (which also supports attachment), to the frontal lobe, which lights up when a mother sees a newborn child. Or, in the words of Thomas Insel, the present director of NIMH, "it's also possible that neural mechanisms that we associate with drug abuse and addiction might have evolved for social recognition, reward, and euphoria, critical elements in the process of attachment" (Insel and Young, 2002, p. 129).

After suggesting how the mechanism of action works, I must answer the question of whether AA is better than a placebo. First, pooling data shows that leading groups, having a sponsor, and going to meetings help relapse prevention. But the argument is then made: "Well, maybe people who go to meetings are just those people that comply with treatment of all kinds and what you're getting here is compliance."

At Stanford, research psychologists Keith Humphreys and Rudolf Moos (1996, 1997) carried out a prospective study that compared compliance with professional treatment to AA attendance. By 8 years the two outcome goals of less drinking and more abstinence were only weakly related to the number of days of professional treatment but were robustly related to AA attendance (Timko et al., 1999). Those alcoholics who attended professional treatment and AA had almost twice the rate of abstinence compared to those who attended professional treatment alone (Timko et al., 2000). In short, the effect of AA does not just rest on compliance with treatment.

The third "scientific" question I must answer is: What are the side effects of AA? Even if it does cure alcoholism, is it safe? Certainly, AA has its detractors. The emotional language and rhetoric of AA horrify social scientists and journalists who understandably fear demagogues and cults. True, cults and AA both take advantage of the fact that people achieve relief from emotional distress when they feel held by what Mark Galanter (1990) calls a "social cocoon." But healing through intense affiliation is hardly confined to cults. Families, sororities, and soccer teams also provide cocoons. Galanter is quite right in accusing AA of a high level of social cohesion. And it's true that, besides recovery and service, the third cornerstone of AA membership is unity. But the dogmatic unity of AA is based on the same principles that drove the 13 original American states to achieve social cohesion. In Ben Franklin's words, "If we don't all hang together, we'll hang separately."

Unlike membership in a cult, following the rigid, sequential steps of AA is like following the rigidly numbered steps of a Nautilus exercise regimen—your participation is voluntary and it is always your turn. The purpose of the rigidity of both postcoronary and AA "step" programs is not, as is the case with cults, to take away your autonomy, but only to provide a disciplined program of relapse prevention so that you won't return to using alcohol and die. I, too, have a profound mistrust of Puritanism, jogging, and diets with too many vegetables. But if such rigid behavior would keep me from dying from heart disease, I just might reconsider.

Nor is AA a religion, and there are several ways AA has avoided becoming a religion. First, the spiritual foundation on which AA arose was based on the fact that James, Jung, and Doctor Bob all hated organized religion but were all deep students of what religions had in common in order to heal.

Another difference is that, unlike religions such as Jehovah's Witnesses and Christian Science, AA does not compete with medical science. AA literature is very clear that it is "wrong to deprive any alcoholic of medication which can alleviate or control other disabling physical or emotional problems" and that "no AA member plays doctor." (AA, 1976, p. 6)

Again, it's hard to belong to two religions at the same time, but in Hindu India, in Buddhist Japan, and in passionately Catholic Spain, AA membership has increased tenfold in the last 15 years. AA membership has also risen exponentially in atheistic Russia. The language of the heart trumps the language of logos and of dogma.

Third, AA has tried to avoid black-and-white thinking, except with regard to abstinence and public anonymity. In the words of cofounder Bob Smith, the famous 12 steps "are suggestions, not dogma." And he could reduce the 12 steps of AA down to just two words: "love" and "service."

Another major difference between AA and religion is that AA has avoided authority. Most jobs are unpaid. The strict rule that requires rotation of roles ensures that no one person accumulates authority; in that way AA is much like the early Christian church, which was, for a brief century, free of past rabbinical authority and free of future papal authority.

A criticism of both AA (and cults) is that in contrast to spiritual programs like

Buddhism, AA encourages dependence. Many observers worry that AA members become as needy of their 8 p.m. meetings as they once were of alcohol itself. And so it is important to distinguish the dependence engendered by AA from the dependence engendered by cults. Dependence can weaken or strengthen us. We are weakened by dependence on cigarettes, slot machines, and junk food. We are strengthened by dependence on exercise, vitamins, and love.

Another feature of AA, which distinguishes it from any cult and from most religions of which I know (including my own faith tradition of psychoanalysis), is that AA has a sense of humor. And humor, by the way, is partially located in the nucleus accumbens. Every meeting of AA that I've ever attended has been filled with laughter. Cults, bishops, and training analysts often fail to observe AA's venerable rule number 62: "Don't take yourself too damn seriously." And it's equally important to note that the other 61 rules don't exist.

Finally, AA, like the Franciscans, strives to stay poor. Unlike cults, universities, and religious denominations, AA owns no property. Outside people can't give money to AA, and members can only leave $2,000 in their wills to AA.

Remember, not only do the positive emotions reflect spirituality, the positive emotions are never all about "me." Nevertheless, skeptical academic minds have tended not to accept the universal importance of spirituality in human life. They wish to keep scientific and spiritual truths separate, insisting that scientific is truer than spiritual. I believe that's a mistake, and the sociobiologist E. O. Wilson (1998) comes to my rescue: "The essence of humanity's spiritual dilemma is that we evolved genetically to accept one truth, and discovered another" (p. 264). With the printing press and then the enlightenment, limbic positive emotion became subordinate to lexical, neocortical science and dogma. However, as the French discovered, with their atheistic—but very scientific—guillotine, the enlightenment was sometimes too true to be good.

Hunter–gatherer humanity evolved to accept the truth that the highest values of humanity could be expressed through enduring spiritual metaphors, and through the enduring guidance of positive emotions. The science that humanity has discovered has evolved the rapid evolution and transmission of culture in order to validate and, when necessary, to invalidate, the perceptions of our five senses. But the difference between neocortical science and limbic spirituality isn't there. They both mediate survival. They simply depend on different parts of our highly integrated, if haphazardly evolved, brain. One truth isn't truer than another.

REFERENCES

Alcoholics Anonymous. (1976). *The AA Member—Medications and other drugs* [brochure]. Retrieved from http://aa.org/pdf/products/p-11_aamembersMedDrug.pdf

Alcoholics Anonymous. (1981). *Twelve steps and twelve traditions.* Retrieved from http://aa.org/twelveandtwelve/en_tableofcnt.cfm

Alcoholics Anonymous. (2001). *Alcoholics Anonymous: The story of how many thousands of men and women have recovered from alcoholism* [Commonly called the *Big Book]* (4th ed.). Retrieved from http://aa.org/bigbookonline/en_tableofcnt.cfm

Insel, T. R., & Young, L. J. (2002). The neurobiology of attachment. *Nature Reviews Neuroscience, 2*(2), 129-136. doi:10.1038/35053579

Sadock, B. J. & Sadock, V. A. (Eds.) (2003). *Kaplan and Sadock's comprehensive textbook of psychiatry* (7th ed.). Lippencott, Williams, & Wilkins: Philadelphia.

Timko, C., Moos, R. H., Finney, J. W., & Lesar, M. D. (2000). Long-term outcomes of alcohol use disorders: Comparing untreated individuals with those in Alcoholics Anonymous and formal treatment. *Journal of Studies on Alcohol and Drugs, 61*(4), 529.

Timko, C., Moos, R. H., Finney, J. W., Moos, B. S., & Kaplowitz, M. S. (1999). Long-term treatment careers and outcomes of previously untreated alcoholics. *Journal of Studies on Alcohol and Drugs, 60*(4), 437.

Wilson, E. O. (1998). *Consilience: The Unity of Knowledge.* Knopf: New York.

4. Higher Goals and Leaving Addiction: Finding Meaning in Life

STANTON PEELE

It's really a great pleasure for me to talk before a group that emphasizes meaning. I wrote a book called *The Meaning of Addiction* that is central to my work. One of the problems I have with the disease model of addiction is that it regards human beings as passive. The disease model states that addictions are: (a) inbred/biological, (b) based on a loss of control, (c) lifelong/permanent, (d) have an inevitable progression, and (e) require medical/spiritual treatment. A disease is something a person has, perhaps that they were born with. It's not anything they're involved in maintaining. But I don't view addiction that way. I view human beings as actively seeking certain kinds of satisfactions in life, and addiction results when their pursuit of those satisfactions mires them down in some bad place, isn't productive, and is in fact destructive. If you've got the wrong view of what addiction is and what its sources are, I don't think you're going to do very well in treating addiction. And I'll talk later about how I see this difference in views of addiction impacting how we treat it.

But let me start out with a basic question: "Why do people get addicted?" This leads to a more fundamental question: "What do people want?" This is basic psychology. And I think that there are some fundamental things that nearly all human beings seek. I think everybody wants to feel *loved*. I think everybody wants to feel *secure*. I think everybody wants to feel *in control* of their lives and their world. And I believe that every human being wants to feel that their life has some *meaning* beyond their individual physical presence on the earth. Let's take those four things—love, security, control, and meaning—and trace out their importance in terms of addiction and addiction treatment.

Let's start with how people usually go about achieving these things. How do you get love? In my experience, people seek love by creating meaningful relationships. Where do they get a sense of security? I think the standard way is to have a well-ordered life where you can count on things being where you want them to be, and count on things progressing in an ordinary way. How do you get a feeling of control? You get a feeling of control, I believe, by having sufficient skills to manage this world around us—you feel control when you feel that you stand some fairly good chance of getting a reasonable amount of what you seek and desire. And how do people get a feeling that there's something in life that extends beyond their mere physical presence? By developing some feeling of transcendence—by finding some way of connecting with something beyond themselves.

So I have identified what I consider to be four fundamental—you could call them "spiritual"—needs, and I've described what I think are the four standard ways that people satisfy those needs. Where does addiction come in? Well, what addiction does is to provide a form of each of these satisfactions.

Addictions can create a sense of belonging and of being valued. For example, people eat or shop as a way to feel better about themselves. People drink or shoot heroin as part of being in a group. It not only makes them feel that they belong to that group, but often the activity itself—as with drinking alcohol—provides them with a better sense that they're appealing to other people. It lessens their defenses so that they feel better regarded. If you ask teenagers why they drink, the answer is effectively "to be loved."

Addictions provide a sense of security. And they provide a sense of security because they create some predictability in your life. The predictability revolves around the rituals required to do what you do. There's a certain place you get your drug or there's a certain place where you perform whatever addictive activity you perform. And addictions are also valuable because they produce reliable effects. People count on drugs producing virtually the same effect each time, and it's the same with drinking: It's something that people count on. So that's the addictive version of security.

If people are seeking a sense of control, which ordinarily is achieved by developing life skills, addictive activities and substances may be thought of as a way of coping with the world and particularly with emotions. We all have a bunch of contradictory feelings and wishes and thoughts about ourselves. Drugs and alcohol and other addictions allow people to mediate those feelings and give them a sense that they're where they need to be. Addictions create a feeling that people control their own inner states.

Lastly, how does addiction give you a sense of transcendence? Well, addictive activities are a way people have of getting outside of themselves. That's obvious in the case of drugs. They give you a sense of being beyond yourself, being separated from who you are. But when people gamble, they also talk about being lost in a whirl of betting, uncertainty, and anxiety—they're not in themselves, they're in some other place. And people really value that. It's a high. It's a very strong motivation.

Let's review. I've described what people want in life, I've described how people ordinarily get those things in life, and I've discussed how addictions provide, in a way, for all of those essential spiritual, emotional, and practical needs. But what makes them addictive? If there's a way to get those things, and if indeed people do need those things, then whose business is it? After all, that's one way to do it. Why do we call that addictive? The obvious answer is that it's an artificial, or external, way of getting those things. It's not a part of who you are in your naked humanity; it's something that you've gone out to get for that purpose. Now that characteristic of addictive activities is shared by something that we don't normally think of as addictive: prescribed psychotropic medications. People don't feel what they think they need to feel about themselves, and so—especially in the United States, and at younger and younger ages—people purchase medications that modify their feelings. So let me provide a second criterion for addiction, which is that the artificial activity must be destructive. By relying on some external way of fulfilling your fundamental needs, you're undercutting your life and your ability to experience those feelings and emotions without the addiction. Those two characteristics are what jointly differentiate addictive from constructive ways of fulfilling fundamental needs for meaning and spiritual fulfillment.

How do people get over addictions? Notice the way that I phrase that: "How do people get over addictions?" I don't ask, "How do people get treated out of addiction?" That's not the way I view it. If you recall, I talked about the problem I have with the disease model, which sees addiction as just being in a passive person, whereas I see addiction as being an effort people make to try and satisfy themselves, but which isn't working very well. And that has direct implications for treatment. It doesn't work for me to think that addiction is some artificial accident—"The doctor prescribed a lot of painkillers for me, and that's why I became addicted." Likewise the answer to an addiction isn't to detoxify.

For example, I'm now writing a book called *Addiction-Proof Your Child,* and in the treatment chapter, the very first thing I discuss is a woman who comes to me and is a single mother with a daughter. They've had a very close relationship and spend a lot of recreational time together. But now her daughter has dropped out of school, and is spending all of her time on the Internet, surfing sexual sites and chat lines, and one day a woman that the daughter is involved with showed up at their house, though neither the daughter nor the mother has ever met this person before. So the mother asks me, "How can I get rid of my daughter's Internet addiction?" You see how she is conceiving of addiction? "Well, my daughter is addicted to the Internet. You're an addiction expert, so stop her from being addicted to the Internet." But what am I going to say to her? I've got a therapeutic problem here, which is that I'm talking with a person who wants me to cure somebody else, so I've got to deal with that. My first question is going to be something like, "Is there anything in your relationship, thus far, that has led to this situation? And since you're the only person here talking to me, is there anything you can change to improve that aspect of your relationship?" That's what I see my job as a therapist as being. But her mistake is a common one: "My daughter has the disease of addiction—cure it!" That's her conception of what we're doing. But my conception is "What's the nature of this girl's life and situation that has led her to seek these satisfactions in a way that's going to be destructive?" An obvious first step is to see that somehow her mother has created a highly dependent individual who's not very good at actively going out and satisfying her needs in a constructive way. And she's still a kid, so is there something the mother can do in interacting with her to assist her to become a more life-seeking, meaning-seeking entity on her own?

So the answer to the question "How do people overcome addiction?" is "People find direct ways to achieve their essential emotional and spiritual needs." They do something that makes them feel more valuable. You can do something positive that other people admire. And how do you get a sense of security? Well, you build some kind of reasonable life structure that allows you to anticipate that things will be okay, and to feel that you're having your fundamental needs satisfied and that you're not going to go down in flames. How do you enhance people's sense of control so that they can fight the addiction? We want to enable and encourage them to develop more successful ways of dealing with the world. In this area in particular, people need coping skills. One reason this girl is on the Internet is that she doesn't feel adequate to meet and talk with people that she actually knows at school, or to go on dates—and those are fundamental ways of relating to people. Or people don't feel that they can cope with stress or difficult situations. When they feel that they can do that—when they're able to develop better coping skills—they're going to become less likely to use their addiction to get these feelings.

And how do you get meaning beyond yourself? Addicts are focused on their own needs. That's always true. When addicts come to you, even the whole therapy process is "Help me, I need something." So there's a kind of a contradiction we have to deal with: Here are addicts feeding themselves, but getting outside of yourself means thinking about people other than yourself. Now, the hardest drug addiction to quit is smoking, and when people do quit, it's usually not as a result of therapeutic or group help. Many people who have quit smoking would have continued if they were on their own. But they might think about their families: "Here are these people, who happen to be genetically related to me, and I want to do something for them, and my addiction is bad for them." People don't give up things. It's like with kids—they don't want to give up that toy; you have to give them a better toy. Likewise, you don't give up whatever you're getting out of an addiction. For better or for worse, you've been doing it for a while, and it's providing these fundamental satisfactions. You're not going to volunteer to give up those fundamental satisfactions unless you see your way beyond the addiction to some higher goal. People are not sufficiently motivated to give up an addiction or a habit simply because it's bad for them or because others want them to stop. But when a habit or an addiction interferes with accomplishing a goal that people want to attain, or something larger that they are committed to, then they're likely to quit.

There are four kinds of meaning beyond oneself that help people to overcome addiction: family, community, accomplishing a goal, and the greater good. Love, intimate relationships, and families are an awfully strong motivation for people to overcome addiction. People smoke, they get married, their spouse doesn't like their smoking, there's some kind of conflict, and eventually they quit—it happens all the time. And then there are children—a guy will say, "I quit smoking because every time I came home, my daughter started crying and saying, 'Daddy, why are you killing yourself?'" That's an effective therapeutic technique. A second way that people get meaning beyond themselves is by having goals—they want to achieve something in life. Again it happens all the time. An ex-heroin addict will say, "I just looked around, I was 25 years old, and what did I have? My friends had jobs and were accomplishing things, and I wanted to as well. So I quit." A third thing is that when people are part of a community, they are much more likely to give up an addiction. They feel that they are part of a family or a culture or a town or some kind of group where they feel their behavior is reflecting negatively on that group, and they want to make some contribution to that group, and they recognize that they're not because of the addiction. Finally, there's the greater good—some kind of mission that people have in life. They just feel that they want to make some contribution to history, or to society, or to the universe.

I talked about the difference between a normal way of satisfying something and an addictive way. So let me focus now on what differentiates between an addiction and a mission or real commitment to something beyond yourself—something we might call genuinely spiritual. It's tricky, because some people will suggest that religion or AA can be addictive. So we need some criteria.

First, a mission or spiritual transcendence deepens your connection with other people and the world around you. It makes you better able to connect to those things that are most important. A man will feel better dealing with his children knowing that he's not smoking—he doesn't feel embarrassed around them, he can take them on car rides, and so on.

Second, it results in real accomplishment. There have to be some kind of concrete indications that this thing is enhancing your ability to accomplish things in the world. It may seem funny to say that the mark of spiritual transcendence is that it produces concrete accomplishment. Without this criterion, you're left with the strange phenomenon of people who have been going to psychoanalysis five days a week for 10 or 12 years, and they think it's going great because they're so much more aware of how much their parents messed them up, but they're a bigger pain than they used to be.

Third, a mission expands your world. What, for example, would be a religion that, by this criterion, didn't provide a spiritual transcendence but rather an addictive one? Well, some people decide that by getting very religious, they've realized how bad most of the people they know are, and therefore they only want to spend time with the good people in their religion. But by the criterion of expanding your world, the difference between a spiritual transcendence and an addictive transcendence is that a spiritual transcendence should expand your horizons and your avenues for meeting your needs. You should be better at dealing with other people, not worse.

Think of love, too. Someone will say, "I'm so in love with Mabel that I've stopped talking to my family," or "I'm so in love with Phil that I've given up all my friends." That makes sense to people, and happens all the time, but also fails by this criterion.

The last, and fourth, criterion for determining whether a way of getting outside of yourself is really transcendent rather than addictive is that it must take you beyond yourself to help others, but at the same time enhance your own sense of self. You should feel better about who you are; your belief in yourself should be greater; you should feel more whole and more competent. If getting outside of yourself means sacrificing yourself, it's not a genuine spiritual transcendence but an addictive one.

5. The Affective Basis of Drug and Social Addiction

JAAK PANKSEPP

Psychoanalysis has recently begun listening to brain research. Unfortunately, brain research is not listening to you; it's not listening to the human experience. That's why there's room for a discipline such as neuropsychoanalysis to be a sanctuary for a tradition whose members truly want to understand the human experience. The main problem that an addict faces is pretty much the same problem that we all face, namely the power of our emotionality, the power of our feelings: We make our choices based on what feels good and what feels bad. This is affective neuro-economics. Neuroscience should be telling us about the deep nature of affect, and about what drugs are doing in the human brain. It's not just reward or reinforcement, those old behavioral concepts. There are many affective experiences. I'm one of those people who have been taking the human emotional experience seriously as a scientific topic. Back when I was a young clinical psychology student, I realized that I would not understand these things by studying human beings, and that, as creatures of evolution, we share these powerful tools with other animals. So I decided to go into animal research.

What took me into emotion research were the 1973 reports on the discovery of the first receptor system in the brain: the opiate receptor system. Finally people had a target for the three main uses of opiates in medicine: pain control, control of coughing, and control of diarrhea. Opiate receptors are all around the brain. They do all sorts of things. The one idea we had was that they were the main messengers of positive social feelings; I think that's now a demonstrated fact in neuroscience. It fits with Stanton Peele's idea from around the same time that love is an addictive process; we become dependent on each other. Here's a postulate: There would be no addictions without affective change. My field, however, is still stuck on this dilemma, a seemingly impenetrable mystery, namely the fact that subjective experience exists in a physiochemical world. But it does so—it's an emergent reality—so let's get on with the business of understanding it! And yet we're stuck arguing about whether it exists, particularly in animals. For example, people doing fear research right now, such as LeDoux and others, say their animals experience no fear; they just have fear reflexes. That's bullshit. We might ask, "Would drug addiction exist if drugs did not change our internal feelings?" In a foreward for a book for Paul MacLean I said: "Clearly the answer is no, and not only for members of our own species. Other animals get addicted to exactly the same drugs for exactly the same affective reasons." And that's why the animal research is so important for everyone working with addiction.

So I take an evolutionary approach to the poppy seed and what it does in our minds. Unfortunately, psychology has become the impoverished stepchild in the neuroscience crusade to understand addiction. The neuroscience crusade comes from behaviorism: "stimulus–response." Once the money for behavioristic research dried up in the 1970s it became "stimulus–brain–response." There was no room for mind, which is unfortunate because one of the main things the brain does is to create mind and mental processes. So currently we have a neuroscience that is fundamentally sterile in terms of its conception of the true nature of reality. Mentality exists. How far back it goes in neuro-evolution we don't know, but all mammals have minds, and the part of the mind that they all share is affective experience. Rats enjoy sweeteners because they produce a pleasurable response. Cats don't care for it. Cats don't care for sweeteners; they like proteins. So there's a lot of variability in detail, but the principles are the same. This spooky thing called "reinforcement" is how affect controls learning. But it was thrown out because affect is spooky, subjective.

Social affect is a source of addictive urges. Social reward is probably the most addictive of the affects because all of our evolutionary progression relies upon having social bonds and social relationships. Evolution therefore has assured that, in a species like ours, where both mothers and fathers are needed to care of their otherwise completely helpless children, mothers and fathers get addicted to each other, at least for a while. The little ones also get powerfully addicted to their parents, to their mothers especially, until they become independent enough to chase other affects. Specifically, this happens when they mature sexually.

This affect system is a general-purpose desire system, perhaps similar to Freud's libido: a life-energy, a desire to chase things in the world that enhance survival. This system doesn't know what to do with itself because it's born really stupid. It has to learn what to do, and there are many things about which it has to learn. And dopamine is at the heart of it. That's why cocaine addiction is so dramatically more habituating than opiate addiction. People can regulate their opiate addictions, as long as they have weak opiates. (Of course, super-powerful opiates have been developed, addiction to which becomes a personal disaster. The old-time opiates were more manageable.)

We have a new measure of appetitive desire in animals: a basic response from rats that says "I like it, I want more." It's a 50 kHz vocalization that we have become notorious for, because we demonstrated that it is an ancestral form of laughter. When little children are anticipating things—for example, if you bring them a present but say they can't have it, holding it just out of reach—they jump, laugh, and are happy. That kind of joy at getting something unexpected, as with jokes, seems to produce a laughter response. Not that rats necessarily have jokes, but maybe they do. Some slapstick or simple, childlike humour, perhaps; no one's studied it before. But they chirp when you tickle them and when they play. It's been the gauntlet I've thrown down in front of my colleagues: "I think it's laughter—you prove me wrong, because we've done serious science for eight years, and there is such a mountain of evidence for it that you have to give us a better interpretation of this." This vocalization measure also turns out to be a superb measure of drug desire. For the first time, we can ask an animal, "Do you really want it?" and when they chirp, "cheep cheep cheep," you know they want it. We have mapped out the system for this in the brain, and it turns out to be the classic Olds and Milner reward/reinforcement system. It runs right along there.

There are some obvious theses concerning the brain, mind, and emotion. The fundamental affective systems of the mind reflect various evolutionary adaptive functions of the brain. They are ancestral tools for living; they are the voices of our genes. In our modern search for understanding the mechanisms of the brain and mind, however, we neuroscientists often choose to forget that widespread neural networks generate various psychological processes that regulate behavior. This is not an idea that is accepted in my field. The National Institute on Drug Abuse (NIDA) is tossing all its money at brain molecules. They believe that's all you need to know about, at least in the animal models. The bottom line, however, is that thinking, perceiving, feeling, behaving, and getting addicted are not simply properties of brain molecules. To truly understand how brains generate addictions, we also need psychological perspectives based on a network doctrine, one that acknowledges complex neuronal networks that are designed to do important things like control affect and emotions. Right now, we're stuck with a neural doctrine. Many of my colleagues trot out this one study by Lamb, in the *Journal of Pharmacology and Experimental Therapeutics*, and claim it as evidence that addiction is unconscious. This study is commonly used to argue that addiction can be sustained by unconscious reward—by unexperienced rewards or reinforcement processes. But go and read that study with a sensitive psychological eye. A careful reading will reveal that the study indicates nothing of the sort. It would take a long time to explain it all, so I will just say that the claims about the unconscious nature of addiction are based on a simple misinterpretation of a very straightforward study that people choose to misuse. So, my conjecture is that, if human pipe dreams or subjective reality were not more enticing than external reality (our affects are built into our system; that's the internal reality), there would be no addictions. Addictions can't exist without affective feelings. That's my bottom line.

So how do we understand these spooky things called affects? We can best access affects through primitive mentality—the psychological properties of the reptilian brain. You have to take a cross-species evolutionary perspective. Here's my image of the triune brain: Paul MacLean's neocortex, limbic system, and reptilian brain. Well, you have a triune, layered, mind, too, and to understand addiction you have to understand the lowest layers of mentality. Addiction is so hard because these lowest layers are very habitual. The feeling of affect initially guides behavior, but then if the behavior doesn't require new adjustments it becomes habitual. It's a very streamlined, affective system. Ultimately addiction is so horrible because it takes over the habitual structures of the brain. Affects provide the comfort zones by which all humans and all animals live their lives. Of course, if everything [in our affective system] is taken care of then we can develop intellectual pursuits, but until that moment it's comfort zones. So this mystery is no longer impenetrable, and it's only penetrable by neuroscience. Experience, thousands of years of human experience, gives us poetry and art but still leaves it as a fundamental mystery.

So we've been studying emotional feelings. There are many other kinds of feelings. And our approach has been simply this: There's an instinctual apparatus in all of our brains, and when this cat is behaving this way, this cat is angry. This is what we call dual-aspect monism; complex networks have several different properties. For example, light has wave and particle functions. Angry behavior reflects angry feelings, and emotions act out into the world in dramatic and dynamic ways so the animal can readjust its behavior depending on what's happening in the environment. So they're all learning systems, and there's a bunch of these systems in the brain, which I've summarized in *Affective Neuroscience*—it's not necessarily a complete list, but one that can be defended with lots of data.

I'd like to talk about contact comfort, the feeling of goodness from a hug, from a touch, from massage, or from sex, which is controlled by brain opioids. Opioids are still the main pleasure molecules of the brain. The opioid system receives lots of pleasures, including the comfort of being held. So we did this study in young birds. When a baby bird is left alone, it cries—"beep beep beep beep"—and when it is picked up, it stops crying. This happens every time. It's just as if it were under its mother's wings. The bird relaxes, its head goes down, its eyes close, and it falls asleep. We know this is an opioid-related response, because if you give antiopioids like naltrexone or naloxone to the bird, the bird does not settle down as well. It takes the animal four times as long to become relaxed. It still becomes relaxed, at least outwardly, but it takes much longer. So a part of contact comfort is opioid mediated, and produces a natural reward. That's why a person in withdrawal deserves a big hug every once in a while. There's many possible interpretations. We assume that this behavioral response has to be a comfort response. I could get stuck in a philosophical argument, so let me move on. All this depends on a convergence of evidence.

I want to talk next about brain opioids and the pleasure of social feelings. There are many affects, pleasures, pains, and sensations that are important as affects but are not emotional affects. For instance, I would not consider the taste of sugar to be an emotional response, even though we can get passionate over a great meal. I would also not consider the feeling of disgust, such as sensory disgust, to be an emotional response, because it operates on an external sensory system. The neat thing about emotions is that the organization is inside the brain. The whole executive organization is an internal brain process. These emotional arousals seem to be linked to the instinctual action apparatus of the animal, and there are a whole variety of postarousal reliefs: "I didn't have breakfast; I was delighted we had a wonderful lunch—it was ok for me that it was late." It is a good feeling to be satisfied again but that is not an emotional category. There's hunger and there's thirst; they're powerful feelings. All of these things are instinctual. We don't learn them; we inherit them. They are the evolved tools for learning. I like the phrase "they are the ancestral voices of the genes." That's what the brain does for us; they're gifts of nature. We might then ask, "How many emotions are there?" "How many basic addictive feelings are there?" There's hardly a discussion about these issues. We have to cover our ambiguities and we have to remember language. A higher rational brain creates the ambiguities so such a question throws us into the realm of ambiguity for a while, and it has to be dealt with scientifically. It is the neocortex, however, that is the source of our ambiguity. These processes themselves are not ambiguous. The baby bird mentioned earlier will run to my hand to be picked up. If my hand were bad, it would not run to it. Fear is built into the system, and anger is built into the system, as well as various other wonderful social processes. We have been mapping joy on the surface of the brain by studying the playfulness of animals. There are powerful circuits involved with play. If spiritual movements can tap into joy, it is the most powerful of animal and human feelings, once everything else is satisfied.

To understand drug addiction, we must understand the nature of affective processes. Affective states of the nervous system are emergent evolutionary properties of complex neural dynamics that need to be talked about and linked to brain processes. We've developed in my field a tradition of using words like "reward" and "reinforcement." Edward Thorndike, in *Animal Intelligence*, explained learning roughly this way: "Of several responses made to the same situation, those which are accompanied or closely followed by satisfaction to the animal or human will, other things being equal, be done more when the same situation occurs. Those which are accompanied or closely followed by discomfort or annoyance to the animal will, other things being equal, be reduced." Here's the point: "Satisfaction" was changed to "reinforcement" and "discomfort" was changed to "punishment" in the law about affect. Was this transformation made because of scientific knowledge? No, it was brought about by a committee of priests who liked certain words better than others. It was not based on a scientific reasoning. It was because reinforcements were in the world, where you could see them, and satisfactions were inside of people, where you couldn't see them. Discomforts were also inside, but punishments were outside. That was the basis for the decision. They didn't care about the brain and they didn't care about the mind.

The person that brought us this disaster for almost a hundred years was Jacques Loeb. He went to the University of Chicago, where a young student, John Watson, fell in love with him. Watson went on to become the father of behaviorism. On the east coast, B. F. Skinner was trained by Crozier, who was also a student of Jacques Loeb. It was thus that the engineering view of mental life took over. These men said that they didn't care about understanding the mind, that all they cared about was how to control behavior. They were explicit. This radical behaviorism took over American psychology, and to this day that dogma rules. Its proponents are not as loud as before, however. Now they're called behavioral neuroscientists, and they do wonderful work, but the one thing they will not talk about is emotional feeling or affective experience.

Why did this whole thing emerge? It started with Karl Ludwig and the Berlin Biophysics Club, back before we had the kind of medical schools we have right now. These guys said, "Doctors' training is pretty spooky. They talk about vital principles, but they don't understand anything. We have to understand physiology, biochemistry, and anatomy." Ludwig joined with other famous physiologists like Helmholz and Ernst Brücke. (Ernst Brücke's most famous student was Sigmund Freud.) What the Berlin Biophysics Club did was to take vital principles out of the scientific game. It took life out of the process. Life became molecules and things that could be studied with good tools. This thinking gave us our modern medical schools, which have achieved so much, but it also spilled over into psychology in the form of radical behaviorism. Consequently, we had a psychology without a mental life. Karl Ludwig also had a famous student: Ivan Pavlov, the physiologist who gave us classical conditioning. Classical conditioning was a wonderful technique, which reflected a lot of good science, but with it, affects disappeared. Sigmund Freud was the only one who tried to maintain a psychology with affect at the heart of the equation. He could never tell us what affects really were, however, because that required brain research, and brain research wasn't mature. The 19th-century battle between vitalism and materialism, though good for medicine for a while, was a disaster for psychology. It led to the belief that the only thing we needed to understand was neuronal firing and stimulus–brain response. But now we need a network doctrine that connects up with psychology.

How did the fox lose its fear? Because we love ruthless reductionism: "It's nothing but molecules; there is no mind." Mind is completely biological, I think, but it has to be part of the equation. In addiction, if you don't bring the mind into the equation, you simply can't understand it.

I'd next like to focus on social affect as a source of addiction. In one of the first fMRI studies on rats, the researchers wondered, "When a mother rat is allowed to suckle her babies, what parts of her brain get aroused?" It turns out that the mom gets a lot of arousal in the dopamine terminal fields from her pups. The remarkable thing is that it is exactly the kind of response you get if you take a virgin female rat and give her cocaine. When they gave these mothers cocaine, however, they did not get a kick out of it. Additionally, the mother doesn't seek cocaine. She has everything she needs—pups, love, good feelings—so she doesn't need an artificial thing. Also, if you look in the brain, you'll see that cocaine doesn't have the same access to the brain that it would have had before she had pups. The opiates here are part of the social rewards system.

This pleasure system is a very fuzzy concept, because there are so many different kinds of pleasure. For instance, take the pleasure of companionship. What could be more pleasurable than social play and social interaction? It is the biggest joy that children have once their tummies are full. Play systems exist in the brain. Play allows the young child to become fully socialized because the genes do not provide that. The genes only provide a couple of simple-minded tools to become a human being. Enculturation uses these tools to knit the child into a social fabric. If a child is well-knit into the social fabric, that child is much less likely to become addicted. That's why the poor individuals that have posttraumatic this or that are left with a chronic feeling of pain. It's because they weren't cared for, or other bad things happened. Those experiences get built into the nervous system; we can pretty well demonstrate it now. And when you carry that pain with you, you're in a state where other people cannot provide that satisfaction as readily. So there's a constitution that becomes addiction-prone, and people with that constitution find that molecules, like those from the opiate poppy, can provide the satisfaction that they're not getting in their lives.

So endogenous opioids are part of the social reward system. When they're low, they produce increased social interaction. We measured the release of opioids during play, and found that there is lots of release during natural social play. So there are similarities between opiate addiction and social dependence. Back in the 1970s, we generated this idea that the main characteristics of opiate addiction are similar to characteristics of social dependence, particularly the love phase or bonding phase, as is the tendency of the feelings to diminish.

In the classic case of opiate tolerance, an addicted person requires higher and higher doses of the drug, and in social dependence, the great feeling you had from certain interactions with a loved one all of a sudden diminishes and tends to disappear. It's a natural part of the system. It leads young people to leave their families and look for other sources of gratification. It is also very effective as a blind evolutionary process for dispersing genes. So perhaps people should recognize that this happens naturally, and do whatever is possible to minimize it—like taking vacations apart.

But, in both these situations, even if tolerance does occur, a hole has opened up. If you don't get the opiates, you have this characteristic opiate withdrawal pattern, and if you lose a loved one that you're not even getting a punch from anymore, you still have powerful, powerful feelings of loss, loneliness, crying, loss of appetite, depression, sleeplessness, and irritability. The symptoms of these two experiences were so similar that we did many studies simply asking "can opiates alleviate separation distress?"

The principle is this: people and animals eventually, and primarily, seek opioids to alleviate pain—psychological pain. The initial pleasure is not that which mediates the addiction; ultimately people just want to feel normal again, and the molecules allow them to feel normal. We studied this in dogs. If you separate a puppy from its mother, it cries, cries, cries, and cries, 700 times per 15 minutes. But tiny, miniscule doses of morphine alleviate the distress completely. Big behavioral effects were seen with the smallest amount of opiates. The young brain is extremely sensitive to opiates. We did this in lots of species. It's a general principle.

Eventually, after testing every molecule that a psychiatrist uses and that is available on the shelf for experimental pharmacology, we found that practically nothing works as effectively as the opioids. For instance, with neuroleptics and antipsychotics, the animal can be staggering around, but it still cries. You can give it barbiturates or other anaesthetics, but if the animal is still awake, and perceives itself to be alone, it cries intensely, even though it might be staggering around and barely conscious. But with a tiny dose of opiates, the animals are totally normal. As a matter of fact, at these low doses of opiates, they play more. Why should they play more? Because play requires confidence. If you're feeling internal pain, you can't have confidence. Opioids melt the internal pain; therefore, the animals play more.

Then we discovered oxytocin, the "love molecule," which is very effective at reducing separation distress. Oxytocin, by itself, is not an addictive molecule. It's a magical item that will come out of brain research to perhaps alleviate addiction urges, because it maintains the sensitivity of the opioid system physiologically, so that the system doesn't show tolerance. I think that's what an addict may need: to reestablish the sensitivity of the internal opioid system to counteract the massive insensitivity produced by pharmacology.

The third main item that alleviated separation distress in these studies—not surprisingly from an evolutionary point of view—was prolactin, the molecule that manufactures the milk of human kindness. So prolactin, which releases milk to the child, oxytocin, and opioids make up the general pleasure system of the brain. Those were the three molecules that dramatically alleviated separation distress. So we think that both oxytocin and prolactin, which are not addictive by themselves, are targets for drug development for treating addiction, because they can alleviate the social pain that people want to control. The feelings of alienation and isolation are the main reason for taking these kinds of drugs. Remember, also, that depression is a pleasure deficit. Opioids are superb antidepressants. They were used before the 1950s brought us MAO inhibitors and tricyclic antidepressants.

I want to talk briefly about play. It's what animals do when they are spontaneously given the opportunity. It becomes as powerful a reward as any reward that animals have in the world. A famous emotion researcher, Rob Plutchik, was in the lab one day, and I told him, "Rob, I want to show you a behavior." I didn't tell him what I was going to show him. I put two animals in a cage and they started play fighting. He asked, "How did you train the animals to fight that way?" and I said, "Rob, I didn't train them; evolution did. And, by the way, they're not fighting, they're playing," This is a real emotion system in the brain. I think this system generates social joy. The more we understand this system, the more we can use it. In George Vaillant's words, "The emotions are spiritual systems." If used well, the positive emotions, and joy is the most positive of emotions, can be used to help treat addictions. If you can capture that joyful impulse again, whatever that may require, then I think you're on the road to recovery. The more a person will laugh with others in a positive way, the more they're on their way to recovery, I think, and to being whole in a human way.

Natural joy is highly addictive. I mentioned the chirping laughter that we discovered in rats. When we listened in, we could tickle animals and generate a lot of vocal activity that appeared to be laughter. These animals would begin to enjoy our company and they would start to play with our hands and wherever we would put our hands they would follow it. And when we tested these animals to determine whether they were enjoying this kind of activity, the unambiguous answer was "yes." And once an animal has chirped like that with you, it will follow you and seek you out and, you know, basically be your friend. That's why we love pets, because certain animals have very responsive systems like this for our social interaction.

Let me end with one of my favorite quotes. In Principles of Psychology, William James noted: "We are spinning our own fates, good or evil, never to be undone. . . ." Well, hopefully not. James continues:

> The drunken Rip Van Winkle. . . excuses himself for every fresh dereliction by saying "I won't count this time!" Well! He may not count it, and a kind heaven may not count it; but it is being counted nonetheless. Down among his nerve cells and fibers the molecules are counting it, registering and storing it up to be used against him when the next temptation arises.

Like George Vaillant said, ultimately the best approach is to rejoin the human family. I think AA and those approaches allow that to happen.

6. The Many Faces of Spirituality

J. SCOTT TONIGAN

There's been over two thousand years of talk about spirituality and alcohol. The Bible has references to alcohol as a sacrament as well as proscriptions against alcohol. So it's always been a yin-yang thing. There has been a divided nature to alcohol, and, by generalization, to illicit substances. In New Mexico, for example, they use peyote in the national Indian church. But the historical relationship between academics and the study of spirituality has been a little bit difficult. We have this thing called "tenure review," and if you study spirituality you are putting yourself at risk. And then once one moves to the study of spirituality, you never quite feel like you're in the same herd. But I'd like to share with you what we currently know empirically; it's very exciting to me.

Just to give you some background, there are about 36 National Institute of Health-funded projects right now studying spirituality as relating to addictions, either as a primary or secondary focus. The mechanisms of research vary considerably. There are what they call "K awards," which are individual investigator awards, and then there are larger studies called "R01s," which are multimillion-dollar studies of spirituality.

I'd like to give you some idea of what the empirical field has done in research on Alcoholics Anonymous (AA); much of this work has centered on the 12 steps because of the spirituality in the core membership. In clinical trials like those for the Consortium of Social Science Associations, an average of about 43% of the participants will attend AA at some point during or after treatment. It's important to point out that several of these studies were pharmacotherapy trials. These were not trials encouraging people to attend AA; people voted with their feet. In the last five years there has been quite an explosion of interest in the area.

In general, meta-analytic studies—studies that quantitatively combine the results of different studies—have found that, on average, we can see about a .31 correlation between AA attendance and later abstinence. As you might recall, a correlation can range from -1 to 1. So if it's on the positive side, it means there is a positive association. And if it's negative, it means the association is reversed; as one variable increases, the other decreases. What we see 68% percent of the time, if we apply the normal curve, is that for people who do attend, we can anticipate relatively little benefit to a modestly positive benefit. Now and again someone says, "Well, my mother and father went to AA and never drank again." Or, "When my mother and father went to AA, it didn't work, and they left." When we deal with the idiographic, there will, of course, be exceptions to all I'm going to say today. All of these analyses are based on nomothetic or group comparisons.

More recently, we've had a number of very important prospective trials. For those of you who are interested in looking at the published literature in this area, Project MATCH, John Morgenstern, a Veterans Affairs study by Keith Humphreys and Rudy Moos, and most recently Project COMBINE have all looked directly or indirectly at the association between AA attendance at Time 1 and drinking at Time 2. That's very important, because if we look at drinking and attendance at the same time, then we have the difficulty of self-selected samples. In other words, those who no longer stay may be drinking, so we can't say that AA is beneficial. Or they might be leaving and being abstinent and we would attribute that benefit to AA when we should not; so it's very important to have temporal ordering to say what is beneficial and what is not. These are very good studies to begin to address some of those questions.

I'll give you some background on the 12-step program. It was developed in the 1930s. It has two texts as its core literature: *Twelve Steps and Twelve Traditions* and the *Big Book*. This core literature has very clear hypotheses and very clear prescriptions about what one is to do; and then the "12 and 12" is more about how one should practice the fellowship of AA. Dr. Toscoba and I read the core literature and we developed what we thought were five spiritual axioms in AA literature. Firstly, there is a belief in a transcendent or higher power. Secondly, and very critically, one has a personal relationship with this higher power, unfettered by institutions, churches, or congregations. Thirdly, mysticism is central to AA's spirituality: the sense of divine intervention, most clearly explained through the gift of sobriety, the gift of abstinence. Fourthly, faith in a higher power should begin anew each day—if one attends the meetings, one will often hear the statement, "You can't win today's games by yesterday's points." Finally, distress is a sense of one's incongruity with the wishes and purposes of a higher power.

Now we all know that myths help us understand the world. They may be true and they may be false. And there is a great deal of mythology surrounding AA in the popular media and in what we hear from people. So I'd like to take a moment to go through a couple of myths before returning to spirituality.

Myth number one is that all AA meetings are alike; that is, AA is the same wherever you go. "90 meetings in 90 days" is often prescribed to people when they are first initiated into AA. What one often hears is "Bring the body and the mind will follow." I'd like to show what our research shows about that. We sampled three AA groups. On average, members had done about seven to nine steps and had been sober for three to five years, so our sample was a fairly stable group. They were, on average, attending quite a high number of meetings, approximately every other day in a typical month, and the percentage of the sample that had a sponsor was quite high in two of the groups and low in the third group. These meetings we would call mainstream AA meetings; they were not specialty meetings at all. We administered the Group Environment Scale. In other words, we asked these members, "How do you perceive the functioning of your groups?" "To what degree is spirituality emphasized?" "To what degree is orderliness described?" "To what degree is self-disclosure described?" "How expressive, cohesive, independent, aggressive, or innovative are your groups?" One group was very expressive and cohesive, and the others were kind of all over the board. Groups can't be both cohesive and aggressive—that's basic social group dynamics. We also asked the groups about the degree to which the program or prescribed behaviors were stressed in the group. What we saw was that the highly expressive group reported significantly higher endorsement of the prescribed program in meetings. In other words, highly cohesive, supportive groups also tended to prescribe what we, as experimenters, would call the "active ingredients" of AA, namely the 12 steps. So, not all meetings are alike. The practice of AA differs.

As clinicians we say, "You go to 90 meetings in 90 days." What we find in a treatment-seeking population is that at about 60 days, reports of involvement decline—they plateau. In other words, if the advice is meant to get maximal involvement, it should recommend 60 meetings in 90 days, or attending a meeting on about two thirds of the days. Now, I said this once, and someone afterwards took me to the woodshed. And for good reason. I always say this ever since that one incident: This does not speak to the social benefit of a sobriety-supportive group; this speaks of the degree to which one is involved in the prescribed behaviors. So 90 in 90 might have value in ways other than getting one involved in the prescribed behaviors.

Now regarding the thought, "Bring the body and the mind follows," we measured frequency of meeting attendance and degree that one was involved in AA at three points in time, namely, end of treatment, 3 years posttreatment, and 10 years post treatment. The degree of one's involvement in AA was a multidimensional measure which assessed, "Do you have a sponsor? Do you read the literature? Do you celebrate AA birthdays," etc.—it was a composite score. What we saw, to no one's surprise, was that one's score at Time 1, the end of treatment, predicted later AA attendance. Yesterday's behavior predicted tomorrow's behavior. And again, AA involvement and attendance at end of treatment were positively related. However, what happened was very interesting. From end of treatment to 3 years, attendance predicted attendance, but involvement did not predict involvement. Attendance predicted involvement from 1 year to 3 years. Involvement did not predict attendance. On the other hand, what we saw at 3 to 10 years was just the reverse. This is very important to stress. What we saw was that involvement predicted long-term commitment and attendance; attendance at 3 years did not predict 10-year involvement whatsoever. So in other words, "Bring the body and the mind follows" was true for the short term, but not long term. Over the long term, it's involvement and belief system that keep people in AA.

So, the myths are neither wholly true nor wholly false. They're functional. The program is constant—I have seen very few changes to the core literature in the 15 years I've been looking at AA, and great debates are held about changing just one or two words—but the fellowship is significantly different across groups. Likewise, 90 in 90 is time dependent. It's true initially, but not in the long term, and does not enhance AA-related engagement beyond 60 in 90. The mind-body idea is also time dependent.

Now, what about drying out and spirituality? Treatment is focused on a targeted behavior, whereas meaning, spirituality, and sense of purpose tend in my mind to be issues of therapy. How can a treatment provider, in a brief period of intensive outpatient treatment, be expected to fully enhance and propel one into a successful life—one of integrating one's inner emotional reality with the outer world to have a sense of purpose that makes one a citizen in its fullest terms and makes one happy and content? In other words, treatment, I would submit, can provide abstinence, but only long-term therapy would provide sobriety. I've put that purposefully in the larger term, not in a 12-step term, although that's where it originally emanates from, in their distinction between abstinence and sobriety.

We have to be very clear, when we're talking about spirituality, about the perspective we're discussing it from. We can talk about spirituality as a dependent measure. How does one's sense of meaning in life and meaning through a higher power or God change throughout the addiction, following addiction, and in recovery? We can also talk about spirituality as an independent variable. How could a change in spirituality affect my later substance abuse? How might it enhance my abstinence into what we might term sobriety? Spirituality can be considered as a mediating variable through such questions as, "How would spirituality explain or enhance two other variables?" or as a moderating variable, for example, "How might one's spirituality influence one's receptivity to a spiritual-focused treatment?"

So we have to be very clear about how we're referring to spirituality. It's very easy to get confused.

What are we measuring in spirituality? Historically, researchers have used three perspectives and ways of assessing it. The most historical of these, used perhaps 50 years ago, is the reliance on religious affiliation measures. A more recent perspective, used in the 1990s, started looking at multidimensional measures, distinguishing between religiosity and spirituality, and looking at the many dimensions of spirituality (e.g., forgiveness, prayer, meditation, daily spiritual practices). Most recently, we've begun to look at mechanisms related to spirituality: "What is forgiveness?" "What function does forgiveness serve?" "Is it a coping mechanism?" and so on.

And there are many psychometrically validated instruments for substance abusers that measure different dimensions of spirituality. What is the underlying structure of (a) measures that distinguish between spirituality and religiosity, and (b) AA-specific measures that focus on the nature and extent of spiritual experience? I had my fantasy come true about a year ago when we had a sample and seven or eight measures of spirituality and religiosity; collectively there were about 10 scales. And I wondered what would happen if I put them all together. I did something called confirmatory factor analysis, which tells me the correlational underlying structure of these responses. And what I found was very surprising. Theoretically, all of these scales should be distinct. Every author said they had something new to measure about spirituality. But that was not the case. They were basically organized into three domains. One domain focused on practices—prayer, meditation, mindfulness, etc., all grouped together. We then had a factor, which I'll call "relational," which helped define one's relation to God. The final domain was affective state—for example a sense of meaning or forgiveness.

SPIRITUALITY AS A DEPENDENT MEASURE

Let's now go through these four perspectives or ways of considering spirituality. First I will talk about spirituality as a dependent measure.

I want to put this in the context of Project MATCH. This was a very large randomized clinical trial of 1700 people at 11 sites across the United States. It was very simple. Project MATCH recruited people presenting for treatment in outpatient sites and recruited inpatient clients seeking aftercare. They randomized 1700 clients into one of three treatment conditions: cognitive behavioral (CBT), motivational enhancement therapy (MET), and 12-step facilitation (TSF). They delivered 12 weeks of treatment, and then they followed them for up to 12 or 15 months. And then we did a 3-year follow-up with the outpatient sample, and we did a 10-year follow-up for the sample in Albuquerque. The CBT condition was very research based; researchers loved it. The MET was a brief therapy consisting of four sessions over 12 weeks. The 12-step facilitation, which was not the favorite of the researchers, was a community-based treatment with 12 sessions over 12 weeks, modeled after the core literature of AA. It had a clear spiritual focus. Its primary objective was to facilitate the person into AA, find a sponsor, and work through the first three steps. Looking at the 3 years, we saw an enormous climb in self-reported God-consciousness in the 12-step group, plateauing post treatment. But we also saw modest increases in both other groups. We also saw, to our surprise, a steep increase in religious practices—reading religious scripture and religious attendance—in the 12-step facilitation group. And, again, there were modest increases in the MET and CBT groups.

We could also look at this in another way by saying, "Let's forget about treatment group assignment, and let's just look at who reported AA attendance," because many clients assigned to MET and CBT reported AA attendance. (Therapists were instructed not to tell people that they could not go there.) Surprisingly, many clients in MET, a program designed to mobilize clients to accept their problem and to do something about it, said, "I think I need to go to AA." So there was quite high participation for those in that group. For those who reported consistent AA attendance over a 10-year period, we see a continuous climb in God consciousness. For those who had attended AA in the past but no longer did, we saw a leveling of God consciousness. And for the no-AA group, we saw an ever-so-gradual increase. I would consider that to be due to maturation. As we approach the abyss, and get closer to our Maker, we start thinking a little bit more about these things. For religious practices, likewise, we see a steady increase for those who are consistent attenders of AA, and for the other groups (past-but-not-current AA and no AA), we saw an initial jump and then a plateauing. Similar longitudinal trajectories can be reported all day long. These are just particularly interesting ones.

One could wonder, "Well, these are treatment-seeking people. What about the real world? What about people who are just recruited out of AA?" Today we are doing a study with 189 people. What we're seeing from it is the relationship between reporting the importance of a higher power and practicing prescribed behaviors. These two were very highly correlated at the time of study recruitment. At three months following, we again saw a very strong relationship between these variables, again very stable, but we saw that practicing does not predict importance; rather importance predicts practicing. Belief drove behavior; behavior did not drive belief. This ties in to the "60 in 90" observation mentioned earlier. What we see is that it may be beneficial, as a clinician, to encourage high rates of attendance, but that will not sustain long-term affiliation.

To reiterate, we generally have large increases in spirituality as a dependent measure. Narrowly specified dimensions, though present, are not orthogonal—that's a researcher way of saying they overlap considerably. Also, spiritual beliefs, or meaning, seem to drive the practice of behaviors, and not the reverse.

SPIRITUALITY AS AN INDEPENDENT MEASURE

What is the value of spirituality as an independent variable? In the core literature, it says very clearly that one will be defenseless against the first drink; one's defense must come from a higher power. This implies, from a scientific perspective, that spirituality is a shield—a coping mechanism, something that will protect one from relapse. At first blush, what we found looks to be supportive of that. Project MATCH tracked the proportion of people avoiding a first drink, following them from end of treatment to 90 days after, 180 days, 270 days, and 360 days. We saw an immediate drop off—a very large number of relapses immediately after treatment, and then a plateauing. The clients assigned to TSF had a significantly longer time to relapse than those in the other two treatment conditions (MET and CBT). Now—and this has been empirically validated—time to first drink might be longer in the TSF condition, but when drinking occurs there is an abstinence violation effect, and the drinking is heavier. That's the other side of the coin, because what they've been told in AA is that they'll have a loss of control, and certainly when they drink, they have a loss of control. Again, belief drives behavior. So one may think that, in a spiritual-based treatment, spirituality is the independent variable. But what we see—and this is controversial, but I think it really has to be said here—is that, in prospective studies, that is, studies that measure spirituality at Time 1 and behavior at Time 2 (which is basic causal ordering), and looking at about 17 studies in the literature, we have a relationship of .09. That is virtually zero. There is no relationship between spirituality, as an independent variable, and later drinking or abstinence.

To give you a bit more of the nitty-gritty, our examination shows that there is a slight positive association between religious practices and abstinence (.13), and there is a slight negative association with drinks per drinking day (-.12); there is again a very modest association with days to first drink (.07), days to first heavy drinking day (.05). Similar things are true of God relation and spiritual meaning. In the scientific world, we're talking about probabilities of less than one in twenty. Would you, for later abstinence, recommend a spiritual experience to a family member, based on the magnitude of these relationships? I don't think I would. We have modestly better prediction of drinking outcome by spiritual/religious measures in Project MATCH; those were about 0.15 relative to the point unknown. But again, would you really clinically tell a client, "We're going to work on a spiritual experience to keep you sober?" Looking again at the results from the longitudinal study with 189 subjects, we saw slightly stronger correlations between recovery and self-rated importance of a higher power, and between recovery and prescribed AA behaviors (e.g., step work, reading core literature), but they were still very modest.

Continuing with the results of the longitudinal study, we'll now focus on Pargament's Spiritual Coping Questionnaire. He has one construct for a person having a deferential relationship to a higher power (e.g., "I do what God leads me to do. I follow God's will"; compare this to the third step prayer: "Thy will, not mine, be done"). He also has another construct for spiritual coping having a cooperative style (e.g., "When I am confronted with a problem, I seek God's counsel, and I move forward"). For both these constructs in this naturalistic sample, again we saw very modest relationships between spiritual measures at Time 1 and the drinking measures at Time 2. However, when I looked at people's spiritual trajectory, rather than where they were at a given time, I did begin to see significant correlations.

Does spirituality or religiosity predict other positive outcomes? Now we're getting to the therapy issue. Aside from the target behavior, what do we know about spirituality? Lee Ann Kaskutas has developed what's called a Helping Activities Checklist. She looks at community activity behaviors (volunteer community behaviors), general activities (e.g., family activities, "I pick up my children," "I help drop them off," "I help around the house"), and recovery activities (this is 12-step focused). With confirmatory factor analysis with measurement models, we see that total religiosity at Time 1 significantly predicts helping behaviors at 10 years (.46). So, one's religious beliefs and practices were significantly predictive of the extent to which one was later involved in community activities, general living activities, and recovery activities. This is a big correlation. We can say that if one wants a client to become engaged as a citizen, spiritual change has value.

SPIRITUALITY AS A MEDIATOR

Is the positive relationship between AA attendance and later drinking reduction mediated by spirituality? This is a difficult one to understand. We know there is a positive relationship between AA participation and abstinence. Also, we know that there is a positive relationship between AA attendance and spirituality as a dependent measure. What we don't know is whether spirituality explains the relationship between participation and abstinence.

In our examination of this, we had as a baseline the following measures of client functioning: the AUI-G scale, which addresses the general involvement that one has with alcohol; the ASI-Psychiatric Severity measure; the AUDIT Alcohol

Dependence measure; and motivation/readiness for change (URICA, SOCRATES). I think most clinicians would regard them as important dimensions in treating a substance abuse problem. And what we find is that we can model these dimensions as a latent construct that we could call "problem severity." So that's our baseline.

We're going to consider a client with high problem severity at Time 1 (intake). What does this client do at Time 2, nine months later? Well, we found that there is a positive relationship between problem severity at Time 1 and being committed to the AA program at Time 2. And AA commitment is measured multidimensionally. It includes the degree to which participants report step work, the degree to which they practice prescribed behaviors, the frequency of their AA meeting attendance, and their God belief. All of these correlations are positive. Earlier we discussed how there was a .31 correlation in a meta-analysis. Well, there is a .30 correlation here too (between severity and AA commitment), in a different sample—it's amazingly robust.

We also saw that AA commitment predicts abstinence at months 10 through 15. Again, that's not a big surprise. However, in this particular model, when we accounted for commitment, problem severity does not predict the degree to which a person will be abstinent 10 to 15 months later. Now, let's make it more complicated. Let's look at who will attend AA and who will not. My wife, a clinician, said this one's a no brainer; those who are high in severity do not have social networks that support continued drinking, but if they happen to have such a network, there is a negative relationship between that support and the person going to AA. In other words, those who are highly dependent on alcohol and have networks supportive of continued drinking will not go to AA.

And here's the big one. AA commitment predicts abstinence (.24), and AA commitment predicts increased God belief (.25), but we found that God belief did not predict abstinence (.04). In other words, God belief did not mediate the relationship between AA commitment and abstinence or the relationship between problem severity and abstinence. So we asked ourselves, "Why not?" We had to go back to the drawing board. My take from reading the core literature is that AA is fundamentally a very eclectic, pragmatic program. (Even the development of the term "the Big Book" is fundamentally pragmatic. When they wrote the first edition, there was a great deal of controversy about whether they should charge or give it out free. It was decided eventually that they had to sell it so that they could keep publishing it. But Bill Wilson decided he wanted to have it printed on very coarse, cheap paper, so that the alcoholic would think they were getting a big book—more for their money. And that's why it's called the "Big Book.")

We had a hypothesis that we developed, and which I'm very excited about, because it was supported. What we predicted was that spirituality might be a secondary or indirect mediator. Thus far what we've been talking about is how AA participation at 3 years might predict AA participation at 10 years, which it does, somewhat (.26). AA participation at 3 years does not predict 10-year abstinence, but current AA attendance does predict abstinence. That's not too controversial. What is controversial, though, is the same model, except with spirituality mediating the relationship between AA practices at 3 and 10 years. And when we have spirituality in there, AA participation at 3 years does not predict participation at 10 years. In other words, it's belief driven again: AA practice predicts spirituality, spirituality predicts sustained AA attendance, but AA attendance and practices do not predict sustained AA attendance. So spirituality can be seen as a shared ideology that holds members to the fellowship of AA. It's a coping strategy that helps people remain affiliated with one another. Incidentally, it is still the case that AA practice significantly predicts long-term abstinence at 10 years, but again spirituality does not directly predict abstinence.

We find—and I don't think this is very controversial—that spiritual and religious beliefs promote social networks that are supportive of abstinence. One has a sense of community and a sense of attachment, and thus spirituality will lead one to stay affiliated with others. Now, I've spoken with many AA members about these findings, and some have said that in practicing their spirituality they continue to help others. And helping others means that they stay affiliated with AA. That would be their description of this finding. But we also know from Lee Ann Kaskutas' findings that spirituality also helps predict community behaviors and general living behaviors. So one could argue that the function of spirituality is like that of the myths that we talked about. It's not true or false; it sustains right living, which in turn predicts positive outcomes. But spirituality in and of itself does not seem to predict positive outcome.

SPIRITUALITY AS A MODERATING VARIABLE

Does pretreatment spirituality influence the acceptability of spiritual treatment? And does spirituality moderate one's willingness to affiliate with a 12-step program? This is such an important topic that an entire chapter in the core literature is dedicated to it (it's called "We Agnostics"). What we see in 12-step facilitation—which is primarily a spiritually focused treatment—is that, in project MATCH, atheists had the lowest attendance when assigned to TSF. Between agnostics, unsures (I've never figured out the difference between agnostics and unsures—they were unsure if they were agnostic, I guess), the spiritual, and the religious, there were only relatively slight differences (ranging from 59% attendance for agnostics to 68% attendance for the religious), but atheists assigned to the 12-step facilitation certainly attended therapy less frequently (at 43%). When we look at why that might have been the case, we considered the degree to which they liked and felt bonded to their therapist and how far they were in agreement about the tasks and goal of therapy. And again the atheists and the agnostics were clearly the lowest on these measures when assigned to 12-step facilitation. So they attended less and they were less enthusiastic about their therapist. Again, in a treatment strongly encouraging and monitoring AA attendance, over half, or 65%, of the atheists (who were admittedly rather a small group) never attended any AA at all. More than half of the members of each of the other groups did attend to at least some extent, with a gradual decline in nonattendance from agnostics (about 45%) through to the religious (about 30%). Likewise, only a small proportion of atheists attended consistently. So pretreatment spiritual beliefs were very strong moderators to the acceptability of treatment as well as to willingness to get involved in 12-step facilitation.

The twist is that, if you get an atheist to attend AA, they derive equal benefit from it. They're less likely to attend, but if they attend they report the same benefit as do spiritual and religious people. Correspondingly, being religious or spiritual gives you no advantage. Everybody reported relatively equal benefit in terms of percent days abstinent and drinks per drinking day (with average, weighted correlations of .27 and -.24, respectively). So, to sum up: Atheists and agnostics are less likely to attend and sustain AA attendance; there's no difference between religious and spiritual people in attendance; and for those who do attend, atheism is not a disadvantage, nor is religiosity an advantage, in deriving benefit. So it's not straightforward.

Something I want to know about is integration. What about the Ebenezer Scrooge phenomenon—that quantum leap, that sudden hitting of bottom, and that recognition that "All is wrong." It's that moment of clarity when everything is falling apart and simultaneously everything is put together. We know absolutely nothing about that from an empirical perspective. I think therapists have to teach researchers about that. I found that, in going through the core literature, the promises of AA are predictions or hypotheses. If you do these things, such and such will happen. Those are testable things.

What, if any, role does spirituality play in distinguishing between sobriety and abstinence? We don't know. We know that spirituality leads to greater involvement in the community; we know that it leads to more involvement in the family; we know that it leads to various such behaviors; but is that sobriety? We did something very interesting. We have in Albuquerque a very good relationship with the AA community. We have some careful prescriptions in terms of how we approach them for research, and there's a mutually respectful relationship. And after we do our studies with them, we go back and show them our PowerPoint presentations, and they always say, "Yeah, we knew that." But they've given their time and effort, so we provide that to them.

We did a very interesting study where we asked our group to write down who in that group was sober and who was abstinent, and we told them we wouldn't share the answers with anybody else. So we gathered all the lists together, and some people were mentioned on four or five lists. We decided, okay that person has sobriety. At the same time, we measured all of them on measures of depression, adjustment, and well-being. What we found is that while there was a clear group identified as sober versus abstinent, the measures were all the same. There was no relationship between being abstinent or sober and the scores for depression and well-being. So there's something very elusive there and, again, I think therapists need to teach us about it.

One of the most curious areas for me is whether spirituality mediates other change agents, like social networks or other change agents that are not target behaviors or addiction behaviors but are factors and behaviors and cognitions and affective responses, that are critical to our functioning. We know very little about that, but it's a very interesting area.

7. Thinking Addiction

FRANCIS F. SEEBURGER

The title I've given to my remarks—"Thinking Addiction"—is intentionally ambiguous. Thinking Addiction can mean, on the one hand, thinking about addiction, perhaps conceptualizing it. However, that is not the only sense my title can have. Thinking Addiction could mean, not thinking about addiction, making addiction the object of the thinking in that sense, but rather in a way that takes thinking as the subject to be talked about, and the addiction of my title being a matter of addiction to thinking, an addiction from which those afflicted by it would presumably need to recover. That is, just as we talk about "drug addiction," and mean by that addiction to drugs, so by speaking of "thinking addiction" we might mean addiction to thinking.

There is also a third possible dimension to my title. That's one that some of you who may be familiar with some of my earlier work on addiction might already have thought of. What I'm referring to is the idea I've raised before (Seeburger, 1993) that all addiction, whether to alcohol, narcotics, or whatever, is rooted in an addiction at the level of thinking as such—that the root of all addiction is a root addiction to attribution, to searching around for something to pin our experiences on, allowing us to manage them by making them seem explainable to us. What I suggested then was that we are all, in effect, addicts at the level of searching for ways to account for, and explain, our own experience.

At this point, I will use the writings of David Hume (1740/1967) to give a brief illustration of what I have in mind. Hume taught that there is no rational ground for the belief that every event has a cause. Nevertheless, he went on to argue, we cannot escape our habituation to thinking that all events do have causes. Regardless of the validity of his overall argument, philosophically considered, I would say Hume was right that our everyday reliance upon what Kant (1790) would later call the "universality and necessity" of the causal connection is more a matter of something we cannot help but believe than something we believe on the basis of reason. We are powerless over that belief, powerless even to give it up at our own choosing. It is something we cannot stop doing even when we want—and try—to, which is precisely characteristic of an addiction.

In talking about the various senses of my title, Thinking Addiction, please note how I have already found myself talking about addiction itself, and about one way of beginning to think about addiction. In short, it is a way of thinking about addiction in which thinking itself is seen to have something of an addiction to it, to the extent that thinking is concerned with offering accounts or explanations of things. Alternatively, it's also a way of thinking about addiction in which addiction always has something of thinking to it. So "Thinkers as Addicts, Addicts as Thinkers" might be an alternative title for this talk. Anyway, one of the thoughts about addiction that I want to share with you is that thinking and addiction are somehow inextricably linked.

There are also a couple of other thoughts about addiction that I would like to share with you in the process. One of them is my development of the idea that addiction is the human norm, rather than an exception to the norm, which is how we most commonly think about it.

I am hardly the first to suggest that addiction is the human norm. For example, in *Addiction and Grace*, Gerald May (1988) said that it is part and parcel of the human condition to be addicted to something. So addiction, for him, is universally human. He says that what differs between us as individuals, however, is precisely what it is each of us becomes addicted to; only some of us become addicted to any one thing, given easy exposure to it, whether it be heroin, alcohol, sex and love, or the Internet, for example. May believed that not only our environment but also our genes play sizeable roles in determining just what it is that we individually become addicted to, but I will not address that topic today.

A moment's reflection will surely show how the idea that addiction is the human norm follows easily enough from the first one I've already mentioned, the idea that there's something of thinking to every addiction and something of addiction to all thinking. Since thinking itself is common to all human beings, at least according to the longest standing mainstream Western definition of the human being, it would follow that, if thinking always has something of addiction to it, then addiction is no less universal for all human beings.

My third is, like the one I've just articulated, contrary to what I take to be our customary ways of thinking about addiction. Whenever we think about our own addictions, or the addictions of those we love, or the incidence of addiction in a given population with which we are concerned (North Americans, teenagers, minorities, middle-class white heterosexual males, or whatever), we tend to identify addiction as some sort of problem for which we need a solution. Well, the third idea about addiction is that we might profit from trying to view addiction not as a problem, but as the solution to a problem (whether a good solution, or a bad one,

I'll leave open for now). I want to share with you some of my reflections on just what problem it might be to which addiction presents itself as offering a solution.

What I want to do is share some reflections with you about each of the three ideas I've mentioned, and then about how they may interconnect to tell us something of interest about the treatment and prevention of addiction. My discussion will hardly exhaust any one of them, let alone their interplay. Rather, I will share with you no more than some preliminary and exploratory speculations, in the best, most positive, philosophical sense of that term. I will begin with the idea that there is always something of thinking to addiction, and of addiction to thinking.

EXCESSIVE THINKING

Various strands from diverse traditions of 20th-century thought, from existentialism to structuralism to psychoanalysis (above all as reworked by Lacan, 1992, and in his wake) to postmodernism to cognitive science, might fruitfully for my purposes today be brought together in one idea. That is the idea that there is something *excessive* about thought itself. I don't mean an excessiveness peculiar to just some particular forms of thinking—for instance, to what we call obsessive thinking. Rather, I mean an excessiveness of all thinking, to thinking as such, regardless of its more specific form. Just as Lacan speaks of there being something in me that is "more than me," so we could say that there is something in thinking that is always a bit more than thinking itself, something always a bit in excess of the thinking in thinking, so to speak.

That would be especially so if we were to take thinking in general as the business of looking for explanations for things, which would include the very sort of thinking that Hume was concerned with, the sort that searches for causes. In fact, one way of putting the point of Hume's analysis of causal thinking might be to say that there is something *uncaused* in such thinking. Causal reasoning, by his analysis, is a reasoning beyond the possibilities of providing any rational justification for itself. So it's reasoning that escapes reasoning itself. It's something *in*conceivable at the heart of all conceivability, something *un*conceptualizable at the heart of all conceptualization, something *un*thinkable at the root of all thought. It's that in thinking which is too much for thinking itself: the excess of thinking over itself.

As I understand them, some problems that surface in contemporary cognitive science point to another example, one more recent than Hume. Some cognitive science, in trying to give an evolutionary account of consciousness, comes up against something I call *evolutionarily excessive* regarding consciousness. In short, to account for the emergence of consciousness in terms of natural evolution, we need to be able to account for consciousness having sufficient survival value that, once it appeared by mutation, would be naturally selected for reproduction. The rub, however, is that any account of consciousness along those very lines risks leaving unexplained just what added survival value one brings to an adaptive behavior by making that behavior conscious, rather than just leaving it unconscious. If we can imagine nature providing the same thing, the same survival value, without introducing consciousness as would be granted by the same process with it, then we cannot see any good reason for evolution to select out consciousness at all. Yet the idea that, in order to avoid such a consequence, we must be able to argue that consciousness introduces something new, something which could not have been produced in just the same way without consciousness, seems to run against the very principle of all evolutionary accounts.

The principle at issue is that an evolutionary explanation is one that begins precisely by bracketing out the very teleology or intentionality that is phenomenologically definitive of consciousness itself. That is, the very idea of giving an evolutionary account of something entails accounting for that something in terms of purely mechanical processes of environmental selection working upon mutational changes, the very sorts of processes that occur without consciousness. Thus, the attempt to offer an evolutionary account of consciousness would flounder upon the evolutionarily excessive nature of consciousness itself.

I will venture to give yet one more example of what is at issue in the excessiveness of thinking. This time my example is from Freud. At one point in his opus, Freud (1909/1953, cited in Santner, 2001) wrote:

> We are not used to feeling strong affects without their having any
> ideational contents, and therefore, if the content is missing, we
> seize as a substitute upon another content which is in some way or
> other suitable, much as our police, when they cannot catch the right
> murderer, arrest a wrong one instead. (pp. 102–103)

As far as I can see, such a search for what Freud called "ideational content" is the same general process as what I am calling attribution.

I will call thinking, then, insofar as it involves the search for explanations or reasons of some sort, whether as causes, or as what Freud calls ideational content, or in any other form, *attributive* thinking. Causal thinking in the more limited sense that Hume had in mind in his analysis, for example, will then be one form of attributive thinking, albeit perhaps the most important form, at least when it comes to science. However, attributive thinking will also include various other forms besides causal thinking. It will include such things as looking for motives to explain someone's behavior. Many philosophers, including the late Wittgenstein, distinguish between motives and causes. For another example, the premises of a valid syllogism provide *grounds* for its conclusion, although it would be uncustomary to call the premises the *causes* of the conclusion.

At any rate, I invite you to entertain the idea that attributive thinking arises from, and in a sense is nothing but, the attempt to address the very absence of any adequate, ultimate reasons or grounds for thinking itself. Alternately put, I invite you to view attributive thinking (the constitution or construal of the ultimate groundlessness of the process of attribution itself) *as a lack requiring to be made good*—a sort of always-outstanding debt insistently demanding repayment. Attributive thinking would then also be the subsequent attempt to find something to make up for that perceived lack, to repay that perceived debt. To put it slightly differently, the idea that attributive thinking arises from—or is itself—the concrete consciousness of consciousness itself is somehow excessive, precisely in the sense of lacking something, which attribution then seeks to remedy.

In passing, let me call attention to the paradoxical sound of calling *excess* a *lack*. After all, to be lacking is to be missing something, to have too little of it, whereas to be excessive is to have a surplus of something, to have too much of it. Yet by a long philosophical tradition that goes back to Aristotle and the old idea of virtue as a mean between extremes, both too much and too little of something have often been characterized in terms of the failure to hit the mark (which is the original meaning of the term *sin*), that is, as an absence or lack of moderation. It is just by such mainstream Western ways of thinking, at least in its classic forms, that the idea of excess has been treated as a lack of something. We might put the idea most simply by saying that what is excessive is lacking in limits or boundaries.

Now, that brings me to a couple of related points I want to make before resuming my main course of reflection. First, I want to call attention to this: Absence as such does not necessarily constitute a lack. In general, an absence becomes a lack only in cases where what is absent is taken to be something that in some sense should be there. Applied to the idea that there is an absence of sufficient grounds or reasons for consciousness itself, the observation that not every absence is a lack would mean that the presumed absence of such grounds for consciousness itself becomes troubling only if consciousness is taken to be something that should have such grounds.

That brings me to a second observation I want to make before resuming my main line of thought: There is really nothing at all obvious about the idea that consciousness—or, for that matter, anything else—*should* have grounds or reasons. Why these two observations are worth keeping in mind, will, I hope, emerge as I proceed.

What I was saying before making these observations was that attributive thinking can itself be understood as the very experience of consciousness itself as somehow excessive, as lacking something—namely, lacking an explanation for itself in terms of grounds or reasons. By such a way of thinking about thinking itself, thinking insofar as it is attributive would be defined as the endeavor to make good on that lack. However, by my same line of thought, the very excessiveness, or lack, at issue is itself definitive of attributive thinking as such. Accordingly, like the tippler on one of the planets Antoine de Saint Exupery's Little Prince visits, who drinks because he is so ashamed, and is so ashamed because he drinks, attributive thinking would be caught in a circle. The more ground or reason attributive thinking attributed to itself, the more radically it would experience its own continuing lack, and the more it would need to go on attributing to try to make good on that lack. Indeed, since such a circle is characteristic of addiction, it would not be too far-fetched to call such thinking an *addiction*.

Insofar as attributive thinking "thinks itself," then it will, precisely as attributive, seek the grounds for its own occurrence, and will encounter itself as lacking grounds and in need of them, until and unless it can discover some. If it can discover no such grounds for itself, it will hardly be surprising if, as suggested in the quote by Freud (1905/1953) cited earlier, out of the very experience of itself as in need of them, it endeavors to supply them, or at least a "sufficient substitute" for them. And it will tend, as do all addicts, carefully to "protect the supply." What is more, as is once again true for addiction in general, just because the very provision of such a supply will add fuel to the fire of the continuing need for more of the same, attributive thinking will, above all, never be able to supply itself with "enough" of that to which it is addicted. Attributive thinking will never be able to break free of its "habit" on its own. It will never be able even to discover the reality of its condition—at least not until it somehow "bottoms out," and is forced to do so by the situation itself.

In my talk here today, I will not speculate much about what that process of the bottoming out of attributive thought might look like. I will let two remarks suffice.

The first is that what Nietzsche (1887a) called "the death of God" might plausibly be read as just such a process of collective, historical bottoming out on attributive thinking. If so, it might also behoove us to remember Nietzsche's own repeated warnings that the death of God is such a momentous event that it may well take a few thousand years for word of it to spread fully.

My second remark is that the story of the last century and a half of philosophy in its continental European current from Nietzsche himself to such so-called "postmodern" thinkers as Michel Foucault, Jean-Francois Lyotard, and Jacques Derrida in France, Gianni Vattimo and Giorgio Agamben in Italy, and Richard

Rorty and Stanley Fish in the United States, has often enough been told—by such postmodernists themselves—as the story of the attack upon the presumed foundationalism of modern philosophy from Descartes, or even back to the ancient Greeks, up to Nietzsche. I would like merely to observe that this story too might easily be retold precisely as the story of the bottoming out of the addiction to attributive thinking.

Having made those two remarks, I will now move on to the second idea about addiction I will address today: the idea of addiction as the human norm rather than the exception.

NORMING ADDICTION

Let me begin by briefly addressing what we might gain by treating addiction as the human norm rather than the human exception, independently of whatever grounds there may be for asserting that it actually is. If we assume for a moment that addiction is indeed the human norm, not the exception, then one consequence of that would be a corresponding shift in our understanding of what it is pertaining to addiction that really needs to be explained, that truly calls out for an account.

What would most invite investigation and most require explanation would no longer be how some people become addicted. To be sure, there would still be something about "becoming addicted" for which we might well still try to provide an explanation. But now what we would thus be trying to explain is how, for example, addiction might, counterintuitively, have had sufficient survival value for the human species that it would be environmentally selected out for reproduction. In that way, questions about how humans came to be addicted in the first place would, therefore, still be good to ask, even if we took addiction for the human norm.

However, once something is established as the norm, then what above all calls out for explanation, after and apart from how it came to be the norm, is how, if at all, any exceptions to that norm might occur. Just as now, under the dominant assumption that addiction (as an exception to the human norm) is what we most need to explain, if we make the contrary assumption that addiction itself is the norm, then what most calls out for explanation becomes how, if ever, anyone can deviate from that norm. What would most demand inquiry would be any cases in which someone managed to escape addiction, either by some sort of innate immunity to it, or by recovery from it.

It has long seemed to me an experiment well worth conducting to see what we would turn up if we investigated, with even half of the financial and other resources we currently devote to investigating the causes of addiction, the different question of the causes of recovery, or of even rarer cases in which someone never becomes addicted in the first place. Instead of asking why certain individuals become addicted or certain populations display high rates of addiction, we would ask why certain individuals do not become addicted, or why certain populations display low rates of addiction. If, as William S. Burroughs (1953, p. xv) said long ago, one drifts into addiction from lack of any strong motivation to the contrary, then what provides such motivation?

That is, of course, a matter of focus, rather than of two mutually exclusive enterprises. Nevertheless, it is a profound shift of focus, with potentially massive consequences. At any rate, with those brief observations about what might be gained by regarding addiction as the human norm, I will now turn to some reflections pertaining to whether addiction really is such a norm.

First of all, I want to note that the idea that addiction is the human norm, the normal human condition, certainly may sound strange at first hearing, since it means treating a negative state or condition as the norm, rather than as a deviation from some positive norm. However, it loses much of its strangeness if we recall, to give one major well-known example of indeed taking a negative state as normative, the [Christian] Biblical notion of "the Fall," according to which all human generations since Adam and Eve start out already fallen. Through Augustine, the story of the Fall became the orthodox Western or Latin Christian doctrine of so-called original sin, the idea that all human beings (save Jesus himself and, perhaps, his mother, if a Roman Catholic doctrine is to be accepted) are born into sin and as sinners, prior to and apart from any specific evil deeds they may deliberately perform.

By bringing up such a religious notion, I do not at all wish to suggest that we should view addiction as sin. To be sure, I have learned from moral theologian Patrick McCormick's (1989) discussion of "Sin as Addiction," in his book of that name, and I think such reflections as his could and should significantly affect how we think when we reverse direction, and try to sort out what is "sinful" in addiction. But I am bringing up the notion of sin here, merely to help remove the air of implausibility that may surround the idea that a negative state or condition might be the universally normal human condition.

Toward that same end, I will supplement the example of the Biblical Fall and the Christian notion of original sin by referring to two thoroughly secularized sources: Freud and Heidegger. Both Freud and Heidegger can be read as repeating, in radically secularized ways, the old biblical notion of the fallen-ness of the human being, with Heidegger even choosing to use that very way of speaking of it (falling, *Verfallen*).

With regard to the Freudian legacy, we have, for instance, the notion of "primary repression." Primary repression is not just one more thing repressed, not even the first one. Rather, it is a truly originating repression in that it is constitutive of the full human psychic economy itself. In some later psychoanalytic thought, such as Lacan's, that is taken to mean that such primary repression is constitutive of human consciousness as such. Accordingly, it is a repression which could never be overcome, as a matter of principle, without at the same time overcoming the human condition, defined as it is by such consciousness.

What I have in mind from Heidegger, is his notion that not just occasionally and in some part but "at first and for the most part," as he liked to say, the human being—what he called Dasein—is in-authentic (*un-eigentlich*), becoming authentic (*eigentlich*) only at and for rare moments of insight (which he took very literally, by the way). Heidegger, it is important to note, made it clear that what he called inauthenticity is not a condition in which human beings only occasionally find themselves, or one from which they might be able somehow ever to purge themselves entirely. Rather, he insisted that human beings can never altogether escape inauthenticity, and that authenticity is always only a modification of inauthenticity itself, from which it arises and to which it returns.

Interestingly, Caroline Knapp (2003), who earlier wrote a best-selling memoir concerning her struggles with alcoholism, made a very similar point in *Appetites*, her memoir about her battles with anorexia, basing it on Lacan. She wrote:

> There is something, [Lacan] suggests, fundamentally insatiable about being human, as though we come into the world with a kind of built-in tension between the experience of being hungry, which is a condition of striving and yearning, and the experience of being fed, which may offer temporary satisfaction but always gives way to new strivings, new yearnings. Once satisfied, the goal always leads on to another goal, and then another and another. (p. 165)

Lacan also taught, if I understand him rightly, that it is of the very nature of desire itself to seek its own continual replication: Whatever object desire may focus upon, from a sexual partner to a plate of good spaghetti, desire is always also and above all the desire of itself as desire, the desire to desire. Hence, it continually seeks its own repetition as desire, by finding any object of desire it does manage to obtain somehow inadequate, still somehow lacking something. The something that Knapp called "fundamentally insatiable" in the human being would be human desire itself. Fully human desire would be precisely the desire always to go desiring, the never having enough of desire itself. By that construction, the last thing desire really wants is satisfaction, since that would bring desire itself to an end, a cessation.

Accordingly, the human being, as a creature defined by desire, would be an addict, so to speak, even before finding any object of addiction, anything to get hooked on. Indeed, I have long toyed with the idea that a good way to think about how the individual person selects, as it were, her own object of addiction, her own individual drug or compulsive behavior to get hooked on, is by searching and searching, trying one thing after another as it presents itself in her experience, until at last she finds the one thing of which she can never possibly have enough, that one thing of which, no matter how much she has, she still wants more. For the alcoholic, that would be alcohol; for the junky, junk; for the cutter, cutting. As May (1988) said, everyone would be an addict, but what hooked one person would not necessarily hook others, each of whom has to search for her own object of addiction.

In fact, from such a perspective, we might even want to say, at least as a provisional, first cut at the issues involved, that those who are typically classified as addicts, those diagnosed by others or by themselves as alcoholics, junkies, or whatever, are actually the lucky few. They would be fortunate enough to have succeeded at the universal human quest. That is, they would have been the happy ones who managed to find the one thing of which they could never get enough, so that they are free to go on building—replicating and increasing—their desire, with no risk of ever sating it.

As I said, that might be a good first cut at just how viewing addiction from the perspective I've been exploring would force us to rethink how it stands between those presently labeled addicts and the rest of us. It also provides me with a first cut at addressing just what problem it may be that addiction solves, or at least presents itself as solving. That brings me to the third idea I promised to address today, the idea that addiction is not the problem, but is, rather, in some sense the solution—or at least presents itself as being a solution. Accordingly, I will now turn to that third idea.

THE PROBLEM OF ADDICTION IS ALSO A SOLUTION

In one clear sense, the idea that addiction presents itself as a solution to some other problem is not new or unusual. Thus, it is actually quite common to hear addicted persons in such settings as 12-step meetings describe their own addictions to whatever they came to be addicted to, be it heroin, or alcohol, or the Internet, in terms of how "using" provides them with what seem at the time to be solutions to their own standard life problems. To my mind, one classic statement of the idea is already to be found in "The Doctor's Opinion" in the *Big Book* of Alcoholics Anonymous (1939/2001), where William D. Silkworth wrote that alcoholics are "restless, irritable, and discontented, unless they can experience again the sense of ease and comfort that comes at once from taking a few drinks" (pp. xxvi-xxvii).[1]

Many self-accounts by recovering addicts offer descriptions of how their "using" served as a coping mechanism for getting through their daily lives. By such accounts, addiction is what one relies on to cope when, in effect, one can't cope. Addicts will often testify that their addictions indeed served them well for a long time as such coping mechanisms. Indeed, they will sometimes attribute literal survival value to their addictions. They will tell how, as they perceive it, the alcohol, or the dope, or the acting out, was for a long while the only thing that really allowed them to keep going and to function at all in their ongoing lives.

Correlatively, the literature of addiction often tells us that addiction rates rise as individuals experience themselves as somehow lacking effective agency in their own daily lives. Addiction rates across various segments of the population suggest that, when individuals experience themselves as lacking in opportunity significantly to affect the circumstances of their own daily lives through their own choices and actions, they turn to addiction far more often than those who experience themselves as reasonably effective agents. So, for example, numerous authors have linked the high incidence of addiction within African-American communities in the United States to the pervasive sense among members of those communities, especially in urban or suburban ghettos, of not being in control of their own destinies. Black feminist cultural critic bell hooks (1998) gave one eloquent statement of this position. Generalizing, she wrote:

> A culture of domination undermines individuals['] capacit[ies] to assert meaningful agency in their lives. It is necessarily a culture of addiction, since it socializes as many people as it can to believe that they cannot rely on themselves to meet even their basic human needs. . . . Living without the ability to exercise meaningful agency over one's material life is a situation that invites addiction. (p. 68)

As far as I can tell, hooks conceptualized addiction under such circumstances as an attempt to escape from such an unacceptable reality. She treated recourse to drugs or other objects of addiction (from substances to such processes as compulsive shopping or even compulsive manipulation of others) as a means of numbing or anesthetizing oneself against such oppressive lack of agency. In contrast, I will argue for what I think is an equally plausible, but far more fruitful, conceptualization in accordance with which addiction is not an escape from such experiential reality, but is instead the assertion of agency in the only way still experientially open,

---

1 I have an alcoholic acquaintance now in recovery who likes to tell how, in the days of his drinking, this sense of ease and comfort did not even require actual drinking to have begun. As soon as he could make it into the bar and get his order placed, he says, he felt peace and relief settling gently down upon him, as if some internal switch had been flipped.

namely, by the direct manipulation of one's inner milieu.

Such an alternative account is one I find suggested by a wide variety of references, only some of which I will briefly touch upon here. First, take the following remark from Augusten Burroughs's (2003) best-selling memoir of his alcoholism, aptly entitled *Dry.* After observing that he didn't "drink like a normal person" (p. 3), Burroughs went on to make a very illuminating observation. "I use booze," he began, "like an escape hatch" (p. 83). So far, then, what he said accords well enough with such common ideas as those of bell hooks, that people turn to addiction as a means of escaping from reality when that reality becomes experientially unacceptable to them. However, what Burroughs immediately added to complete his sentence points in a suddenly new direction: "I use booze like an escape hatch," he wrote, "*and also like a destination*" (p. 83, emphasis added).

As I have written elsewhere (Seeburger, 1993), one can capture the difference between the mere use of something, on the one hand, and addiction to the same thing, on the other, along the very lines Burroughs (2003) suggested: As long as one remains in an instrumentally rational relation to the drug-taking or other behavior at issue, one has not yet crossed the line over into addiction. That is, as long as one truly is taking drugs or engaging in another behavior as a means toward some other end—which is to say as long as one really does have sufficient reasons for doing whatever it is one is doing—then one is not yet addicted. Addiction occurs only when one persists in the behavior even in the absence of any sufficient reason in terms of means and ends, and begins engaging in the practice for its own sake. At that point, one ceases to have or need any further reason for engaging in the behavior. Rather, the behavior itself becomes the reason for doing other things, as it were. After all, any person who is addicted will be happy to latch on to any convenient excuse to use. Once addiction has developed, the addictive behavior itself has been freed of all connection to instrumental rationality. Of course, it may well be that addictive practices may continue to pay additional benefits, besides the sheer joy of pursuing the practice for its own sake. The narcotics to which a given person is addicted may well continue to provide relief from chronic pain, for example. But after addiction has set in, that relief is really only a nice side effect, as it were, and not the continuing reason for the behavior, which no longer needs any such reason. As Burroughs (2003) said, the addiction has become a destination of its own, not just a road to elsewhere; but his remark also makes clear that becoming such a destination of its own is perfectly compatible with still continuing to provide a road to other places.

Along such lines, Margaret Bullitt-Jonas (1998) wrote *Holy Hunger,* about her food addiction and her recovery in Overeaters Anonymous. In the book, she told a joke that was a favorite for her alcoholic father:

> My father loved to tell the joke about a yacht speeding out of the harbor and overtaking a sailboat. The yachtsman leans over the side to yell triumphantly, "I'm going to get there in one hour, and it's going to take you ten!" The sailor looks up calmly and smiles, "Ah, but you don't understand. I'm already there." (p. 204)

Accordingly, the popular view, that addiction is a means for addicts to escape from experientially unmanageable situations, is at best only half the truth, and, as is so often the case with half-truths, it actually conceals more than it reveals. The other half of the truth, captured by Augusten Burroughs' (2003) notion that the addictive practice is its own destination, whatever else it may simultaneously provide as a means to some other end, is the more important half.

Before pursuing that thought further, however, I want to back up for a moment and add a couple of other references to go with the remarks from hooks (1998) and Burroughs (2003)—references that provide important additional perspective. The first has to do with the often-noted paradox that smokers universally report that they find the experience of smoking calming when they are nervous or stressed by external circumstances beyond their direct control. Yet the objective evidence is clear that the physiological effects of nicotine are, in fact, anything but calming. Therefore, the question such reports engender is how it could be that smokers would find themselves calmed by increased excitation.

An answer I find convincing is that, by manipulating their own internal levels of excitation, smokers give themselves something to concentrate upon besides the external circumstances over which they experience lack of control. By allowing smokers to concentrate on the manipulation of their own internal condition, smoking thus calms them experientially, not just despite, but even by means of, increasing levels of physiological excitation.

A second, related phenomenon worth noting is one that I have discussed already elsewhere (Seeburger, 1993). The rates of addiction to both stimulants and depressants are roughly equal, despite the fact that they have opposite mood-altering effects. For both, these rates of addiction are significantly higher than for hallucinogens, although the latter also regularly alter mood. I think the explanation is to be found in the difference of predictability of effect for the user, with the effects of both stimulants and depressants being considerably more predictable than the effects of hallucinogens.

A third item I will bring up concerns the phenomenon of "cutting," the practice of self-mutilation, the incidence of which is particularly high among adolescent and young adult American women. If confronted by emotional or mental pressure for which she experiences herself as without effective means to cope, especially by just enduring it, the cutter will resort to the blade. She will find immediate relief through acting upon her own body, even in such painful and self-destructive ways as self-mutilation, in situations where she experiences herself as otherwise blocked from all effective agency.

In fact, the *assertion of effective agency* in situations where the exercise of such agency is experienced as otherwise blocked is precisely what I see as the key common element in all three cases I have just mentioned—smokers finding smoking calming, despite nicotine functioning as a physiological excitant; rates of addiction to stimulants and depressants, relative to one another and to hallucinogens; and the phenomenon of cutting. Nietzsche (1887b) both began and ended the third and final essay of his *Genealogy of Morals* with the famous remark, "Lieber will noch der Mensch das Nichts wollen, als nicht wollen," which translates as, "One would rather will the naught, than naught will." We need not subscribe to Nietzsche's entire metaphysics of the will to power to find a valuable insight in that remark. In effect, the three cases I've mentioned all show, to paraphrase Nietzsche, that any assertion of agency, even if only in self-destructive ways, is humanly preferable to giving up all agency. If, as one experiences one's situation, the only way left open for one to assert oneself as an efficacious agent is to kill oneself, then one will kill oneself before relinquishing the claim to agency. Indeed, in some circumstances, which I would argue are exactly those under which addiction most flourishes, the greatest agency one can still exercise may turn out to be what the contemporary French phenomenologist Jean-Luc Marion (2002) in a different context, called "*lifelong* suicide" (emphasis added). What could be more descriptive of addiction?

Most of us, caught up in our daily lives, experience ourselves as having and exercising significantly effective agency within those very lives. If we assume that the issue of experiencing effective agency is the crucial factor in addiction, then we would predict addiction rates and intensity to increase dramatically in situations where individuals experience themselves as lacking such agency. Under such conditions, addiction would be the final, desperate effort to maintain the sense of having such agency, by exercising it on oneself.

The consequences of such exercise as judged from the outside may be entirely negative. They may be disastrous. They may even lead to death. None of that would matter, however, from the standpoint of the person practicing the addiction, since, as Nietzsche saw, it is better to be an agent of destruction, even one's own destruction, than not to be an agent at all. By that analysis, addiction would be so addicting, that is, human beings would be so tempted to become addicted, because addiction would indeed offer a solution to an underlying problem. Addiction would provide the solution to the problem of asserting agency in one's own life, just when, and to the extent that, one no longer experiences that life as one's own.

CONCLUSION: SOME IMPLICATIONS FOR RECOVERY, TREATMENT, AND PREVENTION

Adopting the perspective that addiction provides a solution to the problem of preserving effective agency in situations where it is otherwise blocked will profoundly change the general way of addressing the whole issue of prevention, recovery, and treatment. Take prevention first. From the perspective that addiction is itself a solution to the problem of gaining a sense of agency in an experiential reality that otherwise restricts it, prevention efforts would need to focus on remedying that underlying reality, rather than on trying directly to prevent addiction itself without changing that reality. Attention would need to be focused upon providing new, hitherto experientially unavailable, options for the exercise of meaningful personal agency, options besides addiction. If, as William S. Burroughs (1953) said in his preface to *Junky*, one just "drifts" into addiction for lack of any "strong motivations in any other direction" (p. xvi), then prevention of addiction requires the provision of such strong alternative motivations. And since the drift into addiction occurs because, to those experientially void of such alternatives, addiction provides the way to continue to exercise agency in one's own life, those alternatives must be in the form of avenues for the genuine exercise of such personally meaningful, efficacious, agency. Mere distractions and entertainments, or meaningless busywork, however complex and otherwise involving, will not do. At most, such things would only offer the escape from reality that addiction is mistakenly taken to provide. Rather, what would be needed is real opportunity for the continuing enjoyment of the exercise of agency in personally significant ways within one's daily life. If we were to address preventing addiction from such a perspective, we would need to provide systematically for ongoing regular active employment of agency at all levels, particularly in daily living routines.

The same thing follows for treatment of addiction and recovery from it. For those who are addicted, just saying no will never be enough. In fact, in order to keep on saying no, addicted persons must find what AA's *Big Book* (1935) called a "sufficient substitute" (p. 152) for the addictive practice. If the key to addiction is how it provides for the exercise of agency when other avenues seem blocked, only by reopening those other avenues and then keeping them open will any truly permanent substitute—and recovery—be possible.

In many cases, a great deal of the work of prevention, as well as of treatment and recovery, would need to take the form of practical education about alternative ways for exercising agency in daily real-life settings. Many addicts grow up in or into situations in which options for meaningful exercise of personal agency in nonaddictive directions are indeed clearly present—but only to an outside observer and not to the addicts themselves. If they are not seen to be available by the addicts themselves, however, they may as well not be there at all. In such affairs it is always the subjective aspects of the experiential situation that matter.

So far, I have been addressing the implications of the idea of viewing addiction as the solution to an otherwise insoluble problem of personal agency. From my last few remarks I can now go back to an earlier idea—that addiction is the human norm, not the human exception. Insofar as that is so, any serious attempt to treat and, especially, to prevent addiction cannot take the *reactive* approach of trying merely to remove occasional limitations to the exercise of meaningful personal agency. Rather, the approach must be an *active* one of strongly correcting in advance the universal human drift toward addiction. The occlusion of nonaddictive options would belong to the basic human condition as such, not just to variable historical circumstances that reinforce the already-operative drift.

Even assuming the drift toward addiction to be universally human, however, the occlusion of options that opens the door to addiction can be strongly reinforced and worsened by such specific historical factors. From slavery to all the various forms of economic exploitation of some people by others, from limited access to health care and educational opportunities, to racial, gender, and other biases, there are many ways in which sociocultural institutions can exacerbate the presumed universal human tilt toward addiction. This can include physical, emotional, and mental disabilities, differences of intelligence, talent, skill, or character, and tastes or preferences, at the level of individuals within a society. Social institutions can aggravate such individual factors, promoting the tendency toward addiction. Rising rates of diagnosed addiction in the contemporary world strongly suggest that the institutions of the emerging global society bring just such aggravation.

However, institutions can also contribute toward providing counterweights against this drift toward addiction. If contemporary addiction rates are indeed higher today than in past societies, the study of those institutions of bygone social forms which may have provided the needed counterweight to addiction could be an important resource to draw upon in learning how we might give modern guidance to similar institutions today.

But what does *thinking* have to do with all this, to come all the way back to the first of the three ideas I've been discussing today, the idea of an inseparability of attributive thinking and addiction? The drive to attribution, the addictive compulsion to be able to provide attributive explanation to all things, would be a manifestation of the very occlusion at the heart of the human condition, the occlusion at the experiential level that obstructs the nonaddictive exercise of meaningful personal agency.

One way we might put the point is to revisit the unlikely pairing of Freud with Heidegger. Despite their many differences, both assigned a universal generative role in human life to *anxiety* (although one of the points of difference between them concerns just how anxiety is to be conceptualized).

In addition, Heidegger went on expressly to characterize the proximate and primary (*zunächst und zumeist*) human response to anxiety as *anxiety in the face of anxiety itself*—the anxious flight *not* to know what anxiety *gives* us to know. What Heidegger later came to call "conceptual," "calculative," or "representational" thinking, and which corresponds with what I am calling attributive thinking, is precisely thought that springs from, and then serves, that very anxious flight of the human being in the face of humanly definitive anxiety. It is thinking that cannot but heed the demand of *der Satz vom Grund*, the principle of reason. That is the principle that for everything there is a sufficient reason. In its final form (first stated in clear, explicit terms by Leibniz, according to the story Heidegger told) it is the principle in accordance with which all thinking is under the imperative actually to provide the sufficient ground or reason for whatever it encounters, pointedly including thinking itself. Attributive thinking, the thinking that is bound in such a way to the flight of anxiety in the face of itself, would be the form that thinking takes when it experiences itself blocked from all other ways of manifesting itself except by perpetually struggling in vain to ground its own groundlessness.[2]

Complete freedom from addiction would, accordingly, require the liberation of thinking from the imperative of providing the sufficient reason for all things, including itself. I earlier noted Heidegger's insistence that the authentic self is not the substitution of a new, different, true self for an old, inauthentic, false one, but is, rather, a different way of taking up the one and only self, the very one we *are* at first and for the most part in an inauthentic way. I recall that insistence now to caution against supposing that the liberation from the imperative to provide sufficient reasons, that is, the liberation of thinking from attribution as an addiction, necessarily means giving up all attribution. Rather, the model Heidegger provided for the conversion from inauthenticity to authenticity suggests that thinking freed of attribution as an addictive practice, might very well go right on attributing, only now hold itself in a different relationship to its own incessant attributions. In effect, it would be a thinking that had recovered itself from its fall into an addictive fixation upon its own attributions.

I have a number of thoughts about what such liberation of thinking from

---

2   From this standpoint, thinking is the most human of all types of agency.

attribution and, therewith, what such *recovered* thinking—and, furthermore, the connections it would have to a recovered society—might look like. However, I will have to leave that for another occasion, perhaps to a talk I might give some day as a sequel to this one on "Thinking Addiction," a sequel I might call "Thinking Recovery."

REFERENCES

Alcoholics Anonymous. (2001). *Alcoholics Anonymous: The story of how many thousands of men and women have recovered from alcoholism* [Commonly called the *Big Book*] (4th ed.). Originally published in 1939. Retrieved from http://aa.org/bigbookonline/en_tableofcnt.cfm

Bullitt-Jonas, M. (1998). *Holy hunger: A woman's journey from food addiction to spiritual fulfillment.* New York: Alfred A. Knopf.

Burroughs, A. (2003). *Dry.* New York: St. Martin's Press.

Burroughs, W. S. (1953). *Junky.* New York: Penguin Books.

hooks, b. (1998). *Sisters of the yam: Black women and self recovery.* Boston: South End Press.

Hume, D. (1740/1967). *A treatise of human nature.* Oxford: Oxford University Press.

Kant, E. (1790). *The critique of judgement* (J. H. Bernard, Trans.). Retrieved from http://files.libertyfund.org/files/1217/0318_Bk.pdf

Knapp, C. (2003). *Appetites.* New York: Counterpoint.

Lacan, J. (1992). *The seminar, book VII. The ethics of psychoanalysis, 1959–1960* (J.-A. Miller, Ed., D. Porter, Trans.). New York: W. W. Norton.

Marion, J.-L. (2002). Evil in person, in S. E. Lewis, Trans., *Prolegomena to charity.* New York: Fordham University Press.

May, G. G. (1988). *Addiction and grace.* San Francisco: Harper & Row.

McCormick, P.M. (1989). *Sin as addiction.* New York: Paulist Press.

Nietschze, F. W. (1887a). *The gay science* (W. Kaufmann, Trans.). Retrieved from http://ia701205.us.archive.org/35/items/Nietzsche-TheGayScience/Nietzsche-GaySciencewk.pdf

Nietschze, F. W. (1887b). *The genealogy of morals* (H. B. Samuel, Trans.). New York: Boni & Liveright. Retrieved from http://archive.org/details/genealogyofmoral00nietuoft

Santner, E. L. (2001). *On the psychotheology of everyday life.* Chicago: The University of Chicago Press.

Seeburger, F. F. (1993). *Addiction and responsibility: An inquiry into the addictive mind.* New York: Crossroad.

8. Transforming the Addicted Person's Counterfeit Quest for Wholeness
Using Wilber's Transpersonal Spectrum of Development: A Clinical Perspective.

GARY NIXON

Abstract

A transpersonal therapeutic approach calls for the person with addiction issues to become aware of his or her counterfeit quest for wholeness, and in recovery, begin to search authentically for meaning and wholeness by working through the different developmental levels as set out in Wilber's spectrum of consciousness framework. A second stage of recovery beyond abstinence is proposed, in which the person with addictions embraces and works through the emotional underbelly beneath the addictive process. Eventually, a third stage of recovery entails letting go of the addiction to the separate self and the mind by embracing nondual living. Wilber's transpersonal model of development is utilized, including 10 levels and three overall stages of development. Possible pathologies and treatment interventions are reviewed for each level including specific addiction and recovery implications. Case studies and anecdotal accounts are used to illustrate this process.

It is the perspective of transpersonal psychology that all human beings are on a quest for wholeness, whether consciously or unconsciously (Cortwright, 1997; Wilber, 1977). Some 80 years ago, Jung remarked that craving for alcohol was a low-level spiritual thirst for wholeness and union with God (Leonard, 1989). Transpersonal therapist Christina Grof (1993) wrote of the discovery that her own alcohol addiction was a misguided thirst and quest for wholeness. Thus, from the perspective of transpersonal psychology, addictive processes can be seen as a counterfeit quest for wholeness (Grof, 1993; Nixon & Solowoniuk, 2008), a path paradoxically tread to recover lost elements of soul. With the plight of the alcoholic, we see a person who has not brought this quest for wholeness and individuation into conscious awareness (Singer, 1994). Instead, the alcoholic forsakes intuitive self-worth and takes a "short cut" to wholeness by indulging in "spirits" (Leonard, 1989).

A transpersonal therapeutic approach calls for the person with addiction issues to become aware of his or her counterfeit quest for wholeness, and in recovery, to begin to search authentically for meaning and wholeness by working through the different developmental levels as set out in Wilber's spectrum of consciousness framework. A second stage of recovery requires the individual to embrace and to work through the emotional underbelly beneath the addictive process. Eventually, a third phase of recovery entails letting go of the addiction to the separate self by embracing nondual living. Throughout this article, case studies and anecdotal accounts from clients are used to illustrate this process.

THE UNDERBELLY OF ADDICTION

At their training workshops, Firman and Gila (1997) ask participants to imagine a situation during which they begin to feel the urge to engage in their addiction, and imagine rather than acting out with their addiction, to just "sit in" the feelings and to be mindful of them. Next, they ask participants in their fantasy to fully engage in the experience of acting out with their addiction and to be mindful of the positive experiences they sought in their addiction. In summarizing this exercise, Firman and Gila see the addictions process as a method by which we attempt to climb out of the realm of negative experience into a realm of positive experience. It is evident that, by utilizing the addiction process, we are trying to escape unresolved feelings such as pain, nonbeing, abandonment, and worthlessness. These negative feelings fuel our attempts at addictive self-repair.

The impact of neglect and abuse can magnify this negative dynamic (Firman & Gila, 1997). If we look at the central feelings of these experiences we can see how much hidden shame, abandonment, and emptiness drives the addictive cycle. It seems imperative, in the recovery from addiction, that clients address this underlying core (Wolinsky, 1999). The challenge of recovery then begins with Stage 1 in which, through our behavior and abstinence, we "dam up the flood of addiction" (Kasl, 1992), and maintain abstinence and strategies for survival living "one day at a time." The tasks of finding a place to live, paying the rent, keeping or finding a job, coping with relationships, going to counseling sessions and meetings, and dealing with triggers can keep the person in Stage 1 recovery occupied. But this is clearly not enough. The danger is that there is tremendous relapse potential in Stage 1 as a person can live the life of a "dry drunk" (Larsen,

1985), Thus, at some stage in the recovery process the person needs to move into the deep emotional underbelly of addiction and deal with what could be called Stage 2 recovery.

STAGE 2 RECOVERY

Stage 1 recovery may successfully focus on abstinence from alcohol or drugs, but may not address underlying issues that perpetuate addictions, such as chronic dependence on others, fear of pain, helplessness, hopelessness, self-abandonment, and mindlessness (Nixon, 2005; Tessina, 1991). In using the term dry drunk, Larsen (1985) observed that people who are still in that stage have not dealt with the central question of "Why did we have all that pain in the first place?" (p. 14). The pain underlying the addiction must be dealt with.

In this second stage, a person learns to make relationships work (Larsen, 1985). Intimacy, rather than alcohol, becomes the central issue. Here the issues underlying the addiction need to be addressed. Previously learned self-defeating behavior such as caretaking, people pleasing, or being a martyr must be confronted. To change behaviors, people must examine carefully the habits which have made their reality comfortable. These habits are based on past patterns of dealing with feelings and help define what is "normal" for them. The unresolved feelings and issues now become central to the healing process (Larsen, 1985).

In this second phase of recovery, Tessina (1991) stressed the need for a person to move beyond addiction and dependency by learning skills of effective communication, taking risks, solving problems, coping with failure, facing pain, and forgiving others and self. With these new skills, a person learns self-reliance, self-determination, self-motivation, self-confidence, self-esteem, and self-love. Through these new skills, a person acquires the emotional strength to be free of dependency, identifies healthy relationships through the new emerging relation to self, and gains an understanding of self-responsibility (Tessina, 1991).

The avoidance of second-stage recovery can, in some cases, have fairly tragic consequences. A recent example from my clinical practice illustrates this point. Ralph, a 52-year-old male, had been in recovery for over 10 years, but never worked on his issues beyond focusing on abstinence. So, while Ralph was able to stay sober, his underlying emotional issues of self-righteousness, narrowness, rigidity, and rage, as well as deeper levels of insecurity and trauma from his past, had not been worked on. By the time he came for counseling, his job was in danger; his supervisors had given him numerous warnings and were preparing to have him fired in his social services position. He was seen as a very unpopular nonteam troublemaker and his coworkers were hoping that he would be fired.

As well, his fiancée had recently broken up with him as she had grown tired of his self-preoccupation, rigidity, emotional flatness, and very tightly wound-up rituals. Having his world collapse around him forced Ralph into counseling but his delay in working on his dry drunk issues was already causing havoc in his life.

Given the necessity of second-stage recovery (Bewley, 1993, 1995; Brown, 1985; Larsen, 1985; Kasl, 1992; Kurtz & Ketcham, 1992; Nixon, 2005; Straussner & Spiegel, 1996; Tessina, 1991), we will now consider how transpersonal models of counseling can help facilitate this second stage of recovery, and, ultimately, a third stage of recovery.

TRANSPERSONAL APPROACHES

Maslow (1968), the founding father of transpersonal psychology, called for the recognition of the higher or transcendent possibilities occurring at the farther reaches of human nature. This necessitated the development of a fourth force of psychology, *transpersonal psychology*: "transpersonal, transhuman, centered in the cosmos rather than in human needs and interests, going beyond humanness, identity, self-actualization, and the like" (pp. iii-iv). The transpersonal perspective assumes that our essential nature is spiritual, consciousness is multidimensional, and humans have valid urges towards spiritual seeking, expressed as a search for wholeness, through deepening individual, social, and transcendent awareness. As well, it is assumed that contacting a deeper source of wisdom and guidance within is both possible and helpful to growth, and that altered states of consciousness can be an aid to healing and help make our life and actions more meaningful (Cortwright, 1997).

Extensive work has now been done in the area of transpersonal psychology in Western psychology with the development of: the spectrum of consciousness approach of Ken Wilber (1977, 1986, 1990, 1995, 1997, 2000, 2006); the innovation of Michael Washburn (1988, 1994) which centered on Jung's analytical psychology; the diamond approach of A. H. Almaas (1996, 2008); the psychosynthesis of Roberto Assagioli (1973); the holotropic therapy of Stanislav Grof (1985, 1988); as well as existential, psychoanalytic, and body-centered transpersonal approaches (Cortwright, 1997; Hixon, 1978; Walsh & Vaughan, 1980, 1993).

Transpersonal models of development offer the opportunity to recognize the full range of human issues in recovery. Maslow's (1968) hierarchy of needs progresses through lower order needs of physiological, safety, belongingness and love, and self-esteem, before moving on to self-actualization and self-transcendence. Whitfield (1985) pointed to the hierarchy of consciousness in accordance with the perennial philosophy as providing a map of recovery. Similarly, Small (1982) described seven levels of chakras, or energy centers, based on Eastern systems of growth that need to be worked through during the journey of transformation from addiction.

More recently, Almaas (1996) has developed a model of growth based on a transformation of narcissism. This model has exciting implications for long-term recovery as typical issues, such as self-preoccupation and psychic inflation, can be worked through in the counseling process. Pivotal steps of the transformation of narcissism include such themes as: discovering the empty shell and fakeness; becoming aware of the narcissistic wound; working through the great betrayal, narcissistic rage, and the great chasm; discovering a place of loving beingness; and the realization of the essential identity. Almaas' model, with its focus on moving from reliance on the false self to relaxing into essence, highlights many of the developmental issues of long-term recovery.

Examination of the developmental model of the spectrum of consciousness of Wilber (1977, 1986, 1990, 1995, 1997, 2000, 2006) will provide a more detailed examination of the transformation of addiction and self-preoccupation and the movement towards integration and wholeness during the second and third stages of recovery.

WILBER'S SPECTRUM OF CONSCIOUSNESS APPROACH

Wilber (1977, 1986, 1990, 1995, 1997, 2000, 2006) has developed a spectrum of consciousness developmental model which incorporates both conventional psychology and contemplative traditions. What is exciting about the Wilber model is that, while it was not explicitly developed for addictions, it offers an exciting opportunity to work with underlying issues during recovery from substance abuse, and moves the client into a second stage of recovery, and (hopefully) later, a third stage.

Wilber's (1977, 1986, 1990) spectrum of consciousness model mapped out 10 principal levels of the psyche in a developmental, structural, holistic, systems-oriented format. Wilber (1986) synthesized the initial levels from cognitive, ego, moral, and object relations lines of development of conventional psychology represented by such theorists as Piaget (1977), Loevinger (1976), and Kohlberg (1981), and the final four transpersonal levels from Eastern and Western sources of contemplative development, such as Mahayana, Vedanta, Sufi, Kabalah, Christian mysticism, Yoga, Aurobindo, and Zen. This transpersonal model of development can be separated into over 20 lines of development (Wilber, 2006).

Over time, in reaction to severe criticism and the need to be more comprehensive, Wilber (2000, 2006) has acknowledged limitations to conventional lines of development and integrated alternate perspectives, such as the work of Gilligan (1982) on female moral development, the spiraling aspect of development through streams and waves rather than levels and lines captured in such theories as Kegan (1982), and spiral dynamics set out by Beck and Cowan (1996). As well, Wilber (1995, 2000, 2006) has developed a four-quadrant model of knowledge based on interior vs. exterior and singular vs. plural perspectives. The upper left quadrant, the interior-singular, is recognized as the interior "I," the psyche, and this quadrant of inner psychological development will be the focus of this paper.

In focusing on Wilber's model of psychological development, we see that Wilber's model is unique in that not only is it a developmental spectrum of prepersonal, personal, and transpersonal consciousness, it is also a spectrum of possible pathologies as developmental barriers are possible at each stage (Wilber, 1986). It is a model that allows us to integrate many of the Western psychologies and interventions. Originally used for mental health issues (Wilber, 1986), it has now been applied to substance abuse issues (Nixon, 2001a), second-stage recovery (Nixon, 2005), hopelessness (Nixon, 2001b), and gambling issues (Nixon, 2003; Nixon & Solowoniuk, 2008).

The 10 levels of Wilber's spectrum of development model will now be outlined along with corresponding pathologies and treatment interventions. We will see that each of these levels has implications in terms of addiction, and in particular the second stage of recovery. There are three phases of ego development: prepersonal, personal, and transpersonal (Wilber, 1986).

Prepersonal Levels of Stage 1

1) **Sensoriphysical**. The first level, *sensoriphysical*, consists of matter, sensation, and perception. Pathologies at this level need to be treated with physical, somatic interventions. In addictions, the physiology of the chemically addicted person is stabilized by sending the person to detox to get the drugs out of his or her system.

Much can be done at this level for a person in recovery. Beyond the obvious physical aspects of abstinence many initiatives can be undertaken, including attention to diet, weight training and working out, long distance running, yoga, martial arts, and complementary therapies, to name a few. As Glasser (1976) emphasized, the person needs to develop positive habits of wholeness maintenance. The neurochemistry of the recovering person can be naturally enhanced to replace the previous habits of self-medication. Judith (1996) described how the opening up of energy chakras can open up and energize the mind-body.

An example from clinical practice can show the power of methods that focus on the physical. Lynn, a practicing family counselor, came for a consultation over her concern that, after many years in recovery, she was now in a period of low energy and low-grade depression. In our session together, before exploring the emotional reasons behind her current state, we looked at what was going on now in her life that was different from before, and we found out she had stopped her physical exercise over the last six months. She no longer had an avenue to give catharsis to the negative energy, blocks, and primal pain she picked up in life, as well as in working as a counselor. I encouraged her to restart her long-distance running plan immediately. Two weeks later, when I talked to her again, she reported feeling much better, having energy at her disposal, and feeling herself again. She had been running intensely over the last two weeks, including some intense hill work which acted as an intense energetic catharsis.

Unfortunately, not all issues of those experiencing the symptoms of the dry drunk and its accompanying emotionality can be easily resolved through a physical remedy. We will now turn to explore some of the developmental levels which capture the emotional underbelly issues of long-term recovery.

2) Phantasmic-emotional. In the second level, *phantasmic-emotional*, the individual begins to develop emotional boundaries of self through the development of a separated-individuated self (Wilber, 1986). The self-other orientation can be problematic when the self treats the world as an extension of itself (narcissistic), or by being constantly invaded by the world (borderline). People with severe addiction issues often regress back to this level as their world is reduced to their connection with their addiction. To facilitate growth at this level, psychodynamic interventions focus on structure-building techniques, such as in object relations and psychoanalytic therapy. Twelve-step groups can help give structure and self-other connections for the person who has been completely preoccupied with his or her addiction.

While there can be some movement at this level in the first phase of recovery, it is common for the person who had regressed into chronic addictions issues and then gone into recovery to have some difficult issues to face in this second level. Clients can be immobilized in self–other pain and emotional wounds which they had previously covered up through their substance use. It is essential to work on this basic self-other stance and try to reclaim basic trust (Almaas, 1996). The key for therapists here is to model acceptance of pain as an alternative to the client's attempts to escape pain. Experiencing our pain bodies allows us to become consciously aware rather than let our pain bodies unconsciously take over (Tolle, 1997).

In short, we are teaching our clients to sit in their pain. This is an unusual step because we have been conditioned that our pain is unbearable and we have been taught to never look directly into the face of our pain. To their surprise, clients find that, by being one with their pain through adopting a nonjudgmental stance, that the sting of pain dissolves, and they find a healing essence within it (Nixon, 2005). The transformation of pain into healing essence releases the need to escape from it through some addictive process or to be attached to it (Gangaji, 2005).

At this core level, Wolinsky (1999) described how we can become aware of a false *core driver* and a false *compensatory system* that has been at play in the greater part of our life. It can be a shock to realize that we have been driven our whole life by a core belief that we have mainly kept out of our awareness. Here, by asking the client to examine what the worst part of a troublesome experience is, we can help discover a core belief that the client has inadvertently taken on and made central to his or her psychological system. Common examples of this are such statements as "I am worthless," "I am bad," "I am out of control," "I am unlovable," and "I am deficient," and even such intense statements as "I shouldn't have been born." We lose this awareness through what Wolinsky called our "false self-compensator. . . [that] attempts to heal, transform, psychologize or spiritualize itself in an attempt to overcome the false core" (p. 116). Our attempts to overcome the false core through our defensive systems only reinforce the false core as, at a deep level, we accept the false core conclusion. Simply letting clients become aware of these core statements, and letting them dissolve by simply being mindful and present, can help long-held core beliefs dissolve. The key here is that we have to sit in our false core directly and let it dissolve through nonjudgmental awareness.

A clinical case example will illustrate the healing of the false core. Amanda, in her early twenties, was in recovery for codependency and resultant substance abuse and sexual addiction issues. She had been running tapes in her life of perfectionism, idealized body image, and codependency for many years. The one place she did not want to go was to a deep sense of abandonment and to feeling unlovable, which resulted from being adopted and being displaced early in her life by her adoptive mother. Sitting in her feeling of abandonment, and the sense of "I am unlovable" is something she had avoided as long as she could remember, as this would have been too painful to process. In therapy, she was invited to go to this awful place which she had avoided for many years, and to just breathe and to be mindful. Initially, a huge panic attack came over her as it felt like this pain of abandonment was too intense to handle. As she was reminded to stay mindful without judgment, the experience started to transform itself. As she started to feel abandonment as just vast aloneness energy in the moment, and soon discovered to her amazement that she could feel peaceful and spacious in a previously feared place of abandonment. This shift, at her core level, resulted in a pronounced shift in her everyday life. For the first time, she was relaxed in her aloneness, and did not desperately need to cling to the validation of others. A deep issue of emotional pain had been healed and great progress had been made in Amanda's second level of recovery.

In the next developmental level, we will turn to look more fully at the psyche's tendency to split into separate parts which are in conflict with each other.

3) Rep-Mind. The third developmental level, the *rep-mind*, represents the development of the intrapsychic representational self (Wilber, 1986). In Freudian psychology, this is typified by the development of the id, ego, and superego and the resulting intrapsychic conflicts between these parts, such as inhibition, anxiety, obsession, guilt, and depression. Interventions focus on intrapsychic resolution of these internal conflicts through reintegration of repressed, disassociated, or alienated aspects of being (Wilber, 1986). At this level, substance abuse is seen as the false path of intrapsychic conflict resolution. Thus, the person who has been soothing anxieties and fears with chemicals must recognize that this is a false path of internal conflict resolution. Interventions can focus on resolution of intrapsychic conflict through reintegration of repressed, disconnected, or alienated aspects of being as well through curtailing overused aspects.

As we work on this level, it becomes clear that clients may have set up psychic splits internally to deal with trauma experiences. Ironically, it is usually the case that it is not the experience itself that keeps us frozen, but our own judgmental critical voice that says "This is terrible" and the resultant avoidance of the experience altogether. Experientially, it can be important for clients to heal the split through dropping the critical judgments while experiencing and letting the energy work through and flow (Greenspan, 2003; Nixon, 2005).

At this level of the internal mind, an effort can be made to recover and reclaim the lost aspects of self. A great deal of our own inner resources and energy can be dammed up, frozen, or repressed from day-to-day life. We no longer feel we have all of our resources at our disposal. For example, an assertion exercise can be done to help the recovering person reclaim energy through a Jungian–Gestalt exercise of using anger energy that previously was available but is now being repressed out of conscious awareness and into what the Jungians would call the shadow (Perls, 1969; Schwartz, 2007). The shadow of so-called "dark energy" can serve as a vital reservoir of repressed energy that needs to be released, energy that can be reintegrated into conscious awareness.

For example, Wendy, a young woman in her early twenties, had been in recovery for five years after a turbulent adolescence, but had been begging for acceptance from her father, a corporate executive. She had been withholding her authentic voice from him for many years, and in an acted-out role play, was encouraged to embrace her shadow self, and express her anger to her dad, who was sitting in the empty chair. The emotional catharsis that followed was intensified when Wendy was asked to raise her voice and express loudly to her dad "I am angry at you dad. It's over; I can't beg for your acceptance any more." Soon Wendy was loudly saying to her dad, "Screw you, Dad! I have to live my own life!" When it was over, Wendy was shocked at how energized and exuberant she felt. She had been reacquainted with how much energy she had at her disposal.

Related to this opening up of one's internal energy is the issue of dismantling the inner critical voice (Nixon, 2005). Often, to help clarify the situation, it can be helpful to put the critical voice in an empty chair, and then have the client move over and express the typical critical voice dialogue to the waiting self. When the client is asked to take his or her original seat, it can be quite liberating for the client to defeat the critical voice, to tell it to "Leave me alone!" or whatever it takes to dismantle the voice. This process takes it further than cognitive therapy (Burns, 1981), which tries to rationally debunk the critical voice by having the client experience an energetic and emotional catharsis in defeating the voice and getting a sense of freedom beyond it.

This process can even be taken a step further, when the client realizes that the critical voice of another person has been introjected (Nixon, 2005). A client can externalize the voice by role playing the person it has come from, and then switch back to being him or herself, and be assertive to that other person and set boundaries with that critical voice. An emotional catharsis experience can be created to help the person experience the freedom of being when the internalized critical voice of another person is no longer inside them. A person can have carried a parent's or spouse's voice inside for many years, so it can be very liberating to experience the self without the entrenched critical voice.

The essence of this level is dealing with intrapsychic splits internally that have caused the client to lose touch with his or her natural mind–body energetic resources. By working at healing the split, a client can regain the sense of emotional wholeness that was lost long ago.

Stage 2: Personal Levels

We will now turn to the ego-consolidation phase. These personal levels represent the mature ego-developmental phase.

4) Rule/Role Mind. Wilber's fourth level of development, and first personal level, is the *rule/role* phase. It is highlighted by individual development of rules and roles to belong. A person's stance is becoming less narcissistic and more sociocentric (Wilber, 1986). Because problems at this level are experienced as a fear of losing face, losing one's role, and breaking the rules, typical interventions center on script pathology, using techniques such as transactional analysis, family therapy, cognitive therapy, and narrative therapy. Therapies at this stage uncover false scripts including compulsive reliance on substances or other addictive processes, or unhelpful family-of-origin or relationship scripts that contribute to the pain underneath the addiction.

From a Jungian standpoint, the rule/role developmental stage epitomizes the creation of the mask or persona that an individual creates as a result of becoming a civilized creature so as to meet the requirements set forth by the collective society (Jung, 1959). Thus, the individual can be caught between being true to the inner self vs. meeting the ego's demands, the latter of which are manifested through personal goals or the maintenance of a sense of self that is appreciated by others.

While the initial addictive process may have served as a misguided quest for wholeness (Nixon, Solowoniuk & McGowan, 2006), the person in Stage 2 recovery is confronted by his or her underlying social anxiety that formerly was overcome in substance use with alcohol as a form of liquid courage. The alcohol facilitated a sense of fearlessness, connection, belongingness, overcoming alienation, and fitting in. Now in recovery, it is typical for recovering persons to have to face an underlying social anxiety, which in the moment can be experienced as a terrible and pathetic begging for social acceptance. We can constantly be in a state of watching others watch us, and self-consciously perform in a way that we hope will be met with social approval (Nixon, 2005). The tragedy (and vicious cycle of this pattern) is that other people are loathe to approve of individuals who are desperate for social approval. Thus, the recovering person needs to learn how to directly risk being authentic in social and intimate relationships as exemplified by the following clinical case example.

Mark, in recovery from cocaine addiction for about five years, was in coun-seling working on freeing himself up to embrace all that life had to offer him in the present moment. As Mark started to let go of his past, it became clearer how Mark "de-selved" himself in relationships (Lerner, 1985). It seemed that Mark was rarely in touch with his own essence and beingness while interacting with his friends and acquaintances. He gave up vital aspects of himself, including his feelings, perceptions, and opinions, to please others. I pointed out to Mark how he was constantly watching his external environment for cues to see how it was watching him. Because Mark felt he had never really socially fit in, he was continually looking for external cues from others, and trying to give others what he perceived they wanted. In short, he was caught in self-consciousness and de-selving through his desire for guaranteed social acceptance. In our sessions, we worked together on this issue, and Mark began to see that this constant watching and manipulating for validation was both a form of begging and a hopeless pattern. This pattern always kept Mark in a place of unease and self-consciousness as acceptance from others was rather unpredictable, much like stormy weather. Mark began to see that if he dropped his begging, he could experience his essence directly. Rather than watching me or anybody else for cues of acceptance, Mark could directly experience and express where he was coming from.

With this insight, Mark began to make changes in his intimate relationship. He realized that he had fallen into the codependent pattern of trying to figure out and anticipate what his girlfriend wanted him to say, do, or feel. With this insight, he started to risk being true to himself by articulating where he was at. So rather than relying on his pattern of self-described "doting," he risked sharing his own emotions (including his anger) and even setting boundaries by sometimes being able to say "no." He began to see that begging for acceptance actually resulted in the opposite and, as well, disconnected him from his own self. To his surprise, these risky changes were met for the most part with approval from his girlfriend who welcomed the direct expression of emotions and energy from Mark.

As this social level is worked out, and a person in Stage 2 recovery learns to authentically risk articulating vital aspects of self in social, family, and intimate relationships, the core issue of ego identity can be worked on in the next developmental level.

5) Formal-reflexive. The next personal level, and fifth overall, is the *formal-reflexive*. It represents the development of the mature ego (Wilber, 1986). People at this level have a highly differentiated reflexive self-structure and have developed the capacity to reason, assert themselves, and conceive of new possibilities for the future, based on their own desires, passions, and intellectual capacities. Therefore, during therapy, the underlying identity of an addict can be challenged. People need to let go of false identities, such as being an "addict," "street smart," or a "partier," or even very negative identities, such as being "a loser" or "a hopeless case."

Wilber (1986) observed that the central defining problem of development in the fifth level is one of introspection:

> That is, the central and defining problems of F-5 development involve neither psychoneurotic repression nor immersion in pathogenic scripts, but the emergence and engagement of the formal-reflexive mind and its correlative, introspective self-sense (with its particular vulnerabilities and distresses). (p. 135)

The therapist's task at this level, in Wilber's view, is to engage, activate, and draw out the client's reflexive introspective mind and developing self-sense (Wilber, 1986). We see the growth to a more expansive and inclusive self-sense in the following case example.

Cindy was a long-term drug addict who had been in recovery for close to six years. She had hung onto her identity of being "an addict in recovery" throughout her recovery, but now was becoming aware of the narrowness and limitations of that label. In our sessions, we brought this whole identity into question. To do this, we worked on an area we had previously started, which was moving the mythic journey from an unconscious to a conscious level (Feinstein & Krippner, 1988). We looked at the essential archetypes that make up the client's journey (Leonard, 1989; Pearson, 1989). As Cindy looked at her journey, she could see that she identified with many archetypes, not just the addict and the recovering addict; she was also a "helper," a "Mother," a "lover," a "warrior," and a "trickster," to name a few.

Intense questioning and deconstruction of this level took place. We embraced self-questioning using Katie's (2002) four questions centered on "Is it true?" Cindy was tired of the addict label and was quite ready to let go of the narrowness of this label, as she saw herself as a much more expansive person than that. However, it became evident that, beneath the addict identity, Cindy was hanging onto her sense of being a "victim." As she began to get in touch with a deeper sense of her authentic self, Cindy was ready to challenge her identity of being a victim and see it as another way she was hanging on to a sense of ego or narcissistic specialness. In responding to the question, "Is it absolutely true that you are a victim?" Cindy could see that it was not absolutely true. She had been hanging on to this victim identity and creating crystallized stories about it.

As emphasized by Almaas (1996), in transforming narcissism the betrayed person must begin to accept that, despite the very real betrayal experienced, the betrayed must own some responsibility for the current situation. In fact, the greatest betrayal had been done by self to self in the form of "selling out." Because of all the work we had already done, Cindy was able to let this in. In looking at what aspects she was responsible for, Cindy sighed and said that she had given up early in her adolescence and stopped recognizing her essence. Instead, she had manipulated people through addiction and codependency patterns to get her needs met. So, although she was not responsible for the abuse she suffered, she recognized her own part in losing connection with her essence. With this recognition, Cindy seemed to come unstuck from her victim identity and became more in charge of her own life.

Cindy's working through and letting go of attachment to archetypes, in her case the addict and the victim in particular, also left her with a profound sense of deficient emptiness in that she no longer knew who she really was. This deconstruction becomes an invitation to embrace the next level. We will now turn our attention to the existential level of Wilber's spectrum of development.

6) Vision-Logic. The next level of development, the final ego phase, and sixth overall, is the *vision-logic*, or *existential* level. Here, the integrated body-mind confronts the reality of existence. This level represents the development of the existential self. To deal with an individual's encounter with existence, existential therapy encourages authenticity, coming to terms with one's own finitude, fundamental self-responsibility, intrinsic meaning, and self-resoluteness (Frankl, 1965; Wilber, 1986; Yalom, 1980). Kurtz (1982) observed that the experience by an addicted person of "hitting bottom" is a realization of the existential limitations to self. Breaking through unconscious feelings of immortality and realizing the preciousness of life can be an important existential shift in moving out of the rut of an addiction lifestyle.

Stage 2 recovery allows for the working through of the emptiness and inauthenticity beneath all of the addictive acting out. Morgan, a recovering sex and substance-abuse addict, in his second year of recovery got to this true problem at the depth of his existence. We got to the emptiness that was behind all of his sexual acting out and partying. In short, because Morgan had kept himself busy with his preoccupations he had never really come to grips with the emptiness which lay underneath his acting out. As he began to slow down, he began to realize that at the heart of his acting out was an underlying existential depression and crisis of emptiness and world collapse. Up to this time, he had not dealt with what Wilber (1986) called the core issues of the existential self—the potential for autonomy, authenticity, and self-actualization, as well as the problems of finitude, mortality, and apparent meaninglessness.

It became clear that we needed to work on the client's pervasive avoidance of the reality of his own death and mortality. Yalom (1980) wrote about the importance of confronting one's own personal mortality to recover a zest for life and to authentically embrace life and to get out of the assumed immortality pattern of perpetual postponement. In relation to this, Heidegger (1962) pointed out two modes of existence: the usual mode of a state of forgetfulness of being, and a state of mindfulness of being. In the usual mode of forgetfulness of being, one lives in the world of things and is lost in the concerns of everyday life. In the second mode, however, one is continually aware of being as one lives with the reality of freedom and nothingness. This transition to the second level of being is of utter importance on the existential path. It usually takes a shocking experience to make the transition, yet as Yalom (1980) observed, the paradox of being is that "the *idea* of death saves us; rather than sentence us to existences of terror or bleak pessimism, it acts as a catalyst to plunge us into more authentic life modes, and it enhances our pleasure in the living of life" (p. 33). As the existential reality of personal mortality and inevitable death came fully into Morgan's awareness, he discovered his own crisis of beingness and, with that, he decided to embark on a quest of what life was all about. Morgan traveled extensively for six months, and undertook a couple of treks. During this time, he kept a journal and read some existential classics. Getting in touch with questions of being and authenticity caused a huge shift in Morgan's approach to his work as a teacher. He began to translate his own quest for beingness into an interest in the philosophy of teaching and how to connect with his students on the meaningful questions of life. This lit the fire for his teaching for the first time, and his intensity was mirrored back by his students.

We see at the existential level that the clients in Stage 2 recovery must confront the underling emptiness and meaninglessness beneath their addictive processes. Here, the integrated body-mind confronts the reality of existence (Wilber, 1986). Thus, we see a concern for the overall meaning of life, a grappling with personal mortality, and an effort to find the courage to *be*. This process can often be very tenuous; nevertheless, it represents a critical developmental milestone that exemplifies the climax of the existential stage of consciousness development (Yalom, 1980). This is a pivotal step, as the existential level is also the transitional stage to the higher psycho-spiritual levels.

The first six levels culminating in the vision-logic or existential level represent conventional Western psychology. To this conventional scheme of development, Wilber (1986, 1990) has added four levels of transpersonal contemplative development, and we will now turn to these transpersonal levels and see how they offer a chance for a client to embrace a third stage of recovery.

Transpersonal Levels And Stage 3 Recovery

Wilber (1986) goes beyond the existential realm to describe four levels of transpersonal contemplative development integrated from Western and Eastern sources. To the conventional, Western, scheme of development, Wilber (1986, 2000) added four psycho-spiritual levels of transpersonal development integrated from Western and Eastern sources of introspective contemplation. Each of the stages represents a progressively fuller working through of the separate self-sense (Wilber, 1986).

Wilber (1986) pointed to Adi Da and Ramana Maharshi as examples of mystical teachers who pointed out the importance in the transformational journey of releasing the contraction that constitutes the separate self-sense. Seeing this contraction usually entails some sort of overt or covert inquiry into the separate self-sense. Others (Carse, 2006; Renz, 2004; Tolle, 1997) have described transformational experiences in which the sense of separate self is lost, for some on a permanent basis.

Adyashanti (2004) and Almaas (1996) see the addiction to the separate ego self as the underlying addiction of the human condition. The process of releasing ego, however, is rarely a sudden one, and evolves over time, usually going through a number of phases. Using the four transpersonal levels mapped out by Wilber (1986), we can move from the emotional healing of Stage 2 recovery to an integrated psycho-spiritual being of Stage 3 recovery. Kasl (1992) summarized the process of this third stage of recovery as one of moving beyond method and becoming integrated and tuning deeply into nonseparate being in day-to-day life:

> This is where we move beyond the method. Instead of being a good "program person," one is simply an integrated person, instead of being good at prayer or seeing oneself as spiritual, life and spirituality merge, as we bring consciousness to daily activities. . . . We're no longer going somewhere so much as tuning in more deeply to where we are. . . . We do not see ourselves as separate from other people and other forms of life. Thus nonviolence is an intrinsic part of this stage, because to harm another would feel like harming ourselves. Love is not seen so much as something we get, but as a way we live and feel on the inside. (pp. 364-366)

We will now turn to consider each of the transpersonal stages of Wilber's developmental model separately as we consider the possibility of moving into Stage 3 recovery.

7) Psychic. The first level beyond the mind-body integration of the existential level and the seventh overall is the *psychic*. This level symbolizes the yogis (Wilber, 1986). In this phase, cognitive and perceptual capacities, which used to be narrowly personal and individualistic, can expand to a more pluralistic and universal perspective.

A preliminary spiritual experience can be the impetus to break through the shell of the isolated separate ego self. Wilber (1986) pointed out that this often can take the form of a nature mysticism experience, as reported in the following recovery account:

> I will never forget my last day at treatment. . . . I remember the head honcho; he wouldn't talk to me. He knew that I was a people person; it was a part of my addiction. So the last day, he grabbed me by the

neck and takes me to the door. He's a big guy and he shakes my hand, he's like, "Congratulations." It's six in the morning and we're up early. And then the door opens, the sun is coming up, eh. I will never forget how beautiful that was, man. . . . I could smell the winter air, and I could see the trees with no leaves. What a sense of freedom! (cited in Wilber, 1986, p. 135)

Tolle's (1997, 2003) groundbreaking work on the power of now can be a powerful beginning spiritual practice for recovering people. Individuals can begin to witness by focusing on the now, how much they have been pulled into the past or the future in their thought processes, and learn to be mindful and return to the power and intensity of the present moment. Clients can benefit from the insight that psychologically, the present moment is all we have, as life is always experienced in the present moment. Thus they can begin to see that healing always happens in the present moment. The focusing on the present moment can be an easy form of meditation in which clients learn to be mindful. Tolle (1997) observed that, over time, people can re-realize that they are not their thoughts and they can begin to live beyond the mind-created ego self:

Identification with your mind creates an opaque screen of concepts, labels, images, words, judgments, and definitions that blocks all true relationship. It comes between you and yourself, between you and your fellow man and woman, between you and nature, between you and God. It is the screen of thought that creates the illusion of separateness, the illusion that there is you and a totally separate "other." You then forget the essential fact that, underneath the level of physical appearances and separate forms, you are one with all that is. (p. 15)

A simple homework exercise for clients can be as simple as focusing on staying in the now. This can be mirrored back to clients in counseling sessions as demonstrated by the following account in working with Mark, in recovery from cocaine and sexual addiction.

Using Tolle's (1997) work, *The Power of Now,* as a guide, we started to conclude our sessions with a short 10-minute meditation on merging with the present moment. Mark also practiced this at home for homework. Like all new meditators, Mark struggled at first to slow his mind down, but after a few sessions, he began to experience the power and energy of the present moment. He had been so busy with his habits from the past, such as ruminating about his wounds and judging life, he had lost track of the healing presence of the present moment. He began to see the transformational potential involved in living in the now. To his surprise, he discovered a luminous interconnecting energy and an inner radiance in the moment. He had been so caught in his mind that he had not seen it before. He laughed to himself because this expansive feeling of love and at-ease was what he had been seeking in all of his years of using drugs.

As clients open up to the spiritual openings available in the present moment, it is common for problems of ego ownership and inflation to emerge from the process of the opening up of universal–transpersonal energies. For example, Tom, a coach in recovery, had some powerful opening-up and blissful experiences that convinced him that he was on the path of being a spiritual teacher. Tom had developed into an "energy phenomenon." He loved going to bars and coffee shops and talking to people and displaying his intense spiritual energy while pointing out the meaninglessness of people's typical preoccupations. It took him quite a lot of processing within our sessions to begin to realize that this behavior was really only an egoic display, or what Wilber (1986) called *psychic inflation* of the beginning spiritual practitioner. The Tibetan Buddhist teacher Trungpa (1973) coined the phrase "spiritual materialism" to describe this type of ego self-aggrandizing behavior and saw the overcoming of this tendency as being central to spiritual practice:

> It is important to see that the main point of any spiritual practice
> is to step out of the bureaucracy of ego. This means stepping out
> of ego's constant desire for a higher, more spiritual, more transcen-
> dental version of knowledge, religion, virtue, judgment, comfort, or
> whatever it is that the particular ego is seeking. One must step out
> of spiritual materialism . . . . Our vast collections of knowledge and
> experience are just part of ego's display, part of the grandiose quality
> of ego. We display them to the world and, in so doing, reassure
> ourselves, that we exist, safe and secure, as "spiritual" people. (p. 15)

Tom's suffering was actually the catalyst for growth here. His attempts at displaying spirituality were met with much resistance. Friends and strangers alike sabotaged Tom's efforts to establish his spirituality, and at other times, Tom had little energy to bedazzle anybody. He found this very painful. Through this pain, he began to realize that his efforts to assert his spirituality were merely efforts to validate his spiritual "specialness." With that awareness, he was able to begin to let go of his need for spiritual recognition.

Seeing through the ego's shell and the ordinariness of spiritual experience can be an important insight for clients in recovery (Almaas, 1996). A useful client exercise can be for clients to review spiritual experiences they have been hanging on to from the past, and re-realize that these experiences are open to all, that what is past is past, and to see the ordinariness in these experiences. This practice cuts through the tendency of the ego to hang on to spiritual experiences to establish one's specialness, the essence of the ego game.

8) Subtle. The next transpersonal level, and eighth overall, is the *subtle* and is referred to as the level of the saints (Wilber, 1986). Here, subtle sounds, audible illuminations, and transcendent insight and absorption can be experienced. In certain traditions, such as Gnosticism and Hinduism, this is the level of direct phenomenological apprehension of personal deity form (Wilber, 1986). This realm has also been referred to as pseudonirvana and refers to the realm of illumination, rapture and transcendental insight (Goleman, 1988). Recovering persons can have wonderful transformational "white-light" experiences at this level, yet struggle to integrate these experiences into everyday life. Here is an example of Pam, a person in recovery, whose subtle experience was brought on by the healing touch of two missionaries:

> I remember them saying: "We bless you that you will be able to
> give your children what your mother never gave you." I sat on the
> couch after they left and cried for two solid hours and I felt that love
> pouring through me. That love coming through there [sic] hands,
> and I felt for the first time in my life that God was with me, that God
> actually loved me and I could feel the presence of the spirit.

Bill Wilson, the founder of AA, had a pivotal white-light surrender experience as he had come to the end of his rope with his addiction, and turned his power over to a Higher Power in his apparently hopeless case (Kurtz, 1982). Christina Grof (1993) observed, "There are many ways to describe surrender: 'admitting defeat,' 'becoming powerless,' 'ego-death.' Bill Wilson called it the shattering of the ego" (p. 119). Surrender is a process of death and rebirth, as Grof made clear:

> What dies in this process is the part of us that holds on to the illusion
> of control, the part of us that thinks we are running the show, that
> we are in charge. What disintegrates is the false identity that operates
> as though we are the center of the universe. . . . We can die inwardly,
> and still remain alive; if we die emotionally, psychologically, and spiri-
> tually, we are reborn into a new existence. (p. 120)

The danger of this level is that, as a person opens themselves up to transpersonal energies through surrender, prayer and meditation, experiences of white light, illumination, rapture, and transcendental insight can give a person a sense of false awakening or result in an expectation or demanding of ongoing spiritual experiences (Wilber, 1986). A further danger in recovery is that we can fall once again into addiction's mentality and be constantly reaching for bliss and heaven as we also try to avoid and escape from any hell or dark experiences. We fear the dark night of the soul experience (Wilber, 1986). The dark night of the soul has long been recognized as a difficult problem along the crossroads of spiritual awakening.

Accounts of how St. John of the Cross or Phillip Kapleau weathered this phase are recommended as being helpful (Wilber, 1986). At this time, the seeker can have experienced subtle pseudorealizations that are extremely pleasurable and seductive, making ordinary life appear as meaningless suffering.

A way out of this is to embrace choiceless awareness and acceptance of what is (Krishnamurti, 1954), which can be a potent remedy for the tendency to try to change one's emotional state by escaping from what is to some other ego-preferred state. The escaping from what is for some other emotional state is a deeply ingrained emotional management strategy of the person with addiction issues. A powerful exercise is to have clients learn to accept the dark night of the soul and sit in what is, even in the dark emotions of grief, depression, fear, and hopelessness (Greenspan, 2003; Krishnamurti, 1954; Gangaji, 2005).

Even with powerful awakening experiences, at this level the separate ego self has not been totally burned through, despite a person's false claims of enlightenment (Wilber, 1986). There is much work to be done as the person is still caught in dualistic conceptions of self and other, and can fall easily into the trap of attempting to manipulate present experiences or to demand spiritual experiences to change what is (Adyashanti, 2004).

9) Causal. The *causal* level, known as the level of the sages, is the realization of the unmanifest source or transcendental ground of all the lesser structures (Wilber, 1986). In various traditions, it is referred to as the abyss, the void, and the formless (Wilber, 1986). People can prematurely experience this level of cosmic consciousness and struggle to integrate this formless awareness into everyday life.

In working at this level, clients will often report experiences of tremendous anxiety and panic attacks as they begin to merge with the abyss and absolute emptiness of existence but hang on to their ego selves at the same time. In a recent therapy example, Crystal, a graduate counseling student and mother who had been in recovery for over five years, recounted her recent woes. Crystal had already experienced a pivotal surrender experience a few years ago, but now described her total befuddlement of having the sense of a lost self and not knowing who she was any more. I asked her just to get a sense of how that was experienced in her body. As she relaxed into her belly, she said she felt like she had contracted upon herself and was now suspended over a black abyss. She was afraid if she let go she could really crash into, and hurt, herself. The abyss did not have the presence of a soft, loving, holding energy, but seemed to her to be almost like a wall.

I encouraged her just to stay with her belly, but now to let go of any judgment of the situation. As the famous Zen teacher Sosan stated, she was to have no choice or preferences, just be at one with the situation (Osho, 1994). I encouraged her to accept what is, instead of trying to frantically save herself or pick herself up by the bootstraps in some way.

As we sat in our chairs, she felt herself clinging and contracting upon herself over the black abyss, feeling she could be smashed by its murky bottom. I invited her to just relax into the deep abyss, as it was in fact her own energy. It is what Almaas (1996) called the loving black chasm of being:

> When the student finally settles into this experience of deficient emptiness, allowing it without judgment, rejection, or reaction, she sees that it is a state of no self, or, more specifically, no identity. When we fully experience this state of no identified self, it transforms naturally and spontaneously into a luminous vastness, a deep spaciousness, a peaceful emptiness. (p. 336)

As Crystal sat there, it was clear by a relaxing of her energy that she was letting go. She described herself as feeling like she had broken through the bottom of the wall of blackness, and now she was resting in blackness. Strangely, for her this terrifying abyss was transforming. She reported that she was feeling held. She described this experience as being something very new to her, the vastness of inner spaciousness. As we sat there in the meditative stillness of the moment, she reported "It's like an inner spaciousness has opened up for me."

She also expressed surprise that surrender could happen so instantaneously, in a few moments. I responded to her that true surrender is in the intensity of the now. We just sat there in our chairs, and I invited her to see that she could approach the world from this sense of inner spaciousness and she did not have to cling to her separate ego self. When Crystal reported back two weeks later, she reported her life had been transformed as she no longer felt lost, and was not fighting the inner spaciousness that had been growing inside her.

The experience of opening up to the cosmos, and becoming one with it, can leave a person with a subtle dualism as one witnesses the vastness of existence, and finds him- or herself pulled into these realms and away from everyday existence (Wilber, 1986). The invitation becomes for a person not to withdraw, but rather to learn to participate fully in all aspects of life, as suggested by the next level.

10) Nondual. Wilber's developmental spectrum does not stop at the causal level; the final stage is the *nondual*, which is an integration of form and formlessness (Osho, 1978). "The center of formlessness is shown to be not other than the entire world of form" (Wilber, 1990, p. 99). The extraordinary and the ordinary, the supernatural and the mundane, are precisely one and the same. In this level of complete integration of formlessness and form, as well as all prior levels as they arise, the former seeker is now able to enjoy the "suchness" of all levels (Wilber, 1986).

Losing one's attachment to the separate self and integrating all levels of existence lead to this final phase of "nondual" living. At this level, the former addict
is well aware that his or her addiction was nothing more than a desperate attempt
at establishing a separate sense of self. Therefore, with this awareness individuals
are able to accept themselves for who they are, find peace in just being, and rest
in Stage 3 recovery.

As nondual clinical therapist Prendergast (2003) described, problems are
unpacked and people discover a

> profound sense of emptiness that has been fiercely defended against.
> They discover that their problems were all outcomes from and
> compensatory expressions of this defense against what at first appears
> to be annihilation and in time reveals itself as unconditional love.
> (p. 7)

Everything is accepted and embraced simply as it is: "As awakening deepens, the
judging mind loses its grip and attention becomes increasingly innocent, intimate,
and impersonally affectionate" (p. 8).

For example, Cherry had been in recovery for over 10 years. She had worked
hard, initially going to treatment, and then being involved with counseling and
12-step groups for many years. At first, typical of Stage 1, her efforts focused on
abstinence. After a couple of years, she began to work on the emotional underbelly
of her addiction, working on such issues as family-of-origin, trauma, archetypal
roles, codependency, as well as authenticity and meaning. As she became healed
in these areas, she began to make a transition as she approached her 10th year of
recovery into Stage 3 issues, such as surrender of her ego self, integrating all levels,
and moving beyond the addict identity to one of a fully integrated human being.

In our work together, we were now working on nondual living from a different
position: Cherry began to see the natural nondual state of surrendered flowing
energy as her natural state, and instead we looked at what pulled her out of this
state. Initially, as Cherry opened up to the nondual relaxed-presence state of
total flow and surrender in which she felt one with existence, she asked me the
classic question, "How can I keep this state going?" I suggested she review how
clinging to the separate self had occurred once again because she was now trying
to permanently hold this wonderful state. "Really," I said, "there is nothing you
can do. You have to just keep surrendering self in each moment." This made sense
to Cherry as she had long learned that dealing with her addictions issues was a
matter of one day at a time, and over time it grew to be one moment at a time.

Still, the mind can be an elusive and problem-making mechanism. In a
recent session, Cherry summarized her concerns by saying, "What is the meaning

and purpose of life, then?" I laughed, and said, "In the moment, when you are surrendered and feeling your joyous energetic connection with everything, do you need a purpose? You are already the loving energy in the moment." She laughed in relief and agreement.

Cherry continues to work on her issues, as there is no final point of having everything finished and completed. As nondual teacher Papaji commented, there is no final surrender as one is, in fact, surrendering in each moment until the physical body dies (Poonja, 2000). And so, similarly, Cherry had experienced the state of nondual awareness and the letting go of her separate self, but now she had to learn to embrace and let go in the relative reality of each moment. Cherry is learning to stay in her flowing state while she deals with issues of work life, an aging mother, supporting siblings, and dealing with health concerns. The whole range of life issues must continue to be faced, though hopefully now from a place of resting in ego-transcendent being.

CONCLUSION

Wilber's spectrum of consciousness development model, with its accompanying pathologies and interventions, offers an addictions practitioner a useful map for facilitating long-term recovery in working with clients who want to move beyond the identification with a dry drunk archetype. The behavioral abstinence of Stage 1 recovery can be enhanced by working through a range of prepersonal and personal emotional issues of Stage 2 recovery, such as dissolving the false core driver and reestablishing basic trust, reintegrating the shadow, dismantling the internal critic, burning through social anxiety and codependency patterns, dismantling the crystallized ego, and embracing existential issues of meaning and authenticity. This process can be taken further, as clients make the transition to Stage 3 recovery. Here, working through Wilber's ego-transcendence transpersonal levels, clients learn to let go of their separate-self egos in each moment to embrace nondual living. Thus they embrace all levels of living as fully integrated beings. The long journey of transformation has turned the descent of addiction into a wondrous place of beingness for the person who has now fully embraced Stage 3 recovery.

REFERENCES

Adyashanti. (2004). *Emptiness dancing*. Boulder, CO: Sounds True.

Almaas, A. (1996). *The point of existence: Transformations of narcissism in self-realization*. Berkeley, CA: Diamond Books.

Almaas, A. (2008). *The unfolding now: Realizing your true nature through the practice of presence*. Boston: Shambhala.

Assagioli, R. (1973). *Psychosynthesis*. New York; Hobbs, Dorman.

Beck, D. & Cowan, C. (1996). *Spiral dynamics: Mastering values, leadership, and change.* Cambridge, MA: Blackwell Publishers.

Bewley, A. R. (1993). Addiction and meta-recovery: Wellness beyond the limits of Alcoholics Anonymous. *Alcoholism Treatment Quarterly, 10*(1), 1–22. doi:10.1300/J020V10N01_01

Bewley, A. R. (1995). Wellness beyond AA: Testing the theory of meta-recovery. *Alcoholism Treatment Quarterly, 13*(1), 1–15.

Brown, S. (1985). *Treating the alcoholic: A developmental model of recovery.* New York: John Wiley & Sons.

Burns, D. (1981). *Feeling good: The new mood therapy.* Boston: Signet.

Carse, D. (2006). *Perfect brilliant stillness: Beyond the individual self.* Shelburne, VT: Paragate Publishing.

Cortwright, B. (1997). *Psychotherapy and spirit: Theory and practice in transpersonal psychotherapy.* Albany, NY: State University of New York Press.

Feinstein, D. & Krippner, S. (1988). *Personal mythology: The psychology of your evolving self.* Los Angeles: Jeremy P. Tarcher.

Firman, J. & Gila, A. (1997). *The primal wound: A transpersonal view of trauma, addiction, and growth.* Albany, NY: State University of New York Press.

Frankl, V. (1965). *Man's search for meaning.* New York: Beacon.

Gangaji. (2005). *The diamond in your pocket.* Boulder, CO: Sounds True.

Gilligan, C. (1982). *In a different voice: Psychological theory and women's development.* Cambridge, MA: Harvard University Press.

Glasser, W. (1976). *Positive addiction.* New York: Harper and Row.

Goleman, D. (1988). *The meditative mind: Varieties of meditative experience.* Los Angeles: Jeremy P. Tarcher.

Greenspan, M. (2003). *Healing through the dark emotions: The wisdom of grief, fear, and despair.* Boston: Shambhala.

Grof, S. (1985). *Beyond the brain: Birth, death, and transcendence in psychotherapy.* Albany, NY: State University of New York Press.

Grof, S. (1988). *The adventure of self-discovery.* Albany, NY: State University of New York.

Grof, C. (1993). *The thirst for wholeness.* New York: Harper and Row.

Heidegger, M. (1962). *Being and time.* New York: Harper and Row.

Hixon, L. (1978). *Coming home.* New York: Anchor.

Judith, A. (1996). *Eastern body, Western mind.* Berkeley, CA: Celestial Arts.

Jung, C. G. (1959). *The archetypes and the collective unconscious (Collected Works of C. G. Jung, Vol. 9 Part 1).* Princeton, NJ: Princeton University Press.

Katie, B. (2002). *Loving what is.* New York: Harmony.

Kasl, C. D. (1992). *Many roads, one journey: Moving beyond the twelve steps.* New York: Harper Collins.

Kegan, R. (1982). *The evolving self: Problem and process in human development.* Cambridge, MA: Harvard University Press.

Kohlberg, L. (1981). *Essays on moral development, vol. 1.* San Francisco: Harper & Row.

Krishnamurti, J. (1954). *The first and last freedom.* New York: Harper and Row.

Kurtz, E. (1982). Why AA works; the intellectual significance of Alcoholics Anonymous. *Quarterly Journal of Studies on Alcohol, 43*(1), 38–80.

Kurtz, E. & Ketcham, K. (1992). *The spirituality of imperfection.* New York: Bantam Books.

Larsen, E. (1985). *Stage II recovery: Life beyond addiction.* San Francisco: Harper Row.

Leonard, L. S. (1989). *Witness to the fire: Creativity and the veil of addiction.* Boston, MA: Shambhala.

Lerner, H. (1985). *The dance of anger.* New York: Harper & Row.

Loevinger, T. (1976). *Ego development.* San Francisco: Jossey-Bass.

Maslow, A. (1968). *Toward a psychology of being.* New York: Van Nostrund Reinhold.

Nixon, G. (2001a). Using Wilber's transpersonal model of psychological and spiritual growth in alcoholism treatment. *Alcoholism Treatment Quarterly, 19*(1), 75–95.

Nixon, G. (2001b). The transformational opportunity of embracing the silence beyond hopelessness. *Voices: Journal of the American Academy of Psychotherapists, 37*(2), 56–66.

Nixon, G. (2003). Using a Wilber development approach in working with Mary. *eGambling: Electronic Journal of Gambling Issues, 8.* Retrieved from http://camh.net/egambling/issue8/case_conference/responses.html

Nixon, G. (2005). Beyond "dry drunkenness": Facilitating second stage recovery using Wilber's "spectrum of consciousness" developmental model. *Journal of Social Work Practice in the Addictions, 5*(3), 55–71. doi:10.1300/J160v05n03_05

Nixon, G., Solowoniuk, J., & McGowan, V. (2006). The counterfeit hero's journey of the pathological gambler: A phenomenological-hermeneutics investigation. *International Journal of Mental Health and Addiction, 4*(3), 217–232. doi:10.1007/s11469-006-9021-0

Nixon, G. & Solowoniuk, J. (2008). A transpersonal development approach to gambling treatment. In M. Zangeneth, A. Blaszczynski, & N. Turner (Eds.), *In the pursuit of winning: Problem gambling theory, research and treatment.* New York: Springer Publications.

Osho. (1978). *The heart sutra.* Pune, India: Osho International Foundation.

Osho. (1994). *Hsin hsin ming: The book of nothing.* Pune, India: Rebel.

Pearson, C. S. (1989). *The hero within: Six archetypes we live by.* New York: Harper & Row.

Perls, F. (1969). *Gestalt therapy verbatim*. Moab, Utah: Real People Press.

Piaget, J. (1977). *The essential Piaget*. New York: Basic.

Poonja, H. W. L. (2000). *The truth is*. York Beach, ME : Weiser.

Prendergast, J. (2003). Introduction. In J. Prendergast, P. Fenner, & S. Krystal (Eds.), *The sacred mirror: Nondual wisdom and psychotherapy*. St. Paul: Paragon House.

Renz, K. (2004). *The myth of enlightenment: Seeing through the illusion of separation*. Carlsbad, CA: Inner Directions.

Schwartz, S. (2007). Jungian analytic theory. In D. Capuzzi & D. Gross (Eds.), *Counseling and psychotherapy: Theories and interventions* (4th ed.) Upper Saddle River, NJ: Pearson Prentice Hall.

Singer, J. (1994). *Boundaries of the soul: The practice of Jung's psychology* (2nd ed.). New York: Anchor Books.

Small, J. (1982). *Transformers: The therapists of the future*. Marina del Rey, CA: Devorss & Co.

Straussner, S., & Spiegel, B. (1996). An analysis of 12-step programs for substance abusers from a developmental perspective. *Clinical Social Work Journal, 24*(3), 299–309.

Tessina, T. (1991). *The real thirteenth step*. Los Angeles: Jeremy P. Tarcher.

Tolle, E. (1997). *The power of now: A guide to spiritual enlightenment*. Vancouver, B.C.: Namaste Publishing.

Tolle, E. (2003). *Stillness speaks*. Vancouver, B.C.: Namaste Publishing.

Trungpa, C. (1973). *Cutting through spiritual materialism*. Berkeley, CA: Shambhala.

Walsh, R., & Vaughan, F. (Eds.). (1980). *Beyond ego*. Los Angeles: Jeremy P. Tarcher.

Walsh, R., & Vaughan, F. (Eds.). (1993). *Paths beyond ego: The transpersonal vision*. New York: Tarcher/Putnam.

Washburn, M. (1988). *The ego and the dynamic ground*. Albany, NY: State University of New York Press.

Washburn, M. (1994). *Transpersonal psychology in psychoanalytic perspective*. Albany, NY: State University of New York Press.

Whitfield, C. L. (1985). Stress management and spirituality during recovery: A transpersonal approach. Part III: Transforming. *Alcoholism Treatment Quarterly, 1*(4), 1–54. doi:10.1300/J020V01N04_01

Wilber, K. (1977). *The spectrum of consciousness*. Wheaton, Ill.: Quest.

Wilber, K. (1986). The spectrum of development. In K. Wilber, J. Engler, & D. Brown (Eds.), *Transformations of consciousness* (pp. 65–159). Boston: Shambhala.

Wilber, K. (1990). *Eye to eye: The quest for the new paradigm* (rev. ed.). Boston: Shambhala.

Wilber, K. (1995). *Sex, ecology, and spirituality: The spirit of evolution*. Boston: Shambhala.

Wilber, K. (1997). *The eye of spirit: An integral version for a world gone slightly mad.* Boston: Shambhala.

Wilber, K. (2000). *Integral psychology.* Boston, MA: Shambhala.

Wilber, K. (2006). *Integral spirituality.* Boston, MA: Integral Books, Shambhala.

Wolinsky, S. (1999). *The way of the human, Vol. 2.* Capitola, CA: Quantum Institute.

Yalom, I. (1980). *Existential psychotherapy.* New York: Basic.

9. Beyond the Spiritual Wading Pool: A New Approach to Religion and Spirituality in the Healing of Addictions

LINDA MERCADANTE

SPIRITUALITY AND RELIGION: HOW ARE THEY CONNECTED?

For a very long time, the fields of psychology and medicine—places where addiction is often discovered and treated—virtually ignored both spirituality and religion. In fact, as one researcher discovered, "the word spirituality did not even appear in Medline until the 1980s" (Mills, 2002, p. 1). Fortunately this is changing, for in just the last decade or so, spirituality and even religion have become hot topics in both the medical and psychological fields.

As Paul Mills (2002) stated in the *Annals of Behavioral Medicine*:

> Attention to topics of spirituality, religiousness, and health has
> increased substantially in medical and graduate school curricula,
> clinical practice, and research. . . . Of the many interesting aspects
> of this phenomenon, perhaps the most remarkable is the observation
> that medical science, the field of inquiry that initially separated mind
> from body. . . now finds it compelling and perhaps even necessary to
> reexamine the relationship among spirit, mind, and body. (p. 1)

In fact, he added, "In recent years, every major medical, psychiatric, and behavioral medicine journal has published on the topic" of religion and health or spirituality and health (pp. 1–2). This is not just in journals, but also in curricula: "Nearly 30 U.S. medical schools now offer courses on religion, spirituality and health" (Sloan et al., 2000, p. 1913). While this is an exciting development, a problem exists. For these fields are still trying to hold spirituality and religion apart from each other, treating them as two distinct things that can be pulled apart and examined. From this seemingly "safe" perspective, spirituality seems nicely generic and individual, while religion seems too particular and collective.

Spirituality seems nondogmatic and open-ended, while religion seems judgmental and prescriptive. I will shortly discuss why I see these divisions as rather arbitrary and artificial. Nevertheless, it is quite understandable why people try to separate religion from spirituality.

First, and most obvious, religion is a very diverse thing. It is not unilateral in either beliefs or practices. Even people in the same congregation may understand their faith very differently. The second most obvious factor is that religion can function along a wide continuum, ranging from the highly functional role of providing solid values and healthy behavioral norms, to the low point of being dangerously dysfunctional and leading to—or playing into—neuroses and delusions. While these issues make religion a difficult subject to deal with, there is one very important thing that is constant about religion: Throughout human history, religion has existed to provide a framework of meaning for people, making sense of life and death. In fact, across time and culture, religion has been the most constant source of meaning for humanity. To say that because religion can be used harmfully it should be avoided is like saying that we should not eat food because some of it is junk.

But religion also presents practical problems for counselors, therapists, and medical personnel. First, there are ethical concerns—it is not right to impose your own value system or religious perspective on a client. Second, there are issues of diversity; clients will come to you from many different backgrounds, and rather than do them a disservice, it seems safer to stay with some kind of generic experience that all can relate to. Third, and most important, there are issues of expertise. It is hard enough to master even one religious perspective, much less to claim you understand all, or many, of them. Even a trained minister feels daunted in trying to understand the religious and value system that each congregant brings with him or her.

But when people try to separate spirituality and religion, not only is it artificial, it also leads to stereotypes. Many articles go through considerable effort in order to define religion and spirituality as separate and distinct from each other. However, a by-product of this effort is that writers often are forced to create false or at least arbitrary dichotomies. David Moberg (2002), in the *Journal of Adult Development*, found three types of separation, "three polarizations that differentiate religiousness from spirituality (organizational religion vs. personal spirituality, substantive religion vs. functional spirituality, and negative religiousness vs. positive spirituality)" (pp. 47-48).

The last of these false dichotomies is the most problematic and probably the most common in the public imagination. This popular stereotype says that religion is ritualized, dogmatic, and dead, while spirituality is personal, pure, and positive. These polarizations are quick and dirty, cut and dried, simple and simplistic. And they do not take into account many things.

First, both religion and spirituality are so interwoven with each other that hardly anyone experiences them completely apart. Second, both aspects are multifaceted and thus require an integrated perspective to do them justice. Third, if all of life is sacred, we cannot find much practical difference between the two concepts in real-life terms. If I were forced to consider religion and spirituality separately, then as an analogy I would have to say that spirituality is like gasoline, with religion being the vehicle; you can't drive without both.

Or even better, I would say that religion is like language. Spirituality may be the meaning, but you can't separate them. For when we learn our native language growing up, we also learn how to think, how to feel, and how to understand reality from inside that linguistic framework. A person who has studied a foreign language—especially a very different one, like Hebrew—will realize that a whole new perspective on reality is gained in the process.

But you can't cleanly pull spirituality and religion apart. In the end, what we call spirituality also comes to us in the vehicle of some religious framework, whether that religious framework is traditional or nontraditional. In the end, separating religion and spirituality trivializes and minimizes religion and makes spirituality overly generic and amorphous. It is not just scholars in the field of religion who think this. For recent studies and polls are showing that it is very difficult—in real life terms—to break apart these two things. There is increasing evidence that Americans are both spiritual *and* religious. Here is some data compiled by researchers from various surveys (Powell, Shahabi, & Thoresen, 2003; Miller & Thoresen, 2003):

- Belief in God is held by about 96% of the American public.
- Prayer is common, with 9 out of 10 people asserting that they pray, most of them (67% to 75%) on a daily basis.
- Many respondents claim that faith is a central guiding force in their lives.
- Interest in spirituality is high and growing: In 1994, 58% of respondents expressed interest in spirituality; by 1998, there was nearly a 25% increase, as 82% expressed interest.
- Religion is claimed as "very important" in the lives of 67% of people surveyed.
- Over two thirds (69%) reported that they were members of a church or synagogue.
- And 42% attend services regularly.

RELIGION IS IMPORTANT AND IT'S GOOD FOR YOUR HEALTH

It is a good thing that spirituality and religion are so intertwined in real life, because recent studies are showing that the practice of religion brings amazing health benefits. Even if we bracket ideas of salvation and union with God—which are closer to the heart of religion than any of its more tangible this-worldly benefits—being religious is good for you on the purely emotional and physical levels.

Of course, it helps if you believe that religion can help you heal from physical problems. And many people do. A 1996 poll of 1000 adults found that 79% "believed spiritual faith can help people recover from disease" (Miller & Thoresen, 2003, p. 664). But it's not just the power of positive thinking. Powell, Shahabi, and Thoresen (2003) reported the findings of seven studies, each of which discovered that church attendees had a 25–30% reduction in risk of mortality during the studied period. And that was just for showing up. They speculated that if these people actually practiced what they heard during the rest of their week, the figures would go higher still.

ADDICTS AND RELIGION

What about addicts? Not surprisingly, a very high percentage of addicts are alienated from religion, and often from any form of personal spirituality as well. Researcher William Miller (1997) stated:

> As in other health fields, the addiction literature generally indicates that spiritual/religious involvement is a protective factor against the development of problems. There is also evidence that persons currently suffering from alcohol and other drug problems tend to show particularly low levels of spiritual/religious engagement and the relative lack of a sense of meaning and purpose in their lives. The process of recovery is often associated with corresponding improvement on spiritual measures. . . . Certainly there are those, including the vast community of Alcoholics Anonymous (AA), who would argue that spiritual changes are a part and prerequisite of enduring recovery from addictions. The addictions field is, in fact, one of the few health fields where enthusiasm for spiritual factors in recovery has never been lost. (pp. 37–38)

That's good, but not good enough. Even people with many years of sobriety—people in deep recovery—are still very likely to insist they are "spiritual but not religious." Counselors sometimes encourage them in this stance, and sometimes recovery groups do as well. But although it is a remarkable achievement to move addicts towards a spiritual stance, it is not enough to promote deep spiritual recovery. For if addiction is, in the end, a spiritual as well as a physical disease, spiritual recovery is desperately needed even once the physical addiction is under control.

To summarize: We cannot artificially separate spirituality and religion. Doing this does a disservice to both, forcing us into a nonintegrative, reductionist, and artificial stance. And being overtly religious is good for you, in terms of both protection and healing. The practice of religion has benefits which can be observed and even measured. And while the source of these benefits is more intangible, the results are not. Recovering people should not be denied these benefits.

Bill Wilson, the founder of AA, insisted that it is only a "spiritual kindergarten." If this is so, why do we encourage people to stay in kindergarten? Shouldn't we help them graduate to first grade and beyond? Shouldn't we work to get them involved in a recognized, legitimate, and real religious tradition? I contend that we should and we must. If we don't, we are denying them the very real benefits of active religiousness. One gift of recovery—especially the 12-step version first promoted by AA—is that it helps people get their feet wet, spiritually. It eases them into the wading pool. But many remain afraid indefinitely of getting their faces wet and truly learning to swim. What can we do to encourage them to go deeper, little by little, until they are true spiritual swimmers?

A SUGGESTED SCHEMA: A CIRCLE OF SPIRITUAL GUIDANCE

My contribution as a theologian is to propose a schema that may help counselors introduce people to spirituality in a way that does not bracket out religion. Instead, it can serve as the channel that—if it is practiced fully—inevitably leads there. This schema can help people wade, then go to chest height, and then finally put their faces in and swim. I call this a "circle of spiritual guidance," for it is intended to lay the groundwork for religious involvement of some sort. The ultimate goal is to help recovering persons to become engaged with a responsible, stable, and compassionate community of faith. This would include active involvement in larger benevolent causes, ongoing mutual commitment, and a positive foundation for life meaning that will last.

The schema is designed to do four things: (a) allow people to enter at whatever place they can; (b) take into account diversity of background and tradition; (c) not minimize or trivialize religion; and (d) recognize that, while not everyone has the expertise to be a religious and spiritual mentor, everyone can make a contribution to spiritual healing.

Although I can assert that this schema connects well with Christian theology, I don't want to claim that it connects seamlessly with other religious traditions. But I do think it has potential here as well. For what is it about religion that keeps people healthy? There are many factors, some tangible—like enlarging your circle of friends—and some intangible. The most important intangibles, researchers have said, is having meaning and purpose in your life and having the values that promote this. So we may ask: How do people find meaning in life? What values keep people sober? I offer four active values that will help each person discover the meaning of his or her own life and connect with others, and hopefully lead them on into a recognized responsible and stable religious community. These four active values are:

1. ***Risk for good.*** Take the risk that good will prevail. Contribute your effort to make it happen. The highest good is One who insures good will prevail. Risk that there is this One.

2. ***Hope actively.*** Hope even against hope. But hope actively. Your hope must help bring about what you hope for—it must be mediatorial. Your hope rests on the belief that there is someone who will make it come out right in the end. But your help is needed.

3. ***Accept accountability.*** Choose, will, and/or accept your connection to others. Recognize how your life affects others. Becoming accountable is a simple recognition of this fact. But you have to live it.

4. ***Seek higher ground.*** Don't stay in the flood plain. Keep moving toward higher ground. Your goals are not high enough. Keep pushing yourself beyond your present goal, to something even better. Ultimately the goal will be so large that you will need lots of help, both human and divine.

These are not steps. They are a circle. You can enter anywhere. If you risk for good, you are instinctively hoping that there is a guarantor of your actions—that it won't be a waste, and that it won't be fruitless. If you accept your connection to others, you must have higher goals than just your own self-interest. If you search for higher ground, you are involving more people, just naturally. To do this, you must take the risk that good will win in the end, that this is worth it. If you see your connectedness, you can also see that you can pull each other down. So you need to hope that good will prevail and actively use your efforts to contribute to that. Your example and encouragement will catch up other people in this quest and action.

Risking for good is ultimately counting on the fact that there is a good God, or benevolent foundation, for all reality. Hoping actively is lending your hand to making good prevail. That's eschatological. Accepting your connection to others and living it out is realizing that we are all community to one another, under God's gaze, and loved by God. This can become your entry to a church, synagogue, temple, or mosque. If you search ever higher, you will arrive at God's goals, at an acceptance of them, and at a desire to help out in any way you can, in ways you are best suited to help. So you are also accountable to yourself because you must know what you have and can contribute. There is no point in promising what you can't deliver. Others are counting on you. So knowing yourself is part of accountability.

To summarize again: It is artificial and counterproductive to separate religion and spirituality. Religion is good for you. Even on the physical and emotional levels, it is both protective and healing. So we should help all people, perhaps most especially those who are recovering, to actively connect with a religious tradition. And on that point, there is a crucial note. You will never find the perfect congregation. While some are better than others, some are more functional and healthy and some less. Congregations are like families: They all have their issues, their group dynamics, their strengths and weaknesses. Although you can't choose your family, at least in North America, you can choose your congregation. But, nevertheless, don't wait until you or a client can choose the perfect one, because it doesn't exist. Just like the "good enough" parent, look for the "good enough" religious group.

But how do we help people, particularly those who are addicted, move in that direction? Especially when addicted persons are often not bent that way? I believe we need to start using something like this proposed "circle of spiritual guidance" to encourage spirituality without discouraging religious involvement. We can no longer encourage people to say they are spiritual but not religious. That is a start, but it is not going to be enough. Instead of keeping people in the spiritual wading pool, we must help them learn to swim in the deep water of God's grace.

REFERENCES

Miller, W. (1997). Spiritual aspects of addictions treatment and research. *Mind/Body Medicine: A Journal of Clinical Behavioral Medicine, 2*(1), 37–8.

Miller, W., & Thoresen, C. E. (2003). Spirituality, religion, and health: An emerging research field. *American Psychologist, 58,* 24–35. doi:10.1037/0003-066X.58.1.24

Mills, P. J. (2002). Spirituality, religiousness, and health from research to clinical practice. *Annals of Behavioral Medicine, 24,* 1–2.

Moberg, D. O. (2002). Assessing and measuring spirituality: Confronting dilemmas of universal and particular evaluative criteria. *Journal of Adult Development, 9,* 47–60.

Powell, L., Shahabi, L., & Thoresen, C. (2003). Religion and spirituality: Linkages to physical health. *American Psychologist, 58,* 36–52. doi:10.1037/0003-066X.58.1.36

Sloan, R. P., Bagiella, E., VandeCreek, L., Hover, M., Casalone, C., Hirsch, T. J., . . .Poulos, P. (2000). Should physicians prescribe religious activities? *New England Journal of Medicine, 342,* 1913–1916. doi:10.1056/NEJM200006223422513

10. Grief and Addictions

NANCY REEVES

I've worked in the area of trauma, grief, and loss for 28 years now. In the early 1980s I was asked to do a half-day training session at a provincial government drug and alcohol workshop, and when I arrived in the lobby of the hotel, I started hearing some grumbling: "Don't we have enough to deal with without having to add grief and loss to it. Addiction is hard enough already!" I heard this repeatedly. So I started my workshop, and I asked the participants what losses they experienced in working in addictions. For a minute or so people were shrugging, and then slowly it started coming: They suffered their own losses when their desires for healing for the people they were working with were not fulfilled, they realized that many addicts started their addictive behavior after an unresolved loss, and they shared the losses brought about by the addiction itself. Finally I had to stop them so that we could get on to other issues and strategies. But of course now I don't have to do that, because you all know that there's so much loss.

My definition of loss is any experience that restricts us. That can be as concrete as a death or a chronic illness, and it can be as nebulous as the shattering of a dream or expectation. And just because a loss is nebulous doesn't mean the grieving will be easier or shorter; it might be even more difficult, because it's often some of the nebulous losses that are marginalized by our society. We say, "You shouldn't be grieving for that: Grieving for your alcohol or drug is not okay." And yet I find that it's very hard for people to disengage completely and move on if it is not honored that this was a coping mechanism; yes, it was hurtful, but it was also a big part of their lives.

I don't work in an addiction treatment program. I work in private practice, and I teach at universities and seminaries. But I find that many people come to me with trauma and loss in their lives, and after they start to feel some healing, they are then able to admit for the first time that they have an addiction. I can then refer them, or I can work with them in conjunction with other programs, but I find that often it's when people get a sense of hope for the first time, or feel that they have some resources or can work through things to some extent, that they're then willing to admit something which was obvious in their lives for years but which they wouldn't talk about. So in the short time we have I'd like to present some of my models for working with grief and some concepts and issues; I hope that they'll be useful for you in your work.

Here's a short exercise I do. I'll ask individuals to close their eyes, turn inward, and bring their attention to some distress, pain, or grief that they are carrying—something around their addiction. They focus on it, get a sense of where it is in their body, and then give it a rating from 1 to 10, depending on how distressing it is. Then I'll have them think of a symbol of support, comfort, or guidance, perhaps something from their faith tradition, perhaps a person, or an object, or a word or phrase. Once they are open to it, I'll have them write it down on a piece of paper and set it down. Then I'll have them close their eyes again, and focus again on the distress or pain. I'll have them see if there's any change, and rate it again out of 10. Now the response is different for different people. There might be no change, or the distress may have eased considerably. However, I find in many cases that people have been avoiding their symbol of comfort, and that once they are open to it, they'll report that it has given them the courage to confront their pain, even if that pain is now more vivid. So I work a lot with symbols, because symbols are powerful.

If we see a heart-shaped box, and it's the beginning of February, we're probably going to think: "Love!" And yet, if our best friend is waiting for open-heart surgery and we don't think she's going to make it, we're not going to see love when we see that box. So I know that if someone has a symbol for their addiction, or for their loss, or for themselves, that is really dysfunctional or restrictive, then as long as they're holding on to that, I can't do anything to help them shift, because that's their truth, and they won't let it go. So rather than ripping that away, I try to help them find other symbols that are healthier and more empowering. I really trust that, as they live into those new symbols, they will start to use them when a choice point comes and they are forced to decide what to do to protect themselves or to give themselves comfort. As a therapist, I want to make sure that I have symbols that are living and working for me. I also need to be aware that symbols that worked in the past may not still be alive in me, though I keep them out of habit.

The same goes for affirmations. I try to help people find affirmations that are true for them. But I never provide an affirmation, because if I come to something like "When one door closes, another one opens," and it has deep meaning for me, and is freeing and empowering, that's great. But if I then take my beautiful symbol and say to someone else, "I want to give you a present: You know, when one door closes, another opens," I'd better jump back fast, because this guy might punch me out. It becomes a rationalization and a minimizer if it's given to someone else. So I invite people to look for affirmations that will be supportive for them.

I also am very clear with people that I'm not in the cure business. I want to be one of their healing resources. And I look at the healing that is already taking place in their lives, and at the qualities they have that can be used for healing. I'll give you an example: I did a lot of work with bereaved parents early on in my career, and I'd been told about this young couple, Bonnie and Chris, who'd had a baby die from sudden infant death syndrome, or SIDS. I was told that their marriage was on the rocks, that they were not talking to each other, and that they were full of guilt. He was starting to drink heavily. And yet they wouldn't see me—I was at that point working at the Queen Alexandra Hospital for Children, and they could have seen me for free there, but, no, they didn't want to. Now just over a month after the baby's death, I get a phone call from Bonnie. I tell her I'm very glad she's called and ask whether she'd like an appointment, and she says,

"Oh, no. I'm fine, and Chris is fine."

"OK, then what can I do for you?"

"Well, we're really worried about our dog, Lucky."

"You're worried about your dog?"

"Yeah, Lucky loved the baby, and slept by his crib, and her grief has gotten so bad that she's not eating, she's getting real skinny, she's shedding hair, and she's peeing all over the house. So do you know anybody who works with dogs?"

So I think fast, and say, "Well, sure, I could work with dogs." So she asks for an appointment, and I tell her, "I can see you tomorrow afternoon, but dogs are pack animals, and to do individual grief therapy with a pack animal doesn't really work, so I need to see them with their pack."

There's a long pause. "That would be Chris and I, and we don't want to come to counseling."

Now obviously it would be very unethical to trick people into therapy, but in those few quick seconds of thinking, what came to me was the thought that the dog was probably not grieving the baby after a month—the dog was grieving the estrangement of her people. If I took her out of that dysfunctional family and did whatever I did, and then put her back into that situation, her symptoms would return. So I hoped that, with their presence, they could help their dog—and maybe get something for themselves. So, I promise her that I won't ask anything about their own pain, or about the baby, and will only talk about the dog. She makes me swear to it, which I do. And I suggest that I go to their house, because Lucky will be more comfortable in her own house—and because I don't want an incontinent dog in my office!

So the next day I go to the house. Lucky hears me and starts barking; I shake Chris' hand, and look at this very skinny, woebegone-looking dog, who flops down in the middle of the living room as we go in. Chris sits on the sofa, and Bonnie comes in from the kitchen with a chair, and sits down on it as far away from Chris as she can. They're both looking at their dog anxiously, but aren't looking at each other. Now my way of working is by seeing where the energy is, by using what's accessible. So I get down on my hands and knees and start talking to the dog. I tell her about the grieving process. I stroke her. I tell her what a good girl she is. I tell her a little about SIDS. With my warm voice and my attention on her, she relaxes and rolls onto her back so that I can rub her tummy. I say, "You know, people and animals need information about the grieving process, they need support and acknowledgment of their pain, and sometimes they need touch."

Bonnie says, "Well look, it's working! She hasn't been like this since the baby died."

And Chris says, "We haven't been giving her any of those things. It's been really rough."

I say, "Yeah, but look how she's accepting it from me, and I'm obviously a stranger. When you're able to give this to her, she'll really appreciate it."

Without another word, Chris gets down and starts stroking Lucky's long tail, and Bonnie gets down and starts stroking her head. They still aren't looking at each other, but they're closer, and they're connecting with the dog, who is now happy.

I back off a bit, and watch them do this, and then I say, "There are other things about grief I'd like to tell you. One is that over 80% of people grieving any kind of loss experience some level of guilt. And when it's something like this, it's closer to 100%. So could you let Lucky know that you don't blame her for the baby's death? You said that she was sleeping in the room at the time, so she might have a sense that she's done something wrong."

Bonnie says, "Oh Lucky, you would never have hurt the baby—we know that! Don't blame yourself. You're a good dog. If anyone's too blame, it's me, because I'm the mom, and I should have known."

Chris stops stroking Lucky's tail, and looks at his wife with total bewilderment. "I thought you weren't speaking to me because you blamed me. I didn't know you felt guilty. You have no reason to."

And she says, "How could I ever blame you? It's the mother that should have a sixth sense about this."

"Oh, my love," he says. He puts his arm out, and she leans into him.

Lucky gets up, goes into the kitchen, and we start hearing her chewing on her squeaky toy, completely happy. Now I sit and I watch for a while, but it gets boring fast. "I love you, I love you, we should have. . . etc." I'm a fifth wheel now, so I tell them, "Look, I'll come back." And I did. I saw the pack probably three or four times over the next couple of weeks. And it was a pack. Lucky always started with us. But when she saw that they were connecting, she would move off.

Now I see that the healing power there is the quality we call *love*. Chris and Bonnie could not love themselves because they felt too guilty. They loved each other, but couldn't show it because they were sure the other would blame them, or was blaming them. But they could love their dog, and by loving and being concerned for their dog, they gained the courage to reach out for healing—for the dog, so they thought, but it turned into healing and growth for themselves. So I find that I really want to be there in their grieving, and get a sense of what qualities people are living, and support those, and see how those qualities are bringing healing. I make sure that people know that I'm not there to cure them, or to take away their pain or fix them, but that I'm there to help them get in touch with the healing that's already present.

For me, the grieving process is not a series of phases or stages or anything like that. It's a spiderweb of meanings and implications. When someone is grieving, the implication that they are first in touch with is probably the one that is most important at that moment. Sometimes it's also the safest one to deal with. So, for example, someone may say, when told that their partner has died in a car accident, "That means we don't go to the movie tonight." You think, "Whoa, what kind of a relationship did you have?" But what they're not able to say is, "I'm grieving the interpersonal implication of this loss." Nevertheless that's what they're grieving: That bond and connection is shattered. So I listen to the words and pay attention to the implications, and try to support them in those.

I worked with a group of counselors from Veterans Affairs some years ago, and they were saying, "It's so hard; it's mostly widows we're working with, and we want to tell them about the government benefits, and help them work out the finances, and they always want to pull us away to memories, or they want to show us his garden." And I told them, "You're fighting implications here. Your implication is financial; that's what's most important. Theirs is something else. Maybe it's intrapersonal, maybe it's interpersonal, maybe it's a change in role or status, but it's something that needs to be heard and honored. And I bet that if you give them a few minutes and honor the implication they're grieving, they will then kindly move over to yours." I was lucky enough to see this same group six months later, and I asked how it was working. "Like a charm," they said. You've got to support the healing energy which is around a particular implication that the person is experiencing.

One thing with the spiderweb theory is that I can be dealing with the financial implication for a while, and then I can move over to dealing with the change in my role in my family, and then at some point I find that I'm dealing with the financial one again. It doesn't mean I've regressed, or that I didn't do it right—it's just that obviously we don't simply deal with issues in our lives and never have to worry about them again. But people get nervous, and think they're doing something wrong. The other thing is that we revisit the same emotions. Many people have the idea that, when you're grieving, you go through anger, and then you go through depression, and so on—and suddenly they're "back" to anger. I say, "No, you're not 'back' to anger—you're ahead to anger. So what are you angry about now?" Also, some meanings and implications may not come up for years. It's ridiculous to say to someone early on in their grief, "When you get to be the same age as your parent who died, you may have some issues come up, so grieve it now and get it over with." No, you have to wait for that time. But it's also very scary if you don't realize that grieving goes in waves, and that a new implication may bring a big wave up; you think, "I've done it wrong—I thought I was dealing with this, and obviously I'm not." So it's very empowering to understand the grieving process.

Ken Doka talks about two styles of grief: the intuitive and the instrumental. Not all, but many men are instrumental. They find that their grieving goes better by not talking about it a lot, by not sharing their emotions, but by doing something productive, something meaningful, and while they do that, their thoughts and feelings and issues are coming up and being sorted through. If there's somebody else there that they can mention something to briefly, that's great. But intuitive grievers—often women, but not always—do not find it helpful in the early days of their grieving to be doing things, because it takes them away from their issues and their processing. So in the classic scenario the woman is sitting in the living room crying her eyes out, Kleenex all over the place, and feeling like she's moving through it, but saying, "He doesn't love me, because he's in the basement building something." He's in the basement processing things, and thinking, "She's just wallowing in it." And two people who should be supporting each other are instead judging each other, thinking they're not going to work it through. And as therapists we've got to pay attention to what our own style is, because if we're intuitive, we may try to encourage clients to be intuitive too. If we're instrumental, we may try to encourage that. So honoring our own style is important. A lot of people I work with, particularly people with addictions, just don't have a clarified style of grieving. They've bumbled into it, as most people do, from looking at the people who were important in their lives as they were growing up. They've learned to grieve in a certain way, and sometimes it doesn't work.

There's a normal process that happens when we first hear about a loss, called "emotional anesthetic"—we numb out, we may disassociate—and it's protective. If the full impact of a loss hits us all at once, it's an emotional and physical overload. But people don't realize that's normal, and they're scared of it, or don't even know it's happening, and they immediately reach for alcohol or drugs or medication or something that might do the same job, but not as well. I do a lot of crisis intervention after trauma and sometimes on the scene someone spaces out, and I'll say, "Great, I'm glad that can happen!" Usually their response is, "Oh, I'm so sorry, I don't know where I was." I say, "You were not here, because you needed to be somewhere else. You have wisdom inside you that said, 'OK, I've had enough.' So let's work with that." Sometimes that means asking them if they need more physical space. With some adolescents, I'll kick my secretary out of her office, and use that office to call the adolescents in my own, and we talk for an hour and they share all sorts of things. But if I'm in the same room, they'll just sit there with their arms crossed.

Early on, people who had suffered a loss asked me, "How do I know when I'm psychologically ready to make a major change?" I didn't have the slightest idea, and I couldn't find anything helpful in the literature. So I started watching, and I realized that it had a lot to do with a person's energy. By "energy," I just mean that force that allows us to be and to think and to do; nothing fancy. Now some of us have a lot of energy, and some of us have less, but when someone first hears of, or is first really impacted by, a loss, most of their energy goes into grieving or readjustment. They're eating, breathing, and sleeping their loss. A small portion of their energy goes to survival functions: They can do some things, but they usually need a lot of help. Some people are able to do even less of that, and need to be put on respirators; they can't even breathe on their own, they're so much in shock.

At some point we move along, and all the energy we need for survival is intact, though we've still got a lot of energy going into grieving and adjustment—it's about 50/50 between survival and grieving. This is the place where I find that most people come for counseling, because they say that they feel worse than they did a few weeks or months previously. This is also where I think that a number of people really start to abuse substances, because they start to feel some despair—"Isn't it ever going to end? It just seems to be getting worse." And it's actually not worse, but the emotional anesthetic is wearing off. This is positive—they have enough energy now to deal with things. They feel worse because they're able to monitor themselves and think about their issues more clearly.

But at some point there is some life enhancement, and you might have 10% or 20% of your energy available for this. Some people say it happens almost overnight: They wake up one morning feeling some lightness. I had one client who had been in quite rough shape but had made some progress, and one day she came in and said,

"You're pregnant!"

I said, "Yeah, I'm eight and a half months pregnant."

"What? Did you just start showing?"

"No."

"Did I know you were pregnant?"

"Remember our first session, when I said I'd have to be stopping my practice?"

"Oh yeah. . . how come I didn't notice?"

I said, "Because that's life enhancement stuff, and you weren't ready for it."

Or many clients will come in and say, "Did you get new lighting? It doesn't seem as dark in here." That's life enhancement. So people can wake up feeling a sense of lightness; they can start adding new things to their lives, not to deal with pain, but just because they've got some energy freed up. Or they may find that what they're already doing for survival is enhanced; they'll play with menus rather than just cook and eat because they know they need to.

Now I would love for there to be some research on the rebound effect after the breakup of a relationship, because I see it a lot. A guy will be telling me for months, "I hate them, I'll never have anything to do with them, I'll never get into another relationship." And then he experiences this little bit of life enhancement. He feels some lightness, and the birds are singing, and he looks out the window, and instead of saying, "Bah! Humbug! It seems beautiful but there's so much pain in the world," he looks out and just says, "Isn't it beautiful out!" He takes his dog for a walk, meets someone walking her dog, they smile at each other, and he feels something. "True love!" he says. They get into a relationship that isn't based on anything healthy, and the first time he has to commit, or work on it, he doesn't have the energy for it. And he's out of there: "Burned again!" People will take that little bit of energy from life enhancement, use it up, and then they feel even more depressed and more discouraged.

As time goes on, people may find themselves in a fourth situation in which about 50% of their energy is going to survival, and 40% to life enhancement— though again people with ongoing issues may still have to put more like three quarters of their energy into survival. But there will always be some energy still going to grief, and it may be more energy at significant times, or when certain issues arise. When people tell me that they don't want anything to trigger their sense of loss again, I tell them that, well, that person did die, and nothing short of a reversal of that is going to end all their grief. We're human beings. And it can be bittersweet to have that energy suddenly flowing into certain feelings and memories. For example, you may see your daughter walking down the aisle, and wish that her natural father were there, but those memories can also bring you closer together: If you remember beforehand, she could perhaps wear something that represents him. So it's possible to honor that surge of grief, and not see it as something negative.

It takes a lot of energy for people to change jobs, treatment programs, relationships, or schools, and not just physical energy, but mental and emotional and spiritual energy. When we're moving from one status to another, we're in a liminal place, a vacuum that we don't know how to occupy. We're no longer totally one thing, but not yet the new thing either, and that's scary: We could lose ourselves. That takes a lot of energy, and we need something to support us; hopefully we have a community. Now if I try to make these changes while I'm in one of the first two situations I've discussed, where all of my energy is going to survival and grieving, I'm going to be pulling my energy away from grieving. In those cases I'm not going to heal well, or I'm going to pull it away from survival, and I won't be able to do what I had been doing, which will really affect my self-esteem and self-image. If I wait until I have just a bit of life enhancement energy, then the feeling of lightness I've had will suddenly be gone again, and I'll be extremely discouraged. I'll do anything to try to get that back, and I'll think that maybe that drinking could do it. So it's best to wait until somewhere between the third and the fourth states. For some people, that means a few days; for others, it means a few weeks, a few months, or even a few years.

I find that what people are most concerned about is getting stuck. If they have a sense of movement, a sense that they're dealing with things, even if they go back and forth a little bit, that will be empowering; they won't find it so problematic that it's taking a while. And if they realize that they need to be doing something soon, but are able to think about how to intentionally give up or delegate some of their survival functions—they might give up some of their roles, for example—that can be very empowering as well.

Now I think that any emotion that comes up naturally as part of the grieving process is there to help us. Emotions give us information about implications or about things that need to be done. If I feel anger and give it a voice, I may realize that I need an advocate. I may need to confront someone or work something through. But if I say, "Oh, I don't do anger—I'm a good Christian/Buddhist/whatever," it doesn't go away; it just take a bunch of energy to repress. On the other hand, if I think, "This anger really helps; I'm getting my needs met, and I'm going to go in for more of it!" then I'm going to put a lot of energy into magnifying it. Either way, it takes a lot of energy. I call these "expensive emotions." These are attempts to deal with the situation, but these attempts don't allow the natural emotion to emerge; instead, they represent an attempt to control it. Repressing anger turns it into bitterness and resentment; people who are bitter will not admit to having an issue, and yet they spew poison all over the place. Magnified, anger turns into vengeance and hate, creating an oppositional "us vs. them" attitude.

So repression and magnification are expensive in terms of the energy the person has to put in, which takes them away from healing. They're expensive in that they produce a very negative orientation towards life. I often see sadness becoming expensive as it turns into despair, or I see a longing for healing turning into envy and jealousy of people who seem to have a better life or an easier time. Feeling blocked often turns to helplessness. I don't try to take away those expensive emotions, but to help people learn how to handle the original emotions better. As they do that, they'll start to realize that it's less expensive. And I may do some of that by asking them to remember times when they were angry and bringing that into the present.

When somebody comes to me feeling guilty—they've got this addiction, or they've done this thing—my usual response to them is, "Good." This gets their attention, because they expect me to say, "Oh, you don't need to feel guilty—you're only human," and they know how that conversation will unfold, and we won't get anywhere with it. So I say "Good," and sometimes they get mad, or they're startled, and they ask me what I mean by it: Do I want them to feel guilty? Well, no, but feeling guilty means you have a conscience, and I like working with people who have a conscience!

Guilt is a motivator: It invites us to look at a situation and find out what needs to be done to change our attitudes and behavior in order to live safer, healthier, freer, more empowered lives. We generally don't do guilt well. We don't say, "What are you trying to tell me, guilt?" We just say, "Oh, I've done wrong!" and we start punishing ourselves. It's like not even giving yourself a trial. So what I'll invite someone to do is to move deeper into the guilt to get a sense of what we need to learn from it.

I have a three-part process for working with guilt. I do some prison work, and I had one fellow come along who was just about to get out. He had finally done some jail time for maybe the 15th car accident he had been in while driving impaired. On the last occasion he had hit a little girl. She hadn't been killed, but she was severely injured; she had lots of orthopedic injuries and required a number of blood transfusions to save her life. And he told me, "I've done a lot programs in here, I've been sober and will continue to be, I've got a good connection with AA and with a church, but I still feel guilty." He had already worked on this model somewhat with his chaplain, because I had done a workshop at the prison some months earlier. They had done the first step, where they spent a number of sessions looking at the guilt and what the guilt was saying. For many people that's all that is needed; by just opening up and moving into it, they start to balance themselves or to realize what needs to be done and taking action.

Then he went to the second step, which is reeducation: What do you need in order to live in a healthier, better way? And he said that he had done AA and assertiveness programs, and had worked on communication skills; he had done a number of things that he was confident were going to help him, and he told me about how he had changed a lot of his attitudes. "But the guilt is still there?" I said. "It's less," he said, "but I'm going to walk out of here with a 'kick me' sign on my back, I know that." "OK," I said, "the third step is reconciliation." "Oh, I have done that for years," he said, and then he started telling me how he's punished himself. No, I told him, punishment is a restriction. Reconciliation is using some of your qualities, your resources, talents, and gifts to give to the world, but also to yourself, because you can't do one without the other. I asked him whether he'd been doing that. "Well, a little bit," he said, "I've been mentoring some of the new guys, but it hasn't been specifically about this." I told him that it must be intentional: You need to do your reconciliation because of your offense.

Now some people talk to me and it's just irrational. They claim they have not offended, though in their mind they have. I don't fight with them about that. If they believe they have done something wrong, we can work through this process, and it's freeing. And this man had done something wrong. So with the chaplain's help, he contacted the family through the police first, and then through their lawyer. And he told them, "I don't know if you want any contact with me or not, but I'm trying to think of something to give back, and to do reconciliation because of what has happened; if you have any input on that, I would really appreciate it." And what they told him was, "We want to tell you our story. We want you to hear what it was like for us. And then maybe we can come up with something else." So they had a meeting—a restorative or transformative justice meeting—and both parties and support people were there. The daughter told her story about how scary it was: "The light was green, and it said walk, and I looked both ways, and did everything I was supposed to, and all of a sudden I saw this car, and it hurt so much." And the parents told about how scary it was for them, thinking that their daughter might die. Of course he said that hearing the story was worse than any jail time. He listened, he used his communication skills, and when they finished, he said, "What else can I do?" They talked about it, and the girl decided that he could give blood, since she had needed so much blood. Perhaps moving a bit out of the restorative justice mode, she asked him if he liked needles, and he said no, he tried to avoid them, and she said, "Good, you can give blood!" He said, "I'm going to give blood for the rest of my life in your name." The chaplain was wise enough to caution that the reconciliation would become a punishment pretty quickly if it took the form of a "should" like that. So together they thought about a good symbolic time, and decided that he would give blood 10 times, because she was 10 years old, and because reaching those double digits is very important for kids. So once he was released, he gave blood 10 times, and he wrote a letter that the lawyer gave to the family, in which he said, "I have done what I said I would do for you. My guilt feels much less, and I thank you for that. Again, I'm so sorry for what I've done to you. But I'm going to keep giving blood. I'm not going to give it for you anymore; I'm going to give it because I have a new community—I've finally met some people who don't drink all the time. In fact, one of the guys that frequently goes at the same time as me said that he might get me a job, which is really hard when you're just out of prison." The right reconciliation does that. It uses a gift that a person has in a way that will support and sustain them, and it reconnects them with their community. If we had just said to him, "Go out and start to create some new social networks," he wouldn't have done it. But he was doing this for her, not thinking that he was getting anything out of it for himself, and yet he is getting something out of it.

A lot of the people I work with are holding on to grudges, resentments, or are actively in a vengeful mode because of abuse that has happened in their past. If someone says they have forgiveness issues, I do the guilt work first, if necessary, because a person who is not able to forgive one's self is not going to able to forgive somebody else. I also do an exercise with people who have forgiveness issues, where I ask them to close their eyes and remember a time, it could be from when they were children, or it could be more recent, when they did something wrong, it doesn't matter whether or not it was intentional, or how big it was, and when they were forgiven. They have to have truly *felt* that forgiveness. And I'll ask them to give me some words or phrases that speak of what it was like to be forgiven. Then I'll also ask them to remember a time when someone else, a client, friend, family member, or a stranger wronged them, and they truly forgave; truly, and not just because they felt they should as a good person or because their faith tradition said they should. And I'll ask them for some more words expressing that feeling of having forgiven. Now the thing is that when you look at these two groups of words, they'll be the same; in both cases you'll get words like "relief," and "peace," and "freedom." And I find that when I do this exercise with someone who wants to forgive, but is scared to—they think they'll have to give up power, or let someone else off the hook, or diminish themselves in some way, or make themselves more vulnerable—they can see that it means getting back to the original emotions that can help them. They're free to feel anger, or to set limits, or to protect themselves. The expensive emotions of vengeance, resentment, and hate keep you bound. True forgiveness is as beneficial for the forgiver as for the one who is forgiven; it might even help the forgiver more.

11. The Importance of Assessing Meaning in a Clinical Population

KIMBERLY A. MILLER
DARRELL L. BUTLER

There has been much debate about what constructs constitute a need and what constructs qualify as truly universal needs. One of the most scrutinized has been the need for meaning. Although many researchers have argued that having a sense of meaning is an essential human need that exists separate and apart from other needs (Alderfer, 1969; Galtung, 1980; Mallmann, 1980; Maslow, 1943; Ryff, 1989; Volkart, 1951), and many existentialists believe the search for meaning or purpose in life is the greatest need that exists in humanity (Binswanger, 1975; Buber, 1947/1968; Frankl, 1946/1984; Heidegger, 1927/1962; Kierkegaard, 1849/1989; Maddi, 1970; Sartre, 1957; Tillich, 1952; Wong, 1998; Yalom, 1980), many of the major motivation theorists have neglected to include this construct in their theories (e.g., Deci & Ryan, 1985; Murray, 1938; Volkart, 1951). The exclusion of this need in theories of human motivation is surprising, given that lack of meaning has been connected to many manifestations of psychological distress. For example, addictions are a disorder frequently associated with lack of meaning (Coleman, Kaplan, & Downing, 1986; Harlow, Newcomb, & Bentler, 1986; Hutzell & Peterson, 1986; Jacobson, Ritter, & Mueller, 1977; Kinnier et al., 1994; Marsh, Smith, Piek, & Saunders, 2003; Maxwell, 1951; W. R. Miller, 1998; Newcomb, Bentler, & Fahey, 1987; Newcomb & Harlowe, 1986; Orcutt, 1984; Padelford, 1974; Sadava, Thistle, & Forsyth, 1978; Waisberg & Porter, 1994). In addition to these studies, Burrell and Jaffe (1999) found that using drugs enables individuals to escape from the emptiness and lack of meaning they are experiencing in their lives. Several other researchers concluded that there is an inverse relationship between alcohol and drug use and meaning in life (Hutzell, 1994; Kinnier, 1994; Tonigan, Miller, & Conners, 2001). The results of these studies suggest that the absence of meaning in some way is related to the development of addictions. Therefore, although no conclusive evidence has been produced that indicates that lack of meaning *causes* addictions, its continued assessment in clinical populations is warranted.

127

However, a thorough review of the instruments developed to assess meaning and other psychological needs indicates that these instruments would be inappropriate to use for the current study for a number of reasons. First, the majority of instruments developed to assess psychological well-being have originated from theoretically flawed propositions. As such, these instruments have been inherently limited in their ability to accurately measure basic need fulfillment. Second, psychometric studies have not provided evidence that any of the instruments designed to measure meaning and other psychological needs are reliable or valid.

Thus, a new measure of psychological needs was developed (Miller Needs Assessment; K. A. Miller, 2005) in order to effectively assess meaning and other psychological needs in both a clinical and nonclinical population. The needs that were chosen for inclusion in this instrument were meaning, relatedness, autonomy, competence, and physical needs. These were chosen because they have received the most support for universality and have all been inversely related to alcohol and drug addiction. Although all the subscales were found to have excellent psychometric properties, and much more can be said about the implications of the results as a whole, only the meaning subscale will be discussed.

METHOD

Participants were 1,358 individuals (604 clinical subjects recruited from addiction treatment centers and 754 nonclinical subjects recruited from various businesses) from the Midwest. The clinical sample consisted of 156 females (26%) and 443 males (74%) who ranged in age from 18 to 79 ($M = 39.77$, $SD = 11.89$). Approximately 18% identified as African American, 77% Caucasian, 1% Native American, 2% Hispanic American, and 2% identified as multiracial. The main reasons clinical participants reported receiving mental health treatment were alcohol (53%) and drug (55%) addiction (many participants reported more than one problem so the total percentage is well above 100%). Approximately 28% of the clinical sample had been receiving treatment for one month or less, 20% one to three months, 11% three to six months, 7% six to nine months, 5% twelve to eighteen months, 3% eighteen months to two years, and 19% reported receiving treatment for at least two years.

The nonclinical sample consisted of 431 females (57%) and 318 males (43%) who ranged in age from 18 to 77 ($M = 40.40$, $SD = 12.46$). Approximately 5% identified as African American, 91% Caucasian, 1% Native American, 1% Hispanic American, 1% Asian American, and 1% multiracial. In the nonclinical sample, 164 individuals (22%) had received mental health treatment previously; mental health treatments included depression (44%), alcohol addiction (9%), drug addiction (2%), bulimia (1%), anorexia (2%), compulsive overeating (2%), anxiety (17%), and other (23%).

ANALYSES

Four types of analyses were conducted on the data. An exploratory factor analysis (EFA), a statistical procedure used to discover the underlying factor structure of an instrument, was conducted on the nonclinical data. Multiple regression (MR) is an explanatory, theory-driven procedure used to test the effects of one or more independent variables on a dependent variable, and was used to determine which of the five needs explain significant variance in participants' self-esteem scores. Predictive discriminant analysis (PDA), a procedure used to predict group membership from a set of continuous predictors, was used to determine if the instrument discriminates between the clinical and nonclinical samples. Finally, an analysis of variance (ANOVA) and calculation of effect size were conducted to determine if there was a significant difference between the clinical and nonclinical participants' scores on the meaning subscale.

RESULTS

Results of the EFA suggested an appropriate criterion for evaluating item loadings was $\geq .3$ due to the presence of many items with high loadings, and the use of this criterion resulted in no cross-loading items. The initial eigenvalues for the five factors (Meaning, Positive Interpersonal Relations, Competence, Interpersonal Support, and Ability to Adapt) were 15.771, 2.127, 1.681, 1.517, and 1.301, respectively. While Meaning accounted for 39% of the variance, the remaining four factors accounted for 5%, 4%, 4%, and 3% of the variance respectively, with a total of 55% being explained by all five. Alpha coefficients were: Meaning ($N = 12$) $\alpha = .94$, Positive Interpersonal Relations ($N = 8$) $\alpha = .85$, Competence ($N = 4$) $\alpha = .79$, Interpersonal Support ($N = 8$) $\alpha = .83$, and Ability to Adapt ($N = 8$) $\alpha = .86$.

The MR ($N = 1207$) contained three factors (Meaning, Supportive Interpersonal Relations, and Ability to Adapt) and resulted in a significant regression, $R^2 = .57$, $F(3, 1203) = 529.02$, $p < .001$, and SE of the estimate = 3.67. All three factors explained significant variance in participants' self-esteem scores (Meaning: $\beta = .239$, $t = 7.25$, $p < .001$; Interpersonal Support: $\beta = .217$, $t = 7.66$, $p < .001$; Ability to Adapt: $\beta = .372$, $t = 11.55$, $p < .001$).

The PDA demonstrated all five factors (Meaning, Positive Interpersonal Relations, Competence, Interpersonal Support, and Ability to Adapt) and correctly classified 76% of the participants into their respective groups (clinical or nonclinical).

An ANOVA was calculated in order to determine whether there was a significant difference between the clinical and nonclinical participants' scores on the meaning subscale. Results indicated there was a significant difference between the two groups, $F(1, 1186) = 201.59$, $p < .0001$. In addition, an effect size was calculated in order to estimate the magnitude of the difference found in the ANOVA. Results indicated that there is a large difference between the scores of the clinical and nonclinical participants ($d = .81$).

DISCUSSION

A major purpose of this study was to establish the psychometric properties of a new measure of need fulfillment and determine the extent to which meaning in life was related to alcohol and drug addiction. Although all subscales had good reliability, the meaning subscale had the highest internal consistency coefficient ($\alpha = .94$), which provides strong evidence for its ability to measure this construct consistently. In addition, the PDA demonstrated that all subscales were able to correctly classify 76% of participants into their respective groups. This ability to discriminate is important because it provides evidence of construct validity of the instrument; in this case, the ability to discriminate those in distress from those who are not.

The EFA demonstrated that the meaning subscale accounted for the most variance (39%) among the five factors, which indicates that the presence or absence of meaning in life greatly influences the general well-being of participants. Not surprisingly, the MR indicated that the participants' meaning scores also explained significant variance in their self-esteem scores. This result is not surprising considering that many researchers believe that level of self-esteem is reflective of an individual's general level of psychological well-being. Finally, the results from the ANOVA and effect size demonstrated a significant difference between the clinical and nonclinical populations. Although this is not surprising given past findings on the relationship between meaning and addictions, it provides further support for the psychometric properties of the instrument and also suggests that this is an important construct to assess in clinical populations.

CONCLUSION

The field of human motivation and need assessment has a long and controversial past, and although the more modern theories have come to some agreement on need states, there is still uncertainty. This study was conducted to shed some light on this uncertainty and offer some important suggestions for treatment and future directions for research. There are three specific implications this study has for treatment of psychological disorders. First, it is clear that individuals who reported experiencing psychological distress were experiencing lower levels of meaning than those who did not. With this in mind, addressing a client's meaning in life should be an important focus of treatment, no matter what the diagnosis. If the previous research is correct, in that lower levels of meaning lead to manifestations of psychological distress, it is logical to conclude that addressing this unfulfilled area should ameliorate, if not eliminate, the symptoms of distress. Addressing these areas could include psychoeducational classes and focused group and individual therapy. By directly addressing the underlying causes of clients' difficulties, it is likely they will not only experience a reduction in their symptoms, but also have the skills necessary to deal with life more effectively.

Second, although the majority of current psychological assessment measures assist clinicians in diagnosing clients, few provide insights into the origins of the client's distress. Specifically, most instruments describe clients' symptoms but do not provide a starting point for therapy (e.g., addressing the underlying problems that manifested the symptoms). This inability to go beyond a diagnosis is a significant weakness of current psychological assessments. Individuals may manifest symptoms (e.g., alcoholism, depression, eating disorders) for a variety of reasons, but the instruments used to classify these disorders only assess current level of symptoms and not the specific reasons clients are experiencing them. Without gaining an understanding of the underlying causes of distress and directly addressing these in treatment, clinicians are doing a disservice to the clients they serve. One purpose of the current instrument was to go beyond symptom classification and tap into the underlying deficits that create these psychological manifestations. The results of this study suggest this instrument has the ability to do so and thus has a promising future not only as an assessment instrument, but also as a guide for the development of more effective treatments. Finally, although it is clear from this study that the assessment of meaning is critical in a population that has an addiction diagnosis, if the patterns seen in the current clinical participant sample prove to be consistent with other disorders (e.g., depression, eating disorders), it is possible the assessment and treatment of these disorders could also be made more effective.

REFERENCES

Alderfer, C. P. (1969). An empirical test of a new theory of human needs. *Organizational Behavior and Human Performance, 4,* 142–175. doi:10.1016/0030-5073(69)90004-X

Binswanger, L. (1975). *Being-in-the-world: Selected papers of Ludwig Binswanger.* London: Souvenir Press.

Buber, M. (1968). *Between man and man.* New York: The Macmillan Company. (Original work published 1947)

Burrell, M. J., & Jaffe, A. J. (1999). Personal meaning, drug use, and addiction: An evolutionary constructivist perspective. *Journal of Constructivist Psychology, 12,* 41–63. doi:10.1080/107205399266217

Coleman, S., Kaplan, J., & Downing, R. (1986). Life cycle and loss: The spiritual vacuum of heroin addiction. *Family Process, 25,* 5–23. doi:10.1111/j.1545-5300.1986.00005.x

Deci, E. L. & Ryan, R. M. (1985). *Intrinsic motivation and self-determination in human behavior.* New York: Plenum Press.

Frankl, V. (1984). *Man's search for meaning.* New York: Washington Square Press. (Original work published 1946)

Galtung, J. (1980). The basic needs approach. In K. Lederer (Ed.), *Human needs: A contribution to the current debate* (pp. 55–126). Cambridge, MA: Oelgeschlager, Gunn, & Hain Publishers.

Harlowe, L., Newcomb, M., & Bentler, P. (1986). Depression, self-derogation, substance abuse, and suicidal ideation: Lack of purpose in life as a mediational factor. *Journal of Clinical Psychology, 42,* 5–21. doi:10.1002/1097-4679(198601)42:1<5::AID-JCLP2270420102>3.0.CO;2-9

Heidegger, M. (1962). *Being and time* (J. Macquarrie & E. Robinson, Trans.). New York: Harper & Row. (Original work published 1927)

Hutzell, R. R. (1994). Adapting the Life Purpose Questionnaire for use with adolescent populations. *International Forum for Logotherapy, 17,* 42–46.

Hutzell, R. R., & Peterson, T. (1986). Use of the Life Purpose Questionnaire with an alcoholic population. *International Journal of the Addictions, 21,* 51–57. doi:10.3109/10826088609063437

Jacobson, G., Ritter, D., & Mueller, L. (1977). Purpose in life and personal values among adult alcoholics. *Journal of Clinical Psychology, 33,* 314–316. doi:10.1002/1097-4679(197701)33:1+<314::AID-JCLP2270330171>3.0.CO;2-Y

Kinnier, R. T. (1994). Adolescent substance abuse and psychological health. *Journal of Alcohol & Drug Education, 40,* 51–56.

Kinnier, R. T., Metha, A. T., Keim, J., Okey, J. L., Adler-Tapia, R. L., Berry, M. A., & Mulvenon, S. W. (1994). Depression, meaninglessness, and substance abuse in "normal" and hospitalized adolescents. *Journal of Alcohol and Drug Education, 39,* 101–111.

Kierkegaard, S. (1989). *The sickness unto death.* London: Penguin Books. (Original work published 1849)

Maddi, S. R. (1970). The search for meaning. In M. Page (Ed.), *Nebraska symposium on motivation* (pp. 137–186). Lincoln, NE: University of Nebraska Press.

Mallman, C. A. (1980). Society, needs, and rights: A systematic approach. In K. Lederer (Ed.). *Human needs: A contribution to the current debate* (pp. 37–54). Cambridge, MA: Oelgeschlager, Gunn, & Hain Publishers.

Marsh, A., Smith, L., Piek, J., & Saunders, B. (2003). The Purpose in Life scale: Psychometric properties for social drinkers and drinkers in alcohol treatment. *Educational and Psychological Measurement, 63,* 859–871. doi:10.1177/0013164402251040

Maslow, A. H. (1943). A theory of human motivation. *Psychological Review, 50,* 370–396.

Maxwell, M. A. (1951). Interpersonal factors in the genesis and treatment of alcohol addiction. *Social Forces, 29,* 443–448. doi:10.2307/2572723

Miller, K. A. (2005). *Human motivation and psychological well-being in a sample of clinical and nonclinical adults* (Unpublished masters thesis). Ball State University, Indiana.

Miller, W. R. (1998). Researching the spiritual dimensions of alcohol and other drug problems. *Addiction, 93,* 979–990. doi:10.1046/j.1360-0443.1998.9379793.x

Murray, H. A. (1938). *Explorations in personality: A clinical and experimental study of fifty men of college age by the workers at the Harvard psychology clinic.* New York: Oxford University Press.

Newcomb, M. D., Bentler, P. M., & Fahey, B. (1987). Cocaine use and psychopathology: Associations among young adults. *International Journal of the Addictions, 22,* 1167–1188. doi:10.3109/10826088709027479

Newcomb, M. D., & Harlowe, L. L. (1986). Life events and substance use among adolescents: Mediating effects of personal loss of control and meaninglessness in life. *Journal of Personality and Social Psychology, 51,* 564–577. doi:10.1037/0022-3514.51.3.564

Orcutt, J. (1984). Contrasting effects of two kinds of boredom on alcohol use. *Journal of Drug Issues, 14,* 161–173.

Padelford, B. (1974). Relationship between drug involvement and purpose in life. *Journal of Clinical Psychology, 30,* 303–305. doi:10.1002/1097-4679(197407)30:3<303::AID-JCLP2270300323>3.0.CO;2-2

Ryff, C. D. (1989). Happiness is everything, or is it? Explorations on the meaning of psychological well-being. *Journal of Personality and Social Psychology, 57,* 1069–1081. doi:10.1037//0022-3514.57.6.1069

Sadava, S. W., Thistle, R., & Forsyth, R. (1978). Stress, escapism and patterns of alcohol and drug use. *Journal of Studies on Alcohol, 39,* 725–736.

Sartre, J. P. (1957). *Existentialism and human emotions* (B. Frechtman, Trans.). New York: Philosophical Library, Inc.

Tillich, P. (1952). *The courage to be.* New Haven, CT: Yale University Press.

Tonigan, J. S., Miller, W. R., & Conners, G. J. (2001). The search for meaning in life as a predictor alcoholism treatment outcome. In R. Longabaugh & P. W. Wirtz (Eds.), *Project MATCH hypotheses: Results and causal chain analysis* (pp. 154–165). Project MATCH Monograph Series, Vol. 8. Bethesda, MD: National Institute on Alcohol Abuse and Alcoholism.

Volkart, E. H. (1951). *Social behavior and personality: Contributions of W. I. Thomas to theory and social research.* New York: Social Science Research Council.

Waisberg, J. L., & Porter, J. (1994). Purpose in life and outcome of treatment for alcohol dependence. *British Journal of Clinical Psychology, 33,* 49–63. doi:10.1111/j.2044-8260.1994.tb01093.x

Wong, P. T. P. (1998). Meaning-centered counseling. In P. T. P. Wong & P. S. Fry (Eds.), *The human quest for meaning: A handbook of psychological research and clinical applications* (pp. 395–435). Mahwah, New Jersey: Lawrence Erlbaum Associates.

Yalom, I. D. (1980). *Existential psychotherapy.* New York: Basic Books, Inc.

12. Addiction: Theory & Practice

GEOFFREY R. THOMPSON

Abstract

Mainstream theories of addiction have not led to any systematic advancement in our understanding of addiction, and mainstream therapies have not produced compelling results. Their focus is that of the outsider, desperately attempting to come to terms with why individuals repeatedly return to behaviors that cause them severe and chronic suffering. The most popular answer today is that addiction is brain pathology, but other popular answers include conditioning, maladaptive learned coping skills, and theories of rational choice, such as behavioral economics and self-medication. But these neatly packaged answers conveniently neglect research from other perspectives that do not share the mainstream's positivist assumptions. The greatest omission is the insider's perspective. For two centuries, beginning with De Quincey's (1821/1986) *Confessions of an English Opium Eater*, drug users have described their lived experience of intoxication. Existential-humanistic psychologists have interpreted addiction beyond behaviorist conditioning, faulty cognitions, immediate motivations, neural adaptation, and cultural imperatives. Addiction, in this view, is a response to boredom, alienation, loneliness, lack of control over one's life, and other symptoms of what Frankl (1984) labeled the "existential vacuum" (p. 124). This paper ends with the proposal that using *personal meaning* as an organizing construct can allow us to bring coherence to a problem that has thus far baffled our best efforts at understanding and treatment.

INTRODUCTION

Hundreds of books and more than 65 scholarly journals from various disciplines focus on addiction (PARINT, 2011). Almost all of these observations arise from biological, behavioral, cognitive, and motivational psychologies, including a handful of cross-disciplinary perspectives such as behavioral economics. The problem with current addiction theories is that there are too many of them. The presence of many rival contenders means that any individual theory appears dubious, unable to account for findings from its rivals. There is no universally accepted conceptual framework to guide systematic research, with the result that theorists may be at the same table, but they are playing solitaire. The behaviorist, armed with classical and operant conditioning, avoids the behavioral economics theorist focused on drug use as a rational choice. And the rational choice theorist avoids the biopsychologist's insistence that the motivation to use substances is a compulsion generated in the mesolimbic dopamine pathways. West (2006) suggested that integrating theories was too much work for most theorists, since integration demands expertise in various disciplines. Whatever the reason, theorists apparently feel no urgency to confront opposing views.

It is hardly surprising that treatments engineered from such a patchwork of theories have been relatively ineffective. Vaillant (Chapter 3, this volume) pointed out that cognitive-behavioral and psychodynamic therapies have never shown success in longitudinal studies. Similarly, the traditional Minnesota model (Owen, 2000), used in more than 90% of addiction facilities, has achieved only modest statistically significant success, and only in short-term studies (Lemanski, 2001; Polich, Armor, & Braiker, 1980). Hester and Miller (2003) ranked 99 treatments by performance outcomes. According to their ranking scheme, only 19 had any beneficial effect, and these outcomes were generally short-term. Health Canada (1999) ranked 35 treatments and concluded that only 11 had evidence of effectiveness; again, only in short-term studies. It has not gone unnoticed that, although experts agree addiction is a chronic problem, we study outcomes as if it were an acute one (McLellan, 2002).

Complicating matters, studies from the human sciences (with their postmodern epistemologies) have challenged the mainstream's positivist approach. Ethnographic and anthropological research on drug use has presented convincing evidence that addiction is a cultural construction (Heath, 1995). The cultural meanings of intoxication determine whether the individuals succumb to addiction, regardless of how much of a substance is consumed per capita. If we accept the mainstream assumption that addiction is a consequence of drug effects on the individual, we are baffled when we discover Italian-Americans have a lower alcoholism rate than Irish-Americans, even though the Italians consume more alcohol and the Irish promote abstinence (Vaillant, 1995).

Perhaps the greatest problem with our current catalogue of addiction theories is that they have studiously avoided the big observations from existential-humanistic studies. Third-wave psychologists have learned from the works of the Romantics, James (1902/1999), Huxley (1956/1990), and others who did not tar drug use as immoral or necessarily pathological. They appreciated fully that addiction led to severe suffering, but when they examined the lived experience of intoxication, they heard little of disease, conditioning, faulty cognitions, lack of motivation to live a better life, or cultural forces. Rather, drug users described the perceived benefits of intoxication. Drugs and the drug lifestyle were salves for boredom, loneliness, and alienation. Users described a transcendence of their mundane lives. As James (1902/1999) taught, "Not through mere perversity do men run after [alcohol]" (p. 421).

If we are to have a convincing theory of addiction, we need to integrate different perspectives. A mere handful of theorists have attempted this. The most impressive is West (2006), who proposed that addiction was a matter of motivational dominance, a synthesis of 30 mainstream theories. But West's synthetic theory neglects the big observations from the human sciences and from existential-humanistic studies. Another impressive theorist is Orford (2001), who incorporated several theories, including those that highlighted social influence. But Orford organized his theory around the addict's conflicted attachment to the drug. His integration of several specific theories is useful, but unconvincing as an account of cultural imperatives or existential-humanistic insights on self-transcendence.

The implications of finding a coherent theory are profound. Among the more obvious are better use of the billions of tax dollars spent on research and treatment each year, reduced cost to the health care and criminal justice systems for dealing with the aftermath of addiction, and delivering more effective treatment programs. I propose that using personal meaning as an organizing construct may provide the most promising conceptual framework for explaining the big observations from mainstream, human science, and existential-humanistic perspectives.

MAINSTREAM PSYCHOLOGICAL THEORIES AND THERAPIES

In a telling example halfway through his book, *Theory of Addiction*, West (2006) presented the heading, "A reminder of what we are talking about" (p. 23). His reminder was an addict's narrative:

> I woke up in the night because the drink has worn off and my nerves are screaming out. . . . I swear that I'm never going to put myself through this again. I feel like death—in fact I pray for it. But somewhere inside myself I know that by evening I will be drunk again. (p. 123)

This sort of negative experience is what mainstream theories of addiction have taken as their mission to explain. How can anyone who suffers because of his or her own behavior return repeatedly to that behavior?

Mainstream theories are those heralded in the literature as the most scientific and, thus, most valid interpretations of addiction. They arise from empirical research based on positivist assumptions. A survey of these theories leaves the impression that they are a patchwork of different ideas, with no advancement based on systematic research. Surprisingly, only a handful of scholars have admitted this publicly (e.g., Ballinger, Matano, & Amantea, 2008; Bickel & Potenza, 2006; West, 2006).

Mainstream Theories

Mainstream theories on addiction follow from biopsychology, behaviorism and social learning theory, cognitive psychology, and motivational psychology. West (2006) catalogued 30 models, under four overarching approaches: addiction as choice (12 models), impulse and self-control (7 models), habit and instrumental learning (8 models), and population theories (3 models). He summed up the struggles of scholars to come to terms with addiction theory:

> There are many [theoretical models of addiction] and almost all
> of them are insightful and capture important elements of what we
> understand as addiction. The problem is that each theory seemed to
> stem from an innovative idea that accounted for selected aspects of
> the problem but did not account for other features that existing theo-
> ries already catered for quite well. There was little sense of progress in
> our understanding; little sense that we are engaging in "incremental
> science." (West, 2006, p. 1)

Webb, Sniehotta, and Michie (2010) contributed 10 theories on behavioral change from social and health psychologies, which the authors applied to addic-tions. These included control theory, goal-setting theory, model of action phases, strength model of self-control, and various social cognition models. Although Hester and Miller (2003) were interested primarily in treatments, they briefly described theoretical positions derived from the history of treatment (though several models did not arise from empirical studies). Thus, to West's 31 theories (including West's synthetic theory), and Webb, Sniehotta, and Michie's 10 theories, we can add Hester and Miller's moral, temperance, spiritual, dispositional disease, and public health theories.

The following section examines clusters of theories under three umbrella theoretical categories: disease, cognitive-behavioral, and motivational.

Disease Theory. The medical/brain pathology model is the most potent force in addiction theory today. The current version is based on two factors: (1) genetic predisposition, and (2) mechanisms by which intoxication affects the brain.

According to the American Society of Addiction Medicine (ASAM, 2012), the body that is generally recognized as providing the medical definition of addiction,

> Addiction is characterized by inability to consistently abstain, impairment in behavioral control, craving, diminished recognition of significant problems with one's behaviors and interpersonal relationships, and a dysfunctional emotional response. Like other chronic diseases, addiction often involves cycles of relapse and remission. Without treatment or engagement in recovery activities, addiction is progressive and can result in disability or premature death.

Addiction, according to ASAM, has its etiology in physical abnormalities in the brain. It is important to note that the label of *disease* is the medicalization of addiction. Many neurobiological reductionist theorists do not accept the disease label. Vaillant (1995), for example, pointed out that some experts are unwilling to accept the disease definition because medicine changes how it defines disease. Despite labels, however, in disease theory addiction is brain pathology.

According to an older version of the disease definition, addiction is in the drug. It is the drug that does the addicting. Developed by Jellinek (1960), this idea means, for example, that the alcoholic is the person who drinks enough alcohol enough times until he or she becomes addicted. The person begins as a social drinker, but continued use plunges him or her into addiction. The modern version argues that those who succumb to addiction have a neurobiological predisposition (e.g., Dick and Agrawal, 2008; Thatcher & Clark, 2008, Yuferov et al., 2009). Precisely how much of the variance genetic predisposition accounts for is debated, but heritability estimates are in the 50% to 60% range (West, 2006; Dick & Agrawal, 2008).

Combined with psychological and environmental influences, genetic predisposition suggests that not everyone who uses drugs becomes an addict. Someone may drink a lot, but this is not a defining criterion for a diagnosis of substance dependence. The *DSM-IV-TR* (American Psychiatric Association, 2000) listed a second category for substance disorders, *substance abuse*. Abuse is not dependence but rather the use of a substance to deal with, for example, grief over the loss of a loved one. It can also refer simply to too much partying, such as watching the Super Bowl over a few beers and then being arrested for DUI. The difference between the disorders is the key criterion for dependence: "Despite recognizing the contributing role of the substance to a psychological or physical problem (e.g., severe depressive symptoms or damage to organ systems), the person continues to use the substance" (American Psychiatric Association, 2000, pp. 195).

The second neuroscience approach that guides brain pathology theories examines the effects of drugs on the brain. Essentially, the argument is that the addiction is a *compulsion* (Leshner, 1997). Researchers have proposed three major theories on how drugs affect the brain, revolving around the meso(cortico)limbic dopamine pathways. One proposal argued that drugs provide hedonic reward (Volkow et al., 2007). Another theory proposed that the power of drugs is the brain's anticipation of reward (Baars & Gage, 2010; Volkow, Wang, Fowler, Tomasi, Telang, & Baler, 2011). A third major theory, which has assumed the dominant mantle in drug studies, argued that the mesolimbic dopamine pathways enhance motivational wanting (as opposed to hedonic liking), leading to irresistible drug cravings. Biopsychologists T. E. Robinson and Berridge (1993; 2001; 2003; Berridge & Robinson, 2006; Berridge, 2012) formalized this idea as incentive-sensitization theory (IST). Drugs, particularly stimulants and opioids, sensitize the nucleus accumbens and associated structures, which is the biological basis of compulsive behavior.

All three theories have great heuristic value, providing a neurobiological basis for addiction and for the popular idea that addicts are powerless over their addiction. IST has added explanatory power because many addicts report that they use drugs even though they desire to be abstinent.

Cognitive-Behavioral Theory. Under the umbrella of cognitive-behavioral theory are many variations. More dated theories pinned addiction's motivating force on classical conditioning. Environmental cues associated with intoxication elicit cravings (Drummond, 2001), in the same way that Pavlov's dogs salivated when cued by a bell. Others added instrumental learning. Intoxication is particularly pernicious because it offers positive reinforcement through the rewarding effects of the drug, and negative reinforcement through the desire to prevent withdrawal (Childress, McLellan, Ehrman, & O'Brien, 1988; Schulteis, Heyser, & Koob, 1999). Biopsychologists discovered a neurobiological basis for both forms of conditioning (Tomkins & Sellers, 2001). Baars and Gage (2010) and West (2006) described the neurobiological foundation for the well-known behaviorist principle that reinforcing addictive behavior on an irregular schedule is particularly compelling for those addicted to gambling.

Beyond classical and operant conditioning, Marlatt (Marlatt & Donovan, 2005) added Bandura's (1986) social learning theory. Like behaviorists, social learning theorists focus on behavior, but they add a cognitive component. Social learning theory examines the effects of cognitive processing on goal-directed behavior. The rewarding nature of the drug is different for each person and depends on the drug user's history, traits, and life circumstances. Marlatt proposed that much drug craving was based on the cognitive process of anticipating the consequence of intoxication; a positive drug expectancy triggers a motivation to use the substance. His work showed that drug placebos achieved results similar to the real substance (Marlatt, Demming, & Reid, 1973). Marlatt also proposed the abstinence violation effect, which is a cognitive process of attributing a relapse to some failure in the recovering addict. This cognitive attribution of failure leads to increased guilt and a perception of powerlessness, from which the addict could *learn* to relapse.

More cognitively-oriented theories place less weight on cue-elicited cravings and more weight on decision making. Addiction is a choice. Again, many approaches inform rational choice theory, but two have gained prominence. Becker and Murphy (1988) applied economic theory to the psychological dynamics of drug taking. While their theory of behavioral economics involved many variables, its essential thesis was that drug users are no different than consumers of other commodities. If the individual finds benefit in using drugs, he or she will use them, creating stable behavior over time. Utility of drug use is reinforcing. Individual differences are the result of unique variables (that is, those values plugged into the economic equations) such as tolerance and financial resources.

A second rational choice approach interprets drug use as a form of self-medication (Suh, Ruffins, Robins, Albanese, & Khantzian, 2008). Several models have been proposed, but Khantzian's (1997) psychoanalytic approach is generally recognized as the foundational theory. Khantzian noticed that heroin addicts often had psychological struggles before succumbing to addiction. He proposed that heroin addicts (and, later, cocaine addicts) consciously use heroin to curb their anger, depression, and other painful symptoms. The theme running through all self-medication theories is that potential addicts suffer from some underlying condition, and they make a conscious decision to use a substance to alleviate psychological symptoms. In some cases, the underlying symptom is physical pain. The drug user uses opiates until he or she becomes physically dependent. Tolerance develops, and the user begins taking the drug at levels well beyond pharmacological protocols.

Although West (2006) expended many pages on "addiction as a choice" (p. 29), rational choice theory has not gained much currency in Canada or the United States. North American experts prefer the idea that drugs hijack the cognitive components of the brain, the foundation of the brain pathology models. While mainstream theories trumpet abstinence as the solution to addiction (since drugs hijack the brain), the implications of all choice theories are that controlled drug use is a viable option, that individuals have the right to choose how to live their lives, and that intoxication is not the defining criterion of addiction nor abstinence the defining criterion of recovery. These and other assumptions are the basis for what has become known as *harm reduction*. With few exceptions, Marlatt's (1998) book on harm reduction had little influence on mainstream North America. If the problem of drugs is their impact on the brain—rendering the addict powerless over drug use—then it made little sense for disciples of abstinence to pay attention to any theory that implied drug use was a choice and addicts could learn to use socially.

Despite the disciples of prohibition, rational choice has scholarly support. Philosophers seem particularly attracted to it, as for example with Fingarette (1988) and Seeburger (1993). Psychologists outside North America, such as West, have held it in esteem, and even some North American psychologists rely on it. Most recently, Heyman (2009) surveyed the evidence of addiction and determined that it was a choice. After highlighting logical inconsistencies in the disease model, he appealed to behavioral economics, among other theories, to explain addiction as a normal choice process. People make decisions based on the better current option. The problem with addicts is that they choose the local option rather than view the overall benefit across a series of options. Again, however, such an affront to the dominant brain pathology models promoted by the medical profession and the National Institutes of Health did not generate much enthusiasm.

Motivational Theory. W. R. Miller (W. R. Miller & Carroll, 2006; W. R. Miller & Rollnick, 2013) is generally regarded as the main force promoting addiction in terms of motivational psychology. Unlike, for example, T. E. Robinson and Berridge (2001), whose neurobiological reductionist theory stated that motivation is not within the control of the drug user, W. R. Miller and Carroll (2006) declared that "drug use is a behavior, chosen from among behavioral options" (p. 295). Motivational psychology argues that addicts use drugs for some reason (experimentation, peer pressure, self-medication) and then succumb to the effects of the drug on the mesolimbic dopamine system. Their brains have not been hijacked; rather, their locus of control is external, and they lack intrinsic motivation to recover.

Integrated Theories. A handful of theorists have integrated mainstream theories. The World Health Organization (WHO, 1981) attempted integration under a biopsychosocial framework. Its thesis was that consistent use of substances may create physiological responses (as opposed to neurobiological responses). Over time, these responses can become classically conditioned. Negative effects of withdrawal, such as anxiety and stress, can also become associated with drug use, as can environmental cues such as social events. Indeed, most accounts attempting to integrate theories are rudimentary, intended more to convince the reader that addiction is complex. A typical example is Ogborne (1997), who simply listed the various biopsychosocial components without any substantive theoretical integration.

Herrnstein and Prelec (1992) proposed a rational choice theory of addiction, integrating the destructive dynamics of addiction with economic theory that presupposes individuals pursue behaviors for maximum (positive) utility. The benefits of drug use are often reserved for individual instances, but the consequences of addiction are often distributed in various life areas. The distribution of consequences, in a sense, dilutes them.

In his survey of theories, West (2006) mentioned two attempts at integration: Orford's (2001) excessive appetites theory and Blaszczynski and Nower's (2002) pathways model. Orford maintained that mainstream theories—such as IST— were too focused to encompass multiple levels of motivation, social norms of the person's social group, and population analyses. According to Orford, the impaired cognitive processing, depression, and alienation so prevalent in the literature are a result of conflict within the addict. This conflict explains how individuals could find appeal in the drug but, at the same time, feel guilt and anger over using. Although applied only to problem gambling, Blaszczynski and Nower's pathways model similarly recognized heterogeneity in addiction and multiple levels of motivation. Their model attempted "to integrate decision-making, environmental factors, personality, and instrumental learning mechanisms" (West, 2006, p. 121).

West (2006) approved of both theories because "counter-examples are difficult to find" (p. 118), but he complained that they did not sufficiently integrate the various influences on the individual. The importance of synthesis is that it can account for the big observations and also for the assumptions of specific theories. West synthesized his theory under the unifying construct of the "human motivational system" (p. 147). The motivational system comprised, according to West, plans, responses, impulses/inhibitory forces, motives, and evaluations, to which he gave the acronym PRIME. These elements do not exert influence on each other randomly. Rather, they exert influence in specific ways:

> For example, motives can only exert influence on responding through
> impulses, and evaluations can only influence responses through
> motives and then impulses. Plans provide a structure to our actions
> but can only influence through motives and evaluations operating at
> the time when they are to be executed. (p. 147)

West's (2006) theory of motivation is more ecumenical than T. E. Robinson and Berridge's (1993, 2001, 2003) motivational wanting. Under West's motivational umbrella are hedonic liking, biological drives, classical and operant learning, social learning, and cognitive processing. All of these influences come into play. Individual differences and contexts shape the person's drive in a given space and time.

West's (2006) theory is thus a theory of motivational dominance. He assumed a fundamental principle that "the human mind has evolved to be inherently unstable" (p. 167). Stability comes from continual adjustments "to prevent it from spiraling out of control" (p. 167). The benefit is, of course, that the mind is highly adaptable to fluid circumstances. The problem of addiction is that it provides an abnormal motivation for drug using; that is, most of the influences that have evolved to keep the mind balanced are subordinated to the addictive motivation.

Mainstream Therapies

Therapies for addiction generally follow from theoretical underpinnings. Yet engineering theories into practice has been a struggle. The modern medical argument that addiction has its roots in an abnormal mesolimbic dopamine system does not easily translate into practical help. Perhaps the most salient treatment principle from this theory is abstinence, and treatment that supports this goal is efficacious. Alcoholics Anonymous (AA), too, is useful, but not because of its spiritual emphasis; rather, it promotes abstinence (Vaillant, Chapter 3, this volume). Family systems therapies, psychodynamic therapy, treatment tailored to the addict's psychological distress, and other therapies that do not focus on abstinence are of limited or no value. Medications could, in theory, provide a significant advance in helping addicts overcome their neurobiological abnormality, but thus far they have met with limited success. The aim of most of these medications is "to shed the powerful mental associations between the drug and pleasurable feelings that underlie craving and relapse" (Shen, Orson, & Kosten, 2012, p. 61).

The engineering problem from brain pathology theories is likely why most treatments rely on psychological theories. There are hundreds of recognized treatments for addiction, too many to describe in this paper. The following presents four umbrella categories that mainstream treatments generally fall under: behaviorism, cognitive-behavioral coping skills, family therapy, and motivational therapy.

Behaviorism: Community Reinforcement Approach. An example of treatment from behaviorist theory is the community reinforcement approach (CRA). Originally developed by Hunt and Azrin (1973), CRA attempts to make a recovery lifestyle more reinforcing than an addictive lifestyle. CRA directly targets the client's environment, putting in place activities and skill sets that positively reinforce the client's goals. The clinical emphasis is to reinforce positive behavior, as opposed to punishing negative behavior.

CRA recommends two basic strategies. First, the therapist conducts a functional analysis of the client's addiction, including an examination of external triggers (people and places) and internal triggers (emotional states, thoughts, and physical sensations) for the addiction. Secondly, the therapist invites clients to agree to a period of sobriety with a time limit and then completes a happiness scale on 10 areas of their lives. The therapist assists each client to identify specific goals in life areas that have been affected by the addiction, such as finances, family relations, communications, and so on. Achieving these goals means training in, for example, communication skills, problem-solving techniques, job finding, and relapse prevention. A typical reinforcing technique is the use of vouchers for clean drug tests or achieving a goal. A more controversial technique is aversion medication, such as disulfiram.

Cognitive-Behavioral Coping Skills Therapy. Cognitive-behavioral coping skills training comprises many therapies designed for those in early recovery. The goal is strictly to help clients overcome triggers to drug cravings through healthy cognitive and behavioral coping skills. In support of reducing or eliminating drug use, the therapeutic focus is on overcoming the cues that lead to cravings, which, in turn, lead to using. If, for example, anger is associated with using, then the plan is to examine the context of the anger, what gives rise to it, and then provide a healthy response.

Bandura's (1986) social learning theory has played a large part in coping skills training for addiction (Annis, Herie, & Watkin-Merek, 1997). He suggested that we observe the behavior of a model and, based on various observer and model characteristics, imitate the behavior. An alcoholic may, for example, take a drink because he or she sees a television advertisement promising good times from a bottle. This is not, however, simple behavioral reinforcement. It gives a prominent role to cognitions, that is, how we respond to risk factors based on motivation, experience, and other thoughts. Bandura (1997) later examined the role of self-efficacy on behaviors and concluded that those with low self-efficacy had more difficulty overcoming a problem. Clinicians could thus help clients by increasing their self-efficacy through a graduated series of mastery experiences, verbal reinforcement, and vicarious modeling experiences.

Marlatt's (Marlatt, 1985; Marlatt & Wikiewitz, 2005) relapse-prevention therapy interpreted relapse as a response to immediate precipitators and covert antecedents. Immediate precipitators are those situations that are high risk, such as going to a bar or getting into an argument. It is not the situations, themselves, that are the danger, but the client's response to them based on their maladaptive skill set. Typically, alcoholics tend to drink because they have developed positive alcohol expectancies or they focus on immediate rewards. Similarly, if an alcoholic in recovery does not think he or she can resist a drink, then he or she will likely relapse when faced with an urge. Covert antecedents are a set of subtle conditions such as testing one's sobriety or living a stress-filled lifestyle. Although they have no direct connection with drinking, these seemingly irrelevant decisions and conditions can combine to make a recovering person vulnerable to relapse. Marlatt also incorporated Bandura's (1997) self-efficacy findings into his relapse prevention program.

Research has shown that coping skills training has statistically significant success and is generally considered to be as effective as other empirically validated treatments (Hester & Miller, 2003).

A relatively new model of behaviorally oriented treatment is Hayes' (2004) acceptance and commitment therapy, which broadens cognitive-behavioral therapy (CBT) to include the influence of mindfulness meditation. Marlatt (Zgierska, Rabago, Chawla, Kushner, Kohler, & Marlatt, 2009) had later included mindfulness as a way of overcoming cravings, but acceptance and commitment therapy proposed a more complex association, based on the assumption that "control is the problem" (Hayes, 2004, p. 19). It is the addict's desperate desire to control his or her emotions, thoughts, and environment that is the source of drug use. Through mindfulness techniques, clients learn that their preconceived ways of making sense of their struggles are the problem. Through, for example, accepting cravings and not trying to control them, and making a commitment to change, the client learns healthy new behaviors.

Family Therapy

Family therapies remain on the periphery of addiction treatments. Boudreau (1997) blamed this on the "widespread view of addiction. . . as a problem that primarily afflicts the individual" (p. 407); most family programs are adjuncts to the main treatment focus on the individual. The matrix model, for example, invites family members to attend one component of treatment. This is intended to help them understand their loved one's struggles and how they can participate in the addict's recovery (Rawson, Obert, McCann, & Ling, 2005).

But more therapists are becoming aware of how important it is to treat the whole family (Steinglass, 2009). Steinglass and colleagues (1987), for example, analyzed the alcoholic family within Bowenian family systems (Bowen, 1985) and showed how families organize themselves around the alcoholic member. Treatment is a matter of reorganizing the system.

Curiously, the most scientifically informed family therapy in the addictions field is very similar to behavioral therapies. Behavioral couples therapy (Fals-Stewart, O'Farrell, & Birchler, 2004; O'Farrell & Fals-Stewart, 2006) is based on behavioral models of addiction; its practitioners interpret addiction as having a primary connection with relationship discord. "Marital and family problems (for example, poor communication and problem-solving, habitual arguing, and financial stressors) often set the stage for excessive drinking or drug use" (Fals-Stewart, O'Farrell, & Birchler, 2004, p. 31). Behavioral couples therapy demands abstinence, and its basic repertoire includes daily sobriety contracts between partners, witnessed disulfiram ingestion (for alcoholics), regular sessions with a counselor to review how each partner has lived up to the contract, homework assignments such as "catch your partner doing something nice," interpersonal communications skills training, 12-step meetings, and drug screens. This therapy assumes, of course, that partners are committed to their relationship as well as to abstinence.

Motivational Therapy

The most famous evidence-based therapy today is motivational enhancement therapy (MET, W. R. Miller, 1995). Motivational treatment "gives intentional change a prominent role" (W. R. Miller & Carroll, 2006, p. 295). The key to change is intrinsic motivation, not extrinsic motivation. According to W. R. Miller (1995), extrinsic motivation, such as punishing clients if they failed to follow rules, leads to client resistance. The "therapeutic style. . . forms the core of MET" (W. R. Miller, p. 2.), and this style uses Rogerian principles as its baseline: "[The] therapist characteristic of accurate empathy, as defined by Carl Rogers and his students. . . has been shown to be a powerful predictor of therapeutic success, even when treatment is guided by another (e.g., behavioral) rationale" (p. 2). Unlike Rogers' client-centered approach, however, "MET is a directive and persuasive method, not a nondirective and passive approach" (p. 7).

Eclectic/Integrative Therapy

Many (perhaps most) therapists use a range of treatments. Precisely how they choose therapeutic strategies and techniques follows a variety of paths of logic. Norcross (2005) surveyed therapy integrations and concluded that they follow one of three strategies: technical eclecticism, common factors, and theoretical integration. Some therapists are convinced that integration can happen only at the level of theory and practice. Dickerson (2010), for example, proposed that it is impossible to integrate epistemologies that inform theory. Richert (2011) was less impressed with technical eclecticism and argued against using interventions from theoretically incompatible ideas.

Norcross (2005) reported that between one-fourth and one-half of U.S. clinicians identified themselves as eclectic or integrative, borrowing ways of understanding human beings from various theories and strategies and using techniques from various modalities. Eclectic therapists choose whatever therapy they believe will accomplish therapeutic goals. Most seem drawn to eclecticism because their major concern is not a theoretical issue but a real-life interest in the client's well-being. As Slife and Williams (1995) pointed out, however, "eclecticism is itself a theoretical position" (p. 46), and carries assumptions about how theorizing should be done.

All this is to say that being eclectic demands considered appraisal of epistemologies and theories that inform strategies and techniques. Eclectic addiction treatment, however, rarely follows any deeply considered logic. Since mainstream theories arise from a positivist epistemology, eclecticism happens at the level of theory and technique. Depending on length of treatment, treatment may start with medical intervention, shift to motivational interviewing (motivational psychology), followed by cognitive-behavioral coping skills training for issues such as anger or depression. Often treatment ends with relapse prevention coping skills. Others use behavioral approaches, supplemented with educational material. Still others rely on Rogerian therapy, supplemented with educational material. In some treatment regimens, a systems approach serves as an adjunct therapy to help client and family rebuild relationships.

Meta-analyses of Therapies

Few studies offer a bird's-eye view of different treatments. The National Institute on Drug Abuse (2009) provided a list of evidence-based therapies. Perhaps because of political exigencies as a tax-funded organization, it catalogued only descriptions of therapies that claimed support from quantitative research. In Canada, the federal government provided similar catalogues, but it, too, offered only descriptions (see, for example, Health Canada, 1999).

The most comprehensive meta-analysis of treatment is Hester and Miller's (2003). Over a decade, they examined 99 therapies for alcoholism, which included 381 controlled trials and 75,000 participants. Hester and Miller concluded that brief interventions (usually motivational interviewing), MET, and the medication acamprosate (a GABA agonist) were the top three modalities. Of the 99 therapies, only 19 showed a positive "cumulative evidence score" (p. 17) determined by variables such as number of published studies, number of participants, use of a control group, effect size, and other factors affecting methodological rigor. Most, including education, relaxation training, and AA, had little or no detectable efficacy (negative cumulative evidence score).

Although there is a significant body of research examining common factors (i.e., beyond technique) in therapy, such as the influence of the therapeutic relationship (S. D. Miller, Hubble, & Duncan, 2007, November/December), mainstream studies generally examine performance outcomes. In the addiction field, researchers determine if the therapy leads to significant positive changes in drug use, physical health, emotional and mental health, occupational readiness, and involvement in the criminal justice system.

Success rates in outcome studies of mainstream treatments have been a sobering reminder of our struggle to treat addiction. Those that measure abstinence as a performance outcome generally show results hovering somewhere around 25% over some period up to a year (N. S. Miller & Hoffmann, 1995). After a year, success plunges. Rand Corporation (Polich, Armor, & Braiker, 1980) published an abstinence rate of 7% over 4 years. Vaillant (1995) reported research pinning the abstinence rate after 5 years at 5%. Because of the high relapse rate, most researchers in the past 2 decades have preferred to study outcomes measuring reduced harm. One of the most famous studies is Project MATCH (1997), which reported that 30% of participants drank during the first year after treatment without bingeing and 20% remained sober. The Baltimore Drug and Alcohol Treatment Outcomes Study (Johnson et al., 2002) reported that participants reduced drug behavior at statistically significant levels over 1 year posttreatment.

Comparing two or more treatments on performance outcomes generally results in the "Dodo bird effect" a term Luborsky et al. (2002, p. 2) borrowed from the Dodo's judgment at the end of the wacky race in *Alice's Adventures in Wonderland*: "*Everybody* has won, and *all* must have prizes" (Carroll, 1920, p. 34). The most famous example of the Dodo bird effect in addiction studies is the 8-year, $27-million Project MATCH (1997), in which relapse prevention, motivational, and 12-step facilitation therapies produced the same outcomes on various performance indicators.

ASSESSMENT OF MAINSTREAM THEORIES

West (2006) analyzed mainstream theories according to how they made sense of the "'big' observations" (p. 1) of addiction, that is, according to what we know from positivist research. This paper takes a broader view, examining West's catalogue as a collection. While different mainstream theories make sense of human nature in different ways, they share many similarities.

Outsider's Perspective

Mainstream theories are based on the outsider's perspective. Kurtz (1999) suggested that this may be a prejudice of modern science, which prefers a positivist approach, and most are neurobiological, cognitive-behavioral, and motivational. Within these theories, there is no room for phenomenology. Perceptions of the individual are shaped by the deterministic forces of the different behavioral, cognitive, and motivational systems. How individuals perceive their reality is a mere epiphenomenon.

Pathology

All mainstream theories assume that addiction is pathological; definitions of addiction include mental or physical afflictions and infirmities. Brain disease, maladaptive learned behavior, faulty cognitive processing, and familial dysfunction are used to explain why the addict continues to pursue behavior that causes him or her repeated and severe suffering.

Determinism

Similar to their pathological bent, mainstream theories tend toward determinism. Within rational choice theory there is room for responsibility, but even these theories reduce to cost-benefit analyses or the product of economic equations.

The clearest example of deterministic theory is T. E. Robinson and Berridge's (1993, 2001, 2003) IST. With the mesolimbic dopamine pathways sensitized by the drug, an irresistible compulsion forces the pursuit of intoxication, regardless of what the addict thinks or desires. Powerful as IST is, it has critics. D. N. Stephens (2006) questioned whether there is sufficient evidence to support this theory, since the same incentive-salience can be induced in rats with food. Thus, the question arises: What is it about drugs that make them so special?

But a more sophisticated critique is based on T. E. Robinson and Berridge's (2003) research design. Their claim to have found a neurobiological basis for compulsion stemmed from comparing stimulant use between a control group of rats and another group induced with incentive salience (through microinjections of a psychostimulant). The sensitized rats used the stimulant more quickly and for a longer period of time than the control group, and T. E. Robinson and Berridge concluded that this was evidence of compulsive drug use. Unimpressed with this conclusion, G. L. Stephens and Graham (2009) argued that comparing groups could never prove compulsion. What was needed was a study of a single creature and how it moved from choice to compulsive use. According to mainstream accounts, drug use is initially a choice, not a compulsion. Only after repeated use does compulsion arise. But Stephens and Graham pointed out that what the neuroscientists had to prove was the point at which a single rat crossed some line into compulsive use. Since brain chemicals are neutral, having nothing to do with motivation, the scientist faced a daunting task: where to draw this line. For example, they might define some level of molar concentration of dopamine in the pathway, beyond which drug use would be compulsive. In other words, they would have to set a normative standard. Stephens and Graham concluded that, since this was impossible, neuroscientists could never prove compulsion.

West's (2006) theory, too, is deterministic. Despite his emphasis that drug use is, in part, a choice, his theory leads inevitably to his major treatment principles:

abstinence, dismissal of the stages of change model (Prochaska, Norcross, & DiClemente, 1995) (there is no value in tailoring treatment to the individual), and "maximum *tolerable* pressure" (West, 2006, p. 188, italics in original) (with, we can predict, high attrition). West relied heavily on neurobiological and operant conditioning to explain motivational dominance. Indeed, operant conditioning can dominate motivations in the sense that "the mechanism [operant conditioning] is not influenced by beliefs about what is good or bad or right or wrong and so can come into conflict with conscious choices" (p. 149). He ascribed cravings and relapse precisely to these unconscious forces. Where choice comes into play is in "plans and 'foraging'" (p. 143). The thinking person only provides flexibility in planning to get and use drugs. If the liquor store is closed, the thinking person focuses on other drug sources; if the addict needs money, the thinking person figures out how to get funds.

Dingel, Hammer, Ostergren, McCormick, and Koenig (2012) provided a curious defense of free will, while adhering to the disease theory of addiction. They defended the disease model against the complaint that the defining criterion of *compulsion* led logically to an all-or-nothing definition of addiction. An individual addict's degree of free will, they argued, exists on a continuum. After five years of ethnographic research on how addiction experts make sense of the disease model, Dingel et al. found that the experts did not intend to absolve addicts of responsibility; rather, they believed that the disease model promoted treatment.

But the argument is specious. First, the brain pathology model was developed from research such as that of T. E. Robinson and Berridge (1993, 2001, 2003), whose thesis was that addiction is a compulsion. More damning, however, and what Dingel et al. (2012) failed to realize, is that their continuum argument falls prey to the same critique that G. L. Stephens and Graham (2009) made of IST. A continuum depends on a normative neurobiological state. The individual's meso-limbic (or mesocorticolimbic) dopamine pathways are *normal* (that is, compulsion does not exist) up to some cutoff point, beyond which they are diseased. There is nothing in neuroscience that suggests such a normative state could be defined, given that all human brains are different.

Nonscientific Influences

Explanations of why we continue to interpret addiction as pathology are generally pinned on prohibitionary zeal, most powerfully found in the United States but also powerful in other countries. Griffin, Measham, Moore, Morey, and Riley (2008), for example, complained of the "persistence of prohibition as an ideological force" (p. 205). Prohibition has attached a stigma to addiction (Luoma et al., 2007). Heyman (2009) pointed out that addiction is the only health condition worthy of two institutes of health (National Institute on Drug Abuse and National Institute on Alcohol Abuse and Alcoholism); at the same time, addiction has its own organization in the criminal justice department (Drug Enforcement Agency). A final example is harm reduction. Although harm reduction is popular in Europe and has much scientific support, it struggled in North American because of the prohibition influence, which demands abstinence.

Sellman (2009) called for "unity between warring factions in the field to use the knowledge already known more effectively for the betterment of. . . patients suffering from addictive disorders" (p. 6). Alexander (2010) described the vigorous resistance he encountered trying to publish Rat Park, which showed that rats had no interest in morphine if they were not locked up in Skinner cages but were free to roam Rat Park (Alexander, Beyerstein, Hadaway, & Coambs, 1981). Many people did not like his conclusion that drugs did not hijack the rat's brain but, rather, served as a salve for boredom and loneliness. Similarly, Weil (1986) described the vituperative reactions he was subjected to at conferences, when he proposed that drugs aided a natural urge for an altered state of consciousness. Lenson (1995) reported that he was unwilling to publish his nonpathological views on addiction until a more favorable political climate was in place, for fear of losing his research funding.

Another issue giving rise to the debate is that, historically, the addiction field was split off from mainstream health care. Studies have shown that those who work in Minnesota model treatment (Owen, 2000)—counselors who are recovering addicts with little advanced training—tend to resist any idea that disagrees with their perspective (Stoffelmayr, Mavis, & Kasim, 1998). This is especially troubling, since it is the treatment of choice for 93% to 95% of programs in the United States (Lemanski, 2001). Perhaps more troubling is that the Minnesota model pays almost no attention to research findings (Hester & Miller, 2003) and little attention to any health care code of ethics (Taleff & Babcock, 1998; W. R. Miller & White, 2007).

The greatest limitation of mainstream theories is that they fail to account for research findings beyond their own frameworks. T. E. Robinson and Berridge's (2001) research stands as an example. They reported that relapse is an inherent problem of addiction. But to relapse, as Heyman (2009) and G. L. Stephens and Graham (2009) pointed out, one must first be clean and sober for an extended period. If compulsion is the defining criterion of addiction, then how is this abstinence possible? Similarly, if abstinence is generally held to be a requirement for recovery, how does one explain alcoholics who became social drinkers?

HUMAN SCIENCE THEORIES

Moving away from the strict psychological and biological models, the human sciences have contributed a growing number of research articles on addiction. They generally reject positivist approaches and key on what Robson (2002) called *real world research*. The real world, in which the researcher is unable to control variables, demanded a new method of study. Human science researchers used qualitative methodologies that had their foundation in postmodern, not positivist, epistemologies.

MacAndrew and Edgerton (1969) published a milestone work showing that alcohol had differential effects on people and even different effects on a single person in different environments. They reported the case of a wild drunk, seemingly out of control, who instantly became polite and deferential when his environment changed. Gladwell (2010, February 15 & 22) summarized the body of work: "Drunkenness is not disinhibition. Drunkenness is myopia" (p. 74). The cultural environment, not alcohol, directed behavior. Getting drunk while watching the NHL Stanley Cup playoffs produced excitement; getting drunk in the basement produced loneliness. Perhaps more importantly, drinking cultures, such as the Italian-Americans, taught their people how to drink civilly.

The human sciences interpret addiction principally as a consequence of social and cultural environment. Spurred by historical examinations, such as Foucault's (1965) *Madness and Civilization: A History of Insanity in the Age of Reason*, a growing number of studies have examined historical interpretations of addiction. Ferentzy (2001) reported that society sees addiction through the lens of contemporary scientific and moral influences, a conclusion reached by many researchers (see, for example, Levine, 1978; Peele, 1986; Rabin, 2005; Roth, 2004).

How can addiction be a biological, bottom-up phenomenon and, *at the same time*, have some of its etiology in social and cultural factors? Vaillant (1995) provided an answer. To make sense of the different views, he proposed that *understanding* alcoholism required "models of the social scientist and. . . learning theorist. But in order to *treat* alcoholics effectively we need to invoke the model of the medical practitioner" (p. 22). From a positivist perspective, Vaillant's argument is, perhaps, the best that can be said.

Assessment of Human Science Theories

Human science has added impressive evidence to help us better understand addiction, but it has clear problems. There is, of course, the problem of providing any sort of treatment based on human science theory. Another issue is that human scientists, like the positivists, do not appear to find any value in addressing the big observations of theories that do not fit their framework. How does an interpretation of addiction based on culture fit with T. E. Robinson and Berridge's (1993, 2001, 2003) neuroscience studies on motivational wanting? The human scientists are silent.

The most pressing problematic issue is an epistemological one. Postmodernists deconstructed absolutes, claiming humans can be free only by dismantling metaphysics and positivist science. There were no deep meanings, and the pursuit of them kept people trapped in a chimera. Despite this stance, human sciences did appeal to an absolute: culture (Eagleton, 2007; Room, 2003).

The result of suggesting that culture is the real force underlying human behavior is that, like mainstream theories, it tends toward determinism. Rather than being pulled by intrapsychic, interpersonal, or neurobiological forces, the individual is pulled by the overwhelming force of culture.

EXISTENTIAL–HUMANISTIC THEORIES AND THERAPIES

In mainstream and human science theories, there is a rampant determinism. West's (2006) theory of motivational dominance is really a balance sheet of internal and external vectors that point inevitably to behavior. It provides no room for messy thoughts or actions, those human qualities that do not conform to the positivist's rules. In human science views we find people at the mercy of cultural forces. In both mainstream and human science perspectives, the individual is lost under the tyranny of the aggregate.

Useful as they may be, positivist and human science interpretations do not account for all the big observations. They remain the outsider's view. If we are to have a reliable theory of addiction, we also need to make sense of the insider's perspective. There is a considerable body of knowledge that interprets addiction in line with the complexity of subjective experience.

West (2006) concluded that "addiction. . . is best defined by repeated failures to refrain from drug use despite prior resolutions to do so" (p. 2). Mainstream theories emphasized powerful motivations and impaired control (Jellinek, 1960; W. R. Miller & Carroll, 2006; T. E. Robinson & Berridge, 2003; West 2006). But the world only provides answers to the kinds of inquiry we pose. If we ask why addiction is bad, we find answers to why it is bad. But to understand the subjective experience of intoxication, existential-humanistic psychologists asked a different question: *What are the meanings that users ascribe to the experience of intoxication?* Compare the mainstream definitions with any number of personal descriptions, such as the one De Quincey (1821/1986) provided:

> I was necessarily ignorant of the whole art and mystery of opium
> taking . . . but I took it;—and in an hour, oh! Heavens! What

a revulsion! What an upheaving, from its lowest depths, of the inner spirit! What an apocalypse of the world within me! That my [stomach] pains had vanished, was now a trifle in my eyes:—this negative effect was swallowed up in the immensity of those positive effects which had opened before me—in the abyss of divine enjoyment thus suddenly revealed. Here was a panacea. . . for all human woes: here was the secret of happiness . . . ." (pp. 70–71)

One more example from a crack cocaine addict:

It's like the whole world, life is beautiful. I feel great. I have a lot of ideas. My mind just opens tremendously. My mind is like really fast and I can think better. I feel good. I feel life is wonderful. I can do anything. (cited in Trujillo, 2004, p. 171)

Researchers who inquired into the subjective experience of intoxication discovered that drug users often perceive intoxication as enhancing their sober lives. Indeed, any clinician who has worked with addicts has often heard a client's confession that *drugs saved my life*.

Transcendent Experience

Users give many meanings to the experience of intoxication. Grasmick and Bursik (1990) suggested that drug use is "rewarding in and of itself, independent of any extrinsic rewards such behavior might produce [e.g., a sense of belonging in a group]" (p. 857). Hunt and Evans (2008) also reported that intoxication provided personal pleasure, but they emphasized its facilitation of social and communal cohesion.

The dominant theme in the literature is, however, that users interpret intoxication as a transcendent experience. Gregoire (1995) stressed that alcoholics drank to transcend the suffering self and find meaning in life. Trujillo (2004) described the meaning that users give to the crack cocaine experience at an ontological level. Intoxication is the supreme, though doomed, form of the feeling of being (*dasein*). This feeling may include transcending the mundane, being awed at the beauty of the world, and freeing the mind to reflect on the self and others.

Such descriptions of the positive effects of intoxication provide a clue to the addict's (or potential addict's) life without substances. A consistent discovery has been that drugs are a salve for a life that is "meaningless, monotonous and boring" (Narcotics Anonymous, 1982, p. 80). The outsider viewed addiction as a matter of morality, conditioning, self-medication from emotional pain, biological dependence, and fear of painful withdrawal. The insider keyed on a lack of belonging, boredom, fear, loneliness, meaninglessness, and other existential struggles.

Addiction as a Spiritual Disorder

Religion/Spirituality (RS) has gained increasing recognition in psychotherapy (W. R. Miller, 1999). RS has found a following in the addiction field (see Morgan, 2002, for a brief history), probably due to the impact of AA's 12 steps. Bill Wilson, cofounder of AA, stated that "An alcoholic is a fellow who is 'trying to get his religion out of a bottle,' when what he really wants is unity within himself, unity with God. . ." (cited in Dick B., 2005). Wilson was heavily influenced by the works of Carl Jung and William James. Jung (1961) told Wilson that alcoholism was a thirst for spirituality; the human being has a "spiritual need," a thirst to transcend the self through appeal to a higher power, which, if left unrecognized, would lead to "perdition," one form of which was alcoholism. According to Jung, there was no medicine for the alcoholic; only "spiritus contra spiritum," a spiritual awakening, could save the alcoholic. Wilson also found intellectual support from James. James (1902/1999) was the first psychologist to interpret a drug-induced altered state of consciousness as a "mystic experience" (p. 413), a variety of religious experience. The attraction of alcohol was "to stimulate the mystical faculties . . . [and drunkenness] makes its votary, for a moment, one with truth" (p. 421). Although hushed up in the AA program, historical accounts have recorded that Wilson used LSD during the 1950s to explore spirituality (Hartigan, 2000).

In the past decade and a half, mainstream psychology has become more interested in RS, catalyzed in great part by the rise of positive psychology (Emmons & Paloutzian, 2003). The American Psychological Association (APA) has published several books on RS, including W. R. Miller (1999), and just published a 1450-page handbook on religion, spirituality, and psychology (Pargament, 2013). These books have major sections on addiction. Beyond the APA, hundreds of journal articles have provided sufficient research for a growing number of meta-analyses of RS and addiction (Chitwood, Weiss, & Leukefeld, 2008; Cook, 2004; Longshore, Anglin, & Conner, 2009). And Geppert, Bogenschutz, and Miller (2007) discussed their development of a bibliography of religion, spirituality, and addictions.

Based on quantitative studies, we can say with confidence that there is some association between RS and addiction and RS and recovery (Connors, Walitzer, & Tonigan, 2008; Chitwood, Weiss, & Leukefeld, 2008; W. R. Miller, 1999). RS appears to be a protective factor against addiction. Jang, Bader, and Johnson (2008) used a developmental approach that concluded religiosity has a cumulative benefit in preventing drug use into the early 20s. RS has also consistently been shown to be associated with recovery. Piderman, Schneekloth, Pankratz, Maloney, & Altchuler, (2007), for example, found an increase in participants' spirituality during a 3-week outpatient treatment for alcoholism. E. A. R. Robinson, Cranford,

Well, and Brower (2007) found significant increases in RS variables during treatment, which were associated with recovery at 6 months after discharge.

In a provocative study, Piedmont (2004) conducted a hierarchical regression examining spiritual transcendence and personality factors in recovery from addiction. He found that spirituality accounted for variance beyond the five-factor model of personality.

Assessment of RS Theory and Therapy

The struggle to understand the link between RS and addiction/recovery is rooted in the struggle to define and measure RS. Concerned that the study of spirituality has to be more rigorous, Chitwood, Weiss, and Leukefeld (2008) declared that "our ability to make major advancements beyond broad statements. . . will be impeded until we become more conversant with the work of our colleagues whose primary work and expertise is in the field of measurement of religiosity and spirituality" (p. 674). Developing instruments is thus a priority for RS studies, and psychologists have so far created scales to measure any number of dimensions of RS, such as cognitive dimension of belief (Idler, 2003) and positive and negative RS coping (Pargament, 2003).

The barrier to progress is that instruments are based on wildly diverse conceptualizations of RS, which has resulted in no clearly defined major threads in the literature. Analyzing RS and drug research, Longshore, Anglin, and Conner (2009) lamented that the literature "lacks a fully emergent empirical framework to guide further study" (p. 177), and their review of the current work revealed that research tested only isolated hypotheses. Commentators routinely blamed this situation on eclectic conceptualizations of RS, which have led to an eclectic collection of studies (Longshore, Anglin & Conner, 2009; McCaroll-Butler, 2005; Rovers & Kocum, 2010).

Similarly, Cook (2004), in an analysis of 265 books and papers on RS and addiction from 1981 to 2001, concluded that definitions of RS were so contradictory that it was more productive for researchers to spend their time distinguishing between different conceptualizations of RS than it was to spend their time distinguishing RS from other constructs. He proposed we eliminate the term *spirituality* from the literature and use his 13 concepts—such as relatedness, transcendence, wholeness, creativity, values, and nonmateriality—which, he maintained, comprise spirituality.

Despite its fragmented interpretations of RS, psychology seems to have imposed limits on how RS is to be conceived. Almost all interpretations are linked to American theistic ideas, including Christian theology (Shorkey & Windsor, 2010) and nondenominational theology (Hill & Pargament, 2008). Even the

construct of spirituality is assumed to have a theistic premise. The typical definition of religion versus spirituality proposed that *religion* comprises some form of
institutionalized spirituality, whereas *spirituality* is a personal search for the sacred
(Hill & Pargament, 2008).

Likely due to the mainstream's narrow theistic conceptualization of RS, treatment programs based directly on RS and addiction research have found little or
no statistically significant effect on outcomes. W. R. Miller, Forcehimes, O'Leary,
and LaNoue (2008) created a 12-session, manualized spiritual guidance program
for alcoholics based on extensive quantitative studies on the link between RS and
addiction. The program had no effect on outcomes (White, 2008). Among other
questions, White (2008) wondered: "Does the essence of spiritual experience get
lost in efforts to artificially define and replicate it within a professional treatment
intervention?" (p. 443). Similarly, Avants, Beitel, and Margolin (2005) created the
spiritual self-schema program to help those in recovery shift from the addict self
to the spiritual self, but current outcome studies found no statistically significant
effects on achieving this spiritual identity (Amaro et al., 2010).

Even in the ubiquitous spiritual model of AA, success due directly to RS is
questionable. Tonigan (2007) summarized two decades of his and colleagues'
major research findings on the association between RS promoted by AA and
abstinence. This pool of research indicated that AA spirituality has little, if any,
direct impact on abstinence. There was, however, evidence of an indirect effect.
An increase in spirituality was positively related to continuing involvement in
AA, which was positively associated with abstinence. Tonigan thus rejected many
of the conclusions of those who argued that AA spirituality and abstinence are
strongly correlated. He pointed out that most of these studies were cross-sectional;
longitudinal studies reported that any link was, at best, modest.

Transpersonal Perspectives

Gregoire (1995), Trujillo (2004), Jung (1961), and Bill Wilson (cited in Dick
B., 2005) declared that the addict uses substances to transcend the self. But it
is a counterfeit transcendence, ephemeral and doomed. Although transpersonal
psychologists have not provided a theory of addiction, they have made a handful
of contributions to treatment. Moxley and Washington (2001) summed up these
efforts: "Ultimately, from a transpersonal perspective, recovery [from addiction]
is transcendent" (p. 256). They suggested that addiction "lowers their [addicts']
aspirations and expectations for themselves and for others" (p. 254) and "can narrow
a person's scope of vision, preventing them from even recognizing their connection
to a higher purpose and higher order" (p. 254). A transpersonal therapy, focused
on the addict's unique strengths and potentiality, within "the idea of recovery as a

heroic journey" (p. 255), would be more beneficial than mainstream treatments.

Nixon (2001; Chapter 8, this volume) applied Wilber's model in therapy. Although a client's drug use had helped him in connecting with others, it now mired him in "role confusion" (p. 87), the first level of the personal stage. By helping the client recognize that he was stuck in a peer-based addictive lifestyle, the client became aware that he was acting inauthentically. The client's narcissism stood out, a typical problem of this level. The client had developed a "myth" (p. 88) that he was a sports hero and party animal, which allowed him to feel a sense of belonging with his peers but which had become so pronounced as to block authentic living. Nixon's approach was to help the client move through this stage.

Amodia, Cano, and Eliason (2005) proposed an integral approach to addiction treatment, arguing that integral spirituality can help those in recovery to grow into transpersonal dimensions and can encompass multicultural conceptions of RS.

More controversially, at least in North America, Dyck (2008) surveyed research carried out in Saskatchewan, Canada, during the 1950s and 1960s, in which LSD was given to alcoholics as a therapeutic agent. According to Dyck, the LSD catalyzed in participants a more salutary perspective on their lives. In one study, 65% of participants quit drinking for at least 18 months, compared with 25% in a control group receiving group therapy. Dyck called for researchers to take a closer look at using psychedelics as treatment for addiction.

Transpersonal approaches have not gained much support in addiction treatment, likely because they are an affront to mainstream interpretations.

Logotherapy

Frankl (1980) reported publicly that he was not an expert in addictions. Despite this, he made comments throughout his books on its nature and treatment. His most direct conclusion was: "Alcoholism. . . [is] not understandable unless we recognize the existential vacuum underlying [it]" (Frankl, 1984, p. 124). Frankl (1980) was convinced that "filling up this vacuum may well be of primordial therapeutic value—nay, a prerequisite for therapeutic success, and in any event a decisive component in the rehabilitation of the chronic alcoholic" (p. x). A handful of theorists and therapists agreed.

Crumbaugh, Wood, and Wood (1980) developed a treatment for alcoholism based on the tenets of logotherapy. Their interpretation of Frankl was essentially a relational view, that "everybody has to have somebody in order to find a personal identity as Somebody" (p. 18). We come to know ourselves through others. In his treatment, Crumbaugh et al. provided a five-step process: choosing your view of life, building self-confidence, creative thinking, encounter, and deflection.

The choice of how to view one's life is either "Man is merely a machine" (p. 48) or "Man is a machine, but he is also infinitely more than a machine" (p. 49). The second and third steps refer to self-efficacy and determination to overcome obstacles, respectively. Encounter means connections with other beings. A belief that one can find meaning in finding the perfect job or playing music is not accurate; the value of these things for meaningful living is that they are vehicles that bring us into contact with others. Dereflection is one of Frankl's therapeutic techniques and, according to Crumbaugh et al., "is the core of the logotherapeutic process of searching for meaning and purpose in life" (p. 103). This technique helps the addict shift focus from failures and shortcomings to abilities, successes, and aptitudes. These were necessary for someone to find new goals and "discover tasks that will bring him into sufficient relationship with the 'significant others' in his life" (p. 103).

Somov (2007) applied logotherapy to his therapy group for addicts. Somov's meaning-in-life groups aimed at helping clients examine the basic principles of logotherapy: meaninglessness, adversity, self, presence, death, freedom, substance use, and transition. Unlike Crumbaugh's (Crumbaugh, Wood and Wood,1980) relational view, Somov believed that his group triggered an "intrapersonal dialogue" (Somov, 2007, p. 323). Arguing that Frankl saw meaning as a personal affair, Somov believed the focus on intrapersonal dialogue was more powerful than interpersonal relationships.

Assessment of Logotherapy

There are two major issues with logotherapy. First, although Batthyany and Guttman (2006) compiled an annotated bibliography of research in logotherapy, including a section on addiction, much more research is needed. Crumbaugh (Crumbaugh, Wood and Wood,1980) and others studied purpose in life in addicted populations; however, most of this research has been on treatments other than logotherapy. But a greater challenge lies in translating Frankl's ideas into psychological terms. Frankl was more a philosopher than a psychologist. His concept of dimensional ontology—of the somatic, psychic, and noëtic dimensions—is, for example, too diffuse and vague to study scientifically.

Despite these limitations, Frankl's (1984) proposition that the pursuit of personal meaning is a fundamental motivation has inspired or lent support to meaning-oriented theories. And Frankl's definition of addiction resonates with the 12-step philosophy.

Other Meaning-Oriented Models

Klinger. Klinger (1977) proposed a theory of motivation based on what he called *incentives*. "An incentive is any object or event that tends to attract a person"

(p. 6), such as an interesting job or merely the enjoyment of eating a sandwich. This was, he argued, the basis of living a meaningful life. "The more kinds of incentives people can respond to, the greater their sense of meaning" (p. 8). But people often hit barriers to achieving incentives. A person may strive hard to achieve something only to find it was not worth it. Or a person may discover that the cost of the incentive is too great. Or there may be insurmountable barriers to reaching the incentive. Such disappointments take a psychic toll. Since the pursuit of incentives conscripts attention, perception, and thought content, disengaging from an incentive "will set in motion a massive reorganization [of psychic life], a kind of psychic earthquake that will send shudders and rumbles through the person's life" (p. 137). Klinger called this the "incentive-disengagement cycle" (p. 138), a predictable sequence of events: invigoration, aggression, depression, and recovery.

He proposed that the artificial manipulation of affect through drugs could be understood as a response to "inadequate or disturbed incentives" (p. 281) or a response to the incentive-disengagement cycle. In other words, those who felt their lives were impoverished and boring, who felt lonely, anxious, or depressed, turned to the substance for positive affect.

Klinger's proposal was, thus, that the motivation to use drugs arose from a lack of meaningful living. Addiction becomes a risk if one's inner experience is a void. Overcoming addiction is a matter of motivation for an alternative incentive and commitment to pursue it (Klinger, 2012).

Narrative. Narrative theorists focus on how individuals construct meaning through narrative (Sommer, Baumeister, & Stillman, 2012). Singer (1997) examined the narratives of addicts in order to come to terms with the nature of addiction. He concluded that addiction was a problem of meaning. Those suffering from "chronic addiction either had never found sufficient meaning in a sober life or through years of addiction had squandered any meaning they had once possessed" (p. 17). In his attempts to make sense of addicts, Singer could "not reduce their struggle to the common denominator of a genetic defect or a physiological problem of control" (p. 17), or connect their psychosocial difficulties to the defects of character noted by AA. To understand addicts, one had to "take in the full dimensions of their lives—to see them as whole individuals struggling to achieve a sense of identity" (p. 17). This lack of identity "leads to a crisis in meaning" (p. 18). Borrowing Yalom's (1980) model, he described addicts as turning to the drug to provide relief from the existential anxieties of death, freedom, isolation, and meaninglessness.

The solution, for Singer, was to help addicts discover a sense of agency and community. He borrowed McAdams' (1993) narrative work on life stories.

According to McAdams, a life story answered two questions: *Who am I?* and *How do I fit in the world?* These are questions of agency and community. The answers addicts give to these questions are not responsive to what they want from life. Reconstructing the clients' stories helps them live according to their personal values, find comfort around others, and, if possible, attach their lives to something bigger than themselves.

Diamond (2000) was highly influenced by postmodernist thought and developed a narrative therapy for alcoholism. The title of Diamond's book, *Narrative Means to Sober Ends,* reflected the influence of White and Epston's (1990) *Narrative Means to Therapeutic Ends*. He proposed that the experience of addiction is a human experience, which has to be understood at an ontological level. As Robbins (2003) described Diamond's view, "We are at every moment of our lives faced with the nothingness that is our existence, with the gaping holes of our futures waiting to be filled" (p. 335). Diamond's therapy helps clients create a new story of their lives, one in which they are not victims of addiction; rather, clients construct a new "story of what it means to be human" (Robbins, 2003, p. 335).

Peele. Peele's (1998, 2004, 2007) work is essentially a meaning-centered model of addiction and recovery. Discontented with the mainstream view of addiction as a neurobiological pathology or a consequence of conditioning—"the compulsion to bypass human experience" (Peele, 1998, p. ix)—Peele maintained that "lived human experience and its interpretation are central to the incidence, course, treatment, and remission of addiction" (p. ix). While he wrote that the source of addiction was often the individual's lack of direction and weak self-efficacy (Peele, 2007), he also pointed out that those in active addiction tended to have superficial relationships and a disregard for others and community. None of this was conducive to living a fulfilling life. In other words, it was not intoxication that was the problem. Rather, drug use was a result of not living a meaningful life.

In treating addiction, Peele (2004; 2007) relied on many cognitive-behavioral techniques to live a balanced life. But he was particularly keen on motivational techniques, because they had the most viable research supporting taking responsibility for oneself. He also emphasized paying attention to "higher goals: pursuing and accomplishing things of value" (Peele, 2004, p. 194). Peele's approach thus highlighted personal responsibility and the pursuit of meaningful goals. The latter reflects the current movement interpreting well-being as *eudaimonia* (as opposed to *hedonia*), Aristotle's term for living a virtuous life. Deci and Ryan (2008) provided a primer on current research, concluding that happiness is likely the by-product of attaching one's life to moral action.

MEANING THEORY AS A THEORY OF ADDICTION

The interpretive frameworks of spirituality, logotherapy, incentive motivation, narrative, and Peele's meaning theory suggest that *personal meaning* may be a candidate for constructing a theory of addiction that encompasses existential-humanistic observations. Craving some transcendent, overarching force that provides meaning to existence, resolving issues of identity and belonging, choosing motivational incentives, achieving personal growth, moving beyond hedonic well-being to eudaimonic well-being, and constructing existence in some fashion that gives meaningful order to life are readily interpreted under the construct of personal meaning. Although different theorists offered different perspectives, they all agreed that "meaning in life thus refers to the understandings that we develop of who we are, what the world is like, and how we fit in with and relate to the grand scheme of things" (Steger, 2012, p. 165).

Addiction, then, as Frankl and Singer stated directly, is a response to living a life that lacks personal meaning. More than this, however, meaning theory is capable of integrating the big observations from mainstream and human science approaches. Such a theory would clearly be the most powerful to account for all the big observations.

Wong (2008; 2009; 2012a) proposed this idea. He maintained that meaning cannot be reduced to a single dimension or understood within a single school of psychology (Wong, 2012a). Rather, like existential psychology, meaning theory is an approach to understanding human beings, closer to an ontology. With its roots in logotherapy, meaning theory is best understood as a positive existential psychology. Wong (2009) reminded us that what makes an approach existential is not the methodologies used but the lens through which a phenomenon is viewed. One of the foundational principles of existential-humanistic psychology is its openness to different ways of knowing. Wong's theory integrates meaning research from different epistemologies and schools of psychology, using *personal meaning* as its organizing construct. This does not mean, however, that there is some unified body of thought on which meaning theory rests. Rather, different thinkers have promoted their own perspectives. Wong's first edition of *The Human Quest for Meaning* (Wong & Fry, 1998) was a major anthology of contributions from different schools of psychology; the second edition (Wong, 2012c) expanded the construct.

Meaning theory thus arises across disciplines and schools of psychology (Steger, 2012; Wong, 2012b). Applied to addictions, it obviates West's (2006) and Orford's (2001) complaint that mainstream theories are parochial and do not attend to ideas and evidence that conflict with the local argument. As we have seen, no organizing construct from mainstream or human science perspectives has been capable of making sense of all the big observations.

This is not to suggest that meaning is a panacea, but rather to suggest that meaning can work with empirical evidence from different theories and different epistemologies. Using personal meaning as an organizing construct welcomes multicultural perspectives. The will to meaning, to borrow Frankl's phrase, exists regardless of social and cultural environments. Wong (2008; McDonald, Wong, & Gingras, 2012) developed his Personal Meaning Profile (PMP) from sources of meaning that middle-class Canadians reported, such as agency, love, community, and self-transcendence. He reported that PMP was also used with different Asian cultures and concluded that "these sources appear to be universal" (Wong, 2008, p. 76). He welcomed Panksepp's (chapter 5, this volume) affective neuroscience research as supporting the meaning construct, though, of course, he refused to reduce a person to chemicals floating about the brain. Spiritual perspectives fit under the meaning umbrella. Pargament (2003) reported that "the search for meaning has also been defined as one of the critical functions of religion" (p. 19). Narrative is integral to meaning: "In its simplest terms, the meaning-centered approach emphasizes the human capacity for narrative construction and the healing and transforming power of meaning" (Dobson & Wong, 2008, p. 179).

All of this is to suggest that meaning theory is capable of integrating the big observations from different frameworks. It does, however, operate from certain assumptions.

Assumptions of Meaning Theory

Using meaning as an organizing construct demands several assumptions, including the following:

1. In line with Frankl (1984), Wong (2008) stated that meaning theory was anchored to the following proposition: "Humans have two primary motivations: (a) to survive, and (b) to find the meaning and reason for survival" (p. 72). If this theory can be considered reductionist, it is at the level of fundamental motivations, as opposed to analysis based on biology, traits or midlevel units of analysis of personality, or intrapsychic forces. The assumption is always that individuals have a need to make sense of their lives.

2. Human beings are "meaning-seeking and meaning-making creatures living in cultures based on shared meanings" (Wong, 2012d, p. 629).

3. Meaning is a multidimensional construct, which includes situational and existential meanings, subjective and objective meanings, and various

operationalizations of meaning, such as hardiness, meaning as relational, vocational meaning, self-determination, and autonomy (Wong, 2012d).

4. Responsibility for navigating through life rests with the individual. Although current psychology has shown that much of our behavior may be unconsciously motivated, we can still ask, with Yalom (1980), "Whose unconscious is it?" (p. 229).

Addiction as a Lack of Personal Meaning

A final assumption, in terms of addiction theory, is that addiction is a response to living a life that has little personal meaning. Although Wong is not an expert in addictions theory or treatment, meaning theory recognizes that addiction operates at the level of fundamental motivations, beyond neural adaptation, conditioning, self-medication, and beyond cultural constructions. This assumption also implies that addiction is not a pathology, in the sense that the mainstream promotes. Rather, it is more a misguided search for wholeness and belonging.

Meaning Therapy

If addiction is a response to a lack of meaningful living, then the solution ought to be to live a personally meaningful life. If true, this would go a long way to account for the poor success rates in current treatments. It does the addict little good to learn new coping skills, extinguish cues for drinking behaviors, and recognize internal conflicts between the motivation to use and the motivation to abstain if the addict cannot find a meaning and reason for abstinence. The benefits of intoxication, so graphically described in recent research (and in literary and philosophical accounts), have to be addressed. Recommending a life of healthy mindedness and good order is too weak to address existential dilemmas of boredom, loneliness, alienation, identity, and belonging (Thompson, 2012).

One controversial issue of using a meaning framework is that abstinence is not the prerequisite or first stage in recovery. Rather, abstinence is the by-product of living a personally meaningful life. Perhaps because this thesis is an affront to mainstream theory and treatment, few researchers have pursued it. One exception is White (2004), who studied how seven alcoholics achieved sobriety. He concluded that they had undergone a "transformational change" (p. 461), which had obviated their desire for alcohol. Similarly, Thompson (2006) described how Nobel Prize-winning author Eugene O'Neill chose to be abstinent only after he recognized that drunkenness was a dissolution of the self. For the writer who heralded the greatness of the single individual, a loss of self was unacceptable.

But the application of meaning therapy in addiction treatment is not well developed. We cannot comfortably conclude that it would significantly improve treatment outcomes, only that it offers promise of injecting a new energy and direction.

CONCLUSION

This survey of addiction theories presented three sets of big observations about addiction. Positivist psychology offers one perspective, which most addiction experts adhere to. Sellman (2009) summarized "the most important things we know about addiction" (p. 6); his top three were: "(1) addiction is fundamentally about compulsive behavior; (2) compulsive drug seeking is initiated outside of consciousness; and (3) addiction is about 50% heritable and complexity abounds" (p. 6). Human science offers another set of big observations, which interpret addiction not as the effects of drugs on the person, but as a cultural construction. Existential-humanistic psychologists offer a third set of big observations, principally derived from a phenomenology of drugs and consciousness.

These three perspectives are difficult to reconcile, and no organizing construct or discipline has yet been proposed that can make sense of them. Interpreting addiction using *personal meaning* as an organizing construct appears to be a good possibility. Arising within an approach to understanding human nature rather than a school of psychology or discipline, and as an existential psychology and thus open to different ways of knowing, meaning theory appears well suited to the task. It is instructive to note that meaning as an organizing principle is not limited to psychology. For example, after philosophy's postmodern turn to linguistics in the 20th century, many philosophers are now looking to meaning to provide some standard for understanding human nature. Eagleton (2007), Flanagan (2007), Levinas (1998), Macmurray (1999), and Polanyi and Prosch (1975) are among those whose focus now is meaning oriented. Meaning as a fundamental motivation in life appears to have widespread attraction.

Interpreting addiction as a response to a lack of meaningful living may also provide a partial answer to Bickel and Potenza's (2006) question, "Why is addiction so difficult to treat?" (p. 8). A therapy that reaches beyond neural adaptation or conditioning and into fundamental motivations may prove more efficacious than our current fare.

REFERENCES

Alexander, B. K., Beyerstein, B. L., Hadaway, P. F., & Coambs, R. B. (1981). Effect of early and later colony housing on oral ingestion of morphine in rats. *Pharmacology Biochemistry and Behavior, 15*, 571–576. doi:10.1016/0091-3057(81)90211-2

Alexander, B. K. (2010). *The globalization of addiction: A study in poverty of the spirit.* New York, NY: Oxford.

American Psychiatric Association. (2000). *Diagnostic and statistical manual of mental disorders* (4th ed., text rev.). Washington, DC: American Psychiatric Association.

American Society of Addiction Medicine. (2012). *Public policy statement: Definition of addiction.* Retrieved from http://asam.org /for-the-public/definition-of-addiction

Amaro, H., Magno-Gatmaytan, C., Melendez, M, Cortes, D. E., Arevalo, S, & Margolin, A. (2010). Addiction treatment intervention: An uncontrolled prospective pilot study of Spiritual Self-Schema Therapy with Latina women. *Substance Abuse, 31*(2), 117–125. doi:10.1080/08897071003641602

Amodia, D. S., Cano, C., & Eliason, M. J. (2005). An integral approach to substance abuse. *Journal of Psychoactive Drugs, 37*(4), 363–371. doi; 10.1080/02791072.2005.10399809

Annis, H. M., Herie, M. A., & Watkin-Merek, L. (1997). Structured relapse prevention. In S. Harrison & V. Carver (Eds.), *Alcohol & drug problems: A practical guide for counsellors* (2nd ed., pp. 141–159). Toronto, Canada: Addiction Research Foundation.

Avants, S. K., Beitel, M., & Margolin, A. (2005). Making the shift from 'addict self' to 'spiritual self': Results from a stage 1 study of Spiritual Self-Schema (3-S) therapy for the treatment of addiction and HIV risk behavior. *Mental Health, Religion & Culture, 8*(3), 167–177. doi:10.1080/13694670500138924

Baars, B. J., & Gage, N. M. (2010). *Cognition, brain, and consciousness: Introduction to cognitive neuroscience* (2nd ed.). New York, NY: Academic Press.

Ballinger, B., Matano, R. B., & Amantea, A. C. (2008). A perspective on alcoholism: The case of Charles. In K. J. Schneider (Ed.), *Existential-integrative psychotherapy: Guideposts to the core of practice* (pp. 177–185). New York, NY: Routledge.

Bandura, A. (1986). *Social foundations of thought and action: A social cognitive theory.* Englewood Cliffs, NJ: Prentice-Hall.

Bandura, A. (1997). *Self-efficacy: The exercise of control.* New York, NY: Freeman.

Batthyany, A., & Guttman, D. (2006). *Empirical research on logotherapy and meaning-oriented psychotherapy: An annotated bibliography.* Phoenix, AZ: Zeig, Tucker & Theisen.

Becker, G. S., & Murphy, K. M. (1988). A theory of rational addiction. *Journal of Political Economy, 96*(4), 675–699. doi:10.1086/261558

Berridge, K. C. (2012). From prediction error to incentive salience: Mesolimbic computation of reward motivation. *European Journal of Neuroscience, 35*, 1124–1143. doi:10.1111/j.1460-9568.2012.07990.x

Berridge, K. C., & Robinson, T. E. (2006). Automatic processes in addiction: A commentary. In R. W. Wiers & A. W. Stacy (Eds.), *Handbook of implicit cognition and addiction* (pp. 477–481). Thousand Oaks, CA: Sage.

Bickel, W. K., & Potenza, M. N. (2006). The forest and the trees: Addiction as a complex self-organizing system. In W. R. Miller & K. M. Carroll (Eds.), *Rethinking substance abuse: What the science shows and what we should do about it* (pp. 8–24). New York, NY: Guilford.

Blaszczynski, A., & Nower, L. (2002). A pathways model of problem and pathological gambling. *Addiction, 97*(5), 487–499. doi:10.1046/j.1360-0443.2002.00015.x

Boudreau, R. J. (1997). Addiction and the family. In S. Harrison & V. Carver (Eds.), *Alcohol & drug problems: A practical guide for counsellors* (2nd ed., pp. 407–418). Toronto, Canada: Addiction Research Foundation.

Bowen, M. (1985). *Family therapy in clinical practice.* Northvale, NJ: Jason Aronson.

Carroll, L. (1920). *Alice's adventures in wonderland.* New York, NY: Macmillan. Available as eBook at http://cs.cmu.edu/~rgs/alice-table.html

Childress, A. R., McLellan, A. T., Ehrman, R., & O'Brien, C. P. (1988). Classically conditioned responses in opioid and cocaine dependence: A role in relapse? *National Institute of Drug Abuse Research Monograph, 84,* 25–43.

Chitwood, D. D., Weiss, M. L., & Leukefeld, C. G. (2008). A systematic review of recent literature on religiosity and substance use. *Journal of Drug Issues, 38*(3), 653–688. doi:10.1177/002204260803800302

Connors, G. J., Walitzer, K. S., & Tonigan, J. S. (2008). Spiritual change in recovery. In M. Galanter & L. A. Kaskutas (Eds.), *Recent developments in alcoholism: Research on Alcoholics Anonymous and spirituality in addiction recovery* (pp. 209–227). New York, NY: Springer.

Cook, C. C. H. (2004). Addiction and spirituality. *Addiction, 99,* 539–551. doi:10.1111/j.1360-0443.2004.00715.x

Crumbaugh, J. C, Wood, W. M., & Wood, W. C. (1980). *Logotherapy: New help for problem drinkers.* Chicago, IL: Nelson-Hall.

Deci, E. L., & Ryan, R. M. (2008). Hedonia, eudaimonia, and well-being: An introduction. *Journal of Happiness Studies, 9,* 1–11. doi:10.1007/s10902-006-9018-1

De Quincey, T. (1986). *Confessions of an English opium eater.* Toronto, Canada: Penguin. (Original work published 1821)

Diamond, J. (2000). *Narrative means to sober ends: Treating addiction and its aftermath.* New York, NY: Guilford.

Dick B. (2005). 1943 [sic] remarks of Bill W. with Dr. Bob on A.A.'s need for God, religion, and the Bible. Retrieved from http://silkworth.net/dickb/remarks.html

Dick, D. M., & Agrawal, A. (2008). The genetics of alcohol and other drug dependence. *Alcohol Research & Health, 31*(2), 111–118. Retrieved from http://pubs.niaaa.nih.gov/publications/arh312/111-118.pdf

Dickerson, V. C. (2010). Positioning oneself within an epistemology: Refining our thinking about integrative approaches. *Family Process, 49*(3), 349–368. doi:10.1111/j.1545-5300.2010.01327.x

Dingel, M. J., Hammer, R., Ostergren, J. E., McCormick, J. B., & Koenig, B. A. (2012). Chronic addiction, compulsion, and the empirical evidence. *AJOB Neuroscience, 3*(2), 58–59. doi:10.1080/21507740.2012.665411

Dobson, W. L., & Wong, P. T. P. (2008). Women living with HIV: The role of meaning and spirituality. In A. Tomer, G. T. Eliason, & P. T. P. Wong (Eds.), *Existential and spiritual issues in death acceptance* (pp. 173–207). New York, NY: Lawrence Erlbaum.

Drummond, D. C. (2001). Theories of drug craving, ancient and modern. *Addiction, 96*(1), 33–46. doi:10.1046/j.1360-0443.2001.961333.x

Dyck, E. (2008). 'Hitting highs at rock bottom': LSD treatment for alcoholism, 1950–1970. *Social History of Medicine, 19*(2), 313–329. doi:10.1093/shm/hkl039

Eagleton, T. (2007). *The meaning of life: A very short introduction.* New York, NY: Oxford.

Emmons, R. A., & Paloutzian, R. F. (2003). The psychology of religion. *Annual Review of Psychology, 54*, 377–402. doi:10.1146/annurev.psych.54.101601.145024

Fals-Stewart, W., O'Farrell, T. J., & Bircher, G. R. (2004). Behavioral couples therapy for substance abuse: Rationale, methods, and findings. *Scientific Practice Perspectives 2*(2), 30–41. Retrieved from http://pmcc.web-t.cisti.nrc.ca/articlerender.cgi?artid=1725895 doi:10.1151/spp042230

Ferentzy, P. (2001). From sin to disease: Differences and similarities between past and current conceptions of chronic drunkenness. *Contemporary Drug Problems, 28*(3), 363–390.

Fingarette, H. (1988). *Heavy drinking: The myth of alcoholism as a disease.* Berkeley, CA: University of California Press.

Flanagan, O. (2007). *The really hard problem: Meaning in a material world.* Cambridge: MIT Press.

Foucault, M. (1965). *Madness and civilization: A history of insanity in the age of reason.* New York, NY: Random House.

Frankl, V. E. (1980). Foreword. In J. C. Crumbaugh, W. M. Wood, & W. C. Wood, *Logotherapy: New help for problem drinkers.* Chicago, IL: Nelson-Hall.

Frankl, V. E. (1984). *Man's search for meaning.* New York, NY: Vintage.

Geppert, C., Bogenschutz, M. P., & Miller, W. R. (2007). Development of a bibliography on religion, spirituality, and addictions. *Drug and Alcohol Review, 26*(4), 389–395. doi:10.1080/09595230701373826

Gladwell, M. (2010, February 15 & 22). Annals of anthropology: Drinking games: How much people drink may matter less than how they drink it. *The New Yorker, 86*(1), 70–76.

Grasmick, H. G., & Bursik, R. J., Jr. (1990). Conscience, significant others, and rational choice: Extending the deterrence model. *Law and Society Review, 24*, 837–861. doi:10.2307/3053861

Gregoire, T. K. (1995). Alcoholism: The quest for transcendence and meaning. *Clinical Social Work Journal, 23*(3), 339–359. doi:10.1007/BF02191755

Griffin, C., Measham, F., Moore, K., Morey, Y., & Riley, S. (2008). The social and cultural uses of ketamine. *Addiction Research and Theory, 16*(3), 205–207. doi:10.1080/16066350801983731

Hartigan, F. (2000). *Bill W.: A biography of Alcoholics Anonymous cofounder Bill Wilson*. New York, NY: Thomas Dunne.

Hayes, S. C. (2004). Acceptance and Commitment Therapy and the new behavior therapies: Mindfulness, acceptance, and relationship. In S. C. Hayes, V. M. Follette, & M. M. Linehan (Eds.), *Mindfulness and acceptance: Expanding the cognitive-behavioral tradition* (pp. 1–29). New York, NY: Guilford.

Health Canada. (1999). *Best practices: Substance abuse treatment and rehabilitation*. Ottawa, Canada: Government of Canada.

Heath, D. B. (1995). An anthropological view of alcohol and culture in international perspective. In D. B. Heath (Ed.), *International handbook on alcohol and culture* (pp. 328–347). Greenwood Press, Westport, CT: Greenwood Press.

Herrnstein, R. J., & Prelec, D. (1992). A theory of addiction. In G. Loewenstein & J. Elster (Eds.), *Choice over time* (pp. 331–359). New York, NY: Russell Sage Foundation.

Hester, R. K., & Miller, W. R. (2003). *Handbook of alcoholism treatment approaches: Effective alternatives* (3rd ed.). New York, NY: Allyn and Bacon.

Heyman, G. M. (2009). *Addiction: A disorder of choice*. Cambridge, MA: Harvard.

Hill, P. C., & Pargament, K. I. (2008). Advances in the conceptualization and measurement of religion and spirituality: Implications for physical and mental health research. *Psychology of Religion and Spirituality, S*(1), 3–17. doi:10.1037/1941-1022.S.1.3

Hunt, G. M., & Azrin, N. H. (1973). A community-reinforcement approach to alcoholism. *Behaviour Research and Therapy, 11*, 91–104. doi:10.1016/0005-7967(73)90072-7

Hunt, G. P., & Evans, K. (2008). 'The great unmentionable': Exploring the pleasures and benefits of ecstasy from the perspectives of drug users. *Drugs: Education, prevention and policy, 15*(4), 329–349. doi:10.1080/09687630701726841

Huxley, A. (1990). *The doors of perception and Heaven and hell*. Toronto, Canada: HarperCollins. (Original work published 1956)

Idler, E. (2003). Beliefs. In *Multidimensional measurement of religiousness/spirituality for use in health research: A report of the Fetzer Institute/National Institute on Aging working group* (pp. 31–33). Kalamazoo, MI: Fetzer Institute.

James, W. (1999). *The varieties of religious experience: A study in human nature*. Toronto, Canada: Random House. (Original work published 1902)

Jang, S. J., Bader, C. D., Johnson, B. R. (2008). The cumulative advantage of religiosity in preventing drug use. *Journal of Drug Issues, 38*(3), 772–798. doi:10.1177/002204260803800306

Jellinek, E. M. (1960). *The disease concept of alcoholism*. New Haven, CT: Hillhouse.

Johnson, J. L., Ahmed, A., Plemons, B., Powell, W., Carrington, H., Graham, J., . . . Brooner, R. K. (2002). *Steps to success: Baltimore drug and alcohol treatment outcomes study*. MD: Baltimore Substance Abuse Systems, Inc.

Jung, C. G. (1961, January 30). Dr. Carl Jung's letter to Bill Wilson. Available at http://silkworth.net/aahistory/carljung_billw013061.html

Khantzian, E. J. (1997). The self-medication hypothesis of substance use disorders: A reconsideration and recent applications. *Harvard Review of Psychiatry, 4*(5), 231–244. doi:10.3109/10673229709030550

Klinger, E. (1977). *Meaning & void: Inner experiences and the incentives in people's lives.* Minneapolis: University of Minnesota.

Klinger, E. (2012). The search for meaning in evolutionary goal-theory perspective and its clinical applications. In P. T. P. Wong (Ed.), *The human quest for meaning: Theories, research, and applications* (2nd ed., pp. 23–56). New York, NY: Routledge.

Kurtz, E. (1999). The historical context. In W. R. Miller (Ed.), *Integrating spirituality into treatment: Resources for practitioners* (pp. 19–46). Washington, DC: American Psychological Association.

Lemanski, M. (2001). *A history of addiction & recovery in the United States.* Tucson, AZ: The Sharp Press.

Lenson, D. (1995). *On drugs.* Minneapolis: University of Minnesota.

Leshner, A. (1997). Addiction is a brain disease. *Science, 278*(5335), 45–47. doi:10.1126/science.278.5335.45

Levinas, E. (1998). *Entre nous: On thinking-of-the-other.* New York, NY: Columbia University.

Levine, H. G. (1978). The discovery of addiction: Changing conceptions of habitual drunkenness in America. *Journal of Studies on Alcohol, 39,* 143–174. doi:10.1016/0740-5472(85)90022-4

Longshore, D., Anglin, M. D., & Conner, B. T. (2009). Are religiosity and spirituality useful constructs in drug treatment research? *Journal of Behavioral Health Services & Research, 36*(2), 177–188. doi:10.1007/s11414-008-9152-0

Luborsky, L., Rosenthal, R., Diguer, L., Andrusyna, T. P., Berman, J. S., Levitt, J. T., . . . Drause, E. D. (2002) The dodo bird verdict is alive and well—mostly. *Clinical Psychology: Science and Practice, 9*(1), 2–12. doi:10.1093/clipsy/9.1.2

Luoma, J. B., Twohig, M. P., Waltz, T., Hayes, S. C., Roget, N., Padilla, M., & Fisher, G. (2007). An investigation of stigma in individuals receiving treatment for substance abuse. *Addictive Behaviors, 32*(7), 1331–1346. doi:10.1016/j.addbeh.2006.09.008

MacAndrew, C., & Edgerton, R. B. (1969). *Drunken comportment: A social explanation.* London, UK: Aldine.

Macmurray, J. (1999). *Persons in relation.* New York, NY: Humanity Books.

Marlatt, G. A. (1985). Relapse prevention: Theoretical rationale and overview of the model. In G. A. Marlatt & J. R. Gordon (Eds.), *Relapse prevention: Maintenance strategies in the treatment of addictive behaviors* (pp. 3–70). New York, NY: Guilford.

Marlatt, G. A. (Ed.). (1998). *Harm reduction: Pragmatic strategies for managing high-risk behaviors.* New York, NY: Guilford.

Marlatt, G. A., Demming, B., & Reid, J. B. (1973). Loss of control drinking in alcoholics: An experimental analogue. *Journal of Abnormal Psychology, 81,* 233–241. doi:10.1037/h0034532

Marlatt, G. A., & Donovan, D. M. (Eds.). (2005). *Relapse prevention: Maintenance strategies in the treatment of addictive behaviors* (2nd ed.). New York, NY: Guilford.

Marlatt, G. A., & Witkiewitz, K. (2005). Relapse prevention for alcohol and drug problems. In G. A. Marlatt & D. M. Donovan (Eds.), *Relapse prevention: Maintenance strategies in the treatment of addictive behaviors* (2nd ed., pp. 1–44). New York, NY: Guilford.

McAdams, D. P. (1993). *The stories we live by: Personal myths and the making of the self.* New York, NY: Guilford.

McCaroll-Butler, P. (2005). Assessing plurality in spirituality definitions. In A. Meier, T. O'Connor, & P. Vankatwyk (Eds.), *Spirituality and health: Multidisciplinary explorations.* Waterloo, Canada: Wilfred University Press.

McDonald, M. J., Wong, P. T. P., & Gingras, D. T. (2012). Meaning-in-life measures and the development of a brief version of the Personal Meaning Profile. In P. T. P. Wong (Ed.), *The human quest for meaning: Theories, research, and applications* (2nd ed., pp. 357–382). New York, NY: Routledge.

McLellan, A. T. (2002). Have we evaluated addiction treatment correctly? Implications from a chronic care perspective. *Addiction, 97*(3), 249–252. doi:10.1046/j.1360-0443.2002.00127.x

Miller, N. S. (1995). History and review of contemporary addiction treatment. *Alcoholism Treatment Quarterly 12*(2), 1–22. doi:10.1300/J020v12n02_01

Miller, N. S., & Hoffmann, N. G. (1995). Addictions treatment outcomes. *Alcoholism Treatment Quarterly, 12*(2), 41–55. doi:10.1300/J020v12n02_03

Miller, S. D., Hubble, M., & Duncan, B. (2007, November/December). Supershrinks: What is the secret of their success? *Psychotherapy Networker* [Online]. Available at http://www.psychotherapynetworker.org

Miller, W. R. (1995). *Motivational enhancement therapy with drug abusers.* [Therapist manual]. Albuquerque: University of New Mexico.

Miller, W. R. (Ed.). (1999). *Integrating spirituality into treatment: Resources for practitioners.* Washington, DC: American Psychological Association.

Miller, W. R., & Carroll, K. M. (Eds.). (2006). *Rethinking substance abuse: What the science shows, and what we should do about it.* New York, NY: Guilford.

Miller, W. R., Forcehimes, A., O'Leary, M., & LaNoue, M. (2008). Spiritual direction in addiction treatment: Two clinical trials. *Journal of Substance Abuse Treatment, 35*(4), 434–442. doi:10.1016/j.jsat.2008.02.004

Miller, W. R., & Rollnick, S. (2013). *Motivational interviewing: Helping people change* (3rd ed.). New York, NY: Guilford.

Miller, W. R., & White, W. (2007). Confrontation in addiction treatment. Retrieved from http://counselormagazine.com

Morgan, O. J. (2002). Spirituality, alcohol and other drug problems: Where have we been, where are we going? *Alcoholism Treatment Quarterly, 20*(3/4), 61–82. doi:10.1300/J020v20n03_04

Moxley, D. P., & Washington, O. G. M. (2001). Strengths-based recovery practice in chemical dependency: A transpersonal perspective. *Families in Society: The Journal of Contemporary Human Services, 82*(3), 251–262. doi:10.1606/1044-3894.198

Narcotics Anonymous. (1982). *Narcotics Anonymous (basic text)*. Van Nuys, CA: NA World Services.

NIDA. (2009). *Principles of drug addiction treatment: A research-based guide* (2nd ed.). NIH Publication No. 09-4180. Bethesda, MD: National Institute of Drug Abuse.

Nixon, G. (2001). Using Wilber's transpersonal model of psychological and spiritual growth in alcoholism treatment. *Alcoholism Treatment Quarterly, 19*(1), 79–95. doi:10.1300/J020v19n01_06

Nixon, G. (2013). Transforming the addicted person's counterfeit quest for wholeness using Wilber's transpersonal spectrum of development: A clinical perspective. In L. C. J. Wong, G. R. Thompson, & P. T. P. Wong (Eds.), *The positive psychology of meaning and addiction recovery* (pp. 77–104). Birmingham, AL: Purpose Research.

Norcross, J. C. (2005). A primer on psychotherapy integration. In J. C. Norcross & M. R. Goldfried (Eds.), *Handbook of psychotherapy integration* (pp. 3–23). New York, NY: Oxford.

O'Farrell, T. J., & Fals-Stewart, W. (2006). *Behavioral couples therapy for alcoholism and drug abuse*. New York, NY: Guilford.

Ogborne, A. C. (1997). Theories of 'addiction' and implications for counseling. In S. Harrison & V. Carver (Eds.), *Alcohol & drug problems: A practical guide for counsellors* (2nd ed., pp. 3–18). Toronto, Canada: Addiction Research Foundation.

Orford, J. (2001). Addiction as excessive appetite. *Addiction, 96*(1), 15–31. doi:10.1046/j.1360-0443.2001.961152.x

Owen, P. (2000). Minnesota Model: Description of counseling approach. In J. Boren, L. Onken, & K. Carroll (Eds.), *Approaches to Drug Abuse Counseling* (pp. 117–126). Bethesda, MD: National Institute of Drug Abuse.

Panksepp, J. (2013). The affective basis of drug and social addiction. In L. C. J. Wong, G. R. Thompson, & P. T. P. Wong (Eds.), *The positive psychology of meaning and addiction recovery* (pp. 37–46). Birmingham, AL: Purpose Research.

Pargament, K. I. (2003). Meaning. In Fetzer Institute, *Multidimensional measurement of religiousness/spirituality for use in health research: A report of the Fetzer Institute/National Institute on Aging Working Group* (pp. 19–24). Kalamazoo, MI: Fetzer Institute.

Pargament, K. I. (2013). *APA handbook of psychology, religion, and spirituality.* Washington, DC: American Psychological Association.

PARINT. (2011). *Resources for authors.* Retrieved June 12, 2012, from http://www.parint.org

Peele, S. (1986). The life study of alcoholism: Putting drunkenness in biographical context. *Bulletin of the Society of Psychologists in Addictive Behaviors* 5(1), 49–53. doi:10.1037//0893-164X.5.1.49

Peele, S. (1998). *The meaning of addiction: An unconventional view.* San Francisco, CA: Jossey-Bass.

Peele, S. (2004). *7 tools to beat addiction.* New York, NY: Three Rivers.

Peele, S. (2007). *Addiction-proof your child: A realistic approach to preventing drug, alcohol, and other dependencies.* New York, NY: Three Rivers.

Piderman, K. M., Schneekloth, T. D., Pankratz, V. S., Maloney, S. D., & Altchuler, S. I. (2007). Spirituality in alcoholics during treatment. *The American Journal on Addictions, 16,* 232–237. doi:10.1080/10550490701375616

Piedmont, R. L. (2004). Spiritual transcendence as a predictor of psychosocial outcome from an outpatient substance abuse program. *Psychology of Addictive Behaviors, 18*(3), 213–222. doi:10.1037/0893-164X.18.3.213

Polanyi, M., & Prosch, H. (1975). *Meaning.* IL: University of Chicago.

Polich, J. M, Armor, D. J., & Braiker, H. B. (1980). *The course of alcoholism: Four years after treatment.* Santa Monica, CA: Rand.

Prochaska, J. O., Norcross, J., & DiClemente, C. (1995). *Changing for good.* New York, NY: Avon.

Project MATCH. (1997). *Matching alcoholism treatments to client heterogeneity: Project MATCH posttreatment drinking outcomes.* Bethesda, MD: National Institute on Alcohol Abuse and Alcoholism. NIH Pub. No. 01-4238.

Rabin, D. (2005). Drunkenness and responsibility for crime in the eighteenth century. *Journal of British Studies, 44,* 457–477. doi:10.1086/429705

Rawson, R., Obert, J. L., McCann, M. J., & Ling, W. (2005). *The matrix model: Intensive outpatient alcohol & drug treatment.* Center City, MN: Hazelden.

Richert, A. J. (2011). Johnson's philosophy of personal meaning and theoretical integration. *Journal of Psychotherapy Integration, 21*(4), 400–412. doi:10.1037/a0026723

Robbins, B. D. (2003). Book reviews: Narrative means to sober ends: Treating addiction and its aftermath. *Janus Head, 6*(2), 333–336.

Robinson, E. A. R., Cranford, J. A., Webb, J. R., & Brower, K. J. (2007). Six-month changes in spirituality, religiousness, and heavy drinking in a treatment-seeking sample. *Journal of Studies on Alcohol and Drugs, 68*(2), 282–290.

Robinson, T. E., & Berridge, K. C. (1993). The neural basis of drug cravings: An incentive-sensitization theory of addiction. *Brain Research Review, 18*, 247–291. doi:10.1016/0165-0173(93)90013-P

Robinson, T. E., & Berridge, K. C. (2001). Incentive-sensitization and addiction. *Addiction, 96*, 103–114. doi:10.1080/09652140020016996

Robinson, T. E., & Berridge, K. C. (2003). Addiction. *Annual Review of Psychology, 54*, 25–53. doi:10.1146/annurev.psych.54.101601.145237

Robson, C. (2002). *Real world research: A resource for social scientists and practitioner-researchers* (2nd ed.). Malden, MA: Blackwell.

Room, R. (2003). The cultural framing of addiction. *Janus Head 6*(2), 221–234.

Roth, M. (2004). The golden age of drinking and the fall into addiction. *Janus Head 7*(1), 11–33.

Rovers, M., & Kocum, L. (2010). Development of a holistic model of spirituality. *Journal of Spirituality in Mental Health, 12*(1), 2–24. doi:10.1080/19349630903495475

Schulteis, G., Heyser, C. J., & Koob, G. F. (1999). Differential expression of response-disruptive and somatic indices of opiate withdrawal during the initiation and development of opiate dependence. *Behavioral Pharmacology, 10*(3), 235–242. doi:10.1097/00008877-199905000-00001

Seeburger, F. F. (1993). *Addiction and responsibility: An inquiry into the addictive mind.* New York, NY: Crossroad.

Sellman, D. (2009). The 10 most important things known about addiction. *Addiction, 105*, 6–13. doi:10.1111/j.1360-0443.2009.02673.x

Shen, X. Y., Orson, F. M., 7 Kosten, T. R. (2012). Vaccines against drug abuse. *Clinical Pharmacology & Therapeutics, 91*(1), 60–70. doi:10.1038/clpt.2011.281

Shorkey, C. T., & Windsor, L. C. (2010). Inventory of spirituality in alcohol/drug research: Psychometric dimensions. *Alcoholism Treatment Quarterly, 28*, 17–37. doi:10.1080/07347320903436227

Singer, J. A. (1997). *Message in a bottle: Stories of men and addiction.* Toronto, ON: The Free Press.

Slife, B. D., & Williams, R. N. (1995). *What's behind the research? Discovering hidden assumptions in the behavioral sciences.* Thousand Oaks, CA: Sage.

Sommer, K. L., Baumeister, R. F., Stillman, T. F. (2012). The construction of meaning from life events: Empirical studies on personal narratives. In P. T. P. Wong (Ed.), *The human quest for meaning: Theories, research, and applications* (2nd ed., pp. 297–313). New York, NY: Routledge.

Somov, P. G. (2007). Meaning in life group: Group application of logotherapy for substance abuse treatment. *The Journal of Specialists in Group Work, 32*(4), 316–345. doi:10.1080/01933920701476664

Steger, M. F. (2012). Experiencing meaning in life: Optimal functioning at the nexus of well-being, psychopathology, and spirituality. In P. T. P. Wong (Ed.), *The human quest for meaning: Theories, research, and applications* (2nd ed., pp. 165–184). New York, NY: Routledge.

Steinglass, P. (2009). Systemic-motivational therapy for substance use disorders: An integrative model. *Journal of Family Therapy, 31*(2), 155–174. doi:10.1111/j.1467-6427.2009.00460.x

Steinglass, P., Bennett, L. A., Wolin, S. J., & Reiss, D. (1987). *The alcoholic family.* New York, NY: Basic Books.

Stephens, D. N. (2006). Animal models/tests of drug addiction: A quest for the holy grail, or the pursuit of wild geese? *Addiction Biology, 11*, 19–42. doi:10.1111/j.1355-6215.2006.00010.x

Stephens, G. L. & Graham, G. (2009). An addictive lesson: A case study in psychiatry as cognitive neuroscience. In M. R. Broome & L. Bortolotti (Eds.), *Psychiatry as cognitive neuroscience: Philosophical perspectives* (pp. 203–220). New York, NY: Oxford.

Stoffelmayr, B. E., Mavis, B. E., & Kasim, R. M. (1998). Substance abuse treatment staff: Recovery status and approaches to treatment. *Journal of Drug Education, 28*(2), 135–145. doi:10.2190/32ar-g628-ahpd-gb6u

Suh, J. J., Ruffins, S., Robins, C. E., Albanese, M. J. & Khantzian, E. J. (2008). Self-medication hypothesis: Connecting affective experience and drug choice. *Psychoanalytic Psychology, 25*(3), 518–532. doi:10.1037/0736-9735.25.3.518

Taleff, M. J., & Babcock, M. (1998). Hidden themes: Dominant discourses in the alcohol and other drug field. *The International Journal of Drug Policy, 9*(1), 33–41. doi:10.1016/S0955-3959(97)00005-4

Thatcher, D. L., & Clark, D. B. (2008). Adolescents at risk for substance use disorders. *Alcohol Research & Health, 31*(2), 168–176. Retrieved from http://pubs.niaaa.nih.gov/publications/arh312/168-176.pdf

Thompson, G. (2006). *A long night's journey into day: A psychobiography of Eugene O'Neill's recovery from alcoholism.* Abbotsford, BC: INPM.

Thompson, G. (2012). A meaning-centered therapy for addictions. *International Journal of Mental Health and Addiction, 10*(3), 428–440. doi:10.1007/s11469-011-9367-9

Tomkins, D. M., & Sellers, E. M. (2001). Addiction and the brain: The role of neurotransmitters in the cause and treatment of drug dependence. *Canadian Medical Association Journal, 164*(6), 817–821.

Tonigan, J. S. (2007). Spirituality and Alcoholics Anonymous. *Southern Medical Journal, 100*(4), 437–440. doi:10.1097/SMJ.0b013e31803171ef

Trujillo, J. (2004). An existential-phenomenology of crack cocaine abuse. *Janus Head*, 7(1), 167–187. Retrieved from http://www.janushead.org/7-1/index.cfm

Vaillant, G. E. (1995). *The natural history of alcoholism revisited*. Cambridge, MA: Harvard.

Vaillant, G. E. (2013). *Alcoholics Anonymous: Cult or cure?* In L. C. J. Wong, G. R. Thompson, & P. T. P. Wong (Eds.), *The positive psychology of meaning and addiction recovery* (pp. 21–30). Birmingham, AL: Purpose Research.

Volkow, N. D., Wang, G.-J., Telang, F., Fowler, J. S., Logan, J., Jayne, M., . . . Wong, C. (2007). Profound decreases in dopamine release in striatum in detoxified alcoholics: Possible orbitofrontal involvement. *The Journal of Neuroscience, 27*(46), 12700–12706. doi:10.1523/jneurosci.3371-07.2007

Volkow, N. D., Wang, G.-J., Fowler, J. S., Tomasi, D., Telang, F., & Baler, R. (2011). Addiction: Decreased reward sensitivity and increased expectation sensitivity conspire to overwhelm the brain's control circuit. *Bioessays, 32*, 748–755. doi:10.1002/bies.201000042

Webb, T. L., Sniehotta, F. F., & Michie, S. (2010). Using theories of change to inform interventions for addictive behaviors. *Addiction, 105*(11), 1879–1892. doi:10.1111/j.1360-0443.2010.03028.x

Weil, A. (1986). *The natural mind: An investigation of drugs and the higher consciousness*. Boston, MA: Houghton Mifflin.

West, R. (2006). *Theory of addiction*. Malden, MA: Blackwell.

White, M., & Epston, D. (1990). *Narrative means to therapeutic ends*. New York, NY: W. W. Norton.

White, W. L. (2004). Transformational change: A historical review. *JCLP/In Session, 60*(5), 461–470. doi:10.1002/jclp.20001

White, W. L. (2008). Spiritual guidance, addiction treatment, and long-term recovery. [Editorial] *Journal of Substance Abuse Treatment, 35*(4), 443–444. doi:10.1016/j.jsat.2008.05.010

World Health Organization. (1981). Factors affecting drug use and abuse. *Bulletin of the World Health Organization, 59*(2), 225–242.

Wong, P. T. P. (2008). Meaning management theory and death acceptance. In A. Tomer, G. T. Eliason, & P. T. P. Wong (Eds.), *Existential and spiritual issues in death acceptance* (pp. 65–87). New York, NY: Lawrence Erlbaum.

Wong, P. T. P. (2009). Meaning therapy: An integrative and positive existential psychotherapy. *Journal of Contemporary Psychotherapy, 40*(2), 85–93. doi:10.1007/s10879-009-9132-6

Wong, P. T. P. (2012a). From logotherapy to meaning-centered counseling and therapy. In P. T. P. Wong (Ed.), *The human quest for meaning: Theories, research, and applications* (2nd ed., pp. 619–647). New York, NY: Routledge.

Wong, P. T. P. (Ed.). (2012b). *The human quest for meaning: Theories, research, and applications* (2nd ed., pp. 619–647). New York, NY: Routledge.

Wong, P. T. P. (2012c). Introduction: A roadmap to meaning research and applications. In P. T. P. Wong (Ed.), *The human quest for meaning: Theories, research, and applications* (2nd ed., pp. xxix–xlvi). New York, NY: Routledge.

Wong P. T. P. (2012d). Toward a dual-systems model of what makes life worth living. In P. T. P. Wong (Ed.), *The human quest for meaning: Theories, research, and applications* (2nd ed., pp. 3–22). New York, NY: Routledge.

Wong, P. T. P., & Fry, P. (Eds.). (1998). *The human quest for meaning: A handbook of psychological research and clinical applications*. Mahwah, NJ: Lawrence Erlbaum.

Yalom, I. D. (1980). *Existential psychotherapy*. New York, NY: Basic Books.

Yuferov, V., Ji, F., Nielsen, D. A., Levran, O., Ho, A., Morgello, S., . . . Kreek, M. J. (2009). A functional haplotype implicated in vulnerability to develop cocaine dependence is associated with reduced PDYN expression in human brain. *Neuropsychopharmacology, 34*, 1185–1197. doi:10.1038/npp.2008.187

Zgierska, A., Rabago, D., Chawla, N., Kushner, K., Kohler, R., & Marlatt, G. A. (2009). Mindfulness meditation for substance use disorders: a systematic review. *Substance Abuse, 30*(4), 266–294. doi:10.1080/08897070903250019

APPENDIX A: THEORIES & PRACTICES CITED

Theoretical Framework	Theory	Practice	Leading Exponents
Behaviorism	Classical conditioning Operant conditioning	Aversion therapy Community reinforcement Disulfiram Niacin Matrix Model	Hunt & Azrin (1973) Rawson et al. (2005)
	Social learning theory	Relapse prevention	Marlatt & Donovan (2005)
	Focus on changing behaviors	Acceptance and commitment therapy	Hayes (2004)
Cognitive	Rational economic theory Self-medication theory		Becker & Murphy (1988) Khantzian (1997)
Cognitive-behavioral	Cognitive-behavioral	Coping skills training	Marlatt & Donovan (2005)
Neurobiological	Mesolimbic dopamine pathway Mesocorticolimbic dopamine pathways Drug substitution	Matrix model Acamprosate Methadone, etc.	Rawson et al. (2005) Robinson & Berridge (2001)
Motivational	Motivational	Motivational enhancement therapy Brief intervention	Miller (1995) Miller & Rollnick (2013)
Systems	Systems	Marital behavioral therapy	O'Farrell & Fals-Stewart (2006)
Eclectic	Eclectic	Minnesota Model Biopsychosocial Education	Owen (2000) Health Canada (1999)
Postmodern	Culture Socioeconomics	Public perceptions Government policy	Heath (1995) Alexander (2013)

Existential-humanistic	Meaning	Logotherapy	Crumbaugh et al. (1980) Somov (2007)
		Peele's model	Peele (2004)
	Narrative	Narrative	Singer (1997) Diamond (2000)
	Spiritual	12-step program	Wilson (AA, 1939/2001)
	Transpersonal Integral		Nixon (2001) Moxley & Washington (2001)
Integrative	Pathways model		Blaszczynski & Nower (2002)
	Excessive appetite theory		Orford (2001)
	Motivational dominance		West (2006)
	Personal meaning	Meaning therapy	Wong (2012) Thompson (2012)

13. A Meaning-Centered Approach to Addiction and Recovery

PAUL T. P. WONG

The problem of addiction has reached epidemic proportions, affecting every segment of society. About one person out of six is dealing with some form of addiction problem. The track record of addiction treatment has not been very promising, with relapse rates hovering around 90%. Many suffer from the revolving-door phenomenon and the false-hope syndrome. Addiction is more than a disease; it is also a societal, economic, and spiritual problem. It can kill the individual, hurt the family, and harm society.

This paper considers the addiction problem in Vancouver, critically evaluates the four-pillar solution and other mainstream treatments for addiction, and proposes the meaning-centered approach (MCA) as a better alternative.

A CRITIQUE OF MAINSTREAM TREATMENT APPROACHES

The Four-Pillar Solution as Advocated by Vancouver

The City of Vancouver has been promoting the "four pillars" of prevention, treatment, law enforcement, and harm reduction as a comprehensive and compassionate solution to the drug problem in the Downtown Eastside. These pillars are: (1) *prevention*, education about the dangers of drugs and how to avoid addiction without the moralistic and unrealistic message of abstinence; (2) *treatment*, a continuum of interventions and support programs enabling addicts to make healthier decisions and to move toward abstinence; (3) *enforcement*, more police in the downtown Eastside and more efforts to target drug dealers and organized crime; (4) *harm reduction*, a pragmatic way of accepting the reality but minimizing the harm of drug use (e.g., with needle exchange and methadone programs). MacPherson (2001) recognizes that abstinence may not be a realistic or desirable goal for certain users, particularly in the short term. Harm reduction instead follows a hierarchy of achievable goals, which, taken one at a time, can lead to a fuller, healthier life for drug users and a safer community for others. This approach is evidence-based and supported by outcome studies (Marlatt, 2000).

The four-pillar solution, however, has not been effective: The addiction problem in the downtown Eastside area is not getting better. Bruce Alexander

(2001) observes that "There has been little impact, because, no matter how well they are coordinated, the four pillars encompass only a small corner of the addiction problem, illicit drugs, and are not founded upon an analysis of the root cause." Two of these root causes are existential vacuum (meaninglessness) and social dislocation. Existential vacuum refers to chronic feelings of meaninglessness, boredom, and despair. The two related aspects of existential crisis are: (1) the existential anxieties of boredom, alienation, despair, meaninglessness, stress, suffering, sickness, and fear of death; and (2) the existential frustrations of the quest for meaning, purpose, fulfillment, and personal significance. Existential crisis is exacerbated by societal malaise. Since we are wired for community, with a strong need for belonging, social displacement can deepen one's existential crisis. Dislocation or insufficient psychosocial integration results from the breakdown of community and the depersonalization of individual.

The societal malaise of modern free market societies is characterized by the following: (1) depersonalization and dehumanization due to global competition and technological domination; and (2) the disintegration of communities, the unraveling of social institutions, and the displacement of individuals.

Pharmacotherapy

Pharmacotherapy is based on the disease model of addiction (Bloom 1992; Heinz et al., 1998). According to this model, addiction is a chronic disease (American Society of Addiction Medicine, 2011) to which some are genetically predisposed. Prolonged drug use leads to structural and chemical changes in the brain (Kalat, 2001; Niehoff, 1999). Medications are used in detox and in reducing withdrawal symptoms. Pharmacotherapy stems from the belief that the cure for addiction will come from neuroscience and the use of medication. But drugs do not cure the social and personal issues that initially trigger addiction.

Cognitive-behavioral therapy

Cognitive-behavioral therapy has long been a standard practice in psychotherapy and addiction treatment. The basic assumption is that addiction is a learned maladaptive coping skill (Marlatt & Gordon, 1985). In this view, addiction is simply a bad habit, not a disease (Peele, 2000). Many addicts report childhood abuse and family dysfunction (Sayette, 1999); addiction is a maladaptive way to deal with the inner pain and anger. Relapse is precipitated by triggers, stress, and cravings.

Treatment focuses on anticipating problems and helping addicts develop effective coping skills. Self-monitoring helps those affected to recognize early signs of drug cravings and avoid high-risk situations for use. Coping skills learned in relapse prevention therapy remain after the completion of treatment (Carroll,

Rounsaville, & Keller, 1991; Marlatt & Gordon, 1985). Mindfulness meditation has been found effective in preventing relapse (Marlatt, 2002). Cognitive-behavioral therapy continues to play a major role in addiction treatment, but it does not address existential and spiritual issues.

Solution-focused brief therapy

In solution-focused brief therapy (S. D. Miller, 2000), the therapist helps clients reframe and reduce problems to small, specific, and solvable goals, and then encourages them to use their own resources to accomplish the treatment goals. The therapist elicits information on how to repeat "exceptions" (periods of time when problems are not experienced) and "instances" (periods of time when problems are experienced), thus giving clients a sense of control. Solutions may have little to do with the addiction problems, as long as they contribute to clients' sense of self-control and awareness of the less remembered positive moments.

Motivational enhancement therapy

Motivational enhancement therapy (W. R. Miller, 2000) is based on the principles of cognitive and social psychology. In this model, change of habit is a process and relapse is part of the cycles of change (Prochaska, Norcross, & DiClemente, 1995). The focus is on intrinsic motivation—the client is the agent of change with some help from the counselor. The approach is largely client-centered, but planned and directed to elicit from clients self-motivational statements of personal decisions and plans for change. This therapy is most suitable for the earliest states of change.

The goal of motivational enhancement therapy is to help clients confront painful reality, reduce their resistance, and initiate change. The therapy helps clients see the discrepancy between their self-destructive addictive behaviors and their significant personal goals. Strategies for decreasing resistance include: asking open-ended questions, using reflective listening (giving voice to the client's resistance), using amplified reflection (taking the client's resistance a step further), reframing (giving new meaning to what the client has said), selectively agreeing with what has been said, eliciting the client's own verbalization of the need for change, supporting the client's expressions for change, and giving a summary reflection at the end of each session. Common themes include good and not-so-good things about drug use, a typical day involving use, reasons to quit or change, and ideas about how change might occur.

Supportive-expressive psychotherapy

Supportive-expressive psychotherapy (Luborsky, 1984) is a time-limited psychotherapy based on principles of psychoanalytical psychotherapy. Supportive techniques help patients feel comfortable in discussing their personal experiences.

Expressive techniques help patients identify and work through interpersonal relationship issues. This therapy emphasizes the role of drugs in relation to problem feelings and behaviors and discusses how problems may be solved without recourse to drugs. Supportive-expressive psychotherapy has proven efficacy with patients in methadone-maintenance treatment with psychiatric problems (Woody et al., 1995).

The Minnesota model

Primarily developed at the Hazelden treatment centre, the Minnesota model is abstinence based and committed to the 12-step approach. It often uses confrontation as a counseling style to break through the client's "denial" and resistance. It then adds medical, psychological, and religious elements. The goal is to treat the whole person in addition to the disease of addiction. Its holistic approach works with the mind, body, and spirit as components of a healthy life. This model is not regarded as a mainstream addiction treatment in Canada because it is based on abstinence rather than harm reduction.

The 12 steps of Alcoholics Anonymous (AA, 2002) form the spiritual core of the Minnesota Model recovery program. In essence, the 12 steps are designed for helping clients to get reconnected with self, others, and a Higher Power. Tonigan, Connors, and Miller (2003) have provided empirical support for the 12-step facilitation therapy.

Critique of mainstream addiction treatments

The same criticisms of the four-pillar approach apply to mainstream addiction treatments as well. One is that they fail to meet clients' existential and spiritual needs, which hinders the long-term efficacy of these treatments. Recovery needs to include spiritual healing: the process of reconnection to true self, others, and God. Recovery also needs to take place in a healing community, where addicts are treated with compassion, respect, and dignity. There is too much emphasis on sobriety and not enough emphasis on healthy living. There is also not enough emphasis on the personal development of counselors and therapists and the need for them to model authentic, meaningful living.

THE MEANING-CENTERED APPROACH

MCA is intended to complement mainstream treatments and address existential and spiritual needs of the clients. This model advocates the benefits of a healing community, which addresses clients' needs of psychosocial integration and continued social support. Because providing hope is crucial to recovery, MCA also provides a tragic sense of optimism (Wong, 2009) that is based on faith and meaning.

The mission of a therapist using MCA is the restoration of the total person to wholeness. The problem of addiction is not the drug, but the person. Treatment goals include not only recovery from addiction but also restoration to fullness of life and reintegration into society.

The treatment goal

According to MCA, addiction represents an inadequate and often self-destructive coping mechanism to escape the inner pain resulting from existential crisis (Frankl, 1959/1985) and societal malaise (Alexander, 2001). According to Frankl (1955/1986), "The feeling of meaninglessness. . . underlies the mass neurotic triad of today, i.e., depression-addiction-aggression" (p. 298). Effective treatment must help people rise above their circumstances, overcome what was inhibiting the defiant human spirit, and discover a clear sense of meaning and purpose.

The treatment goal of MCA is not complete abstinence but complete restoration of the total person to wholeness. Complete abstinence is likely the outcome of complete restoration, but it is not necessary for this restoration. The primary focus is therefore not on substance avoidance, but rather on helping clients discover purpose, embrace the joy of living, and obtain the freedom needed to pursue newfound passions.

There are seven pillars of MCA. 1) It is *holistic*—it treats the person rather than just the disease; it treats each individual as whole, based on the bio-psycho-social-spiritual model. 2) It is *integrative*—it incorporates other evidence-based addiction treatment modalities. 3) It is *meaning centered*—it regards addiction as a symptom of existential crisis and seeks to address the underlying existential and spiritual issues. 4) It is *community oriented*—it considers the healing community as a necessary part of effective addiction treatment. 5) It is *comprehensive*—it makes use of all available resources to achieve treatment goals. 6) It is *psychoeducational*—it teaches clients the underlying issues related to addiction and the need for more adaptive coping skills. 7) It is *optimistic*—it recognizes the bleak reality, but believes that there is hope for every addict.

The treatment and recovery process

MCA can be applied for the entire process of treatment and recovery. Basically, it involves a three-pronged approach: (a) treating the disease process and the harmful effects of addiction; (b) working through the psychological, existential, and societal issues that underlie each individual's addiction; (c) providing a supportive healing community that facilitates healing, restoration, and re-entry. This approach may be captured by the 3 R's for the recovery and restoration of the total person: recovering from addiction and its harmful effects, resolving the underlying issues of addiction, and rediscovering the purpose and passion for living.

The following strategies can be readily adapted to addiction treatment and recovery in individual counseling.

The PURE strategy of pursuing meaningful life

The PURE model provides an ideal framework to restore meaning in an addict's life because it addresses the key components of meaningful living. Meaning is defined in terms of four interrelated components (Wong, 2010): purpose, understanding, responsible action, and evaluation (PURE). This PURE model is holistic because it incorporates all the major human faculties: motivation, cognition, morality, and emotion. It is also capable of incorporating most meaning research. PURE can also be referred to as *the four treasures of meaning therapy* because they represent the best practices of building a healthier and happier future.

- Purpose—*the motivational component*, including goals, directions, incentive objects, values, aspirations, and objectives—is concerned with such questions as: What does life demand of me? What should I do with my life? What really matters in life? A purpose-driven life is an engaged life committed to pursuing a preferred future.

- Understanding—*the cognitive component*, encompassing a sense of coherence, making sense of situations, understanding one's own identity and other people, and effective communications—is concerned with such questions as: What has happened? What does it mean? How do I make sense of the world? What am I doing here? Who am I? A life with understanding is a life with clarity and coherence.

- Responsible action—*the moral and behavioral component*, including appropriate reactions and actions, doing what is morally right, finding the right solutions, making amends—is concerned with such questions as: What is my responsibility in this situation? What is the right thing to do? What options do I have? What choices should I make? A responsible life is based on the exercise of human freedom and personal agency.

- Enjoyment/Evaluation—*the affective component*, including assessing degree of satisfaction or dissatisfaction with the situation or life as a whole—is concerned with such questions as: Have I achieved what I set out to do? Am I happy with how I have lived my life? If this is love, why am I still unhappy? A meaningful life is a happy life based on reflection and judgment.

Each of these components includes a set of intervention skills. Some of the commonly used skills include goal setting, decision making, reality checking, fast-forwarding of the consequences of choices, Socratic questioning, the use of Wong's (1998) Personal Meaning Profile, and challenging irrational or unrealistic thoughts. These four components of meaning work together and form an upward-spiral feedback loop. With each successful completion, one's positivity moves up a notch. However, when one encounters a serious setback or obstacle, one will switch to the avoidance system to manage the negative circumstances.

It is unavoidable that we experience unpleasant events. We need to find a more effective way to overcome them than resorting to old habits of addiction as a way of escaping from pain and suffering.

The ABCDE strategy for overcoming negativity

The ABCDE intervention strategy is the main tool in dealing with negative life experiences. Totally different from the ABCDE sequence involved in the rational-emotive therapy process (Ellis 1962, 1987), this ABCDE is similar to acceptance and commitment therapy in its emphasis on action rather than thinking. (For a more detailed outline, see Wong, 2012.)

Simply put, A stands for Acceptance, B for Belief and affirmation, C for Commitment to specific goals and actions, D for Discovering the meaning & significance of self and situations, and E for Evaluation of the outcome and Enjoyment of the positive results. These components generate corresponding principles:

1. *Accept* and confront the reality—*the reality principle*.
2. *Believe* that life is worth living—*the faith principle*.
3. *Commit* to goals and actions—*the action principle*.
4. *Discover* the meaning and significance of self and situations—*the Aha! principle*.
5. *Evaluate* the above—*the self-regulation principle*.

Wong's 5-step approach to restoring hope

Given the importance of hope in recovery and the common false-hope syndrome in the addiction literature, we need to find a way to instill a realistic sense of hope. Viktor Frankl's (1959/1985) concept of tragic optimism (TO) is uniquely suited for addicts. Through personal communication, I personally know that at least one addict credits TO for saving his life (he is now a graduate student after recovering from a life-long drug addiction).

Wong (2009) has identified five essential components of TO:

1. Acceptance—confronting and accepting the reality of our condition, no matter how bleak or painful. This is the necessary step for healing.
2. Affirmation—saying "yes" to life; believing that life is worth living in spite of the suffering and pain. This is the turning point for healing.
3. Courage—this involves the defiant human will to persist in spite of setbacks, fears, and obstacles. This is needed to see us through.
4. Faith—this is often the only source of strength and hope in a hopeless situation. It is needed to keep us going when everything else has failed.
5. Self-transcendence—the ability to transcend self-interest and reach out to others. This is the manifestation of affirmation, courage, and faith.

The double-vision strategy (e.g., Wong, 2010, 2012)

This is a two-pronged strategy designed to address both the immediate presenting problems and the underlying big picture issues such as death anxiety, the quest for meaning, and the struggle against injustice. Double vision is an important macro strategy for several reasons:

- If we focus on the trees, we may lose sight of the forest. We can gain a deeper insight into our clients' predicaments by looking at the larger context and the big picture issues.
- If we can help restore clients' passion and purpose for living, this will reinforce their motivation to make the necessary changes.
- By looking beyond their pressing, immediate concerns, MCA seeks to awaken clients' sense of responsibility and vision for something larger than themselves.

The usefulness of a double-vision strategy for addiction becomes clearer when we consider how it works with a solution-focused approach. Clients' expressions of a desire to change are translated into concrete plans and actions. This is what solution-focused therapy does. However, when these small solvable goals are related to the addict's larger values, those that really matter in their lives, it provides added incentive for change. Although addicts tend to focus on short-term goals and living one day at a time, deep down, they still have dreams and aspirations. The double-vision strategy empowers them to discover and restore those ideals.

THE HEALING COMMUNITY

Another element of MCA is the inclusion of the healing community in the context of residential rehabilitation. The vision of a healing community is partially my answer to the problem of social malaise. Though we are not in a position to transform society into a more humane and caring place to live, we can start on a smaller scale by creating such a healing community for addicts.

Most treatment facilities exist as an artificial bubble in which clients are sheltered from the stress and seductions of the real world. Furthermore, life within the bubble tends to be highly regimented and controlled. Fear is the primary motivation for the clients to stay clean—fear of reprimand and termination for violating institutional rules or behavioral contracts. In such an environment, therapists do things to the clients and for the clients, but rarely with the clients. Therefore, there is little opportunity for clients to develop self-control and responsible behaviors.

MCA proposes a healing community as a solution to these problems. The benefits of a healing community have been emphasized by AA (1939/1990), Scott Peck (1978), and Michael Picucci (1996). By creating an accepting, caring, and trusting environment, an MCA community provides many opportunities for clients to experience psychosocial integration and learn new ways of relating and coming together.

The healing community in MCA has the following characteristics:

- It goes beyond the healing community modeled after a 12-step recovery program, because it involves all units within and beyond the treatment center: the administration, clinical staff, support staff, clients, and alumni.
- It involves clients' families whenever possible.
- It is based on the guiding principles of compassion, integrity, democracy, and justice.
- It is characterized by the Rogerian principles of client-centered counseling: (a) unconditional positive regard and acceptance, (b) genuineness or congruence, and (c) accurate empathic understanding.
- All members of the community are treated with dignity, respect, and consideration. All clients are treated royally. The quality of relationship with clients is a major focus in the treatment plans; its hallmark rests in the quality of relationships.
- Its corporate culture is characterized by transparency, integrity, and ethical concerns and social responsibility.
- Its climate is supportive, validating, caring, and nurturing, which is needed for both staff and clients to freely explore avenues of healing and growth in their quest for meaning and authenticity.
- It includes a loosely connected healing community outside the treatment center to provide ongoing aftercare support to reduce relapse and reinforce progress.
- It treats the whole person, as well as the illness.

Such a healing community not only provides models for authentic, meaningful living, but also offers opportunities for addicts to rediscover meaning and purpose. These transformative dynamics empower the clients to tap into the defiant human spirit and to develop their capacity for making responsible choices and pursuing a healthy lifestyle. This existential approach to addiction treatment will significantly enhance the prospect of recovery, because it addresses the two fundamental problems that plague mainstream addiction treatment programs.

The healing community concept can be extended beyond the residential treatment facility to Vancouver's Downtown Eastside or any area with a severe addiction problem. Social housing can be planned and organized with a view to fostering the development of a community spirit that facilitates psychosocial integration and the personal quest for meaning.

CONCLUSIONS

MCA complements mainstream addiction treatments, especially in its emphasis on meeting the existential and spiritual needs of addicts. Providing hope is crucial to recovery. MCA provides a tragic sense of optimism that is based both on accepting reality and affirming faith in a more fulfilling future. From a meaning perspective, hitting rock bottom may be the turning point for recovery. MCA describes both the skills and the stages necessary for building a new life.

In addition, MCA advocates the development of a healing community, which will facilitate clients' psychosocial integration and provide a supportive environment for their personal quest for meaning. There is empirical evidence that social and emotional support is important for addiction recovery (Hart & McGarragle, 2010).

The ultimate objective of MCA is the realization of clients' full potentials. Thus, the treatment goals include not only *recovery from addiction* but also *restoration of full functioning and passion for living*. The recovery process needs to move from healing of addiction and brokenness to personal transformation and full integration into society. Complete abstinence is likely the outcome of complete restoration. Through the PURE and ABCDE strategies, MCA facilitates clients' quests for meaning and discovery of life purpose and prepares and supports clients' re-entry and reintegration into society.

Given that addiction is multidimensional with numerous causes, Peele (2000) proposes that an ideal addiction model needs to be holistic and integrative, incorporating pharmacological, experiential, cultural, situational, and psycho-social components in describing and understanding the addictive motivation. MCA represents such an integrative model.

MCA is based on the logotherapy of Viktor Frankl (1959/1985). If addiction is a symptom of meaninglessness, then the restoration of meaning seems a logical approach to treatment and recovery. This paper simply provides an overview of what can be done to combat the problem of addiction.

MCA complements existential programs by equipping clinicians with the fundamental principles and skills to (a) motivate and empower clients in their struggle for survival and fulfillment regardless of life circumstances, (b) tap into clients' capacities for meaning construction in order to help them restore purpose, faith, and hope in their predicaments, (c) provide the necessary tools for clients to overcome personal difficulties/anxieties and achieve their life's mission, and (d) establish a genuine healing relationship with clients.

REFERENCES

Alcoholics Anonymous (1990). *Alcoholics Anonymous*. New York: AA World Services. (Original work published 1939).

Alcoholics Anonymous (2002). *Twelve steps and twelve traditions*. Alcoholics Anonymous World Services.

Alexander, B. K. (2001). The roots of addiction in free market society. Canadian Centre for Policy Alternatives. Retrieved from http://policyalternatives.ca/publications/reports/roots-addiction-free-market-society

American Society of Addiction Medicine (2011). Public Policy Statement: Definition of Addiction. Retrieved from http://asam.org/docs/publicy-policy-statements/1definition_of_addiction_long_4-11.pdf?sfvrsn=2

Bloom, F. E. (1992). Molecular genetics and psychiatry. In D. Kupfer (Ed.), *Reflections on modern psychiatry*. Washington, DC: American Psychiatric Press, pp. 79–90.

Carroll, K., Rounsaville, B., & Keller, D. (1991). Relapse prevention strategies for the treatment of cocaine abuse. *American Journal of Drug and Alcohol Abuse, 17* (3), 249–265. doi:10.3109/00952999109027550

Ellis, A. (1962). *Reason and emotion in psychotherapy*. Oxford, England: Lyle Stuart.

Ellis, A. (1987). *The practice of rational-emotive therapy*. NY: Springer.

Frankl, V. (1985). *Man's search for meaning*. New York: Washington Square. (Originally published 1959)

Frankl, V. E. (1986). *The doctor and the soul: From psychotherapy to logotherapy*. New York, NY: Vintage. (Original work published 1955)

Hart, K. E., & McGarragle, O. (2010). Perceived social support from counselors and client sobriety during aftercare: A pilot study of emotional and functional support. *Alcoholism Treatment Quarterly, 28*, 198–229. doi:10.1080/07347321003648216

Heinz, A., Ragan, P., Jones, D. W., Hommer, D., Williams, W., Knable, M. B., . . . Linoila, M. (1998). Reduced central serotonin transporters in alcoholism. *American Journal of Psychiatry, 155*, 1544–1549.

Kalat, J. (2001). *Biological psychology*. Toronto ON: Addison-Wesley.

Luborsky, L. (1984). *Principles of psychoanalytic psychotherapy: A manual for supportive-expressive (SE) treatment*. New York: Basic Books.

MacPherson, D. (2001). A framework for action: A four-pillar approach to drug problems in Vancouver (Revised). Retrieved from http://donaldmacpherson.ca/wp-content/uploads/2010/04/Framework-for-Action-A-Four-Pillars-Approach-to-Drug-Problems-in-Vancouver1.pdf

Marlatt, A. (2002). Substance abuse treatment and the stages of change. *Addiction, 97*, 607–608. doi:10.1046/j.1360-0443.2002.t01-8-00166.x

Marlatt, G. A. & Gordon, J. R., (Eds.). (1985). *Relapse prevention: Maintenance strategies in the treatment of addictive behaviors*. New York: Guilford Press.

Marlatt, G. A. (2000). *Harm reduction.* New York: The Guilford Press.

Miller, S. D. (2000). Description of the solution-focused brief therapy approach to problem drinking. In K. M. Carroll (Ed.), *Approaches to drug abuse counseling.* Bethesda, MA: National Institutes of Health.

Miller, W. R. (2000). Motivational enhancement therapy: Description of counseling approach. In K. M. Carroll (Ed.), *Approaches to drug abuse counseling.* Bethesda, MA: National Institutes of Health.

Niehoff, D. (1999). *The biology of violence.* Toronto, ON: Prentice-Hall.

Peck, M. S. (1978). *The road less traveled: A new psychology of love, traditional values and spiritual growth.* New York, NY: Simon & Schuster.

Peele, S. (2000). The meaning of addiction. Retrieved from http://peele.net/lib/moa1.html

Picucci, M. (1996). *Complete recovery: An expanded model of community healing.* New York, NY: Mombaccus Publishing.

Prochaska, J. O., Norcross, J., & DiClemente, C. (1995). *Changing for good.* New York: Avon.

Sayette, M. A. (1999). Does drinking reduce stress? *Alcohol Research & Health 23*(4), 250–255.

Tonigan, J. S., Connors, G. J., Miller, W. R. (2003). Participation and involvement in Alcoholics Anonymous. In T. F. Babor, & F. K. Del Boca (Eds.), *Matching in alcoholism* (pp. 184–204). Cambridge: Cambridge University Press.

Wong, P. T. P. (1998). Implicit theories of meaningful life and the development of the Personal Meaning Profile (PMP). In P. T. P. Wong & P. Fry (Eds.), *The human quest for meaning: A handbook of psychological research and clinical applications* (pp. 111–140). Mahwah, NJ: Lawrence Erlbaum.

Wong, P. T. P., & Fry, P. S. (1998). (Eds.). *The human quest for meaning: A handbook of psychological research and clinical applications.* Mahwah, NJ: Erlbaum.

Wong, P. T. P. (2009). Viktor Frankl: Prophet of hope for the 21st century. In A. Batthyany & J. Levinson (Eds.), *Existential psychotherapy of meaning: Handbook of logotherapy and existential analysis.* Phoenix, AZ: Zeig, Tucker & Theisen, Inc.

Wong, P. T. P. (2010). Meaning therapy: An integrative and positive existential psychotherapy. *Journal of Contemporary Psychotherapy, 40,* 85–99. doi:10.1007/s10879-009-9132-6

Wong, P. T. P. (2012). From logotherapy to meaning-centered counseling and therapy. In P. T. P. Wong (Ed.), *The human quest for meaning: Theories, research, and applications* (2nd ed., pp. 619–647). New York, NY: Routledge.

Woody, G. E., McLellan, A. T., Luborsky, L., & O'Brien, C. P. (1995). Psychotherapy in community methadone programs: A validation study. *American Journal of Psychiatry, 152(9),* 1302–1308.

14. A Meaning-Centered Therapy for Addictions

GEOFFREY R. THOMPSON

Abstract

This article describes a treatment for addictions, based on the idea that addiction is a response to living a life that has little personal meaning. First, it presents the theory of meaning-centered therapy (MCT) as developed by Paul Wong, particularly the need to understand intoxication from the addict's perspective. Next, it presents the principles governing clinical application. MCT is a positive, existential psychotherapy, which incorporates psychoeducational, cognitive-behavioral, narrative, and positive psychologies, by using personal meaning as an organizing construct. The article ends with a case study.

INTRODUCTION

Meaning-oriented programs for addiction are not unknown. Most are applications of Frankl's logotherapy (Crumbaugh, Wood, & Wood, 1980; Somov, 2007). Singer (1997) developed a meaning-oriented therapy, based on McAdams' (1993) narrative approach. Yalom (1974) described his existential group therapy with alcoholics, and Ballinger, Matano, and Amantea (2008) presented an existential-integrative approach with an alcoholic.

This paper describes a positive existential therapy recently implemented at the Sunshine Coast Health Center (SCHC) in Powell River, British Columbia. SCHC is a private, licensed, for-profit, residential facility for addicted men.

The program is based largely on the theory and practice of meaning-centered therapy (MCT), developed by psychologist Paul Wong (1998; 2008; 2009). Wong was heavily influenced by Frankl's (1988) proposition that the fundamental motivation in humans is the *will to meaning*, the need of the individual to make sense of his or her life and pursue a personally meaningful existence.

MCT extends Frankl's (1984, 1988) existential psychotherapy, integrating cognitive-behavioral, narrative, multicultural, and positive psychologies under the organizing construct of personal meaning. Recognizing that most mainstream treatment focused only on abstinence or reducing harm, Wong (2006) suggested that a meaning-centered approach could move beyond providing a measure of physical and mental stability:

> Such a positive existential approach recognizes that the goal of addiction treatment is not only recovery from addiction, but full restoration to the fullness of life. . . . The recovery process needs to move beyond healing of brokenness to personal transformation and full integration into society. (p. v)

ADDICTION AS A RESPONSE TO A LACK OF MEANING

Although early psychologists, especially William James (1902/1999), described the positive subjective experience of intoxication, the rise of behaviorism and prohibitionist attitudes shifted the perspective from the insider's to the outsider's point of view (Tart, 1990). Where James (1902/1999) had written that drunkenness "stimulate[s] the mystical faculties of human nature" (p. 421), the new psychology interpreted it as a lack of healthy mindedness. Today, mainstream conceptions of addiction reduce it to a disease (American Society of Addiction Medicine, 2001), brain disease (National Institute on Drug Abuse, 2010), brain disorder (Vaillant, 1995), maladaptive learned behavior (Marlatt & Donovan, 2005), response to family dysfunction (Copello & Orford, 2002), and other deficits. Motivational (Miller & Rollnick, 1991) and solution-focused (Berg & Miller, 1992) therapies provide alternatives to deficit approaches, but even these neglect the introspection and depth psychology that informed James' ideas. The mainstream solution to addiction is to encourage a healthy-mindedness in addicts. Treatment typically consists of an eclectic combination of medications, cognitive-behavioral coping skills, motivation strategies, and other therapies to support the client's shift to a healthy lifestyle. But successful outcomes are generally reserved for short-term studies. It has not gone unnoticed that, despite agreement that addiction is a chronic condition, we evaluate treatments as if it were an acute one (McLellan, 2002). Vaillant has been among the most vocal on this point, arguing that all long-term studies of, for instance, cognitive-behavioral and psychodynamic therapies have shown they are ineffective (Vaillant, Chapter 3, this volume).

A meaning-centered approach is an attempt to improve the effectiveness of treatment by recognizing that substance use operates at the level of fundamental motivations, beyond escapism, maladaptive coping skill, or neural adaptation. The starting point is Frankl's assertion that "alcoholism . . . [is] not understandable unless we recognize the existential vacuum underlying [it]" (Frankl, 1984, p. 129). The existential vacuum arises when the individual's attempts to live a *personally* meaningful life are persistently frustrated. Frankl's emphasis on the unique individual's perspective is essential. Looked at from the outside, many SCHC clients are successful. They have families, social circles, good jobs, and material possessions. But their subjective experience is boredom, anger, depression, and loneliness, the symptoms that Frankl said arise from the existential vacuum. Our clients describe a nagging feeling of emptiness, a hollowness in their lives. Their narratives depict a lack of purposeful living, lost souls wandering about directionless. The addict's life, said Narcotics Anonymous (1982), is "meaningless, monotonous and boring" (p. 80).

In addition to feelings of emptiness and boredom, another example of the existential vacuum is a feeling of not fitting in the world. Recovered addict Eric Clapton's opening line in his autobiography is typical of our clients' life stories: "Early in my childhood. . . I began to get the feeling that there was something different about me" (Clapton, 2007, p. 4). The Nobel Prize winning addict-writer, Eugene O'Neill, recognized that his own suffering arose from a feeling of separateness, a disconnection from others and from a higher power, which could provide meaning in his life. In *Long Day's Journey into Night*, O'Neill, as the 23-year-old character, Edmund, summarizes the nature of his suffering: "I will always be a stranger who never feels at home. . . who can never belong" (O'Neill & Bogard, 1999, p. 812). There is an uneasiness in the addict, a self-consciousness. As another O'Neill character put it, "I learned early in life that living frightened me when I was sober" (O'Neill & Bogard, 1999, p. 692).

When we ask addicts the meaning they ascribe to the positive experiences of intoxication, they confirm Frankl's (1998) thesis. Gregoire (1995) concluded that alcoholics drank in a doomed attempt to find "transcendence and meaning" (p. 339). Trujillo (2004) reported that users of crack cocaine experienced intoxication as the supreme state, though counterfeit, of the feeling of being (*dasein*). This feeling included transcending the mundane, being awed at the beauty of the world, and freeing the mind to reflect on self and others. One of Trujillo's participants described its appeal this way:

> It's like the whole world, life is beautiful. I feel great. I have a lot of ideas. My mind just opens tremendously. My mind is like really fast and I can think better. I feel good. I feel life is wonderful. I can do anything. (p. 171)

Using discourse analysis, Riley, Morey, and Griffin (2008) identified "social and communal togetherness" (p. 218) as a key meaning that young people gave to their experience of ketamine intoxication. Hunt and Evans (2008) conducted a phenomenological study of 276 young people, mainly 18- to 24-year olds, on the benefits of ecstasy intoxication at rave dances. They reported that participants saw ecstasy as "transforming the everyday [and] highlighting the extraordinary or transcendental nature of the experience" (p. 337). Sumnall, Cole, and Jerome (2006) found six major components of drug use based on a survey of ecstasy users. Among these, perceptual alterations, entactogenesis, and prosocial effects were most prominent.

Bill Wilson, the driving force behind the creation of Alcoholics Anonymous, informed the assembled crowd at the Shrine Auditorium in Los Angeles in 1948 that "An alcoholic is a fellow who is 'trying to get his religion out of a bottle,' when what he really wants is unity within himself, unity with God . . ." (as cited in Dick B., 2005). For Wilson, Frankl, Wong, James, O'Neill, and others, addiction is best understood, not as an escape from life, but as an attempt to satisfy a yearning to feel whole and find community. As James (1902/1999) described it, drunkenness "brings its votary from the chill periphery of things to the radiant core. It makes him for a moment one with truth" (p. 421).

But this experience, for the addict, is ephemeral and doomed, because the vacuum remains. Frankl (1980) was convinced that "filling up this [existential] vacuum may well be of primordial therapeutic value—nay, a prerequisite for therapeutic success, and in any event a decisive component in the rehabilitation of the chronic alcoholic" (p. x). MCT is designed to be this decisive component.

THEORY OF MEANING-CENTERED THERAPY

With its roots in Frankl's logotherapy—literally, therapy through meaning—MCT is best considered an existential approach. It should be remembered that what makes an approach existential is not the methodologies used but the lens through which a phenomenon is viewed. One of the foundational principles of existential-humanistic psychology is its openness to different ways of knowing. MCT integrates what we have learned from different epistemological approaches about personality. Indeed, meaning as a benefit to health and as an organizing construct has much empirical support, including meaning research (Wong, 2012), logotherapy (Batthyany & Guttman, 2006; Batthyany & Levinson, 2009), hardiness (Maddi, 2002), spirituality (Hill & Pargament, 2008), and the positive psychology of eudaimonic happiness (Ryan & Deci, 2001).

But the construct of personal meaning requires us to understand the subjective experience of the addict. As such, it shares many of the assumptions of existential psychology.

Existential Principles of MCT

The whole human being is center stage. MCT does not treat an addict or an addiction. Therapists do not assume that by virtue of having an addiction that a client is in denial or narcissistic or has some vaguely defined addictive personality. Existential-humanistic psychology arose as a response to the perceived weaknesses of psychoanalysis and behaviorism. Rollo May (Schneider & May, 1995) had challenged psychologists: "Can we be sure. . . that we are seeing the patient as he really is, knowing him in his own reality; or are we seeing merely a projection of our own theories about him?" (p. 82). In existential-humanistic thought, the individual is not reducible to one or a few traits, states, behaviors, or conditions. Singer (1997) concluded that we cannot reduce the addict's "struggle to the common denominator of a genetic defect or a physiological problem of control" (p. 17); rather, we must "take in the full dimensions of their lives—to see them as whole individuals struggling to achieve a sense of identity [and community]" (p. 17).

The individual is growth oriented. Maslow's (1954) theory of motivation laid the foundation for the principle that the individual has an inherent tendency toward self-actualization. Similarly, Cain (2002) pointed out that, for Rogers, "there is an inevitable directional course in people and all forms of life toward increased complexity, differentiation, evolution, completion, and wholeness" (p. 6). Research has indicated that, if the addicted person can overcome barriers to this growth process, then a transformational change and values may result (Miller & C'de Baca, 2001; White, 2004).

The individual is the author of his or her life. In Existential Psychotherapy, Yalom (1980) described existential responsibility as follows: "Responsibility means authorship. To be aware of responsibility is to be aware of creating one's own self, destiny, life predicament, feelings, and, if such be the case, one's own suffering" (p. 218).

The freedom to choose is, thus, the natural companion of existential responsibility. True, advances in neurocognitive psychology have shown that most of our decisions are unconscious (Myers, 2010), but we must ask, with Yalom, "Whose unconscious is it?" (p. 229). While Yalom's emphasis on responsibility for suffering is, perhaps, too simplistic—is someone's suffering due to a diagnosis of terminal cancer entirely his or her personal responsibility?—most of the clinical effort at SCHC is in helping clients take control of their lives, regardless of circumstances or personal and social limitations.

Almost all existentialists refuse to pathologize clients. May (1983), for instance, stated, "Neurosis is not to be seen as a deviation from our particular theories of what a person should be. Is not neurosis, rather, precisely the method the individual uses to preserve his own center, his own existence?" (p. 26). Pathologizing addictive behaviors tends to encourage therapists to see the client as defective and in need of repair, an attitude that reinforces the stigma of addiction (Luoma et al., 2007) and, from the existential view, disrupts the therapeutic alliance.

Further Principles of MCT

MCT distinguishes itself from other existential models on several levels. In line with Frankl, Wong (2008) stated that MCT was anchored to the following proposition: "Humans have two primary motivations: (a) to survive, and (b) to find the meaning and reason for survival" (p. 72). MCT pays special attention to helping clients find a reason for recovery. For example, most relapse prevention strategies fail because they do not account for the innate urge for meaning. The typical recovery plan includes outpatient counseling to work through issues, to attend self-help meetings, to focus on diet and exercise, and to engage in other healthy-minded activities. What is missing is a *reason* to do all these things. Mechanically following an aftercare plan generally ends in boredom, leading to relapse.

There are little meanings and big meanings. Frankl (1984) maintained that finding meaning in the present moment is more useful than attempting to answer questions, such as "Why am I here?" or "What is the meaning of my life?" MCT tends to focus on the little meanings, helping clients gain awareness that they react to the meanings they ascribe to events and others, rather than to the things themselves. In practical matters, MCT promotes doing the next right thing and acting according to one's values rather than out of fear. But the pursuit of little meanings should not blind us to the fact that we must have a long-term vision. Without such vision, short-term goals are directionless. Wong's (2008) meaning management theory extends Frankl's ideas by proposing that all of us need to manage three processes: meaning-seeking (find meaning in situations), meaning-making (construct meaning through personal action), and meaning-reconstruction (transform a negative into a positive).

Meaning therapy is forward-looking. From his experience in Nazi concentra-tion camps, Frankl (1985) concluded that those able to survive the camps were "oriented toward the future, toward a meaning to be fulfilled by them in the future" (p. 37). Helping clients learn ways to reduce suffering is not enough. They also need awareness that pursuing personal strivings are equally important.

MCT emphasizes the positive givens of existence. All of us confront the negative existential givens of death, inevitability of suffering, recognition that we are fundamentally separate from others, and so on. But human beings have the capacity to dig deep within themselves and find courage, resilience, and other qualities, which Frankl described as the *defiant human spirit*. Even in the worst possible circumstances, human beings are still free to choose the attitude they take toward the situation. Unlike Yalom (1980), for example, who focuses solely on the negative givens and thus on the inherent limitations of people, meaning theory promotes the individual's ability to transcend biological and environmental limitations. MCT emphasizes the capacities of clients to take control of their lives, develop hardiness, find the courage to overcome fears, turn failures into learning experiences, and so on.

A key difference between Wong's meaning theory and other meaning-oriented theories is his argument that the first step in meaningful living is the acceptance of reality, no matter how bleak (Wong & McDonald, 2002). The refusal to accept reality is, essentially, the attempt to make demands on life. Clients early in their recovery often make unspoken demands on life. "I will get recovery if and only if. . ." and then demand "My parents quit nagging me," "I can still have a beer or two when I want," "I don't have to take any risks," and so on. But the reality of recovery makes demands of addicts. MCT therapists help clients shift from the need to control life to listening to what life demands of them. To take ownership of their lives demands that they accept families are angry at them, that having a beer reflects a misunderstanding of addiction, that recovery involves learning to live comfortably in the ambiguities of life.

Example of a Meaning-Centered Interpretation of Addiction

The following example shows how a meaning-centered approach can add insight into the nature of addiction. I have written at length elsewhere about this dynamic (Thompson, 2006), but a brief summary is presented here. Mainstream therapists, with their healthy-minded view of addiction, often dismiss the chaos of the addict's lifestyle as a symptom of drug use. But if we recognize the existential vacuum that underlies addiction, then it becomes clear that addiction has two complementary components: the drug and the drug lifestyle.

Vancouver's notorious, drug-infested Downtown Eastside, the poorest postal code in Canada, has been a concern for politicians, police, and community groups. The mainstream generally tends to interpret the neighborhood as an example of the marginalization of addicts. Local television and newspapers call for taxpayer-supported housing and services to alleviate the suffering. But when we listen to those who live in the Downtown Eastside, we gain another perspective. One nonaddicted resident once put a sign in his window, which read, "This is better than television!" The Downtown Eastside is filled with intensity, action 24 hours a day. Visitors to Vancouver are often eager to visit the area because its notoriety has been promoted in the American and Canadian commercial film industry. The dark side of life has an appeal that middle-class society lacks.

From the mainstream view, the addict is ostracized, forced to live at the margins of society. But what the mainstream fails to recognize is that it is at the fringes of society where life is most intense. And addicts love intensity. According to Narcotics Anonymous (1982), "We made mountains out of molehills" (p. 93). The addict's life is filled with emotional intensity, and addicts do not seem to care whether the emotion is anger, love, hate, happiness, or sadness. As long as emotion is raised to the level of a soap opera, it is good. Yet for all the time, effort, and money spent in getting and using drugs, nothing is accomplished, other than lost health, relationships, jobs, and friends. There is no goal, no purpose to addiction; it serves only to perpetuate itself. To put it another way: *The addict lives intensely as a substitute for living meaningfully.*

The therapist's recognition that the intense lifestyle is actually a response to an existential vacuum has great therapeutic value. Indeed, the lure of intensity must be addressed to provide clients with the best chance of recovery.

MCT THERAPY

Rogerian Environment

One of the most important (perhaps the most important) aspects of SCHC's program is that it provides an environment where clients feel free to be themselves. Carl Rogers (Raskin & Rogers, 2000) was convinced that people would naturally actualize their potentialities if they were provided with the conditions of empathy, unconditional positive regard, and therapist's congruence. Empathy requires the therapist to appreciate the world as the client interprets it, an active immersion into the client's internal frame of reference. Unconditional positive regard invites clients to feel validated regardless of their feelings or state. This validation invites "the client to *be* whatever immediate feeling is going on—confusion, resentment, fear, anger. . ." (Raskin & Rogers, 2000, p. 148). The client must also experience an authentic relationship with the therapist, which demands that the therapist be genuine with clients.

Like all existential-humanistic approaches, meaning therapy is not technique driven. It relies on what Bugental (1976) called "ways of being" (p. xiv) with clients. Different therapists have different ways of being with clients. For Bugental, this was his concept of *presence*, a deeply attentive connection with the client, in which the client becomes aware of his or her being in the here-and-now. For Yalom (1995), this way of being was rooted mainly within interpersonal relationships. For Raskin and Rogers (2000), it was a deep empathic awareness, which resulted in his understanding a client at a deep psychological level, well beyond what the client's words conveyed. Similarly, MCT proposes that an authentic encounter between therapist and client is more important than any school or technique of psychotherapy. Therapy is as much about *process* as content.

SCHC's environment is designed to counter the addict's struggle with community. MCT recognizes that we are relational beings, with basic needs for belonging and attachment (Wong, 2009). A Rogerian environment invites community, providing clients with an authentic experience of what it means to connect deeply with others, including staff members.

Acceptance that the Individual Client is the Author of his Life

Most residential centers have vigorously resisted providing a Rogerian environment. Much of this resistance likely has to do with the demands that a Rogerian approach put on therapists:

> Their faith in the client's potential results in humanistic therapists'
> disinclination to be directive but rather to act in ways that free clients
> to find their own directions, solve their own problems, and evolve in
> ways that are congruent to them. (Cain, 2002, p. 6)

Because of the prevalence of deficit approaches, few addiction therapists appear able to muster this sort of faith in their clients. The matrix model, developed for those addicted to stimulants, for instance, is heavily behavioristic, under the argument that drugs have compromised the prefrontal cortex (Rawson, Obert, McCann, & Ling, 2005). CBT coping skills training leave little room for clients' perspectives (Longabaugh & Morgenstern, 1999), and even motivational therapies, which are used to address each client at his or her point of awareness, are directive (Miller, Zweben, DiClemente, & Rychtarik, 1995). Rogerian principles require therapists to shake off these influences and assume their clients are the best experts on themselves and, given the right conditions, will realize their potential.

Family Program

SCHC's family program is a meaning-centered approach for family members. Families do not tell their loved ones how much they have been hurt under the assumption that their loved ones are in denial. The construct of codependence has no part in our program because of its deficit approach and lack of scientific validity. Rather, the program helps families appreciate they have developed certain coping skills to deal with the abnormal situation and that these coping skills may not be helpful. At a deeper psychological perspective, family members routinely tell us that they have spent so much time and worry on their loved ones that they have lost a sense of themselves. Just as we remind clients that they are the authors of their lives, we also remind families that it is their existential responsibility to make decisions that will influence their lives. Ultimately, we ask family members to consider whether they want to be the expert managers of another adult human being or whether they want to pursue their own dreams and goals.

Psychoeducation

Psychoeducation sessions provide a framework and a language for clients to come to terms with personal meaning. Frankl's eulogy exercise helps them begin the process of discovering what is meaningful to them. We also present clients with research and allow them to make their own conclusions. A typical example is Bruce Alexander's Rat Park studies (Alexander, Beyerstein, Hadaway, & Coambs, 1981), in which rats showed no interest in morphine if they were free to be themselves.

Existential Coping Skills

Clinically, MCT helps clients to manage their lives more effectively. Barriers to an authentic life are addressed, such as immediate concerns (for example, drug cravings), environmental influences (for example, dealing with drug-using friends), and personal issues (anger, depression, and anxiety). Therapy provides avoidance strategies, such as self-regulation techniques for decreasing anger or anxiety. But defensive coping skills are not enough. Therapy must also provide *existential coping* skills (Wong, Reker, & Peacock, 2006). Gaining awareness of who we are, how we fit in the world, our strengths and limitations, and the promotion of acceptance, humility, compassion, and forgiveness provide clients with the best protection against tough times and the best chance of pursuing life goals. As O'Neil and O'Neil stated:

> By managing ourselves we come to know more completely what we want for ourselves, we come to know our priorities, our needs, our wants far more clearly; and this knowledge inevitably brings a greater sense not only of freedom but of security. The person who knows himself or herself, and manages his or her own life, can tolerate a higher level of ambiguity than before, can deal more successfully with anxiety and conflict because he is sure of his own capabilities. (cited in Wong, 2008, p. 243)

If Frankl (1984) is correct, that addiction is a response to an existential vacuum, then we must do more than simply focus on cognitive-behavioral coping skills, motivational techniques, and pharmacological interventions. Practitioners of MCT agree with White (2004), who concluded from a study of sober alcoholics that abstinence may be a *by-product* of meaningful living, not its prerequisite.

Narrative

Narrative is another vehicle that therapists use to help clients work through the existential vacuum. Dobson and Wong (2008) argued that narrative is fundamental to MCT:

> In its simplest terms, the meaning-centered approach emphasizes the human capacity for narrative construction and the healing and transforming power of meaning. It incorporates cognitive behavior theory and narrative psychology as import devices for transforming negative events and thoughts into coherent, positive stories. (p. 179)

The primary therapeutic exercise at SCHC is based on McAdams' (1993) life story work. By deconstructing the client's narrative in group therapy, the client discovers how he has answered the questions, "Who am I?" and "How do I fit in the world around me?" These are questions of agency and community, essential components of MCT. Reconstructing the client's narrative is the process of helping him find new ways of making sense of life, one more responsive to his authentic values.

Action

Yalom (1980) stressed that "In order to change, one must first assume responsibility: One must commit oneself to action" (p. 287). Frankl, borrowing some lines from Goethe, had stressed action over thought: "How can we learn to know ourselves? Never by reflection, but by action" (as cited in Frankl, 1986, p. 56). Although MCT recognizes that many people hide behind action, it promotes constructive action as one of the most potent methods to discover what is meaningful for a client. Daily life at SCHC, such as meal times and recreational activities, is one of the best tools clients have for putting new skills into action.

The Therapist is the Therapy

A key principle of MCT is that *the therapist is the therapy*. Meaning therapy puts demands on the therapist. For instance, meaning therapy demands that therapists be self-aware. Yalom (1980) observed that, although many therapists promote existential responsibility, "secretly, in their own hearts and in their own belief systems, [they] are environmental determinists" (p. 268). At SCHC, we often hear therapists lament, for instance, that a client's parents are to blame for his "stuckness" because they rescue him. Similarly, therapists fall into the tendency of believing that a client's negative behavior makes the center "unsafe" for other clients, rather than believe each adult is free to make choices. MCT promotes the therapist's self-awareness and vigilance in not falling prey to the client's (and their own) willingness to give up responsibility.

CASE STUDY

The first thing that Harry tells me when we meet is that his mother suffered from schizophrenia, and he is afraid that he "may have inherited some of her genes." In less than one minute, he has let me know that he is different than other people and that his problem is essentially some imposed factor (his genes), over which he has no control. Harry uses this to explain why he has suffered from anxiety since childhood. He has many more complaints. He's 40, single, and lives alone because intimate relationships never seem to work out. He's held onto a department store job since he left high school. During 22 years at a job he "hates," he has been promoted to a middle-management position and recently fired for drinking at work. As I come to know Harry, I have the impression that, at some level of consciousness, he deliberately forced his boss to fire him by showing up drunk. Harry is more comfortable when others make decisions about his life. He's here only because of a family intervention.

A mainstream therapist might diagnose generalized anxiety disorder and alcohol dependence disorder. Treatment would likely consist of easing Harry's anxiety with medication and coping skills. Likely, a mainstream therapist would interpret Harry's addiction as a form of self-medication. Indeed, asked why he drinks, Harry tells me it is the only thing that relieves his chronic anxiety. Also evident are adult relationship complications likely stemming from poor mother-child attachment (Schore, 2005).

SCHC's psychiatrist provides the official DSM-IV diagnosis and treats Harry's anxiety. Connecting with others is a challenge for him, but, given time limitations, his therapy will revolve around helping him take control of his life.

The first step is to deconstruct Harry's narrative. Deconstructing means listening to how Harry makes sense of himself and his place in the world. Two salient themes emerge: problematic relationships and the job. He's had two intimate relationships, each of which fell into his lap without effort on his part. Both were long-term relationships; Harry wasn't satisfied with them but didn't do anything about it. The first was 12 years, the second, two years. The first woman was a drinking companion, and she offered the consolation of being with another alcoholic. The second woman had recently ended a long-term marriage. Harry reported that its main benefit was "great sex," not emotional connection. She introduced him to an educated, upscale crowd. Harry became quite animated as he described taking part in social gatherings of lawyers, engineers, and professors, where he was invited to engage in "intellectual conversations," the only venue he experienced for this. But the lifestyle was unearned. When she ended the relationship, she ended the social gatherings, and Harry was left alone once more.

The relationship problems reflect his greater struggles to connect with others at an authentic level. In group therapy, he is superficial. The other group members, having tried to engage Harry without success, pay little attention to him. During our initial individual sessions, he brings his ever-present notebook, in which he has itemized things to tell me. He says he wants to make sure that I really understand him. But such behavior tells me that he's too busy organizing himself to pay attention to the human encounter happening between us in the session, in the here and now.

I'm curious to know why he stayed at a job that he hated. He initially blames external factors, such as the weak job market and difficulty of retraining. Harry prefers to play it safe in life. But it's important for Harry to understand how he exists in his world, which is devoid of meaningful work and relationships. The answer: distracting himself by drinking and living vicariously in his imagination. Harry likes to search for opportunities to ramble on about cosmology, which he learned from PBS television shows. He becomes animated and more alert. This is, of course, his attempt at connecting with me, but it is also one way he distracts himself from looking at his life. When I point out his avoidance behavior, he is resentful at first. We spend time processing his methods of distraction, this thinking about things that have little relevance to the emotional pain that brought him to treatment. He tries to convince me that he does think deeply about his life and shows me his notebook filled with pros and cons of going to university to get a new career. He had researched and thought about it. Harry thinks all the time. At some level of awareness, Harry knows that, despite all this planning, he's too scared to act.

He's afraid he's not smart enough to attend a university. While he tells me he believes he has good esteem, his behavior betrays him. One of the clinical benefits of a residential center is to watch clients outside of the therapeutic hour. Harry engages with other clients only at a superficial level of (pseudo-) intellectual debate. He rarely asserts himself in discussions over, for instance, which television show to watch or what to do on the daily outing. He routinely holds the dining room door open for other clients and is thus the last in the queue. Daily behavior at a residential facility is a gold mine for therapy.

Our deconstruction of his narrative and behaviors has helped Harry accept that his life is one of loneliness, low self-worth, fear of taking action, and allowing others to dictate his life. His is not a purpose-driven life. His past has few nurturing memories. His future exists only in his imagination, with no hope of action. He's condemned to live in the present. Frankl (1986) noted that, for those who live only in the present, "Life consequently loses all content and meaning" (p. 100). As May (1953) pointed out, if the individual "is not growing toward something, he does not merely stagnate; the pent-up potentialities turn into morbidity and despair" (p. 22). It is, perhaps, no surprise why Harry turned to the bottle. His life is meaningless, monotonous, and boring.

The events that brought him into treatment—lost relationship, being fired, family intervention—tell us both that his old narrative has run its course. Harry needs a new narrative, one that is more responsive to what is important to him: a new job that excites him, an intimate relationship. Although we cannot deal directly with the relationship, we can help Harry learn to connect with other clients at the center. I ask him to sit with different clients at meals and ask about what is happening for them. Another homework assignment is to ask each client for feedback on what they see in Harry. I reflect Harry's behavior back to him during sessions. He begins to discover that how he treats others has much to do with how others treat him, which, in turn, influences how he sees himself—one of Yalom's (1995) big points.

The content of therapy is to focus on employment. Harry knows that this means returning to school, but he's afraid to act. We spend a great deal of time processing this, but not as an end in itself. Everything is directed at helping Harry shift from living in his imagination to starting to take charge of his life by going to school. I help him develop a plan and support him with the first step, a phone call to the university. But it will be up to Harry after he is discharged to follow through.

CONCLUSION

When SCHC shifted from a behaviorist model to meaning therapy, several benefits were apparent. Attrition dropped dramatically; in fact, many clients extended their programs. Alumni from the old program, who returned for a visit, remarked on the new positive environment. Treating clients as responsible adults eliminated most behavioral problems. Preliminary studies—client self-report surveys, client evaluations, exit interviews, follow-up surveys—have been promising.

Most clients in early recovery believe that they can stay away from drugs by avoiding what they do not want from life, such as the guilt that accompanies not being there for children, the frustration of family members, the painful liver, the empty bank account. But such defensive coping has only short-term benefits. Frankl (1984) reminded us that addiction was a response to an existential vacuum. What the addict needs for recovery is to live a personally meaningful life.

REFERENCES

Alexander, B. K., Beyerstein, B. L., Hadaway, P. F., & Coambs, R. B. (1981). Effect of early and later colony housing on oral ingestion of morphine in rats. *Pharmacology Biochemistry and Behavior, 15*(4), 571–576.

American Society of Addiction Medicine. (2001). *Public policy of ASAM*. Retrieved from http://asam.org/ppol

Ballinger, B., Matano, R. A., & Amantea, A. C. (2008). EI mediation of addiction: Alcoholism: A perspective on alcoholism: The case of Charles. In K. J. Schneider (Ed.), *Existential-integrative psychotherapy: Guideposts to the core of practice* (pp. 177–185). New York, NY: Routledge.

Batthyany, A., & Guttman, D. (2006). *Empirical research on logotherapy and meaning-oriented psychotherapy: An annotated bibliography*. Phoenix, AZ: Zeig, Tucker & Theisen.

Batthyany, A., & Levinson, J. (Eds.). (2009). *Existential psychotherapy of meaning: Handbook of logotherapy and existential analysis*. Phoenix, AZ: Zeig, Tucker & Theisen.

Berg, I. K., & Miller, S. D. (1992). *Working with the problem drinker: A solution-focused approach*. New York, NY: Norton.

Bugental, J. F. T. (1976). *The search for existential identity: Patient-therapist dialogues in humanistic psychotherapy*. San Francisco, CA: Jossey-Bass.

Cain, D. J. (2002). Defining characteristics, history, and evolution of humanistic psychotherapies. In D. J. Cain. (Ed.), *Humanistic psychotherapies: Handbook of research and practice* (pp. 3–54). Washington, DC: American Psychological Association.

Clapton, E. (2007). *Clapton: The autobiography*. New York, NY: Broadway Books.

Copello, A. G., & Orford, J. (2002). Addiction and the family: Is it time for services to take notice of the evidence? *Addiction, 97*, 1361–1363. doi:10.1046/j.1360-0443.2002.00259.x

Crumbaugh, J. C., Wood, W. M., & Wood, W. C. (1980). *Logotherapy: New help for problem drinkers*. Chicago, IL: Nelson–Hall.

Dick B. (2005). 1943 [sic] remarks of Bill W. with Dr. Bob on A.A.'s need for God, religion, and the Bible. Retrieved from http://silkworth.net/dickb/remarks.html

Dobson, W. L., & Wong, P. T. P. (2008). Women living with HIV: The role of meaning and spirituality. In A. Tomer, G. T. Eliason, & P. T. P. Wong (Eds.), *Existential and spiritual issues in death acceptance* (pp. 173–207). New York, NY: Lawrence Erlbaum.

Frankl, V. E. (1980). Foreword. In J. C. Crumbaugh, W. M. Wood, & W. C. Wood, *Logotherapy: New help for problem drinkers*. Chicago, IL: Nelson–Hall.

Frankl, V. E. (1984). *Man's search for meaning*. New York, NY: Vintage.

Frankl, V. E. (1985). *The unheard cry for meaning: Psychotherapy and humanism* (new ed.). New York, NY: Simon & Schuster.

Frankl, V. E. (1986). *The doctor and the soul: From psychotherapy to logotherapy*. New York, NY: Vintage.

Frankl, V. E. (1988). *The will to meaning: Foundations and applications of logotherapy*. Toronto, Canada: Meridian.

Gregoire, T. K. (1995). Alcoholism: The quest for transcendence and meaning. *Clinical Social Work Journal, 23*(3), 339–359. doi:10.1007/BF02191755

Hill, P. C., & Pargament, K. I. (2008). Advances in the conceptualization and measurement of religion and spirituality: Implications for physical and mental health research. *Psychology of Religion and Spirituality, S*(1), 3–17. doi:10.1037/1941-1022.S.1.3

Hunt, G. P., & Evans, K. (2008). 'The great unmentionable': Exploring the pleasures and benefits of ecstasy from the perspectives of drug users. *Drugs: Education, Prevention and Policy, 15*(4), 329–349. doi:10.1080/09687630701726841

James, W. (1999*). The varieties of religious experience: A study in human nature.* Toronto, Canada: Random House. (Original work published 1902)

Longabaugh, R., & Morgenstern, J. (1999). Cognitive-behavioral coping-skills therapy for alcohol dependence: Current status and future directions. *Alcohol Research & Health, 23*(2), 78–85.

Luoma, J. B., Twohig, M. P., Waltz, T., Hayes, S. C., Roget, N., Padilla, M., & Fisher, G. (2007). An investigation of stigma in individuals receiving treatment for substance abuse. *Addictive Behaviors, 32*(7), 1331–1346. doi:10.1016/j.addbeh.2006.09.008

Maddi, S. R. (2002). The story of hardiness: Twenty years of theorizing, research, and practice. *Consulting Psychology Journal, 54*, 173–185. Reprinted in A. Monat, R. S. Lazarus, & G. Reevy (Eds.), (2007), *Handbook of stress and coping.* New York: Praeger.

Marlatt, G. A., & Donovan, D. M. (2005). *Relapse prevention: Maintenance strategies in the treatment of addiction* (2nd ed.). New York, NY: Guilford.

Maslow, A. H. (1954). *Motivation and personality.* New York, NY: Harper.

May, R. (1953). *Man's search for himself.* New York, NY: Norton.

May, R. (1983). *The discovery of being: Writings in existential psychology.* New York, NY: Norton.

McAdams, D. P. (1993). *The stories we live by: Personal myths and the making of the self.* New York, NY: Guilford.

McLellan, A. T. (2002). Have we evaluated addiction treatment correctly? Implications from a chronic care perspective. *Addiction, 97*, 249–252. doi:10.1046/j.1360-0443.2002.00127.x

Miller, W. R. & C'de Baca, J. (2001). *Quantum change: When epiphanies and sudden insights transform ordinary lives.* New York, NY: Guilford.

Miller, W. R., & Rollnick, S. (1991). *Motivational interviewing: Preparing people to change addictive behavior.* New York, NY: Guilford.

Miller, W. R., Zweben, A., DiClemente, C. C., & Rychtarik, R. G. (1995). *Motivational enhancement therapy manual: A clinical research guide for therapists treating individuals with alcohol abuse and dependence.* NIH Publication No. 94-3723. Rockville, MD: National Institute on Alcohol Abuse and Alcoholism. Retrieved from http://motivationalinterview.org/library/MATCH.pdf

Myers, D. G. (2010). *Psychology* (9th ed.). New York, NY: Worth.

Narcotics Anonymous. (1982). *Narcotics anonymous (basic text)*. New York, NY: NA World Services.

National Institute on Drug Abuse. (2010). *Drugs, brains, and behavior: The science of addiction*. NIH Pub No. 10-5605. Bethesda, MD: National Institute on Drug Abuse. Retrieved from http://nida.nih.gov/scienceofaddiction/

O'Neill, E., & Bogard, T. (Ed.). (1999). *Eugene O'Neill: Complete plays 1932–1943*. Toronto, Canada: Penguin.

Raskin, N. J., & Rogers, C. R. (2000). Person-centered therapy. In R. J. Corsini & D. Wedding (Eds.). *Current psychotherapies* (6th ed., pp. 133–167). Itasca, IL: Peacock.

Rawson, R. A., Obert, J. L., McCann, M. J., & Ling, W. (2005). *The Matrix Model: Intensive outpatient alcohol & drug treatment*. Center City, MN: Hazelden.

Riley, S., Morey, Y., & Griffen, C. (2008). Ketamine, the divisive dissociative: A discourse analysis of the constructions of ketamine by participants of a free party (rave) scene. *Addiction Research and Theory, 16*(3), 217–230. doi:10.1080/16066350801983715

Ryan, R. M., & Deci, E. L. (2001). On happiness and human potentials: A review of research on hedonic and eudaimonic well-being. *Annual Review of Psychology, 52*, 141–166.

Schneider, K. J., & May, R. (1995). *The psychology of existence: An integrative, clinical perspective*. New York, NY: McGraw–Hill.

Schore, A. N. (2005). Back to basics: Affect regulation, and the developing right brain: Linking developmental neurosciences to pediatrics. *Pediatrics in Review, 26*(6), 204–217. doi:10.1542/pri.26-6-204

Singer, J. A. (1997). *Message in a bottle: Stories of men and addiction*. Toronto, Canada: The Free Press.

Somov, P. G. (2007). Meaning in life group: Group application of logotherapy for substance abuse treatment. *The Journal of Specialists in Group Work, 32*(4), 316–345. doi:10.1080/01933920701476664

Sumnall, H. R., Cole, J. C., & Jerome, L. (2006). The varieties of ecstatic experience: An exploration of the subjective experiences of ecstasy. *Journal of Psychopharmacology, 20*(5), 670–682. doi:10.1177/0269881106060764

Tart, C. T. (Ed.). (1990). *Altered states of consciousness* (3rd ed.). New York, NY: HarperCollins.

Thompson, G. (2006). *A long night's journey into day: A psychobiography of Eugene O'Neill's recovery from alcoholism*. Abbotsford, BC: INPM.

Trujillo, J. (2004). An existential–phenomenology of crack cocaine abuse. *Janus Head, 7*(1), 167–187. Retrieved from http://www.janushead.org/7-1/index.cfm

Vaillant, G. E. (1995). *The natural history of alcoholism revisited*. Cambridge, MA: Harvard University Press.

Vaillant, G. E. (2013). *Alcoholics Anonymous: Cult or cure?* In L. C. J. Wong, G. R. Thompson, & P. T. P. Wong (Eds.), *The positive psychology of meaning and addiction recovery* (pp. 21–30). Birmingham, AL: Purpose Research.

White, W. (2004). Transformational change: A historical review. *JCLP/In Session, 60*(5), 461–470. doi:10.1002/jclp.20001

Wong, P. T. P. (1998). Meaning-centered counseling: In P. T. P. Wong, & P. Fry (Eds.), *The human quest for meaning: A handbook of psychological research and clinical applications* (pp. 395–435). Mahwah, NJ: Lawrence Erlbaum.

Wong, P. T. P. (2006). Foreword. In G. Thompson, *A long night's journey into day: A psychobiography of Eugene O'Neill's recovery from alcoholism.* Abbotsford, BC: INPM.

Wong, P. T. P. (2008). Meaning management theory and death acceptance. In A. Tomer, G. T. Eliason, & P. T. P. Wong (Eds.), *Existential and spiritual issues in death acceptance* (pp. 65–87). New York, NY: Lawrence Erlbaum.

Wong, P. T. P. (2009). Meaning therapy: An integrative and positive existential psychotherapy. *Journal of Contemporary Psychotherapy, 40*(2), 85–93. doi:10.1007/s10879-009-9132-6

Wong, P. T. P. (Ed.). (2012). *The human quest for meaning: A handbook of psychological research and clinical applications* (2nd ed.). New York, NY: Routledge.

Wong, P. T. P., & McDonald, M. J. (2002). Tragic optimism and personal meaning in counselling victims of abuse. *Pastoral Sciences, 20*(2), 231–249.

Wong, P. T. P., Reker, G., & Peacock, E. (2006). A resource-congruence model of coping and the development of the Coping Schemas Inventory. In P. T. P. Wong & L. C. J. Wong (Eds.), *Handbook of multicultural perspectives on stress and coping* (pp. 223–283). New York, NY: Springer.

Yalom, I. D. (1974). Group therapy and alcoholism. *Annals of the New York Academy of Sciences, 233*, 85–103. doi:10.1111/j.1749-6632.1974.tb40286.x

Yalom, I. D. (1980). *Existential psychotherapy.* New York, NY: Basic Books.

Yalom, I. D. (1995). *The theory and practice of group psychotherapy* (4th ed.). New York, NY: BasicBooks.

15. Interpreting the 12 Steps of AA from the Perspectives of Ecumenical Christianity and Transpersonal Psychology

KENNETH E. HART

Abstract

A transpersonal orientation to understanding the mind and spirit (the psyche) is used to reenvision the 12 steps of addiction recovery originally developed by Alcoholics Anonymous (AA). Special attention is given to articulating the unique panentheistic approach to 12-step spirituality embodied in the New Thought movement. The first part of the chapter describes panentheism and the core principles of the New Thought worldview. Attention is also given to the historical points of contact between proponents of New Thought metaphysics and the founders of AA during AA's embryonic phase of development in the 1930s. Conventional AA literature is then used as a basis for describing the standard spiritual interpretation of each of the 12 steps that comprise AA's program of spiritual healing. I have termed this approach as the ecumenical Christian perspective. The second half of the chapter provides a unique Eastern understanding and transpersonal reinterpretation of AA's 12-step program. The net result is an expanded appreciation of the diversity of ways of understanding AA's spiritual program of holistic health and healing. It is hoped that the new viewpoint offered by the current chapter's transpersonal perspective will help fill a need that has been left unmet by societal shifts associated with multicultural diversity. If AA's 12-step program can be reframed and presented to non-Christians in a way that is more inclusive, perhaps a wider range of diverse clients may be able to derive benefits from attending this spiritually centered support group.

THE CHALLENGE OF ADDICTIVE BEHAVIOR CHANGE

While the prevalence of addictive disorders continues to soar, the rate with which afflicted people have been seeking professional treatment has remained somewhat flat over time. The growing "service gap" has become a focus of study for community-oriented mental health professionals concerned with reducing the burden of addiction to public health (Tucker & Grimley, 2011). Statistics reliably show that only a very small minority of substance abusers ever receives professional services. There is reason to be optimistic about the fate of those who never enter a formal treatment program. Fortunately, a variety of "natural change" methods exist for overcoming addictive disorders. To date, little is known about the efficacy of these nonprofessional means of change. Examples include highly individualized and idiosyncratic do-it-yourself plans such as the grapefruit diet for weight loss or switching from whiskey to light beer in overcoming a drinking problem. Other types of natural change programs have received more scrutiny from social scientists. These involve affiliation with a group that offers a strategy for change. Some of these groups are paraprofessional in their leadership (e.g., Weight Watchers) and charge a fee, while others are completely nonprofessional such as Alcoholics Anonymous (AA) and have no cost. Collectively, natural change methods of change far outstrip formal treatment as a pathway to remediation.

In this regard, the single most prevalent natural change method for overcoming substance abuse disorders involves affiliation with AA and its 12-step program of spiritual growth (Galanter & Kaskutas, 2008). In a nutshell, the 12-step approach to spiritual rehabilitation and "recovery" involves a number of phases or steps. The first task that is faced by new members of AA is to admit that they are unable to control their compulsive urge to drink alcohol, and to realize that this inability has caused damage and suffering to self and others. The second step involves the acceptance that a Higher Power (God) exists and the acquisition of faith that this Power can and will provide the strength that is needed to abstain, strength that the individual lacks. Another aspect of the 12-step approach to healing from addiction includes giving up the compulsive need to be in control of one's destiny. This spiritual process is called "surrendering" to a Higher Power. Surrender is accomplished in AA by means of removing internal obstacles that stem directly from the insecure ego, which is marked by extreme narcissism. Ego-related barriers to God consciousness are dismantled by a variety of means. For instance, AA members who are "working" the 12 steps will become humble and "teachable" by examining their limitations and imperfections and by recognizing the truth of their existential predicament as being flawed mortal beings who are destined to continue to harm themselves and others unless the ego relinquishes its power and permits a Higher Power to give direction. By relying on the strength and direction provided by a forgiving and loving God, the AA member is encouraged to make amends for falling prey to the character flaws of the imperfect ego. After clearing the obstructed channel that connects the unfettered human will to the Divine Will, the AA member experiences a release from compulsive ruminations involving the urge to drink. The participant also experiences a release from the worries and selfish concerns of the insecure ego. Concern for the welfare of others, rooted in gratitude, begins to dominate as a new priority in a rejuvenated life in the Spirit. Having completed the process of 12-step recovery, the AA member becomes increasingly interested in being of service to people around them, especially to those who still suffer from the damage caused by active addiction.

THE 12-STEP SOLUTION TO THE PROBLEM OF ADDICTION

Meta-analyses (Emrick, Tonigan, Montgomery, & Little, 1993; Tonigan, Toscova, & Miller, 1996) and narrative reviews (Humphreys, 2004; Tonigan, 2008) provide convincing evidence that greater involvement with, and adherence to, AA's 12 steps can contribute to recovery. Though a number of different mechanisms may be operating to account for why involvement in AA exerts its salutary impact on drinking, theory (Grof, 1994) and research suggest that AA might have a healing effect because it enhances spiritual growth. Readers interested in learning more about behavioral science research along this trajectory should consult Connors, Walitzer & Tonigan (2008); Johnson (2013); Kelly, Stout, Magill, Tonigan, & Pagano (2011); Zemore (2007). For a transpersonal conceptual approach to understanding alcoholism and its treatment, see Grof (1994). Consistent with the view of Carl Jung, Grof suggests that, when they are young, persons who are prone to later develop problems with alcohol suffer from a distressing inner emptiness which is subjectively felt as a vague spiritual yearning (e.g., "something is missing," "there must be more to life"). Both Grof (1994) and Clinebell (1963) describe how alcohol intoxication can temporarily satisfy the unmet desire for self-transcendence by providing a counterfeit experience with the vertical dimension of life. Over time, the frequency and intensity of these chemically manufactured "spiritual experiences" diminish. Clinebell describes how awareness of the existential vacuum progressively grows and how drinkers will seek relief through alcohol, which has been transformed from a magical-mystical elixir to an anesthetic which dulls the deep pain of existential despair.

The past decade has witnessed a remarkable surge of empirical interest among behavioral and social scientists in the study of AA's 12 spiritual steps. Mental health professionals who come into contact with addicted clients in the context of formal treatment might be able to support client abstinence and facilitate their emotional sobriety by encouraging them to supplement professional treatment with attendance at AA meetings. Research suggests that clients who benefit the most from affiliating with AA do much more than attend meetings; they have adopted a spirit-centered approach to living life, which stands in marked contrast to a self-centered approach. To date, there has been a paucity of scholarly attention to probing the inner psycho-spiritual workings of AA's 12-step program. In a rare exception to this trend, Swora (2004) adopted an anthropological perspective to describe how AA discourse is sacred in nature. She argues that AA's 12 steps heal the mind, the body, and the spirit by means of a rhetoric of predisposition, empowerment, and transformation. The purpose of this chapter is to complement narrative explanations such as the one offered by Swora (2004). The current chapter offers a discourse which details the spiritual nature of AA's 12 steps and shows the inner psycho-spiritual workings of how healing comes about. Much is yet to be learned about how these processes operate. For simplicity of communication, I have termed AA's self-understanding as an ecumenical Christian perspective.

AN ALTERNATIVE APPROACH TO SPIRITUALITY: THE NEW THOUGHT WORLDVIEW AND TRANSPERSONAL PSYCHOLOGY

For purposes of the current discussion, I am using the term "New Thought" in a specific way. It is not being used in a way that makes it synonymous with "New Age." Instead, the New Thought worldview is typified by an interconnected system of mystical philosophies, theologies, and spiritual practices. It exists, at the sociocultural level, as a cluster of positive-thinking quasireligious spiritual-healing movements. It assumes the existence of a Higher Power or a "God," that can be apprehended personally and directly. Some of the more publicly visible facets of this cluster include "churches" (denominations), such as Science of Mind (led by Ernest Holmes), the Unity School of Christianity (led by Charles Fillmore), Divine Science (led by Emmet Fox), and other related quasireligions, such as Churches of Truth. This amalgam of loosely connected spiritual beliefs and practices, is deeply rooted in a unique blending of Hindu and Buddhist panentheistic belief systems and Western principles and values that emphasize philosophical pragmatism.

The New Thought worldview shares many features in common with transpersonal psychological approaches to spirituality. Both approaches assume a panentheistic worldview and both emphasize the transformative and healing potential of mystical experience. According to Davis (2003):

> Transpersonal psychology is based on nonduality, the recognition that each part (e.g., each person) is fundamentally and ultimately a part of the whole (the cosmos). This view is radically different from psychological approaches founded on the premises of mechanism, atomism, reductionism, and separateness (subject-object distinction).

From this insight come two other central insights: the intrinsic health and goodness of the whole and each of its parts, and the validity of self-transcendence from the conditioned personality (ego-self) to an alternate sense of an experienced identity which is deeper, broader, expansive and more unified with the whole. (p. 6)

The transpersonal worldview assumes the existence of—and places value on—hidden dimensions of reality, dimensions that extend beyond an individual's persona and beyond the reaches of their five senses and their thinking mind. These hidden dimensions are assumed to be sacred in nature because they are of God and in God. Furthermore, they are assumed to be potentially amenable to direct experience by means of nonconceptual (spiritual) awareness. Because spiritual experiences require a loss of (transcendence of) one's ego identity, they are ineffable due to their silent and wordless quality.

In the subtitle of their 1995 book addressing the New Thought approach to religion, philosophers Alan Anderson and Deborah Whitehouse refer to this confluence of the East and the West as "a practical American spirituality." They describe the New Thought orientation as one that emphasizes ego transcendence and mystical awakening, health and healing of the mind, the body and life circumstances, and the use of prayer and meditation as spiritual practices which have the power to resolve problems of daily living and which can contribute to flourishing or thriving in life. Historical figures who helped pioneer modern expressions of New Thought include Horatio and Julius Dresser, Ralph Waldo Trine, Mary Baker Eddy, Henry Drummond, Emma Curtis Hopkins, Thomas Troward, James Allen, and Phineas Parkhurst Quimby. As noted by Anderson and Whitehouse, New Thought owes a particular debt of gratitude to the unschooled Maine clock maker and inventor named Phineas Parkhurst Quimby. Quimby was involved in spiritual healing and had a reputation as a faith healer. He himself attributed his powers to a rediscovery of the lost healing methods of Jesus. Contemporary popular culture authors who epitomize the New Thought approach to spirituality include Deepak Chopra, Wayne Dyer, Eckhart Tolle, Anthony Robbins and Marianne Williamson. *The Secret* (Byrne, 2006) is perhaps the most famous recent Western pop-culture book in this tradition.

New Thought expressions of the panentheistic worldview have no dogma or creed. However, loosely organized principles have been established and have been codified in numerous publications. Braden (1963) provides an authoritative scholarly analysis in his seminal book, *Spirits in Rebellion*. For a more recent review and critique of New Thought practices and principles, see Albanese (2009), and Clayton and Peacocke (2004).

SCIENCE OF MIND, UNITY SCHOOL OF CHRISTIANITY AND THE INTERNATIONAL NEW THOUGHT ALLIANCE

Contemporary descriptions of the principles that underpin New Thought interpretations of the panentheistic worldview can be found on websites maintained by organizations that support the Science of Mind movement and the Unity School of Christianity. These two denominations dominate the contemporary New Thought landscape in American and Canadian culture. A concise introduction to the principles of the Unity Church (2013) can be found on their web site (unity. org). This site identifies the following core principles:

- Heaven is not a place, but is rather a state of consciousness;
- People create their own heaven and hell here and now;
- All people have an innate capacity to directly know a personal god through mystical experience;
- The "Christ" is that spark of the immanence of the ground of being, God that is everywhere present;
- There is a spark of hidden divinity within all people, just as there was in Jesus;
- Prayer works;
- People are here on Earth to help each other awaken to their true identity as a spiritual being.

An equally concise introduction to Science of Mind (2013) teachings can be found on their web site, scienceofmind.com. This site identifies a number of central tenets. These include:

- All that exists owes its existence to a single Reality Principle and Presence, call it Supreme Being, or Infinite Source, etc;
- Each human being is a creation of this Divine Principle and Sacred Presence (i.e., God);
- Each person who has form is an individualized expression of the Supreme Spirit;
- At the core, each person is one with God and one with each other because all is in God and of God;
- There is a unity of all that exists because the manifest world exists because of the Unmanifest Source (God);
- The Source of all that exists is not elsewhere or "out there somewhere," it is within you, and is always right where you are.

A third glimpse into the belief system that underpins the New Thought approach to "religion" can be found by perusing the declaration of spiritual principles published online by the International New Thought Alliance (INTA,

2013). The main purpose of the INTA is to knit together individual New Thought denominations. Through its online presence, its popular culture magazine, and its annual Congress, this umbrella organization serves an ecumenical bridging function. It has published 10 principles that embody a common core set of beliefs shared by the Unity School of Christianity and Science of Mind. These overarching principles are described below. Though they are not intended to be expressive of the spiritual principles that underpin AA, scores of AA members would heartily endorse the INTA declaration as being compatible with their private spirituality. Some of these principles include:

- We affirm God as Mind, Infinite Being, Spirit, and Ultimate Reality.
- We affirm that God, the Good, is supreme, universal, and everlasting.
- We affirm the unity of God and humanity, in that the divine nature dwells within and expresses through each of us, by means of our acceptance of it, as health, supply, wisdom, love, life, truth, power, beauty, and peace.
- We affirm the power of prayer and the capacity of each person to have mystical experience with God, and to enjoy the grace of God.
- We affirm that our mental states are carried forward into manifestation and become our experience in daily living.
- We affirm our evolving awareness of the nature of reality and our willingness to refine our beliefs accordingly.

CONNECTIONS BETWEEN THE NEW THOUGHT WORLDVIEW AND THE ORIGINS OF ALCOHOLICS ANONYMOUS

Before continuing, it might be helpful to clarify some AA terminology which may be foreign to some readers. The *Big Book* is the affectionate nickname AA (1980) has given to its basic textbook, officially known as *Alcoholics Anonymous: The Story of How Many Thousands of Men and Women Have Recovered From Alcoholism*. In the same way as Emilie Cady's (1896/1989) *Lessons in Truth* is the basic text of the Unity School of Christianity, the *Big Book* is the basic text of AA. In addition, AA (1981) has published a book called the *Twelve Steps and Twelve Traditions*; nicknamed the "*12 & 12*," it has expansive essays on the 12 steps of AA, which promote personal recovery. This book also contains essays describing 12 traditions that promote group unity. This second core textbook was written by Bill Wilson, cofounder of AA, in order to provide context for understanding the concise set of "how-to" instructions found in the *Big Book*. Wilson makes it clear that these steps represent a planned program of recovery from alcoholism that was actually followed by early AA members. As such, the 12 steps were lived or embodied as a way of life by the pioneering founders.

The "how-to" instructions necessary to emulate this early way of life were written down and published in the *Big Book* in 1939 (now in its fourth edition as AA, 2001), and these ideas were grouped into 12 principles or "steps." They are offered to new members as an integrated spiritual solution to the problem of alcoholism. Christian members of AA typically have no difficulty accepting the spiritual principles. However, agnostics or immigrants from Eastern cultures are less likely to embrace these ideas. To help overcome any such resistance, a nontraditional approach to understanding AA's spiritual program is proposed in this chapter. In this regard, clients might be more accepting of a New Thought perspective with historical roots in Eastern philosophies, which are inclusive of Buddhist and Hindu approaches to spirituality.

Barger (1991) suggested that, during the early years just prior AA's birth, the founders of AA were exposed to ideas and practices grounded in New Thought teachings. This possibility is supported by other sources (cf. Dick B, 1999). Both Barger and Dick B noted that this exposure occurred during the 1930s, before they wrote and published AA's basic texts. As a result, some New Thought language and concepts can be found embedded in AA's publications, even though AA writings never promoted or acknowledged the New Thought influence directly. In this regard, it is likely that AA's well-known use of the term "Higher Power" originated with Ralph Waldo Trine (1919/ 2006).

Emmet Fox was a well-known minister who provided leadership to the Church of Divine Science, located in New York City. He had a reputation for giving charismatic sermons, first in the New York Hippodrome and then at Carnegie Hall to audiences that numbered up to 5,000. Sikorsky (1990), Barger (1991), and Dick B (1999) noted that Wilson's (AA, 1976) use of the term "conscious contact" could be attributed to the lectures of the Reverend Emmet Fox, who often spoke of "consciously contacting" God. This term is strongly suggestive of a panentheistic God, one which is both transcendent and immanent.

The core textbooks of AA (1980, 1981) use a variety of terms known to have been originally coined by New Thought authors, such as "Spirit of the Universe," "the Great Reality," "Universal Mind," "the Presence of Infinite Power," "Great Spirit," "the Boss Universal," "Creative Intelligence," "Spirit of Nature," "conscious contact," "consciousness of the Presence of God," "God Consciousness," "the All Powerful Creator," "a Living Creator," "the Presence of Infinite Power," "the Fourth Dimension," and "Divine Mind." These terms have a remarkably close resemblance to similar expressions for divinity previously coined by New Thought pioneers such as Ralph Waldo Trine (1919/2006), who refers to "Infinite Power," "The Supreme Intelligence," "Divine Wisdom," "The Voice of Spirit," "Eternal Divine Life," and "God-consciousness."

Braden (1963) documented that Horatio Dresser, an influential historical New Thought writer, received his Ph.D. in Philosophy in 1907. While studying at Harvard University, he received supervision and mentorship from Professor William James. According to Anderson and Whitehouse (1995), Dresser was considered to be one of the most highly trained scholars in what was then a fledgling New Thought movement. Indeed, through his publications and public talks, Dresser served as one of New Thought's most forceful proponents and interpreters. The influence of Dresser on the thinking and writing of William James (1902/1985) is clearly visible in *The Varieties of Religious Experience*, particularly in the fourth and fifth chapters. In these two chapters, James quotes extensively from both Dresser and Trine. James also describes his personal insights into the New Thought approach to spirituality, which he labeled as "religion of healthy-mindedness."

William James' (1902/1982) *Varieties* was read by Bill Wilson while he was hospitalized for withdrawal from alcohol. It is well documented that he had a profound spiritual awakening a few days later, which subsequently led to his conversion experience with "God Consciousness." His experience has been described as a case of spiritual healing; it was so transformative that it resulted in permanent and lifelong sobriety. In the AA literature, it is often referred to as Wilson's "white light" experience.

Wilson (1935/2000) was primarily responsible for writing the AA *Big Book* and the *12 & 12*. James' (1902/1982) book also exerted an influence on other pioneers of AA who had input into these writings. According to historical records documented by AA historian Dick B (1999), James' book was prescribed to AA members as "essential reading" prior to the 1939 publication of their core text, the *Big Book*. Wing (1999), a former personal secretary to Bill Wilson and a retired AA archivist, noted that early AA members in the 1930s and 1940s were strongly encouraged to read James Allen's (1902) book, *As a Man Thinketh*, Thomas Troward's (1904) *Edinburgh Lectures on Mental Science*, and Emmet Fox's (1934/1989) book, *Sermon on the Mount*. These books represent major landmarks on the burgeoning New Thought landscape. In his own writings, Wilson (1935/2000) freely acknowledged the importance of Fox's book to early AA, but insisted that it was no longer needed after the publication of the *Big Book* in 1939.

In his many writings on the topic of spiritual awakening and spiritual growth, Bill Wilson clearly gives credit to James. Both the *Big Book* and James (1902/1982) share a common conception of a panentheistic God who is both immanent and transcendent. The *Big Book*, for instance, states, "We found the Great Reality deep down within us" (AA, 1976, p. 55). Also, the terminology and phraseology of the two books are similar. For examples, some of the terminology and ideas in the follow quote from James also appear in the *Big Book*.

> The *great central fact* of the universe is the spirit of infinite life
> and power that is back of all is what I call God. I care not what
> term you may use, be it Kindly Light, Providence, the Over Soul,
> Omnipotence, or whatever term may be most convenient, so long
> as we are agreed in regard to the great central fact itself. God fills
> the universe alone, so that all is from Him and in Him, and there is
> nothing that is outside. (p. 94, emphasis added)

The AA (1976) *Big Book* uses the same phrase: "the great central fact." Also, in connection with the label or name given to God, James (1902/1982) elsewhere stated, "I care not what term you may use" (p. 50). This idea shows up in the 3rd and 11th steps of AA as "God as we understand Him." Thus, like James, AA strongly endorses the idea that the specific label used to describe "God" is less important than trusting that a Higher Power, however labeled, exists and is the source and sustainer of all life including human life, and all that exists in the macrocosm and microcosm.

In addition to the two main texts of AA (1976, 1981), the imprint of New Thought's seminal influence is found in other AA-approved literature. Dr. Bob, the other cofounder of AA, was similarly exposed to New Thought principles and practices prior to the launch of AA. In *Dr. Bob and the Good Oldtimers* (AA, 1980), it is noted that James' (1902/1982) *Varieties* was a favorite of Dr. Bob's, as was Emmet Fox's (1934/1989) *The Sermon on the Mount*. It was also documented (AA, 1980) that Dr. Bob was influenced by the writing of Charles Fillmore, the founder of Unity Church of Christianity. Unity Church is leading contemporary proponent of New Thought metaphysics. It is evident that Dr. Bob's spiritual quest involved learning about mysticism, world religions, and the metaphysical approach to spirituality and religion.

Thus, it seems clear that both of the cofounders of AA were quite familiar with New Thought principles, practices, and teachers. Importantly, this familiarity was gained prior to 1939, when the first edition of the *Big Book* was published.

THE 12 STEPS OF ALCOHOLICS ANONYMOUS

Although a major purpose of this program is to help alcoholics become and stay abstinent from alcohol, the program attends to much more than merely "being dry." In this regard, it is not uncommon to hear AA members speak about the "dry drunk syndrome." This refers to a rather poor quality of life that can be exhibited in an AA member who is not drinking and who is not "working the steps." Dry drunks are said to be restless, irritable and discontent, and prone to creating chaos in their own life and in the lives of others by way of acting out on their character flaws (personality imperfections such as dishonesty, inconsideration, etc). They are also believed to be prone to relapse and return to drinking. According to AA (Wilson, 1958), the term "recovery" refers to a style of living which goes beyond abstinence. It includes both physical sobriety and "emotional sobriety."

Many people are surprised when they learn the true extent to which the 12-step program de-emphasizes drinking, while at the same time emphasizing the quality of becoming (and staying) "spiritually fit." As will be demonstrated, only the first of the 12 steps explicitly names alcohol; the remainder of the steps are concerned with spiritual processes, such as knowledge of and relationship with a God of one's understanding (or a Higher Power), self-searching, confession, openness to being changed, amends, prayer and meditation, seeking God's will, and carrying the message to others.

In connection with the spirituality of alcoholism and recovery from alcoholism, Carl Jung, another strong influence on the early formation of the steps, has argued that alcoholic drinking is a reflection of the human need gone wrong, a need for spiritual life (cited in Wilson, 1963). In 1961, decades after the establishment of AA, Wilson (1963) reached out to Jung to thank him for his role in the foundation of AA. In a now-famous series of publicized letters between the two men, Jung wrote that the craving for alcohol is the equivalent, on a low level, of the spiritual thirst of our being for wholeness, or union with God (also see Kurtz, 1980; Colwell-Bluhm, 2006). Jung told Wilson: The word "alcohol" in Latin is *spiritus*: the highest religious experience as well as the most depraving poison. In solving the problem of alcoholism, Jung offered the formula *spiritus contra spiritum*, which figuratively translates as "It takes the Spirit of God to overcome the harmful spirit of alcohol" (Kurtz, 1980; Colwell-Bluhm, 2006)

For those who pursue the 12 steps of AA, abstinence signals one thing: embarkation on a planned spiritual program of recovery from alcoholism. This path, or quest, is a continuing cyclic journey to inner wholeness and inner peace ("serenity") together with an altruistic and compassionate outer expression of this wholeness. Spiritual experience and spiritual expression are not by-products of this quest, but the very means by which an alcoholic recovers. Many AA writings, in fact, question whether it is even possible to fully "recover" in a holistic sense by nonspiritual means.

Widespread confusion suggests the term "recovery" needs some clarification. It does not refer solely to abstinence, which is the quality of being dry. Recovery is more encompassing. It connotes an exceptionally high quality of life. Some call this a meaningful life; others, bountiful living. True recovery is not only being dry, but also being "happy, joyous, and free" (AA, 1976, p. 133). Members of AA sometimes describe this state as serene sobriety.

In the AA understanding, the deep core of alcoholism, the hidden root of problematic drinking lies in the flawed and imperfect human personality. This idea is clearly articulated in a key passage in chapter five of the *Big Book* (AA, 1976), which reads, "selfishness, self-centeredness, that we think, is the root of our troubles," (p. 63). AA members habitually use the vocabulary of personal flaws such as grandiosity, resentment, impatience, arrogant defiance, dishonesty, contempt, and self-pity. Practice of the 12 steps brings about a personality transformation characterized by a replacement of primitive ego traits with higher moral/spiritual virtues, such as honesty, humility, patience, love, acceptance, and forgiveness. These virtues have their source in Divine Grace.

ECUMENICAL CHRISTIAN vs. NEW THOUGHT PERSPECTIVES

The value of providing contrasting perspectives for understanding the 12 steps becomes apparent when one realizes how diverse clients are. Some clients might be well suited to a Christian explanation of AA's program, while others might be more apt to resonate with a transpersonal (New Thought) perspective. An expanded appreciation of the spiritual nature of AA's 12-step program may prove especially useful for counselors who are working with agnostic or atheistic alcoholic clients or clients from Eastern cultures. Diverse clients may show resistance or belligerence to Christianity as it has traditionally been presented. To the extent that they identify AA as being for Christians only, such clients may prematurely reject this modality for healing from addiction. It is possible that these clients will more easily accept a nontraditional approach, such as one that is transpersonal or metaphysical. If cognitive reframing can be accomplished and if an alternative mind set can be found that is more appealing, the net result may increase willingness to affiliate with AA. By making AA appear to be more inclusive with a broader base, more diverse clients may be able to derive benefit.

At this point, I will take up the task of examining, in sequence, the inner workings of each of AA's 12 steps. For each step, I will first present the standard spiritual interpretation as described in AA literature. I have referred to this understanding as the ecumenical Christian perspective. Immediately following a discourse on the standard AA interpretation, I will briefly present an additional discussion that reinterprets the step from the vantage point of New Thought metaphysics. As part of the New Thought "spin" that I put on the steps, I have rewritten the steps using metaphysical language and vocabulary. In discussing the reinterpretation, I have drawn heavily on Emilie Cady's (1896/1989) New Thought book, *Lessons in Truth*, the foundational textbook for Unity Church.

Step 1

Step 1 states that "we admitted we were powerless over alcohol—that our lives had become unmanageable" (AA, 1976, p. 30). This step involves recognizing the nature of the problem, which is lack of power:

> At a certain point in the drinking of every alcoholic, he passes into a state where the most powerful desire to stop drinking is of absolutely no avail. . . . For reasons yet obscure, the alcoholic has lost the power of choice in drink. Our so-called will power becomes practically nonexistent. We are unable at certain times to bring into our consciousness with sufficient force the memory of the suffering and humiliation of even a week or a month ago. We are without defense against the first drink. (pp. 24-25)

Step 1 includes a deep emotional recognition that one is in an impossible situation that involves being condemned to keep drinking until one is destroyed. Not surprisingly, this step is associated with a profound sense of helplessness and hopelessness that result from giving up the struggle to control one's drinking and admitting defeat. "Surrender" is a term often used by AAs to describe the first-step experience. In a state of surrender, the prideful ego is sufficiently crushed so as to free the person to seek alternative solutions and ask for help, hopefully from a Higher Power. Thus, in step 1 the person finally stops trying to use the wrong methods to bring the right results. Of course, changing old behaviors requires a change in thinking. In step 1 the person experiences a shift from a nonteachable state of stubborn resistance to a more teachable and receptive state of open-minded willingness.

From the perspective of New Thought, the first step might be reworded as follows: "Admitted that my thinking mind or ego personality is limited, and that trusting this lower self has resulted in a life of bondage to alcohol." One possible metaphysical reinterpretation of the first step suggests that the central problem of the alcoholic is that he or she has lived solely at the lower plane of human consciousness, and because of this, believed all the lies of "the mind of the flesh." As a consequence, he or she has been overcome by lack, limitation, and suffering. Step 1, therefore has to do with gaining a deep experiential understanding of the limits of the thinking mind or human ego. This idea was reflected by Cady (1896/1989), who stated that "sometime, somewhere, every human being must come to themselves and become tired of eating husks" (p. 95).

The first step experience also illustrates how bad results follow false thinking, and how the Spirit of the Universe permits us—through ignorance—to drift into wrong thoughts, and so bring trouble on ourselves. As sentient beings, we are not preprogrammed robots. Thus, in the process of soul growth, our Higher Power allows us to experience our limited false self to get a firsthand knowledge of the associated problems of sickness, sorrow, and poverty of spirit. All of these naturally flow from subjective identification with the limited "animal part" of the self.

The spirit of step 1 also reflects the divine law of supply and demand which holds that the demand must be made before the supply can come forth: "Ask, and ye shall receive" (Matthew 7:7, KJV). Thus, while there is already provided a lavish abundance of every human want, this infinite supply is useless unless we place a demand upon it. Finally, the first step appears to involve a cleansing of the mind of false beliefs which previously had brought sorrow, lack, and limitation, and repudiating beliefs about being more powerful than alcohol. Cady (1896/1989) noted that "the first step toward freeing ourselves from our troubles is to get rid of our erroneous beliefs about ourselves. . . beliefs that have made such sad havoc in our lives" (p. 99).

Step 2

AA (1976) stated that, in step 2, alcoholics "believe that a Power greater than ourselves could restore us to sanity." If step 1 is a recognition of the problem, then step 2 is a recognition of the solution. Because this step presents the still sick and suffering alcoholic with a potential solution, it is often referred to as the "hope step":

> If a mere code of morals or a better philosophy of life were sufficient
> to overcome alcoholism, many of us would have recovered long ago.
> But we found that such codes and philosophies did not save us, no
> matter how much we tried. We could wish to be moral, we could
> wish to be philosophically comforted, in fact, we could will these
> things with all our might, but the needed power wasn't there. Our
> human resources, as marshaled by the will, were not sufficient: they
> failed utterly. Lack of power, that was our dilemma. We had to find a
> power by which we could live, and it had to be a Power greater than
> ourselves. Obviously, but where and how were we to find this Power?
>
> . . .We needed to ask ourselves but one short question. "Do I now
> believe, or am I even willing to believe, that there is a Power greater
> than myself?" As soon as a man can say that he does believe, or
> is willing to believe, we emphatically assure him that he is on his
> way. It has been repeatedly proven among us that upon this simple
> cornerstone, a wonderfully effective spiritual structure can be built.
> (pp. 46-47)

According to AA (1976), in order to drink at all, the sober alcoholic must first deceive himself or herself by telling a lie and then believing it to be true. In this way, "insanity" is understood to be the inability to see the truth, or the ability to mistake false beliefs as true. Step 2 suggests that the Spirit of the Universe can restore sanity.

From the perspective of New Thought, step 2 might be reworded to read as follows: "through the personal revelation of the Universal Spirit that is my Higher Self, I came to believe that I am abundant, whole, and prosperous." The theme of step 2 is expressed in Christian scripture: "all things are possible to him that believeth" [Mark 9:23, AKJV], and "if any man will come after me, let him deny himself" [Matthew 16:12, KJV]. The object of the belief that Mark refers to is one's divine character, or "Higher Self." Thus, from the metaphysical vantage point of New Thought, the alcoholic at step 2 comes to believe that human beings are much more than merely human. The alcoholic shifts to have faith that people are actually spiritual beings, and that there is a higher dimension to them that was formerly hidden from awareness. As Cady (1896/1989) pointed out:

> Man, who is at first living in the selfish animal part of himself, will grow up through various stages and by various processes to the divine or spiritual understanding wherein he knows that he is one with the Father, and wherein he is free from all suffering. . . . Somewhere on this journey the human consciousness or intellect comes to a place where it gladly bows to its spiritual self and confesses that this spiritual self, its Christ, is highest and is Lord. (p. 41)

In summary, a New Thought interpretation of step 2 suggests that the alcoholic comes to draw a distinction between the limited mind expressed in terms of ego-personality (the mind of the flesh) and expansive spiritual (God) consciousness. Furthermore, the alcoholic comes to recognize that faith in the thinking mind has been misplaced because reliance on this limited source of power has been the root of his or her sorrow. Thus, step 2 brings the acknowledgement that one has fallen prey to narcissistic grandiosity, which is akin to admitting one has worshipped a false idol. Finally, the recovering alcoholic develops faith that the Universal Mind or Divine Spirit (or whatever label one likes) has the ability to supersede the "carnal" mind and breathe in a Holy Peace. Step 2 requires a faith that does not depend on physical facts or on the evidence of the five senses, because the type of faith that is required is born of intuition, or of the Spirit of Truth, ever living at the center of one's being.

Step 3

Step 3 involves making a decision: "to turn our will and our lives over to the care of God as we understood Him" (AA, 1976, p. 58). The third-step decision poses the alcoholic with a choice between two alternatives. The first choice is to return to drinking and stay stuck in the problem, and the second choice is to move toward the solution, and to seek to obtain power from a Divine Source.

> Our troubles. . . arise out of ourselves, and the alcoholic is an extreme example of self-will run riot, though he usually doesn't think so. Above everything, we alcoholics must be rid of this selfishness. We must or it kills us! God makes the removal possible. And there often seems no way of entirely getting rid of self without His aid. (p. 62)

From the viewpoint of New Thought, the wording of the third step might be: "Made a decision to experience direct revelation of the Truth of my Soul by detaching from ego-personality and actualizing my oneness with the Divine Self, the Oversoul of all that is." According to this metaphysical interpretation, step 3 expresses a desire on the part of the alcoholic to open more widely the invisible channel ever connecting their awareness to the Spirit within. Moreover, this step involves the intuitive understanding that the individualized expression of the Godhead will work out salvation from all worldly troubles. As noted by Cady (1896/1989), in proportion to the increase in Divine guidance, human guidance must decrease. Because step 3 reveals a willingness to affirm and embody Divine Will and deny human will, it capitalizes on the New Thought "law of mind action," which states that if we replace old thoughts and motives with new ones, the difference will transform our conditions from inside out. Thus, by making a decision to come into greater harmony with the Divine Mind, the alcoholic at step 3 seeks to gain direct access to all the Higher Laws and Higher Forces available only to those who disavow (deny) the power of human consciousness.

Steps 4 and 5

The fourth step reads "made a searching and fearless moral inventory of ourselves," (AA, 1976, p. 58) while the fifth step states that "we admitted to God, to ourselves, and to another human being the exact nature of our wrongs" (p. 58). Generally speaking, the fifth step involves a public confession of the inventory of personality flaws completed in the fourth step.

Given that the fourth step requires the person to engage in some observable action, it is the first action step and is considered by many in AA to be a form of spiritual practice. Thus, it is not just a principle to contemplate or meditate upon. As noted by AA (1976):

> We launched out on a course of *vigorous action*, the first step of which is a personal housecleaning, which many of us had never attempted. . . . Though our (3rd step) decision was a vital and crucial step, it could have little permanent effect unless at once followed by a *strenuous effort* to face, and be rid of, the things in ourselves which

had been blocking us (from God). Our liquor was but a symptom.
So we had to get down to causes and conditions. . . . Therefore, we
started upon a personal inventory. (p. 64, emphasis added)

The AA perspective of the introspective self-appraisal undertaken in the fourth
and fifth steps suggests that the invisible root problem is narcissism or egocentricity,
which gives rise to visible feelings of resentment, anger, fear, guilt, shame, regret,
and remorse. Given this multiplicity in the way that selfishness is expressed in
actual practice, the fourth step actually consists of three different inventories. The
first analyzes the role of self in anger and resentment. A second inventory analyzes
the role of self in fears; a third analyzes the role of self in sex-related harm done
to others. When drafting the fourth step inventory, the AA member is asked to
ignore the wrongs others have done them and to look for places in which they
have been selfish, dishonest, inconsiderate, self-seeking, and grandiose. When
these faults are spotted, they are placed on paper, in black and white.

Regarding the fifth step, the *Big Book* (AA, 1976) states the following:

Having made our personal inventory, what shall we do about it? . . .
We have admitted certain defects; we have ascertained in a rough
way what the trouble is; we have put our finger on the weak items
in our personal inventory. Now these are about to be cast out. This
requires action on our part, which, when completed, will mean that
we have admitted to God, to ourselves, and to another human being,
the exact nature of our defects. . . . We pocket our pride and go to it,
illuminating every twist of character, every dark cranny of the past.
Once we have taken this step, withholding nothing, we are delighted.
We can look the world in the eye. We can be alone at perfect peace
and ease. Our fears fall from us. We begin to feel the nearness of our
Creator. We may have had certain spiritual beliefs, but now we begin
to have a spiritual experience. The feeling that the drink problem has
disappeared will often come strongly. We feel we are on the Broad
Highway, walking hand in hand with the Spirit of the Universe.
(p. 75)

From the perspective of New Thought, these two steps might be reworded
as follows. For step 4, it might read that "I took stock of the limitations of my
false self or ego-personality." For step 5 it might state that "I revealed to the Spirit
of the Universe and another human being the exact nature of the limitations of
my false self or thinking mind." Cady (1896/1989) wrote about the flaws and
limitations of the lower ego-self in a way which was remarkably similar to the
ones identified in the *Big Book*:

> This intellectual man, carnal mind, or whatever you choose to call
> him is envious and jealous and fretful and sick because he is selfish.
> The human self seeks its own gratification at the expense, if need be,
> of someone else. . . . Thus, we begin our journey toward true spiritual
> understanding by cutting off the branches of our selfishness. (p. 62)

This inner journey of introspection and identification of that which has previously been denied or repressed is followed by a type of spiritual purging through "confession" to God and another person. In the purging process, the Soul is purified of some of the obstacles to fuller realization of true Spiritual identity. From a Jungian viewpoint, the fourth and fifth steps clearly represent a person's attempt to explore and befriend the repressed "shadow" part of personality.

Steps 4 and 5 also make practical use of the law of mind action, which suggests that thoughts held in mind manifest after their kind. Thus, to the extent that these steps help to remove negative thoughts and disharmonious emotions from consciousness, they should also result in appropriate actions. In proportion to the amount of release from this type of "bondage of karma," recovering alcoholics are able to experience life more abundant in their daily affairs.

Steps 6 and 7

In the tradition of AA (1976), step 6 states that we "were entirely ready to have God remove all these defects of character," (p. 58) while step 7 states that we "humbly asked him to remove our shortcomings" (p. 58). Step 6 is concerned with the motivational state known as desire or willingness. At step 6, the recovering person is faced with the continuing task of becoming more willing to let go of selfish (dysfunctional) personality traits that stand in the way of fully experiencing and expressing the presence of God. Acquiring the quality of humility requires one to carry out step 7, involving further deflation of the grandiose self-concept. This is because humility, by definition, is the antithesis of narcissism. Humility requires that the thinking mind transcend itself and relinquish its preeminence and place to God or a Higher Power first. This is yet another meaning of the term "surrender." Interpreted spiritually, the recovering person at step 7 is invited to intellectually admit and experience—at the core of their being—that "of myself I am nothing, the Father doeth the works" (AA, 1981, p. 75). Step 7 also presupposes faith in the proposition that God (or a Higher Power) can do for us what our ego cannot do for ourselves.

Of relevance in this connection is a passage from the 12 & 12 (AA, 1981): "The seventh step is where we make the change in our attitude which permits us, with humility as our guide, to move out from ourselves toward others and toward God. The whole emphasis of step seven is on humility" (p. 76).

The alcoholic at step 7 is given two questions to ponder: "Are we now ready to let God remove from us all the things which we have admitted are objectionable?" (AA, 1976, p. 76); and "Can He now take them all—every one?" (p. 76). If the alcoholic still clings to something and will not let go, he is instructed to pray to God to help him to become willing. After pondering these questions for a sufficient period of time so as to respond in the affirmative to both questions, the recovering alcoholic is asked to declare that he or she has acquired sufficient willingness to be emptied of traits such as selfishness, dishonesty, and inconsiderateness. Specifically, the alcoholic is encouraged to affirm, out loud if desired, the seventh step prayer:

> My Creator, I am now willing that you should have all of me good and bad. I pray that you now remove from me every single defect of character which stands in the way of my usefulness to you and my fellows. Grant me strength, as I go out from here to do your bidding. Amen. (AA, 1976, p. 76)

From the vantage point of New Thought, the wording of step 6 might be changed to read as follows: "I became willing to have my Spirit Essence remove from my thinking mind the belief in lack and limitation." Step 7 might be reinterpreted as stating: "I humbly invited my Spirit Essence to give me access to the intuitive knowledge that my poverty consciousness is but illusion." According to this New Thought restatement, steps 6 and 7 are consistent with the recognition that the Great Spirit's will is always for a person's thinking to become uplifted to a previously unknown level of reality. In these steps, the alcoholic becomes ready to let go of the false and limited concept of themselves that they have been clinging to so very tightly, that they are human beings seeking a spiritual experience. The alternative belief offered the recovering alcoholic is that he is a *spiritual being undergoing a human experience*. Trust is a prerequisite for this type of letting go, for the person who lacks trust will certainly be reluctant to detach from the ego. From a New Thought perspective, in step 7 the person invites the individualized expression of the Soul of the Universe to remove the obstacles inherent in his or her limited ego-personality. These obstacles have blocked the recovering alcoholic from a full experiential awareness of Christ Consciousness and mystical awakening.

According to the New Thought perspective, the major barrier to be removed from human consciousness is the ego's culturally conditioned belief in the fiction of lack and limitation, also known as poverty consciousness ("not enough" syndrome). At the wellspring of this tenacious faith in sickness, sorrow and suffering is the sense of separation from the indwelling Divine Supply. This metaphysical reinterpretation of steps 6 and 7 suggests that the thinking mind's perception of itself as an isolated entity—different from other entities—can be disintegrated or transcended. When perceptions of boundaries between self and non-self begin to dissolve, it is that much easier for the recovering alcoholic to have a transformative, unitive experience known variously as "mystical awakening," or "cosmic consciousness," etc.

This radical transformation is consistent with New Thought teachings:

> When you have learned how to abandon yourself to infinite Spirit, and have seasons of doing this daily, you will be surprised at the marvelous change that will be wrought in you without any conscious effort on your own. It will search far below your conscious mind and root out things in your nature of which you have scarcely been conscious, simply because they have lain latent there, waiting for something to bring them out. It will work into your conscious light and life and love and all good, perfectly filling all your lack while you just quietly wait and receive. (Cady, 1896/1989, p. 177)

The metaphysical essence of step 7 is also expressed by Emerson (1986), who stated that man is "by his nature as unconditioned, pure, as perfect and alone as the infinite. But he doesn't know it and the smokescreen of his own conditioning forever fogs him" (p. 251). Thus, in step 7, the person readies himself or herself for Divine Grace to enter and transcend fictional beliefs held by the ego-self.

Steps 8 and 9

The eighth step of AA (1976) states: "We made a list of all persons we had harmed, and become willing to make amends to them," (p. 58) and in step 9 we "made direct amends to such people wherever possible except when to do so would injure them or others" (p. 58). The *Big Book* (AA, 1976) noted:

> We need more action, without which we find that "Faith without works is dead." . . .We have a list of all persons we have harmed and to whom we are willing to make amends. We made the list when we took our 4th step inventory. . . . Now we go out to our fellows and repair the damage done in the past. We attempt to sweep away the debris which has accumulated out of our effort to live on self-will and run the show ourselves. If we haven't the will to do this, we pray to God until it comes. . . . The alcoholic is like a tornado roaring his way through the lives of others. Hearts are broken. Sweet relationships are dead. Affections have been uprooted. Selfish and inconsiderate habits have kept the home in turmoil. We feel a man unthinking when he says that sobriety is enough. . . . Yes, there is a long period of reconstruction ahead. We must take the lead. A remorseful mumbling that we are sorry won't fill the bill at all. . . . So we clean house. . . asking each morning in meditation that our Creator show us the way

of patience, tolerance, kindliness and love. The spiritual life is not a theory. *We have to live it.* (p. 76, 82-83)

These two steps are presented in a manner that highlights their spiritual nature. Specifically, the main spiritual purpose of doing steps 8 and 9 is to further purify oneself in order to be able to carry out the third step decision, which consists of the decision to become willing to let God or a Higher Power direct one's thinking and actions. Completion of these two steps rids the self of guilt, shame, and remorse (unforgiveness of self) as well as bitterness, resentment, and the desire for revenge (unforgiveness of others). These different character flaws all have one thing in common: They block a richer experience in awareness and fuller expression in behavior of the grace of God.

The stumbling block at step 8 is the same as the barrier faced by the AA member at step 4: false pride or narcissism. Freudian psychologists have long known the conceit of the narcissist as an ego defense against unacceptable self-perceptions involving lack of worth and dignity.

At step 9, the recovering alcoholic is asked to make amends to people whom they have held in unforgiveness. Because of this overlap between the fourth- and eighth-step lists, persons working steps 8 and 9 are faced with the difficult but life-transforming task of exhibiting true humility and true forgiveness. The *Big Book* (AA, 1976) suggests that, if needed, the alcoholic should pray to the God of their own understanding for strength to transcend their egocentric focus on their own hurts and thereby develop sufficient willingness to enact the ninth step. This focus on making reparations for how one's own actions caused another to suffer clearly distinguishes it from the conventional understanding of forgiveness as mercy and compassion given by a victim to a perpetrator who has committed an offense against the self. As a result of taking responsibility for harm done to others, the recovering alcoholic who makes amends experiences self-forgiveness as well as a heightened sense of forgiveness from God and other people. After completing steps 8 and 9, a person will often experience a deep sense of humility.

Taken together, these two steps represent a powerful and transformative spiritual practice for accelerating spiritual maturation. This, in turn, enables the recovering alcoholic to be of maximum service to God or a Higher Power and humankind, which is the overarching goal of AA. Thus, AA not only seeks to cultivate private spiritual experience, it seeks to cultivate public expression of this experience in the form of altruistic service to others (i.e., step 12).

From the transpersonal perspective of New Thought, steps 8 and 9 might be reworded. Step 8 suggests that "I became aware of my karmic debt to others, and I developed sufficient willingness to encourage my Spirit–Essence to use my form as a vehicle to erase this debt." Step 9 suggests that "I allowed my indwelling Spirit-Essence to express directly through me to manifest healing and wholeness in my unhealed relationships." From the vantage point of New Thought, steps 8 and 9 represent a sincere desire to transcend the ego's obsessive preoccupation with its own welfare. In the process of reaching out to others to mend broken relationships, the Soul is given the opportunity to express more fully in this earthly plane of reality. The natural expression is manifested in the form of compassion, mercy, and loving kindness for a former adversary. Having undergone the previous seven steps, the recovering alcoholic at steps 8 and 9 has already undergone the preparatory internal experience of acknowledging his or her own human faults and frailty (e.g., steps 4 and 5). Because step 9 can be considered to represent love-in-action, or living the abundant life, it embodies the essential message of New Thought which is not so much a message of words but of works. With its requirement of forgiveness (granting it, seeking it, accepting it) and repentance, step 9 also exemplifies the New Thought proclivity toward the practical application of one's spiritual beliefs to solve problems of daily living.

Step 10

Step 10 states that we "continued to take personal inventory and when we were wrong promptly admitted it" (AA, 1976, p. 58). The emphasis here is on the ongoing nature of working the steps:

> It is easy to let up on the spiritual program of action and rest on our laurels. We are headed for trouble if we do, for alcohol is a subtle foe. We are not cured of alcoholism. What we really have is a daily reprieve contingent on the maintenance of our spiritual condition. Every day is a day when we must carry the vision of God's will into all of our affairs. "How can I best serve Thee—Thy will not mine be done." These are thoughts which must go with us constantly. We can exercise our will power along this line all we wish. It is the proper use of the will. (p. 85)

The *Big Book* directions for working step 10 suggest that a continuous, daily practicing of steps 4 thru 9 is required. The recovering alcoholic is instructed to "continue to watch for selfishness, dishonesty, resentment, and fear" (p. 84) as previously identified in steps 4 and 5. If and when they are found, the book gives instruction to discuss them with another person (step 5). Then, the book instructs the individual to ask God to remove them (steps 6 and 7), and if they have harmed anyone, to make amends instantly (step 9). Thus, step 10 is really a continuous updating of steps 4 through 9 on a one-day-at-a-time basis.

If the 10th step is sincerely worked for a period of time, the alcoholic can expect to reap the fruits promised:

> We will have ceased fighting anything or anyone—even alcohol. For
> by now, sanity will have returned. We will seldom be interested in
> liquor. If tempted, we will recoil from it as from a hot flame. We will
> react sanely and normally, and we will find that this has happened
> automatically. We will see that our new attitude toward liquor has
> been given us without any thought or effort on our part. It just
> comes! That is the miracle of it. We are not fighting it, neither are
> we avoiding temptation. We feel as though we had been placed in a
> position of neutrality—safe and protected. We have not even sworn
> off. Instead, the problem has been removed. It does not exist for us.
> We are neither cocky nor are we afraid. That is our experience. That is
> how we react so long as we keep in fit spiritual condition. (AA, 1976,
> p. 84-85)

From the viewpoint of New Thought, it is possible to read step 10 as follows:
"I continued to take stock of my thinking, and immediately recognized wrong
thinking or erroneous consciousness." A New Thought perspective on the 10th
step involves vigilant scanning of thought processes for the purpose of denying
wrong thinking and affirming right consciousness. Step 10 asks the alcoholic in
recovery to rise in consciousness when needed so as to avoid being punished by
his "sins." From the perspective of New Thought, the term "sin" refers to error
consciousness, or thinking that is off the mark or "off the beam." Because the
10th step helps the alcoholic to uplift or change his or her thinking and keep it
uplifted, it allows the person to "sin no more" one moment at a time. As Emmet
Fox (1934/1989) noted, having a negative thought run across your consciousness is like having a hot burning ash land on the sleeve of your shirt. You can do
nothing and let it burn a hole, or you can brush it off. In the present case, you
can brush it off with a quick application of the 10th step.

Step 11

Step 11 (AA, 1976) states that we "sought through prayer and meditation to
improve our conscious contact with God as we understood Him, praying only for
knowledge of His will for us and the power to carry that out" (p. 58). McQuainy
(1990) noted that step 11 is the culmination of all of the previous steps:

> As a result of the actions of steps 4 through 10, we removed or had
> removed for us the things that were blocking us from God. Now we
> can finally carry out the decision we made in step 3 of turning our
> will and our lives over to the care of God as we understood Him.
> Through prayer and meditation, we can receive God's will for us and
> the power to carry it out. If we can do that, we will have carried out

the decision that we made in step 3. Steps 3 and 11 are the pillars of the steps. We could say that the steps have two crucial points: The decision to turn over our will in step 3 and the receiving of God's will in step 11. (p. 135)

The 11th step prayer appears in the *12 & 12* (AA, 1981). Some readers may recognize this prayer as one widely attributed to St. Francis:

Lord, make me an instrument of thy peace—
that where there is hatred, I may bring love—
that where there is wrong, I may bring the spirit of forgiveness—
that where there is discord, I may bring harmony—
that where there is error, I may bring truth—
that where there is doubt, I may bring faith—
that where there is despair, I may bring hope—
that where there are shadows, I may bring light—
that where there is sadness, I may bring joy.
Lord, grant that I may seek
rather to comfort than to be comforted—
to understand, than to be understood—
to love, than to be loved.
For it is by self-forgetting that one finds.
It is by forgiving that one is forgiven.
It is by dying that one awakens to Eternal Life. Amen. (pp. 99)

From the perspective of New Thought, the 11th step might be reworded as follows: "I sought to enter the silence and experience an inner revealing of the truth of my oneness with the Spirit of the Universe." As I have restated it here, this step is highly consistent with the New Thought belief that "we all have direct access to the Father in us, the central source of our being and the great whole of life, love, wisdom, and power which is God." In step 11, alcoholics seek to be obedient to the "still small voice" of the indwelling presence, knowing that the more they learn to act in harmony with the voice, the more their Spirit Essence is able to find expression. In this connection, Cady (1896/1989) stated:

We can all learn how to turn the conscious mind toward Universal Mind or Spirit within us. We can, by practice, learn how to make this every-day topsy-turvy mind of the flesh be still and let the mind that is God think in us and through us (p. 133)

The importance of resting in the silence cannot be overemphasized:

You may be so busy with the doing, the outgoing of love to help others, that you find no time to go apart. But the command, or rather the invitation, is "come ye yourselves apart. . . and rest awhile" (Mark 6:3). And it is the only way in which you will ever gain definite knowledge, true wisdom, newness of experience, steadiness of purpose, or power to meet the unknown, which must come in all daily life. Doing is secondary to being. When we are consciously the Truth, it will radiate from us and accomplish the works without our ever running to and fro. (p. 210)

Whereas in the third step, the alcoholic seeker made a decision to experience direct revelation of the Truth of his soul by moving away from ego-personality and toward Spirit Being, in the 11th step the alcoholic rests in his secret place and receives intuitive knowledge of his oneness with the Father of Light. In this secret place lies the point of mystical union between the human mind and the Spirit in us, and "each man must for himself wait upon God for the inner illumination which is lasting and real. God alone can whisper the secret to each one separately" (Cady, 1896/1989, p. 27).

Step 12

The 12th step is not a process which contributes to recovery. Rather, it describes an outcome which results from enacting the prior 11 steps. Step 12 states that "having had a spiritual awakening as the results of these steps, we tried to carry this message to alcoholics, and to practice these principles in all our affairs" (AA, 1976, p. 58). This step provides a guarantee that, if alcoholics take the first 11 steps, they will have a spiritual awakening. The *Big Book* provides a detailed and somewhat lengthy description of the meaning of the term "spiritual awakening." While some have a sudden, overwhelming epiphany of God-awareness, that is not usually the case:

Most of our experiences are what the psychologist William James calls the "educational variety" because they develop slowly over the period of time. Quite often friends of the newcomer are aware of the difference long before he is himself. He finally realizes that he has undergone a profound alteration in his reaction to life, and that such a change could hardly have been brought about by himself alone. What often takes place in a few months could seldom have been accomplished by years of self-discipline. With few exceptions, our members find that they have tapped an unsuspected inner resource which they presently identify with their own conception of a Power greater than themselves. Most of us think this awareness of a Power greater than ourselves is the essence of spiritual experience. (p. 570)

From the perspective of New Thought, the 12th step might be reworded as follows: "Having had a spiritual awakening as a result of these steps, I carried the messages of goodness and oneness to others, and practiced the principles of love-in-action in my daily affairs." In the present context, the term spiritual awakening is used to refer to the ineffable intuitive state of knowledge or awareness gained by direct inner revelation of the presence of God and our oneness with him. As Cady (1896/1989) noted:

> In that day when, more than riches and honor and power and selfish glory, you shall desire spiritual understanding, in that day will come to you the revelation of God in you, and you will be conscious of the indwelling Father, who is life and strength and power and peace (p. 101)

Cady elaborated on the idea of a direct, inner revelation:

> In the onward growth, the time will come to every man when he will hear the divine voice within him saying, "come up higher," and he will pass beyond any merely selfish desires that are just for his own comfort's sake. He will desire good that he may have the more to give out, knowing that as good flows through him to others it will make him "every whit whole." (p. 95)

Finally, Cady (1896/1989) resonates with the need for service to humanity, the essence of the 12th step:

> There must be an equal conscious receiving from the Father and giving out to the world, a perfect equilibrium between the inflowing and the outgiving to keep perfect harmony. We must each learn how to wait renewedly upon God for the infilling, and then go and give out to every creature that which we have received, as Spirit leads us to give, either in preaching, teaching or silently living the Truth. That which fills us will radiate from us without effort right in the place in life where we stand. (p. 88)

CONCLUSION

We live in a society marked by increased pluralism. One of the expected benefits of the current chapter's transpersonal perspective is that it can potentially help to accommodate societal shifts associated with multicultural diversity. If AA's 12-step program can be reframed and presented to non-Christians in a way that is seen to be more relevant and more inclusive, perhaps a broader range of clients can derive benefit from attending this spiritually centered support group. This perspective on AA's 12-step program of recovery from alcoholism might prove especially useful for counselors who are working with clients who identify as agnostic, "spiritual but not religious," or non-Christian from Eastern (or other) cultures. Diverse clients such as these may show resistance or belligerence to Christianity as it has traditionally been presented. To the extent that they identify AA as being for Christians only, such clients may prematurely reject it as a viable modality for healing from addiction. It is possible that these clients may find a nontraditional (e.g., transpersonal or metaphysical) approach to understanding AA spirituality more appealing. If cognitive reframing can be accomplished, the net result may be increased motivational readiness to affiliate with AA.

In closing, an empirical question for future research is whether a New Thought/ transpersonal reinterpretation of AA's 12-step recovery program will actually be more effective than the ecumenical Christian approach in recruiting culturally diverse non-Christian drinkers. A related question is: What can mental health professionals do to recruit these people into treatment or facilitate their willingness to attend the AA meetings which are offered in the community in which they live? It is difficult to say whether atheistic alcoholics will find the New Thought approach to AA equally or more offensive than the ecumenical Christian approach. These are questions that public health scholars and professionals ought to be concerned with.

Over the past 20 years, a number of membership surveys conducted in Canada and the US by the world headquarters of AA shows that it is relatively rare for minority group members to attend AA meetings. It is unclear why Caucasians tend to dominate. One likely explanation involves AA's long standing reputation in the general community as a Christian program, or as a program that is most appropriate for people who are "religious." In this connection, mental health professionals who are currently implementing 12-step facilitation programs and who wish to increase the rate of AA uptake by clients who view themselves as "spiritual but not religious" or as non-Christian may wish to reframe AA for these clients using the New Thought/transpersonal perspective articulated in this chapter. For a number of sociocultural reasons, the base rate of these kinds of clients has been growing since the 1960s. Yet, these same clients seem to have been marginalized by addiction-service providers who encourage AA involvement as an adjunct to treatment. The 1960s witnessed an explosion of cultural interest in the West in Eastern and Indian spiritual traditions. This interest seems to be increasing in the new millennium. Thus, concurrent with the rapid decline of the Christian church in the West, we continue to witness a rise of alternative spirituality rooted in Buddhism and Hinduism. The New Thought/transpersonal framework may resonate well with Caucasians who define themselves as "spiritual but not religious" and with immigrants from countries that subscribe to Hinduism and Buddhism. Hopefully, social and behavioral scientists concerned with public health initiatives will consider testing the efficacy of AA recruitment campaigns that are designed to reframe its 12-step program so that a wider range of culturally diverse drinkers see it as a viable solution for their drinking problem.

REFERENCES

Albanese, C. L. (2009). *A republic of mind and spirit: A cultural history of American metaphysical religion.* New Haven, CT.: Yale University Press.

Alcoholics Anonymous. (1976). *Alcoholics Anonymous: The story of how many thousands of men and women have recovered from alcoholism* (3rd Ed.). New York, NY: AA World Services.[1]

Alcoholics Anonymous. (1980). *Dr. Bob and the good oldtimers: A biography with recollections of early AA in the Midwest.* New York, NY: AA World Services.

Alcoholics Anonymous. (1981). *Twelve steps and twelve traditions.* New York, NY: AA World Services.

Allen, J. (1902). *As a man thinketh.* Retrieved from http://gutenberg.org/ebooks/4507

Anderson, C. A., & Whitehouse, D. G. (1995). *New Thought: A practical American spirituality.* New York, NY: Crossroad Publications.

Barger, M. (1991). *New Wine: The spiritual roots of the 12-step miracle.* Center City, MN: Hazelden Publications.

Barger, M. (2000). *My search for Bill W: Biography.* Center City, MN: Hazelden Publications.

Braden, C. S. (1963). *Spirits in rebellion: The story of the beginnings and growth of New Thought and kindred American metaphysical healing movements.* Dallas, TX: Southern Methodist University Press.

Byrne, R. (2006). *The secret.* New York, NY: Atria Books/Beyond Words.

Cady, H. E. (1989). *Lessons in Truth.* MO: Unity Village. (Original work published 1896)

Clinebell, H. J. (1963). Philosophical-religious factors in the etiology and treatment of alcoholism. *Quarterly Journal of Studies on Alcohol, 24,* 473–488.

Clayton, P. & Peacocke, A. (Eds.) (2004). *In whom we live and move and have our being: Panentheistic reflections on God's presence in a scientific world.* Grand Rapids, MI: William B. Eerdmans.

---

1 The excerpts from the *Big Book, Alcoholics Anonymous* and the *Twelve Steps and Twelve Traditions* are reprinted with permission of Alcoholics Anonymous World Services, Inc. (AAWS). Permission to reprint these excerpts does not mean that AAWS has reviewed or approved the contents of this publication, or that AAWS necessarily agrees with the views expressed herein. A.A. is a program of recovery from alcoholism only—use of these excerpts in connection with programs and activities which are patterned after A.A., but which address other problems, or in any other non A.A. context, does not imply otherwise. Additionally, while A.A. is a spiritual program, A.A. is not a religious program, and is not affiliated or allied with any sect, denomination, or specific religious belief.

Colwell-Bluhm, A. (2006). Verification of C. G. Jung's analysis of Rowland Hazard and the history of Alcoholics Anonymous. *History of Psychology, 9*, 313–324.

Connors, G. J., Walitzer, K. S, & Tonigan, J. S. (2008). Spiritual change in recovery. In M. Galanter & L. A. Kaskutas (Eds.), *Recent developments in alcoholism* (pp. 209–227). New York, NY: Springer Science and Business Media.

Davis, J. V. (2003). An overview of transpersonal psychology. *The Humanistic Psychologist, 31*, 6–21. doi:10.1080/08873267.2003.9986924

Dick B. (1999). *The books early AAs read for spiritual growth* (7th Ed). Kihei, HI: Paradise Research Publications.

Emerson, R. W. (1986). *Emerson on transcendentalism.* New York: Continuum Books.

Emrick, C. D., Tonigan, J. S., Montgomery, H., & Little, L. (1993). Alcoholics Anonymous: What is currently known? In B. S. McCrady & W. R. Miller (Eds.), *Research on Alcoholics Anonymous: Opportunities and alternatives* (pp. 41–76). Piscataway, NJ: Rutgers Center of Alcohol Studies.

Fox, E. (1989). *The sermon on the mount.* San Francisco, CA: HarperOne Publications. (Original work published 1934)

Galanter, M., & Kaskutas, L. A. (Eds). (2008). *Recent developments in alcoholism: Research on Alcoholics Anonymous and spirituality in addiction recovery.* New York, NY: Spring Science Business Media.

Grof, C. (1994). *The thirst for wholeness: Attachment, addiction and the spiritual path.* San Francisco, CA: Harper Publishers.

Humphreys, K. (2004). *Circles of recovery: Self-help organizations for addictions.* Cambridge, UK: Cambridge University Press.

International New Thought Alliance. (2013). *Declaration of principles.* Retrieved from: http://newthoughtalliance.org/about.html

James, W. (1982). *The varieties of religious experience.* New York, NY: Penguin Classics. (Original work published 1902)

Johnson, T. J. (2013). Addiction and the search for the sacred: Religion, spirituality, and the origins and treatment of substance use disorders (pp. 297–317). In K. I. Pargament (Ed.), *American Psychological Association handbook of psychology, religion and spirituality: An applied psychology of religion and spirituality* (Vol. 2). Washington, DC: APA Press.

Kelly, J. F., Stout, R. L., Magill, M., Tonigan, J. S., & Pagano, M. E. (2011). Spirituality in recovery: A lagged mediational analysis of Alcoholics Anonymous' principle theoretical mechanism of behavior change. *Alcoholism: Clinical and Experimental Research, 35*, 454–463. doi:10.1111/j.1530-0277.2010.01362.x

Kurtz, E. (1980). *Not God: A history of Alcoholics Anonymous.* Center City, MN: Hazelden Publications.

McQuainy, J. (1990). *The steps we took: A teacher of the twelve steps shares his experience, strength and hope.* Little Rock, AR: August House Publishers.

Science of Mind. (2013). *What we believe.* Retrieved from http://scienceofmind/what-we-believe

Sikorsky, I. I. (1990). *AA's godparents: Three early influences on Alcoholics Anonymous and its foundation: Carl Jung, Emmet Fox, Jack Alexander.* Minneapolis, MN: CompCare Publications.

Swora, M. G. (2004). The rhetoric of transformation in the healing of alcoholism: The twelve steps of Alcoholics Anonymous. *Mental Health, Religion & Culture, 7,* 187–209. doi:10.1080/13674670310001602445

Tonigan, J. S. (2008). Alcoholics Anonymous outcomes and benefits. In M. Galanter & L. A Kaskutas (Eds.), *Research on Alcoholics Anonymous and spirituality in addiction recovery: Recent developments in alcoholism* (Vol. 18; pp. 357–372). New York, NY: Springer Science + Business Media.

Tonigan, J. S., Toscova, R., & Miller, W. R. (1996). Meta-analysis of the literature on Alcoholics Anonymous: Sample and study characteristics. *Journal of Studies on Alcohol and Drugs, 57,* 65–72.

Trine, R. W. (2006). *The higher powers of mind and spirit.* New York, NY: Cosimo Publications. (Original work published 1919)

Troward, T. (1904). *Edinburgh Lectures on Mental Science.* Retrieved from http://gutenberg.org/ebooks/10390

Tucker, J. A., & Grimley, D. M. (2011). *Public health tools for practicing psychologists.* Cambridge, MA: Hogrefe Publ ications.

Unity Church. (2013). *Our philosophy.* Retrieved from http://unity.org/about-us/our-philosophy

Wilson, W. (2000). *Bill W.: My first 40 years.* Center City, MN: Hazelden Publications. (Published posthumously. An autobiography based on audio recordings made in 1935)

Wilson, W. (1958). The next frontier: Emotional sobriety. *The Grapevine,* January, pp. 5–11.

Wilson, W. (1963). The Bill Wilson–Carl Jung letters. *The Grapevine,* January, pp. 8–12.

Wing, N. (1999). *Grateful to have been there: My 42 years with Bill and Lois and the evolution of Alcoholics Anonymous.* Center City, MN: Hazelden Publications.

Zemore, S. E. (2007). A role for spiritual change in the benefits of 12-step involvement. *Alcoholism: Clinical and Experimental Research, 31,* 76–79.

16. A Meaning-Centered 12-Step Program for Addiction Recovery

PAUL T. P. WONG, JESSICA J. NEE & LILIAN C. J. WONG

This chapter provides a meaning-centered framework for addiction recovery based on Viktor Frankl's (1986) logotherapy and Wong's (2010a, 2012b) meaning therapy. For a more detailed discussion of this meaning perspective, please refer to Wong (Chapter 13, this volume) and Thompson (Chapters 12, 14, this volume). In this chapter, we emphasize that activation of the primary motivation for meaning and self-transcendence is the most promising way to achieve full recovery and personal transformation.

At the 2006 Meaning Conference on Addiction, Paul Wong (Chapter 13, this volume) emphasized the need for recovering addicts to be awakened to their true purpose in life and their calling to pursue worthy life goals. This meaning approach is predicated on the belief that addicts not only need to be free from addiction, but also free to be fully engaged in life in a meaningful and productive way. Only a new passion for living is strong enough to replace the old addiction habit.

The following is an e-mail letter from a recovering addict, who is challenging Wong's meaning hypothesis (Chapter 13, this volume). This individual seemed intelligent and knowledgeable about Frankl's (1986) work, but also seemed bitter and hopeless about life.

> From the addicts' view, they sometimes can barely see today. Their future is very much making it through "just for today," sometimes just this moment. They all want the big picture, which is to get a new life like they dream it should be. Trial and error and time tell us that we can only grow one moment at a time and each new day clean is a victory. . . . The biggest mistake an addict can make in recovery is to focus on the big picture too much and miss the steps needed to get there. It's just like learning a profession or trade, go to school one day at a time, one course at a time and make it the most important time of your life. Sometimes you get A's sometimes a D but you haven't failed the course, just that test. Above all it takes Practice, Practice, Practice.

> I think I must apologize for preaching to the expert. I didn't even
> know life was supposed to have a meaning. My life has just been
> something that happened to me. I've struggled alone all my life. That
> includes going through two bouts of cancer. And I've never had a goal
> in my life that was any further ahead than the next meal, or where I
> will sleep tonight. I have no mission, no goal, no purpose. . . . That's
> my "existential vacuum," as Viktor Frankl put it. And there's naught
> to be done for it. . . . And I have no further expectations of life (other
> than "eat more shit"), neither do I find anything of life interesting,
> because nothing stimulates my imagination, curiosity, and therefore
> my interest. . . . And there's no one, of either gender, to share it with.

This individual was correct in recognizing the need to learn how to realize his vision step by step. His biggest problem is his existential vacuum and his hopelessness of finding any life goal. This chapter attempts to apply the meaning principle in a step-by-step manner to facilitate recovery and transformation. We hope that the 12 steps outlined here can evoke an innate motivation for personal growth and self-transcendence in spite of any painful past. We also hope that Viktor Frankl's message will be inspiring: Regardless of life circumstances, there is still the freedom to take full responsibility for one's life and create a more rewarding and meaningful future.

STEP 1: WHO ARE YOU? DISCOVER THE TRUE SELF YOU NEVER KNEW.

Knowing one's true self is the most important first step for recovery. Most people identify themselves in terms of positions, roles, and relationships. But when everything is stripped away, who are you?

No matter how broken you are, and no matter what other people think of you, you need to develop the new conviction that your life has intrinsic value and meaning, because you are a worthy spiritual being with a unique calling to contribute to the greater good. This conviction can become not only the main source of motivation for positive actions, but also a new direction to rebuild your life. The foundation of your future will be built on knowing who you are and who you might become.

You Matter as a Unique Individual

Many people consider themselves to be failures or misfits. They have given up hope and are afraid to look in the mirror. Such a negative self-concept is based on performance rather than the inherent value of being a human. Viktor Frankl (1959/1985), from his experiences as a prisoner in a Nazi concentration camp, observed that even in these camps, some were able to live with human dignity and a profound sense of meaning. He also discovered that those who gave up hope and died on the inside usually succumbed to physical death quickly in the camp. Recent research (Wong, 2012a) has clearly shown that having a clear sense of meaning makes us less vulnerable to harsh realities and more likely to function optimally.

You may wonder: How can I really believe that my life has worth and that I can have a good future, given all the failures I have gone through? How can I change my poor self-concept to a positive one? Frankl (1959/1985) has made the case that you actually matter as an individual in spite of your setbacks and failures, because of your singularity and potential for growth. As long as you have life, you have the spiritual and psychological potential to become what you were meant to be. It may take hard work and determination to discover your unique calling. Your quest for meaning will keep you moving forward through the dark valleys and obstacles until you become what you were meant to be.

Discover Your Authentic Self

The idea of singularity is important for personal meaning in times of suffering, according to Frankl. You are one of a kind because of a unique combination of personal talents, temperament, and experiences. You need to embrace and celebrate your singularity and be true to your unique calling in spite of social pressure towards conformity. The challenge is to find out your true purpose in life. This may be a long and difficult process, but at least you need to start with the conviction that you were born for a reason and that there is a special task, a mission, waiting for you to fulfill.

During your quest for meaning, you may need to hold down various jobs to make a living, but a sense of calling may make your work more meaningful, regardless of the nature of your job. A big part of searching for your calling is self-knowledge of your skills, abilities, and gifts, as well as where your passion lies. It also entails knowing how you should respond to the demands of various situations in life in a responsible way.

Aristotle noted that knowing yourself is the beginning of wisdom. If you do not know who you are, how can you know what you really want? "To thine own self be true," wrote Shakespeare (*Hamlet*, I, 3); if you are not true to your calling, who will be? That is why self-knowledge is the first step on your journey towards healing and flourishing. Once you see yourself as an autonomous, authentic person, free to choose your own destiny and create your own future, you will not easily get confused and overwhelmed by life.

Knowing & Accepting Your Dark Side

Just as important as recognizing the positive, spiritual aspect of your being, it is also important to be aware of the dark side of your personality. If you do not confront your vulnerability, it can trip you and defeat your best effort. Happiness is to know and accept the real you in totality—the good, the bad, and the ugly. There is a dark side to every human being. This has been well documented historically, scientifically, and experientially. We are capable of cruelty, atrocities, and evil. If you cannot confront and accept your weaknesses, you will waste a lot of your energy in defending and hiding the real you. In your futile attempts to escape from yourself, you will feel lonely, alienated, fearful, and miserable.

The brutal fact is that you cannot escape from yourself all your life. You may seek temporary escape through distractions, addictions, or sleep, but such escapes may make your life more painful. Your dark sides are your points of vulnerability, the areas where you need help and remediation. Addiction is clearly a point of vulnerability, a problem that needs to be overcome. It may be helpful to separate you as a person from your addiction problem. You are a person with a history of addiction, but addiction is not your identity. Your true identity is as a human being with a spiritual core; you have the potential to grow and to make a unique, meaningful contribution to society. However, your weaknesses can become your strengths when you learn to accept, transcend, and transform them. You will learn some of the skills in coping with the dark side of life later in this chapter.

Summary

You are a unique worthy human being in spite of your dark side. You are defined by your intrinsic value and inner strengths rather than by your addiction problems.

Exercises:

Self-Reflection. Many people in their moments of crisis and despair may engage in self-reflection, which may in turn lead to self-awakening to the new possibilities in life. Spend some time reflecting on these questions.

- Who am I?
- What am I doing here?
- What kind of person do I want to see in myself five years down the road?
- How would I describe my self-identity?

Self-Acceptance.

- What are the parts of me that I try to hide—or escape—from?
- What parts of me are most difficult for me to face?
- What are some forces that have shaped me?

Life Review of Past Success.

- Name at least two of your strengths.
- Name at least one thing that you have done in your lifetime that you are proud of—it doesn't matter how big or small.
- Think of someone who really values you and cares for you, either in the past or present.

STEP 2: WHAT REALLY MATTERS IN LIFE? SET YOUR NEW LIFE GOALS.

If self-knowledge is the first step towards change, then knowing what you really want in life is a logical next step. Part of your identity is your core values, which can be either self-centered or self-transcendent. What matters most to you reflects your core values. You are defined not by your past, nor by your present circumstances, but by your choice of what really matters.

You may feel too tired to think about your future, having only enough energy to fight for sobriety one day at a time. But sobriety cannot be your sole life purpose. You need a meaningful and achievable life goal to motivate you to move forward. Sobriety will no longer be a problem when you are preoccupied with the passion for living

In this step, you will learn two important lessons: First, you are responsible for deciding on your core values and priorities, and second, you can change your past mistakes and pain into assets in planning for your future.

Taking Ownership of Your Life

If you pause to review your life, you may recall a time when you had dreams and aspirations. Perhaps too many bad things have happened in your life or you have experienced too many broken dreams. You may still be suffering from the aftermath of traumas over which you had no control. Focusing on blame and injustice will not be productive, but taking ownership of your own life will. Ultimately, you are responsible for your own life, if you want to live an authentic and fulfilling life. Your past does not need to be a liability; it can be an asset. Everything that has happened so far in your life can become part of a new story, a story of triumph rather than tragedy. Only you can learn from your painful experiences—mistakes can make you wiser, pain can make you stronger, and faith can make you more hopeful. You can start reviewing your life and writing a new life story.

Setting New Life Goals

After assuming full responsibility for your own life, you may find the task of setting new life goals daunting, either because of too many options or the lack of opportunities. Whatever your circumstances, you can start by setting a clear and achievable life goal on the basis of your past lessons, your best strengths and values, and the demands life makes of you in your present station of life.

Steve Jobs' (June 12, 2005) epiphany is a good example:

> When I was 17, I read a quote that went something like: "If you live each day as if it was your last, someday you'll most certainly be right." It made an impression on me, and since then, for the past 33 years, I have looked in the mirror every morning and asked myself: "If today were the last day of my life, would I want to do what I am about to do today?" And whenever the answer has been "No" for too many days in a row, I know I need to change something.

> Your time is limited, so don't waste it living someone else's life. Don't be trapped by dogma—which is living with the results of other people's thinking. Don't let the noise of other's opinions drown out your own inner voice. And most important, have the courage to follow your heart and intuition. They somehow already know what you truly want to become. Everything else is secondary.

As a young man, Jobs already learned to follow his heart and he became what he was meant to be. We need to become aware of our own calling, either from a transcendental source or from our own inner voice. Awakening is both a turning point and a process. Many things can trigger an awakening—a tragedy, a sermon, a time of reflection, and all have the potential to make you realize that there is more to life than everyday busyness and striving for money or fame. Once you are awakened to the true purpose of your life, you will continue on the path of enlightenment. Research and experience have shown that several areas can endow life with meaning (Frankl, 1959/1985; Peterson, 2013; Wong, 1998); these include family and friends, helping others, developing one's full potential, and contributing to society. You may notice that the common denominator of all these domains is self-transcendence—transcending self-interests and self-limitations to serve a higher purpose and the greater good.

Summary

Your life goals may evolve over time, changing across different life stages and stations, but you need a meaningful life goal to keep you moving forward. No matter how menial your day-to-day work is, the idea that you are moving towards a meaningful life goal will make your work more enjoyable and meaningful.

The take-home lessons for step 2 are to transform your past into stepping stones for moving forward and to choose a life goal that really matters.

Exercises:

Choices. Try to answer the following questions concisely:

- What would you love to do most, if you were free to pursue anything you want?
- What do you really care about? What matters to you? What are the things you have been passionate about?
- What dreams did you cherish before addiction took over your life?

Goal Setting. We can begin with where you are at this moment. Think of the kind of projects you want to do. Write down a list of worthy projects you want to pursue. Select one that reflects your interests and values most; for example, reconciliation with your loved ones or going back to school to complete your education.

It is important that you start engaging in an activity that has intrinsic value—something that is worth doing in its own right, such as volunteering or learning a new skill or subject. The more intrinsic your core values, the less dependent you are on contingencies or external circumstances. The more self-transcending your life goal is, the more meaningfulness you will experience.

Stepping Stones.

- Name one or two of the most helpful lessons you have learned from your painful addiction experiences.
- Name one or two lessons from your journey of recovery.
- How do these lessons help you decide on your future life goals?

STEP 3: HOW DO I LIVE A GOOD LIFE? DISCOVER YOUR MINDSET.

In step 2, we emphasized the importance of doing what really matters and setting worthy life goals. In step 3, we make it explicit that meaningful life goals are primarily based on a life orientation of self-transcendence—a life of serving the greater good.

There are different assumptions of what constitutes a good life. Most people equate the good life with worldly success, but a success mindset will lead you to the same frustrations, despair, anger, and pain that led you to addiction. We propose an alternative life orientation, which is called the meaning mindset (Wong, 2012d).

The Meaning Hypothesis

Since antiquity, in both East and West, human beings have been actively engaged in the quest for the good life. Greek philosophers, such as Plato and Aristotle, and Chinese philosophers, such as Lao Tse and Confucius, have wrestled with such questions as "What are the highest human values for society?" "What is the nature of the good life?" and "What is the meaning of life?" This line of questioning reflects the human yearning for the good life.

Contemporary psychology has paid increasing attention to the ubiquitous presence and the importance of meaning in human life (Baumeister, 1991; Bruner, 1990, Steger, 2012; Wong, 2012a). Regardless of one's theoretical perspective, and regardless of one's religion, there is some consensus that meaning matters in the good life. It is not possible to live a good life that is devoid of meaning and purpose. Interestingly, the same point was made by Tony Robbins in his recent interview with Piers Morgan (CNN Piers Morgan tonight, January 25, 2013).

The meaning hypothesis, as advocated by Viktor Frankl (1959/1985), is that, more than happiness and success, meaning is the most important value or virtue that enables us to overcome our personal demons and live a fulfilling and rewarding life. The present 12-step program is based on the meaning hypothesis. The meaning mindset is one of the essential steps towards developing meaningfulness.

The Meaning Mindset

A mindset is a way of looking at the world, a basic life orientation. Some may call it "worldview" or "frame of reference," which refers to the kind of lens through which you perceive the world or the dominant principle that shapes your life. We hypothesize that a meaning mindset will lead to healing and flourishing, in spite of your circumstances. You may want to complete a brief scale to assess your own mindset (see Appendix A).

If you are primarily concerned with extrinsic motivation, such as possessions, prestige, and power, then success is your core value and your basic life orientation. However, if your primary concerns are about intrinsic motivation, such as developing your potentials and serving the public good, then your basic life orientation may be called a meaning mindset.

Meaning Mindset vs. Success Mindset

One of Frankl's (1959/1985) most important contributions was to challenge people to switch from a success mindset to a meaning mindset. This basic change in life orientation fundamentally changes a person's life direction and liberates one from anxieties about success and failure.

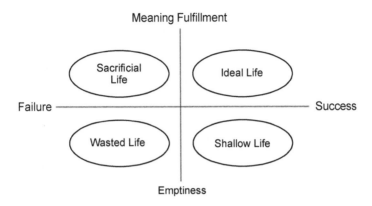

Figure 1. The Meaning Axis vs. The Success Axis (Wong, 2012d)

As illustrated in Figure 1, when you pursue a meaningful life as your vision for the good life and are able to realize it, then you are living an ideal life. But sometimes you may not have the opportunities to achieve your dream or gain recognition. In this case, you will be living a sacrificial life but can still feel fulfilled for living a meaningful life. A good example is the painter Vincent Van Gogh, who never sold a painting in his lifetime but never stopped pursuing his ideal of trying to capture the beauty of nature on canvas. If you choose a success mindset, then you are doomed to live a shallow life, regardless of how successful you are. If you pursue success as your life goal, you are running the risk of wasting your life if success eludes you.

Developing a Meaning Mindset

To fully understand and practice the meaning mindset will take time and effort because it is like forming a new habit. For example, when you start thinking about a situation in terms of how it will benefit you or the likelihood of success, you are under the control of a success mindset. On the other hand, if you start thinking, "What would be the right thing for me to do in this situation?" you are beginning to practice the meaning mindset. You can apply this logic to every situation in your life. Dr. Frankl (1959/1985) has always emphasized that we do not ask what we can expect from life but rather what life demands of us.

A meaning orientation focuses on meaning fulfillment as the ultimate life purpose. In other words, the primary concern of the meaning mindset is the fulfillment of self-transcendence—to fulfill one's potential and calling to serve others. We need to intentionally cultivate loving-kindness and practice the habit of serving others without any concern for personal gain or loss. It requires diligence and consistency until it becomes our second nature.

In the long run, you will be liberated from worries about failure or success and from concerns about self-interest. This is not an easy process and it is not something that can be accomplished in one day. It requires daily practice in thinking about "How can I help someone?" and "How can I make this world better?"

What are those things that are really worth living for? What are the things that matter more to you than a fleeting moment of happiness or temporary respect and recognition? Everyone can live a meaningful life, regardless of circumstances, abilities, or resources. There is no failure in the pursuit of meaning fulfillment. To live a worthy life, you need to set a worthy life goal—a goal that is worth dying for.

According to Frankl (1959/1985), even with little or no resources and in terrible conditions, those in the concentration camps were driven by the purpose of caring for others and found some way to do it:

> We who lived in concentration camps can remember the men who walked through the huts comforting others, giving away their last piece of bread. . . . They offer sufficient proof that everything can be taken from a man but one thing: to choose one's attitude in any given set of circumstances, to choose one's own way. (p. 86)

A meaning orientation sustains us when we are unhappy or unsuccessful, because it gives us a reason for living. A meaning orientation also protects us against temptations and excesses, because our focus is on what really matters. As by-products, we may find that we have also found success and happiness (Frankl, 1959/1985).

Exercises:

Reflection.

- Write a brief paragraph entitled: "This I believe." Describe what you believe are the most valuable and important goals in life.
- What is your definition of a good life? What would you like written on your epitaph?
- What is something that matters more to you than happiness and success?

Serving.

- Each day, look for an opportunity to help someone in need. These needs may be material, psychological, or spiritual. Your job is to express your care in a practical way.
- Don't be disappointed if you encounter rejection or lack of response. Remind yourself that you are simply doing what matters and fulfilling your calling of self-transcendence. Learn from this experience and make it an opportunity to examine whether you have expressed your care appropriately.

Minimalism.

- Suppose you are allowed to take only three things with you to a distant place, what would they be, and why?
- How will you simplify your life so that you have more time and money to serve others?

Intrinsic Motivation.

- How would you motivate yourself to continually improve your work performance?
- Do you know the difference between extrinsic and intrinsic motivation? Why is intrinsic motivation generally more beneficial?

STEP 4: IS LIFE WORTH LIVING IN BAD TIMES? LEARN THE BASIC CONCEPTS OF LOGOTHERAPY.

The first three steps lay a philosophical foundation for building a meaningful life primarily based on Frankl's (1959/1985) logotherapy. In step 4, we will discuss the basic tenets of logotherapy. Viktor Frankl confronted the existential crisis of his time and developed logotherapy as an antidote to the problem of meaninglessness. Applying the principles of logotherapy will greatly help you in your own quest for meaning.

Meaninglessness & Existential Vacuum

"Is life worth living?" This is one of the most important and provocative questions ever asked. During times of despair or bitterness, perhaps you have concluded that there is no point in striving. Here are two classical examples from the Old Testament of the Bible about the problem of meaninglessness.

Job experienced despair and bitterness. He had everything taken away from him; within a short period of time, his possessions were stolen, his children were killed, and he was afflicted with painful sores covering his body.

Solomon had a different problem: meaninglessness. As a king, he had everything he could possibly desire, with tremendous wealth, power, and multiple women, yet he found everything to be empty. The whole world was not enough, because all his achievements and possessions could not fill the hole in his soul. Meaninglessness is simply part of the inescapable human condition. How do we meet this crying need for meaning?

Frankl (1959/1985) was a modern day Job. He was taken away from his home and medical practice and sent to the Nazi concentration camps. His autobiography, *Man's Search for Meaning*, remains the No. 1 best seller in the self-help category of Amazon.com. This book is based on his painful experiences and discovery of the meaning of suffering in Nazi concentration camps. Given his personal experiences and clinical insights, his logotherapy is most helpful to the suffering masses. Frankl's message is that you can say "Yes" to life no matter how difficult, because your life's meaning is stronger than all your suffering, and your mission is greater than your pain. His meaning-seeking model, based on the following tenets, will empower you to overcome your personal demons and achieve your dreams.

The Three Basic Tenets of Logotherapy

The three basic tenets of logotherapy are: (1) freedom of will, (2) will to meaning, and (3) meaning of life.

(1) Freedom of will. "The one thing you can't take away from me is the way I choose to respond to what you do to me. The last of one's freedoms is the ability to choose one's attitude in a given set of circumstances" (Frankl, 1959/1985, p. 12). Freedom of will refers to the basic human capacity for self-determination or autonomy. Ryan and Deci's (2000) self-determination theory has demonstrated that autonomy is essential for well-being and growth.

We have learned in the first three steps that a sense of responsibility is a prerequisite for living an authentic life. Responsibility and self-transcendence are the two pillars of logotherapy. Responsibility is inextricably linked to the freedom of will. In every situation, we need to respond to the meaning potentials of the situation in an ethical and responsible way. We need to be aware that there are four ways to misuse our responsibility: Relinquish it, abuse it, overstep it, or deprive others of their responsibility. The best way to avoid these various forms of abuse is to listen to our inner compass or intuitive conscience.

(2) Will to meaning. A widely quoted statement attributed to Frankl notes that "Life can be pulled by goals just as surely as it can be pushed by drives." The will to meaning refers to both the primary need for meaning, which drives us, as well as the specific life goals that pull us. Meaningful life goals are based on the practice of self-transcendence and self-detachment. We are able to serve others and serve a higher purpose only to the extent that we learn to detach from our own selfish desires or self-centered concerns. Self-transcendence also enables us to transcend our internal and external limitations.

In order to fulfill the will to meaning, individuals need to be prepared psychologically because self-transcendence entails self-sacrifice. To discover one's calling is to find something worth fighting for and dying for. To live out one's calling is to overcome obstacles and oppositions.

(3) Meaning of life. This tenet affirms the intrinsic value and meaning of life in every situation. Therefore, we can discover meaning in life regardless of our life circumstance, even until our last breath. Since the meaning of life is unique and

specific, each person must discover the meaning potential of each situation and life as a whole. However, "the meaning of our existence is not invented by ourselves, but rather detected" (Frankl, 1963, p. 133), because we cannot arbitrarily decide what is meaningful without regard to ethics and values (e.g., the case of Hitler). The discovery of meaning has to be guided by authenticity and time-tested values.

Meaning of life includes both situational and Ultimate Meaning (Frankl, 1959/1985). Situational meaning refers to the moment-to-moment specific demands from each situation. Ultimate Meaning refers to how we fit into the larger scheme of things, relating to questions, such as "What should I do with my life?" "What is the point of all my striving?" or "What will happen to me after I die?"

This affirmation of meaning is based on the spiritual or noëtic dimension. Fabry (1998) wrote: "People's lives will be meaningful to the extent that their human spirit is able to tune in on the 'Ultimate Meaning'. . . in the suprahuman dimension of the Spirit (with a capital S)" (pp. 297–298).

The detection of the meaning of the moment, from situation to situation, can be facilitated by having an overall meaning orientation (Ultimate Meaning). For example, if you believe that your ultimate purpose is to show compassion towards others and share with them God's love, you might see fit to strike up a conversation with a distressed stranger to find out how you can be of help.

Affirmation of meaning also affects your career. Whatever your chosen career, whatever your temporary job, don't forget your calling and don't underestimate the significance of doing ordinary things for a higher purpose. Meaning will make your work more enjoyable.

The Meaning Triangle

On a more concrete level, Frankl (1959/1985) describes the Meaning Triangle as the three avenues that lead to the experience of meaningfulness. These three pathways to meaning are also referred to as the three values of meaning because they represent categories of time-tested, universal values:

Creative values. We find meaning through giving something to the world in service and creative work. It also means staying actively engaged with life. Even cancer patients can still find meaning through creative value such as handicrafts, painting, etc.

Experiential values. We find meaning through receiving from the world, such as appreciating each moment or enjoying the love and kindness of relationships. This is equivalent to learning how to savor the present moment with an attitude of openness and gratitude. You can make sense of things intellectually, but you can only make sense of life by living through it first. If we have never gone through the valleys of life, we will never truly understand the meaning of suffering.

Attitudinal values. We find meaning through our attitude towards suffering and fate. Through our defiant human spirit, we are able to turn tragedy into triumph. In order to create a better future, we need to face our inner demons and external obstacles. This takes tremendous courage and a defiant spirit. We must defy the many things that seek to oppress or defeat us.

Whatever may be troubling you, if you apply this meaning triangle to your problem and meditate on it, you will find a way to overcome or transcend your predicament. For example, the creative value of suffering includes doing something to relieve the suffering of other people. In helping others, your own suffering is reduced. The experiential value includes valuing the social support offered by others and appreciating the presence of loved ones. The attitudinal value of suffering includes taking a heroic stance or trusting in God.

Exercises:

Responsibility.
- Many people think that addiction is a disease. If you agree with this position, what kind of responsibility do you have in coping with your addiction?
- If life has been unfair to you, what is your responsibility in reacting to your experience of injustice?
- Your genes and circumstances may largely shape who you are, but you are responsible for who you will become. What kind of choices will you make now to shape your own future?

Will to Meaning.
- What is the major difference between Frankl's concept of pursuit of meaning and the contemporary concept of pursuit of success and happiness?
- In what ways does the will to meaning enable you to become a better person?
- What is the difference between Ultimate Meaning and situational meaning?
- In what concrete ways are you able to apply the concept of self-transcendence to your life and work?

Meaning of Life.
- In what way does your belief in the meaning of life help you cope with your addiction problem?
- How would you encourage a friend who has lost his job and is in despair?
- If you believe that there is purpose in life and there is a reason for your existence, how would that make you more resilient?

Meaning Triangle.
- Meditate on the meaning triangle and discover how each of the values can help you defeat the demon of addiction or overcome any other problem.

- Sit before a wall and focus on a significant other in your life, discovering what good the person has brought into your life or anything you have done to wrong the person. What will you do to show your appreciation or make amends?
- What kind of freedom can you have in a very oppressive situation, like the Nazi concentration camps?

STEP 5: WHAT ARE THE BASIC COMPONENTS OF MEANING? IDENTIFY THE BUILDING BLOCKS OF MEANINGFUL LIVING.

Everyone talks about meaning—meaningful work, meaningful relationships, meaningful beauty, and meaningful living. But what does meaning really mean? Building on the foundation laid out in previous steps, in step 5 we provide a comprehensive definition of meaning, which serves as a framework for building a meaningful life.

Meaning Defined

The lack of a clear definition of meaning has hindered meaning research and applications. After reviewing all the relevant literature in psychology, Wong (2010a, 2012b) has concluded that meaning consists of four essential components: Purpose, Understanding, Responsibility, and Enjoyment, which can be represented by the acronym PURE. This framework provides clear guidelines for meaningful living.

Purpose—the motivational component. Life purpose is important in clarifying our life direction and core values, organizing our activities and daily plans, and in setting long-term and short-term goals.

Purpose addresses questions such as: What matters most to me? What is my calling? What are my dreams and goals? What are my strengths and passions? Where am I going? What do I want to live for? What would be worth dying for?

When you start rebuilding your life, you need to be very clear and precise on what you want to do with the rest of your life. You need to discover a purpose that is most consistent with your ideals, your values, and calling. If you do not have a clear sense of calling, then it will be easy to go astray and end up in the wrong place. It is also important that our purpose is noble and ethical; it needs to be consistent with the meaning mindset of self-transcendence and intrinsic motivation.

Understanding—the cognitive component. Understanding involves full awareness of the situation and the consequences of one's actions. From the standpoint of Viktor Frankl (1959/1985), it is to listen to our intuitive conscience and respond to the demand quality of the situation. This means knowing right from wrong and understanding legal/ethical principles in decision-making.

It is important to know ourselves and understand our place in the larger scheme of things; this is what Frankl meant by Ultimate Meaning. Self-knowledge of our strengths and weaknesses reduces self-deception. There are tools available for self-assessment regarding strengths, interests, and personality traits.

Finally, understanding involves achieving a sense of coherence in the midst of uncertainties, chaos, and absurdities. We have to make some sense of life, even if we have to create myths.

Responsible action—the behavioral component. Responsibility and freedom go together. Responsibility has moral implications. To be a responsible person is to be a moral agent. Doing the right thing is the surest way to feel good about ourselves.

Having a sense of social responsibility prevents the excesses of the egotistic pursuit of personal happiness and success. Responsible action addresses such questions as: What can I do in this situation? Where does my freedom lie in these circumstances? What are my realistic options that are consistent with my values and beliefs? What is the right and responsible thing to do in this situation? In what ways can I make amends for mistakes I have made?

Enjoyment/Evaluation—the affective component. Enjoyment is the natural result of leading a purposeful and responsible life with a sense of contentment and well-being in all circumstances. But it is by no means definite, because our understanding is less than perfect and our ability to carry out our responsibilities is often hampered by internal and external constraints.

The best part of adopting the PURE way to the good life is that we will not achieve happiness at the expense of others; we can develop our full potential without harming others. The PURE way will lead to the life that is good in every sense, emotionally, intellectually, relationally, and morally.

However, if we still do not experience happiness after practicing PURE, we may need to reexamine our life purpose, understanding, and actions in order to do some fine-tuning. The PURE way is basically a process of self-regulation that requires honest self-reflection and courageous action. Evaluation involves evaluating the first three elements of PURE.

Summary

The meaning hypothesis posits that the pursuit of meaning is the most promising way to repair what is wrong and to bring out what is right. This hypothesis is supported by ample empirical evidence. It will also continue to generate more research (Wong, 2012a). The meaning hypothesis is the basis for meaning therapy (Wong, 2010a, 2012b).

The PURE intervention strategy is a very flexible approach, because it can be applied to relationship (Wong & Wong, in press) and management (Wong, 2010b). We now apply it to addiction recovery.

Exercises:

- Write a simple and concise mission statement for your life, not more than one paragraph.
- Is your life mission stronger than your urge for addiction?
- Do you have a deeper understanding now of how you have gotten into addiction and why you need to stay sober?
- If you are in the process of making an important decision, consider how your decision will affect your future, your family and friends, society, and the environment. If you are religious, you may ask yourself how you would give an account to God about your decision.
- Apply the PURE model to a current situation in your life.

STEP 6: HOW DO I FIND HAPPINESS IN DIFFICULT TIMES? DISCOVER THE SOURCES OF AUTHENTIC HAPPINESS.

Everybody wants happiness, but few understand true happiness. In this step, we emphasize that, when our primary concern is to pursue meaning and virtue, authentic happiness will come in through the back door. Seligman (2002) emphasizes that meaning is just one of the three components of authentic happiness; Frankl (1959/1985) and Wong (2013) elevate the role of meaning and propose that authentic happiness flows from living an authentic life of self-transcendence.

Meaning-based authentic happiness is accessible to everyone who chooses meaning as their primary life objective. It also has more enduring power than hedonic happiness, which is dependent on pleasant circumstances and positive moods. Most importantly, it enables us to enjoy peace and contentment even in adversity.

What is authentic happiness? There are several facets to a meaning-based authentic happiness. We have already discussed self-acceptance, self-transcendence, and the PURE model. Now, consider the importance of virtue and living a balanced life.

Virtue as a Key Component

The ancient sages considered the good life to be a morally exemplary life characterized by virtues that benefit both the individual and society. Aristotle (2004) equated the good life with "eudaimonia," which may be translated as the virtuous life or flourishing life. The four interconnected cardinal virtues according to Aristotle are: prudence, justice, fortitude, and temperance. According to Aristotle, to live the good life is to become what we ought to be as human beings. Thus, his view of the good life is based on living right and fulfilling what we are meant to be rather than on positive emotions and materialistic success.

Confucius equated the good life with the harmonious life, within an ordered society guided by the five cardinal virtues: benevolence, righteousness, propriety, wisdom, and faithfulness or loyalty. The good life consists of both inner cultivation of virtues as well as fulfilling one's proper role within the family and society. Psychological research has shown that we feel good when we do good deeds (e.g., Steger, Oishi, & Kashdan, 2009). One implication of this line of research is that society would become more humane and just if we value and practice altruism and compassion.

Frankl's meaning hypothesis is that we are moral beings living in a moral universe. We cannot flourish without being guided by a moral compass to do what is right and responsible. According to the meaning perspective, happiness rests in fulfillment of one's life purpose of responsibility and self-transcendence.

Another important consideration in meaning-based authentic happiness is living a meaningful life based on balancing different sources of meaning (McDonald, Wong, & Gingras, 2012; Wong, 2012c). In other words, living a balanced life is predicated on the breadth of various sources of meaning (Reker, 1994; Reker & Wong, 1988).

Sources of Meaning-Based Happiness

Wong (1998) asked hundreds of people from all walks of life what would make their lives meaningful if money was not an issue. Based on their responses, he discovered that there are eight sources of meaning:

- Positive affect—feeling satisfied with life,
- Achievement—striving and attaining worthy life goals,
- Relationship—relating well to others and community,
- Intimacy—having family and close friends,
- Acceptance—being at peace with oneself,
- Religion—having a personal relationship with God,
- Self-transcendence—losing oneself in serving others, and
- Fairness/justice—being treated fairly.

It is noteworthy that these sources of meaning are also sources of happiness (e.g., Myers, 1993). The good life is not based on single-minded pursuit of only what one is good at or what one is passionate about. Often ambitious individuals sacrifice their families and friends in chasing after their cherished dreams. Feverish engagement in activities can lead to disillusionment and burnout. Ambition needs to be balanced with relationship. Active engagement needs to be balanced by rest, meditation, and self-reflection. In the face of obstacles and setbacks, striving for accomplishment also needs to be balanced by acceptance of one's limitations and external constraints. Even the virtuous and spiritual act of self-transcendence cannot be one-sided. If one simply keeps giving without any reciprocal appreciation or return, one would experience discouragement and disappointment. Therefore, for the practice of self-transcendence to be sustainable and enjoyable, it needs to be balanced by fairness and reciprocation.

Summary

According to the meaning perspective, you can still have authentic happiness even when you go through trying times, because such happiness is not dependent on external circumstances but on living a meaningful life of self-transcendence. The take-home message of step 6 is that meaning-based authentic happiness needs to be virtuous and balanced.

Exercises:

- Try to help someone who is less fortunate than you. Describe how you feel afterwards.
- If you are bored with pleasurable activities, try something that challenges your intellect, courage, or skill.
- Discover the joy of letting go of something that has been bothering you.
- Is there a balance in your life? Complete the brief PMP (Appendix B) and see if the scores are evenly distributed.

STEP 7: HOW TO MAINTAIN HOPE AFTER TRAUMA? PRACTICE TRAGIC OPTIMISM.

According to the meaning hypothesis, meaning is the key to the good life; happiness and hope are the experiential proof that this hypothesis actually works. In step 6, we concluded that authentic happiness depends on authentic living rather than positive circumstances. In step 7, we show how you can keep your hope alive even when you feel that your world is falling apart. Most recovering addicts are no strangers to tragic events. Some of them know well what it is like to hit rock bottom.

Our daily news reports are full of traumatic events. Some of these traumatic events may be compared to Nazi death camps in terms of the scope of atrocities committed by humans against innocent people. The inmates at the camps were not only subjected to unimaginable degradation and deprivation, they were also threatened with impending death in gas chambers. Out of such a horrible ordeal, Viktor Frankl (1959/1985) developed his concept of tragic optimism (TO):

> an optimism in the face of tragedy and in view of the human
> potential which at its best always allows for (1) turning suffering into
> human achievement and accomplishment; (2) deriving from guilt the
> opportunity to change oneself for the better; and (3) deriving from
> life's transitoriness an incentive to take responsible action. (p. 162)

As we have discussed in step 4, one of the components of the meaning triangle is important in turning suffering into opportunity for heroic achievement: an attitude of the defiant human spirit. This attitude can turn people from despair and defeatism to hope and triumph. It also turns people from feelings of self-pity to realization of responsibility to others. Awakening to one's true purpose and responsibility represents the second basic tenet of logotherapy. Transforming guilt into personal growth highlights the power of meaning making.

The Five Ingredients of Tragic Optimism

TO is the only kind of hope that can survive the worst kind of tragedy and trauma. Based on what happened after 9/11, the Asian tsunami, and more recent tragic disasters, we are more convinced than ever that TO is part of the process of recovery. Meditating on the meaning triangle can help people develop TO in tragic situations. More importantly, Wong (2009) identified five basic ingredients for this construct based on logotherapy and resilience research.

(1) Acceptance of What Cannot Be Changed. It is becoming increasingly clear that we are living in a world full of suffering and tragic events. In this climate, it may be more realistic and healthier to develop a tragic sense of life. All of us grow old, become ill, and eventually die. All of us have either experienced or know someone who has experienced some kind of tragic event. Accepting life as it is or reality as we experience it is a necessary part of developing a tragic sense of life.

We have to learn to accept the fact that no matter how careful we are, bad things sometimes do happen to good people. No matter how much we try to avoid or escape adversity, it is never too far around the corner.

(2) Affirmation of the Meaning and Value of Life, Regardless of Circumstances. This is one of Frankl's basic tenets. Affirmation or belief is a necessary antidote to feelings of hopelessness and helplessness. If we only accept the bleak reality we are in, we naturally feel helpless and depressed. However, affirmation or belief can lift our spirits and empower us to move on. Affirming the intrinsic meaning and value of life is the foundation—an idea that we have emphasized in step 1. We need to return to this foundational belief when our presumptive world is shattered. If we firmly believe that life is worth living no matter what the circumstances, we are more likely to continue the difficult task of recovery.

In this step, we emphasize the importance of believing in recovery, no matter how many times we have failed or how broken our lives have become. The sun will rise again, no matter how stormy the night. We just have to believe that recovery is possible and wholeness is possible.

(3) Self-Transcendence in Serving the Greater Good. In self-transcendence, we lose ourselves in a higher service, and we find meaning by giving of ourselves to others. In fact, the central theme of logotherapy is finding meaning through self-transcendence. In times of crisis, such as 9/11 and the Connecticut school shooting, people naturally come together to help one another in a selfless way. In traditional 12-step recovery programs, sponsorship and small group meetings provide the possibility of self-transcendence.

(4) Faith or Trust in God and Others. Faith in God and prayer have been sources of strength and optimism to countless individuals in practically hopeless situations. It has often been said that man's adversity is God's opportunity. Faith represents a flickering light at the end of the tunnel. Often, it is the only positive expectation in an otherwise dark and hopeless world. Yahne and Miller (1999) referred to faith-based hope as the net that catches one when all else fails. Such hope is vested not in oneself but in a Higher Power (Tillich, 1958). That is why, in the traditional 12 steps, seeking help from God or a Higher Power is an essential step for recovery. In this step, we emphasize the importance of seeking professional help for problems. Denial or delay can exacerbate the problem.

Faith also includes our trust in other people. We gain strength from togetherness. We will elaborate on this in step 11.

(5) Courage to Face Adversity. Courage may be considered as the "master gland," because without it other glands will not function well. It is the pivotal point of TO. All other components hinge on courage: the heroic, defiant human spirit. We need courage to face tomorrow, courage to grow old, and courage to face sickness and death. One cannot be optimistic without the courage to face an unknown and uncertain future. Courage does not mean fearlessness to the point of being reckless. It does mean that you take all the precautions, make all the preparations, pray with all your heart, and then, move forward bravely in spite of fear.

We can cultivate this courage by recalling all the adversities we have overcome. We can also practice what Frankl (1959/1985) called "paradoxical intention" by facing what we fear most through our imagination. We do not know how courageous we are until we are severely tested.

Summary

The above five strands work together to form a strong rope that will not break under any circumstances. TO is the only kind of optimism that can survive the worst kinds of tragic events; with TO, you are on your way to a resilient life.

A recovered drug addict recently wrote to the senior author that the concept of TO has been more helpful to his recovery than anything else; he is now happily married and doing well in graduate school.

Recovery is a hard and steep journey. You travel on it one day at a time and one step at a time. When you fail, you just get back to the healing path. Never lose sight of your life goal. Never lose faith in complete recovery. The psychological scars may still linger. You may still have to cope with the fallout from your past substance or alcohol abuse. You may even suffer from posttraumatic stress symptoms. But you still can have hope for a bright future if you practice meaning-based tragic optimism.

Exercises:

- Think of a tragic situation that you have experienced or witnessed and discover new grounds for hope based on step 7.
- How does meaning make tragic optimism stronger than hopes based on positive thinking and confidence in one's own competence?
- Think of a task that you have been avoiding because of its difficulty and its high risk for failure. How would the concept of tragic optimism empower you to complete this task?

STEP 8: PRACTICAL STEPS TO BUILD RESILIENCE: THE ABCDE MODEL

TO teaches us the foundational attitude that enables us to maintain hope and keep moving forward, even in the most difficult of times. Building on this foundation, the ABCDE model (Wong, 2010a) provides tools to cope with the hardships in life and to transform the negatives into positives. It shows us that what does not kill us makes us stronger.

TO is like stress inoculation that prepares you for the hard life ahead. The ABCDE strategy equips you with skills to cope with the stress and troubles that may come your way. The ABCDE can be used to address a variety of problems and predicaments in life. Some personal problems may stem from deeply rooted unresolved issues. Some may be due to circumstantial difficulties. The ABCDE intervention is an all-purpose coping strategy. ABCDE stands for:

- *Accept* and confront the reality—the *reality principle*,
- *Believe* that life is worth living—the *faith principle*,

- *Commit* to goals and actions—the *action principle*,
- *Discover* the meaning and significance of self and situations—the *Aha! principle*, and
- *Evaluate* the above—the *self-regulation principle*.

Acceptance

Acceptance does not mean resigning or giving up. When we accept our problems, we are no longer in denial. We no longer expend our energy trying to pretend or prove that there is nothing wrong with us. The first step in the 12-step recovery program of Alcoholics Anonymous—acknowledging one's addiction problem—is a case in point. Before we can move forward, we need to face the difficult realities of loss, addiction, weaknesses, limitations, traumas, and existential givens (e.g., our own mortality, alienation, finitude). Acceptance means accepting life as it is. We need to learn to accept the imperfections in ourselves, in others, and in the world in which we live. We also need to learn to accept annoyances, frustrations, and normal anxieties in our everyday lives.

Belief

Belief incorporates the affirmation and faith principles of TO. Belief means affirming one's ideals, core values, and faith in the things that give you hope. It may involve a belief in an Ultimate Rescuer or Higher Power. It could also mean believing in the eventual triumph of good and justice. During difficult times, we need to return to and nurture these beliefs.

Commitment

Commitment refers to moving forward and carrying out one's convictions with determination, doing what needs to be done regardless of feelings or circumstances. It means striving to fulfill one's responsibility, including enduring hardship and pain for a worthy cause.

When we are committed to our mission or life goal, we will not allow temptations to lead us astray or bad habits to lure us back to addiction. Commitment may also involve embracing suffering or personal loss for the sake of a higher purpose or calling.

Commitment is intimately related to the PURE model because both pursuing your life purpose and fulfilling your responsibility entail commitment. Furthermore, applying the ABCDE to cope with obstacles and setbacks also entails commitment.

Discovery

Every challenge presents an opportunity to learn something new about oneself and life. We may discover our hidden courage and strength through striving. Our faith may grow deeper and we may discover the power of spiritual resources in times of great need. We may grasp the complexities of life and see people in a new way. These discoveries may lead us to a richer understanding of life and a greater ability to empathize and to walk with others through similar difficulties. Our meaning-seeking and meaning-making abilities allow us to find a secret gift in our suffering. We may discover ways in which these circumstances can ultimately serve our higher purpose.

Evaluation & Enjoyment

At the end of this process, we reflect on the results. It is a chance to review the situation, assess our progress, consider feedback from others, and make adjustments as needed. We also take time to enjoy the positive results and savor the small successes.

Summary

The PURE and ABCDE models are two pillars for meaningful living and meaning therapy, built on the foundation of Frankl's meaning-seeking model. If you can practice ABCDE, you can overcome solvable problems and transcend problems that are beyond your control.

Exercises:

- What are some things about yourself or your life that you find difficult to accept? What are the barriers to acceptance? Discover what will happen to you when you fully accept that aspect of yourself.
- In what ways does your defensiveness or self-deception prevent you from finding solutions to your problems?
- What are some of the beliefs that sustain you and give you hope during difficult times? Make a list.
- What is the vision you have been pursuing? How would the ABCDE model empower you to overcome opposition and obstacles?

STEP 9: WHAT SHOULD I DO WHEN I FEEL STUCK OR TRAPPED? USE THE DOUBLE-VISION STRATEGY.

The central concept for meaningful living is to be awakened to your responsibility for the higher purpose of self-transcendence. The double-vision strategy (Wong, 2012b) is closely linked to the central concept of self-transcendence. We will not find solutions for our problems if we only focus on our immediate present situation. But when we consider our place in the larger scheme of things, and consider our responsibility to others, it is possible to see our personal problems in a greater perspective and gain new understanding (see also Wong, Chapter 13, this volume).

Do you feel trapped in a bad relationship, lifestyle, dead-end job, or in a painful situation with no way out? Do you feel that the setbacks are insurmountable? In these situations, you may feel stuck and not know how to resolve your personal predicaments. The paradox is that sometimes the more you focus on finding a solution to these problems, the more confused and frustrated you become. The more you give your lives to others, the smaller your personal problems become.

Consider the proverbial frog at the bottom of the well. To this poor creature, the sky is no bigger than the opening of the well. It has no knowledge of the vast world all around it. Also consider the Chinese axiom: "If you step back from your problem, you will see the ocean and the sky open up before you."

What is Double Vision?

Double vision means that while we are confronted with a situational problem, we keep in mind the big-picture issues as well as our dreams (Wong, 2010a). These issues include, for examples, the universal human condition, the injustice of society, and the displacement and alienation of immigrants. These universal issues normalize our personal problems and give us the motivation to work for a better world.

What seems to be a personal problem may be related to a universal human condition. Our personal visions are also part of the big picture. We are more likely to give up and die from within if we stop pursuing our dreams. We are more likely to be motivated to tackle and overcome our obstacles if we maintain our tragic optimism and pursue our life goals.

With the double-vision strategy, we keep one eye on the ball and one eye on the goal, our higher purpose in life. Where are you headed? What is your ultimate goal? When we fix our eyes on our life goals, we will be less likely to be defeated by small setbacks along the way. To use a chess game analogy, we don't mind to sacrifice a pawn in order to checkmate our opponent's king. From time to time, we need to step back, take a deep breath, and consider the big picture. This can create a much-needed space between us and our problems, keeping us from getting lost in the misery of the moment.

At a time when all we can see is our "stuckness," double vision can expand our vision so that we can see things more clearly. New solutions may emerge. These solutions may take the form of practical changes or may simply be a shift in the way we relate to the problem. For example, what we once perceived as obstacles may become opportunities. Alternatively, a sense of the big picture may give us the freedom and courage to change things that we previously thought we could not.

Exercises:

• Think of a situation in which you felt stuck.

- How would you see this problem differently if you used the double-vision strategy?
- How do you relate your personal problem to a larger societal or existential problem?

STEP 10: HOW DO I LIVE LIFE TO THE FULLEST? DISCOVER THE YIN-YANG WAY.

Through the PURE model, we have learned how to build our lives through meaning. Through the ABCDE model, we have learned how to overcome and transform adversities. In this step, we learn how to integrate these two models in order to live our lives to the fullest, regardless of the circumstances.

You have already learned that a meaningful life cannot be based on the hedonic principle of maximizing pleasure and minimizing pain. In this step you will learn that life is about how to manage pleasure and pain that are always present in different measures in every situation. Generally, people tend to make one of two mistakes: Some want to focus solely on the positive and ignore the negative side of the human condition; others focus only on the negative and ignore what is good and beautiful about life. The yin-yang way avoids these two extremes and requires a more philosophical and integrative way to cope with life's vicissitude and challenges.

Yin-Yang

As the symbol of yin and yang demonstrates, life is a balancing act between positives and negatives. In fact, each positive experience contains the seed of self-destruction; similarly, each negative contains the seed of personal growth. The yin-yang approach avoids the excesses of the pursuit of happiness and success, while allowing us to discover the potential benefits of negative experiences. This is an important skill in life. It will not only prevent us from extremes, but also gives us the practical wisdom to practice the middle way, according to Confucius, or the Golden Mean, according to Aristotle.

A famous Taoist story teaches us the wisdom of the interrelationship between fortune and misfortune:

> There was an old farmer whose only prized possession was a
> workhorse. One day, his horse ran away. Upon hearing the news, his
> neighbors came to visit. "Such bad luck," they said sympathetically.
> "We'll see," the farmer replied. The next morning the horse returned,
> bringing with it three other wild horses. "How wonderful," the
> neighbors exclaimed. "We'll see," replied the old man. The following
> day, his son tried to ride one of the untamed horses, was thrown,

and broke his leg. The neighbors again came to offer their sympathy on his misfortune. "We'll see," answered the farmer. The day after, military officials came to the village to draft young men into the army. Seeing that the son's leg was broken, they passed him by. The neighbors congratulated the farmer on how well things had turned out. "We'll see," said the farmer.

Dual-Systems Model

The dual-systems model represents our attempt to translate the yin-yang principle into psychological processes. It focuses on the interaction between our approach and avoidance tendencies, in order to yield the best possible outcome.

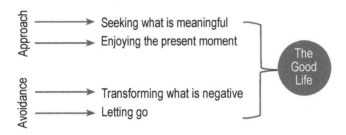

Figure 2. Interaction of approach and avoidance in the dual-systems model.

We can use the PURE model (see step 5) to develop what is good and right about us. However, in your pursuit of a meaningful goal, such as recovery from addiction or developing your professional life, from time to time there is bound to be a bump on the road or some major setback.

The ABCDE intervention (step 8) represents a meaning-centered approach to overcoming or transforming what hinders or troubles us. If you practice the skills related to acceptance, belief, commitment, discovery, and evaluation/enjoyment, you will be able to overcome the obstacle and return to your positive life goals under the umbrella of PURE.

Many people are struggling with their personal demons, financial difficulties, or health problems. For most people, life is hard and complex. There is no simple solution for all life's problems. The dual-systems model emphasizes flexibility and enables us to embrace all of life; it enables us to benefit from both positive and negative experiences. PURE maintains your passion for life and gives you the energy to face obstacles, while ABCDE deepens your resilience and broadens your horizon.

Summary

The take-home message is that, in the process of practicing PURE, you may encounter setbacks, while ABCDE can transform negatives to positives. ABCDE needs to be fueled by the positive energies and visions from PURE to keep going until the problem is resolved.

Exercises:

- Recall a situation in which your belief or faith was the only thing you could hang on to in order to survive?
- In what ways does the dual-systems model give you a sense of freedom or relief when you feel overwhelmed by your problems?
- Can you name some of the benefits resulting from your painful life experiences?
- Can you name some of the dangers or risks when everything is going your way?
- Try to apply the dual-systems model to solve a current life problem.

STEP 11: OTHER PEOPLE MATTER: WHY ARE OTHER PEOPLE ESSENTIAL FOR THE GOOD LIFE?

No man is an island; we cannot live without other people. We are hardwired for each other; intimate relationships are the main source of our security, happiness, and well-being. Happy people have good relationships. Happy organizations and communities are also based on good interpersonal connections. The question is: How do we relate to other people in a way that is best for everyone? If we focus on pursuing a self-centered happiness, we will treat others as tools to meet our own needs and purposes.

However, if we relate to others from the standpoint of transcending our own personal interests and caring for others, we will have a better chance of enjoying good relationships. This meaning perspective treats others as people worthy of respect, not as instruments for self-gain.

Other People Matter

We established in step 1 that you matter as a unique individual. Here we emphasize that other people also matter. Do other people matter to us because we need them to meet our needs? Or do they matter in their own right, regardless of what they can do for us? This is an important question that will determine how we treat others.

Many spiritual teachings claim that we matter because we bear the divine image in our soul. Humanists say that we matter because we belong to each other and we will all be happier if we treat each other well. Other people are neither hell nor heaven—they are us. Ultimately, how we treat others always boomerangs back to us; paradoxically, the best way to love self is to love others. Self-transcendence is not just about politeness or occasionally considering the needs and wants of others; to transcend ourselves, we must fundamentally alter our orientation toward others. We must learn to love others as we love ourselves.

Perhaps the most complete description of love is offered by a passage from the Bible:

> Love is patient, love is kind. It does not envy, it does not boast, it is not proud. It does not dishonor others, it is not self-seeking, it is not easily angered, it keeps no record of wrongs. Love does not delight in evil but rejoices with the truth. It always protects, always trusts, always hopes, always perseveres. (1 Corinthians 13:4-7, NIV)

Such love is focused on the other and enables us to truly see the other. Viktor Frankl (1959/1985) wrote:

> Love is the only way to grasp another human being in the innermost core of his personality. No one can become fully aware of the very essence of another human being unless he loves him. By his love he is enabled to see the essential traits and features in the beloved person; and even more, he sees that which is potential in him, which is not yet actualized but yet ought to be actualized. Furthermore, by his love, the loving person enables the beloved person to actualize these potentialities. By making him aware of what he can be and of what he should become, he makes these potentialities come true. (p. 134)

From "Me" to "We"

One practical way of living out the principle that other people matter is to change our "me" mindset to a "we" mindset. We treat others as if we are on the same team, as if we are on their team. We focus on the common interests we have in a situation, rather than on our competing interests. We reflect on such questions as: "What is motivating the other person? What is it that they hope for or desire? How can I be on their side, helping meet their needs as well as my own?" When we think in terms of "we" rather than "me" alone, we are more likely able to balance the tension between self-interest and the needs of others.

Communication is also essential in relationship. Self-centered communication is often conflictual and destructive, whereas meaning-centered communication builds relationships. Self-transcendence is a major component of meaning-centered communication. Here we contrast the different communication styles:

Self-centered communication style

1. It is accusatory—"You do not meet my needs." "You never listen."

2. It is manipulative—"If you loved me, you would. . . ."
3. It is demanding—"You had better fix this."
4. It is defensive—"It's not my fault."
5. It is boastful of one's own contribution—"I have done this, I have done that."
6. It is critical of the other—"How can you be so stupid?"
7. It is often deceitful—telling half-truths or lies.

Meaning-centered communication style
1. Seeks to understand the other's perspective.
2. Shows appreciation and validation to the other.
3. Expresses one's own need without accusing the other.
4. Communicates trust and understanding.
5. Attempts win-win solutions.
6. Reaches out to help and support the other.
7. Talks about common interests and shared goals.
8. Tells the truth with love.

Summary

Other people matter (Peterson, 2013), because relationships matter a great deal for the good life. To transform an inhumane society into a kinder and gentler community, we need to value people more than self-gains. We all gain at the end when we place other people's well-being above self-centered concerns. Another take-home message is that, if we practice meaning-centered communication, we will more likely achieve better harmony in our relationships.

Exercises:

- Think of a relational conflict in your life. What difference would it make if you thought in terms of "we" instead of "me" in this situation?

- Try to start with "I" rather than "you" to express a negative emotion (e.g., "I feel angry" vs. "You make me angry").

- Focus on an interpersonal conflict you have experienced and recall any self-centered communication you employed in this conflict. Then try to replace the problematic statement(s) with meaning-centered communication.

- Have you ever made amends in order to repair a broken relationship? If not, what holds your back?

STEP 12: LEARN THE MEANING-CENTERED PATHWAYS TO WELL-BEING: A HOLISTIC MODEL

This last step provides a brief survey of the influential models of happiness and well-being with special emphasis on the meaning hypothesis. It identifies several pathways to happiness and well-being based on meaning as the core motivation. For a more detailed discussion of meaning-based happiness, see Wong (2013).

Snyder and Lopez (2007) propose the formula: Happiness + Meaning = Well-being. This summarizes the important role of meaning in well-being as broadly defined. Other psychologists have also proposed more specific definitions of happiness and well-being.

Diener (2000), the foremost authority on happiness, uses the terms "happiness" and "subjective well-being" interchangeably, reflecting a hedonic perspective of subjective well-being. A eudaimonic perspective of subjective well-being focuses on meaning and virtue (Waterman, 1993, 2008).

According to Ryff and Keyes (1995), psychological well-being is based on several dimensions: self-acceptance, personal growth, purpose in life, environmental mastery, autonomy, and positive relationships with others. According to Keyes (1998), social well-being consists of five dimensions: social integration, social contribution, coherence, actualization, and acceptance. Complete mental health includes emotional, social, and psychological well-being (Keyes & Magyar-Moe, 2003), in addition to the absence of mental illness symptoms (Keyes & Lopez, 2002).

Consistent with the meaning hypothesis, some psychologists emphasize spiritual well-being, as measured by the Spiritual Well-Being Scale (Paloutzian & Ellison, 1982). This scale consists of Existential and Spiritual subscales: the former is the quest for personal meaning, while the latter is about one's relationship with God. Research has shown that the Spiritual Well-Being Scale is also a useful indicator of global health and well-being, because it is related to physical, psychological, and relational well-being (Ellison & Smith, 1991).

According to contemporary positive psychology, meaning is a component of authentic happiness, along with engagement and pleasure (Seligman, 2002). Meaning is also considered a component of well-being, according to Seligman's (2011) more recent theory of PERMA (Positive Affect, Engagement, Positive Relationship, Meaning, and Achievement).

Most of the above models of well-being include a component of meaning and purpose. The present meaning-oriented approach makes meaning the overarching framework for well-being and mental health. Even in the absence of positive affect and active engagement, one can still enjoy certain levels of well-being based on meaning, virtue, and spirituality. According to Haybron (2000), "pleasure does not really matter all that much in itself, being merely a by-product that accompanies the achievement of what is truly worthwhile" (p. 20).

A Three-Factor Theory of Meaning-Based Well-being

We have reiterated the importance of will to meaning or need for self-transcendence as the core motivation for the good life. Three major pathways to well-being and positive mental health are:

1. Meaning itself leads to a sense of eudaimonia or happiness. For example, meaningful work and meaningful relationships are intrinsically satisfying.

2. Meaning making and meaning reconstruction help transform negatives into positives. These processes help to repair what is broken and indirectly increase our well-being. Tragic optimism is an example of transforming hopeless situations into hopeful ones through the attitudinal value of meaning. Reauthoring your life story and changing your role from a victim to a victor are other forms of meaning reconstruction.

3. Meaning provides a blueprint for building a better life for self and others. A meaning-centered model for recovery and well-being is holistic. It involves building relationships and being part of supportive community. It involves making contributions to society.

Summary

A meaning-centered holistic model of positive mental health captures all the previous steps. This model differs from other models of happiness and well-being, because (a) it emphasizes self-transcendence rather than the self-centered pursuit of personal happiness and success, and (b) it is dependent on personal meaning more than positive affect and favorable circumstances.

This meaning-centered 12-step program makes good use of the uniquely human capacities for meaning seeking, meaning making, and self-transcendence. The final aim of this program is to develop one's full potential to live a life of self-transcendence in order to serve the greater good.

Exercises:

- What are the advantages of the meaning approach to wellness as compared to the traditional emphasis on happiness and positive affect?
- Identify an unhappy situation in your life. Try to use meaning seeking or meaning making as a way to help you feel better without thinking about addiction for relief.
- Describe an experience in which you felt good about yourself in going through a very difficult situation because of your belief in following your calling and doing the right thing.
- How will you use the meaning approach to help a depressed friend?
- Which aspects of the meaning-centered 12-step recovery program are most helpful to you? Why?

CONCLUSION

To put it all together, this meaning-centered 12-step program will facilitate healing and flourishing. It is not meant to be a simple recipe for recovery, but rather a road map for living the good life in spite of a history of addiction. It may be used as an alternative to the 12-step program of Alcoholics Anonymous (see Hart, Chapter 15, this volume).

It would be more helpful to think of each step described here as a major life task, necessary for living a sober, productive, and rewarding life. As you have already discovered, each task actually involves several skills and lessons.

Paul Wong's (December 5, 2012) *Meaning Manifesto* captures the essence of this chapter. Use this manifesto as a daily reminder that meaningful living can transform self and society:

> Life is much more than the everyday busyness of making a living or striving for personal success. Life is much more than a constant struggle of coping with harsh reality by fighting or escaping. Life can be lived at a deeper level and on a higher plane by adopting a *meaning mindset* as your basic life orientation.
>
> Your life has intrinsic meaning and value because you have a unique purpose to fulfill. You are endowed with the capacity for *freedom* and responsibility to choose a life of meaning and significance. Don't settle for anything less. No matter how confusing and bleak your situation, there is always beauty, truth, and meaning to be discovered; but you need to cultivate a *mindful attitude* and learn to transcend self-centeredness.
>
> Don't always ask what you can get from life, but ask what life demands of you. May you be awakened to your sense of responsibility and call to *self-transcendence*; you become fully human only when you devote your life to serving a higher purpose and your fellow human beings. Let your inner goodness and *conscience* be your guide; let compassion be your motive and may you see the world and yourself through the lens of meaning and virtue. You will experience transformation and authentic happiness when you practice meaningful living. Now, go forward with courage and integrity and pursue your ideals against all odds with the *defiant human spirit*.

We encourage you to study these 12 steps by yourself or with a group. Take time to work on the exercises and apply them to your own life. As we have said before, recovery can be a long and steep road. Do not despair if you relapse or fail in any area of your life. Hang on to the belief that your life has intrinsic meaning and value and you have a unique purpose to fulfill. If you persist, you will make life better not only for yourself, but also for those around you. By practicing these 12 steps, you are contributing to a new paradigm for community mental health.[1]

REFERENCES

Aristotle. (2004). *Nicomachean ethics*. (F. H. Peters, Trans.). New York: Barnes and Noble.

Baumeister, R. F. (1991). *Meanings of life*. New York, NY: Guilford.

Bruner, J. (1990). *Acts of Meaning*. Cambridge, MA: Harvard University Press.

CNN Piers Morgan tonight. (January 25, 2013). Tony Robbins on happiness: "The quality of your life is the quality of where you live emotionally" [Video file]. Retrieved from http://piersmorgan.blogs.cnn.com/2013/01/25/

Diener, E. (2000). Subjective well-being: The science of happiness and a proposal for a national index. *American Psychologist, 55*, 34–43. doi:10.1037//0003-066X.55.1.34

Ellison, C. W., & Smith, J. (1991). Toward an integrative measure of health and well-being. *Journal of Psychology and Theology: Special Issue, 19*, 35–48.

Fabry, J. (1998). The cause of meaning. In P. T. P. Wong & P. S. Fry (Eds.), *The human quest for meaning: A handbook of psychological research and clinical applications* (pp. 295–305). Mahwah, NJ: Erlbaum.

Frankl, V. E. (1963). *Man's search for meaning: An introduction to logotherapy*. (I. Lasch, Trans.). New York, NY: Washington Square Press. (Original work published 1959)

Frankl, V. E. (1985). *Man's search for meaning: Revised and updated*. New York: Washington Square. (Original work published 1959)

Frankl, V. E. (1986). *The doctor and the soul: From psychotherapy to logotherapy* (Second Vintage Books edition). New York, NY: Random House Inc. (Original work published 1959)

Hart, K. E. (2013). Interpreting the 12 steps of AA from the perspectives of ecumenical Christianity and transpersonal psychology. In L. C. J. Wong, G. R. Thompson, & P. T. P. Wong (Eds.), *The positive psychology of meaning and addiction recovery* (pp. 211–240). Birmingham, AL: Purpose Research.

Haybron, D. M. (2000). Two philosophical problems in the study of happiness. *The Journal of Happiness Studies, 1*, 207–225.

Jobs, S. (June 12, 2005). Stanford commencement address. Available at http://youtube.com/watch?v=VHWUCX6osgM

Keyes, C. L. M. (1998). Social well-being. *Social Psychology Quarterly, 61*, 121–140. doi:10.2307/2787065

Keyes, C. L. M., & Lopez, S. J. (2002). Toward a science of mental health: Positive directions in diagnosis and interventions. In C. R. Snyder, & S. J. Lopez (Eds.), *Handbook of positive psychology* (pp. 45–62). New York, NY: Oxford University Press.

---

[1]   Much of the material in this chapter is derived from the lessons created by Paul T. P. Wong for the Toronto Meaningful Living Meetup sessions. More information about this meaning-centered 12-step program is available at inpm.org or directly from Dr. Paul T. P. Wong.

Keyes, C. L. M., & Magyar-Moe, J. L. (2003). The measurement and utility of adult subjective well-being. In S. J. Lopez, & C. R. Snyder (Eds.), *Positive psychological assessment: A handbook of models and measures* (pp. 411–426). Washington, DC: American Psychological Association.

McDonald, M. J., Wong, P. T. P., & Gingras, D. T. (2012). Meaning-in-life measures and development of a brief version of the Personal Meaning Profile. In P. T. P. Wong (Ed.), *The human quest for meaning: Theories, research, and applications* (2nd ed., pp. 357–382). New York, NY: Routledge.

Myers, D. G. (1993). *The pursuit of happiness: Discovering the pathway to fulfillment, well-being, and enduring personal joy.* New York, NY: Avon Books.

Paloutzian, R. F., & Ellison, C. W. (1982). Loneliness, spiritual well-being and the quality of life. In L. A. Peplau, & D. Perlman (Eds.), *Loneliness: A sourcebook of current theory, research and therapy* (pp. 105–119). New York, NY: Wiley.

Peterson, C. (2013). *Pursuing the good life: 100 reflections on positive psychology.* New York, NY: Oxford University Press.

Reker, G. T. (1994) Logotheory and logotherapy: Challenges, opportunities, and some empirical findings. *International Forum for Logotherapy, 17,* 47–55.

Reker, G. T., & Wong, P. T. P. (1988). Aging as an individual process: Toward a theory of personal meaning. In J. E. Birren, & V. L. Bengtson (Eds.), *Emergent theories of aging* (pp. 214–246). New York, NY: Springer.

Ryan, R. M., & Deci, E. L. (2000). Self-determination theory and the facilitation of intrinsic motivation, social development, and well-being. *American Psychologist, 55,* 68–78. doi:10.1037//0003-066X.55.1.68

Ryff, C. D., & Keyes, C. L. M. (1995). The structure of psychological well-being revisited. *Journal of Personality and Social Psychology, 69,* 719–727. doi:10.1037//0022-3514.69.4.719

Seligman, M. E. P. (2002). *Authentic happiness: Using the new positive psychology to realize your potential for lasting fulfillment.* New York, NY: Free Press/Simon and Schuster.

Seligman, M. E. P. (2011). *Flourishing: A visionary new understanding of happiness and well-being.* New York, NY: Free Press.

Snyder, C. R., & Lopez, S. J. (2007). *Positive psychology: The scientific and practical explorations of human strengths.* Thousand Oaks, CA: Sage Publications.

Steger, M. F. (2012). Experiencing meaning in life: Optimal functioning at the nexus of well-being, psychopathology, and spirituality. In P. T. P. Wong (Ed.) *The human quest for meaning: Theories, research, and applications* (2nd ed., pp. 165–184). New York, NY: Routledge.

Steger, M. F., Oishi, S., & Kashdan, T. B. (2009). Meaning in life across the life span: Levels and correlates of meaning in life from emerging adulthood to older adulthood. *Journal of Positive Psychology, 4,* 43–52. doi:10.1080/17439760802303127

Tillich, P. (1958). *The dynamics of faith.* New York: Harper Collins.

Waterman, A. S. (1993). Two conceptions of happiness: Contrasts of personal expressiveness (eudaimonia) and hedonic enjoyment. *Journal of Personality and Social Psychology, 64,* 678–691. doi:10.1037//0022-3514.64.4.678

Waterman, A. S. (2008). Reconsidering happiness: A eudaimonist's perspective. *Journal of Positive Psychology, 3,* 234–252. doi:10.1080/17439760802303002

Wong, P. T. P. (1998). Implicit theories of meaningful life and the development of the Personal Meaning Profile (PMP). In P. T. P. Wong, & P. Fry (Eds.), *The human quest for meaning: A handbook of psychological research and clinical applications* (pp. 111–140). Mahwah, NJ: Lawrence Erlbaum Associates, Inc.

Wong, P. T. P. (2009). Viktor Frankl: Prophet of hope for the 21st century. In A. Batthyany, & J. Levinson (Eds.), *Existential psychotherapy of meaning: Handbook of logotherapy and existential analysis.* Phoenix, AZ: Zeig, Tucker & Theisen, Inc.

Wong, P. T. P. (2010a). Meaning therapy: An integrative and positive existential psychotherapy. *Journal of Contemporary Psychotherapy. 40*(2), 85–99. doi:10.1007/s10879-009-9132-6

Wong, P. T. P. (2010b). The PURE strategy to create lean and excellent organizations. *International Journal of Existential Psychology and Psychotherapy, 3*(2), 1–21.

Wong, P. T. P. (Ed.). (2012a). *The human quest for meaning: Theories, research, and applications* (2nd ed.). New York, NY: Routledge.

Wong, P. T. P. (2012b). From logotherapy to meaning-centered counseling and therapy. In P. T. P. Wong (Ed.), *The human quest for meaning: Theories, research, and applications* (2nd ed., pp. 619–647). New York, NY: Routledge.

Wong, P. T. P. (2012c). Toward a dual-systems model of what makes life worth living. In P. T. P. Wong (Ed.), *The human quest for meaning: Theories, research, and applications* (2nd ed., pp. 3–22). New York, NY: Routledge.

Wong, P. T. P. (2012d). What is the meaning mindset? *International Journal of Existential Psychology and Psychotherapy, 4*(1), 1–3.

Wong, P. T. P. (December 5, 2012). Meaning manifesto. Retrieved from http://meetup.com/Toronto-Meaningful-Living-Group/messages/boards/thread/29354572

Wong, P. T. P. (2013). The positive psychology of meaning in life and well-being. In A. C. Michalos (Ed.), *Encyclopaedia of quality of life research.* New York, NY: Springer.

Wong, P. T. P., & Wong, L. C. J. (in press). The challenge of communication—An integrative-existential perspective. In E. van Deurzen & S. Iacovou (Eds.), *Existential perspectives on relationship therapy.* Hampshire, UK: Palgrave Macmillan.

Yahne, C. E., & Miller, W. R. (1999). Evoking hope. In W. R. Miller (Ed.), *Integrating spirituality into treatment.* (pp. 217–233). Washington, DC: American Psychological Association.

APPENDIX A: THE LIFE ORIENTATION SCALE (LOS)

Wong, P. T. P. (2012d)

Please indicate how much you agree or disagree with each of the following statements by circling a number on the 5-point scale that best corresponds to your personal belief and attitude.

1	2	3	4	5
Strongly Disagree	**Disagree**	**Undecided**	**Agree**	**Strongly Agree**

1. I can find something meaningful or significant in everyday events. — 1 2 3 4 5
2. There is a reason for everything that happens to me. — 1 2 3 4 5
3. There is no ultimate meaning and purpose in life. — 1 2 3 4 5
4. There is no point in searching for meaning in life. — 1 2 3 4 5
5. No matter how painful the situation, life is still worth living. — 1 2 3 4 5
6. The meaning of life is to "eat, drink and be happy." — 1 2 3 4 5
7. What really matters to me is to pursue a higher purpose or calling regardless of personal cost. — 1 2 3 4 5
8. I would rather be a happy pig than a sad saint. — 1 2 3 4 5
9. I am willing to sacrifice personal interests for the greater good. — 1 2 3 4 5
10. Personal happiness and success are more important to me than achieving inner goodness and moral excellence. — 1 2 3 4 5

SCORING

Items 3, 4, 6, 8, and 10 are worded in the negative direction. The higher the total score is, the greater the meaning mindset.

APPENDIX B: THE BRIEF PERSONAL MEANING PROFILE (PMP-B)

McDonald, M. J., Wong, P. T. P., & Gingras, D. T. (2012)

This questionnaire is intended to identify what really matters in your life and measures people's perception of personal meaning in their lives. Generally, a meaningful life involves a sense of purpose and personal significance. However, people often differ in what they value most, and they have different ideas as to what would make life worth living. The following statements describe potential sources of a meaningful life. Please read each statement carefully and indicate to what extent each item characterizes your own life. You may respond by circling the appropriate number according to the following scale:

1	**2**	**3**	**4**	**5**	**6**	**7**
Not at all			**Moderately**			**A great deal**

For example, if going to parties does not contribute to your sense of personal meaning, you may circle 1 or 2. If taking part in volunteer work contributes quite a bit to the meaning in your life, you may circle 5 or 6.

It is important that you answer honestly on the basis of your own experience and beliefs.

1. I believe I can make a difference in the world.		1 2 3 4 5 6 7
2. I have someone to share intimate feelings with.		1 2 3 4 5 6 7
3. I strive to make this world a better place.		1 2 3 4 5 6 7
4. I seek to do God's will.		1 2 3 4 5 6 7
5. I like challenge.		1 2 3 4 5 6 7
6. I take initiative.		1 2 3 4 5 6 7
7. I have a number of good friends.		1 2 3 4 5 6 7
8. I am trusted by others.		1 2 3 4 5 6 7
9. I seek to glorify God.		1 2 3 4 5 6 7
10. Life has treated me fairly.		1 2 3 4 5 6 7
11. I accept my limitations.		1 2 3 4 5 6 7
12. I have a mutually satisfying loving relationship.		1 2 3 4 5 6 7

13. I am liked by others.	1	2	3	4	5	6	7
14. I have found someone I love deeply.	1	2	3	4	5	6	7
15. I accept what cannot be changed.	1	2	3	4	5	6	7
16. I am persistent and resourceful in attaining my goals.	1	2	3	4	5	6	7
17. I make a significant contribution to society.	1	2	3	4	5	6	7
18. I believe that one can have a personal relationship with God.	1	2	3	4	5	6	7
19. I am treated fairly by others.	1	2	3	4	5	6	7
20. I have received my fair share of opportunities and rewards.	1	2	3	4	5	6	7
21. I have learned to live with suffering and make the best of it.	1	2	3	4	5	6	7

SCORING

Please indicate the score you circled for the indicated question number in the cells below. Add up the scores in each row.

Subscale	Score	Score	Score	Row Total
Achievement	(Q5)	(Q6)	(Q16)	
Relationship	(Q7)	(Q8)	(Q13)	
Religion	(Q4)	(Q9)	(Q18)	
Self-transcendence	(Q1)	(Q3)	(Q17)	
Self-acceptance	(Q11)	(Q15)	(Q21)	
Intimacy	(Q2)	(Q12)	(Q14)	
Fair treatment	(Q10)	(Q19)	(Q20)	

Lightning Source UK Ltd.
Milton Keynes UK
UKHW010636280223
417789UK00001B/14